This book explains the changes in industrial leadership from Britain to the United States earlier in this century and from the United States to Japan more recently in terms of the changing investment strategies and organizational structures of business enterprises in these nations. It then criticizes economists for failing to understand these historical changes. The book shows that this intellectual failure is not inherent in the discipline of economics; there are important traditions in economic thought that the mainstream of the economics profession has simply ignored. The intellectual problem inheres in the static methodology and individualist ideology that mainstream economists call "science." The book shows how, through historical analysis and the consideration of the changing relation between individuals and organizations in leading capitalist economies, economics as an academic discipline can get back in touch with the real world.

Business organization and the myth
of the market economy

Business organization and the myth
of the market economy

WILLIAM LAZONICK

CAMBRIDGE
UNIVERSITY PRESS

Published by the Press Syndicate of the University of Cambridge
The Pitt Building, Trumpington Street, Cambridge CB2 1RP
40 West 20th Street, New York, NY 10011-4211, USA
10 Stamford Road, Oakleigh, Melbourne 3166, Australia

First published 1991
First paperback edition 1993
Reprinted 1994

Printed in the United States of America

Library of Congress Cataloging-in-Publication Data
Lazonick, William.
Business organization and the myth of the market economy / William
Lazonick.
p.   cm.
Includes index.
ISBN 0-521-39419-8 (hardcover)
1. Free enterprise – History – 20th century.   2. Capitalism –
History – 20th century.   3. Economics – History – 20th century.
I. Title.
HB95.L39   1991
330.12′2–dc20   91-8865
                                                        CIP

British Library Cataloguing in Publication Data
Lazonick, William
Business organization and the myth of the market economy.
1. Economic conditions
I. Title
320.9

ISBN 0-521-39419-8 hardcover
ISBN 0-521-44788-7 paperback

To Kathy

Contents

vii

Figures

ix

Acknowledgments

The essays that make up this book were written and revised between 1986 and 1991. I have, however, been exploring the central ideas – the historical dynamics of capitalist development and the making (and remaking) of an outmoded market mentality – since I was a graduate student in economics at Harvard University in the early 1970s. From the mid-1970s to the mid-1980s, as a faculty member in the Harvard Economics Department, I shared my ideas with many students who (often trying only to find a way to fulfill the department's economic history requirement) found their way into my courses. I like to think that I helped a precious few future economists confront the myth of the market economy, just as they helped me clarify my own thinking. Susan Helper, Robert McCauley, Perry Mehrling, and Mohan Rao stand out. Among my colleagues in the Harvard Economics Department, I enjoyed the intellectual company of Stephen A. Marglin and David S. Landes. It was also at Harvard that I began my collaboration with Bernard Elbaum on the analysis of British economic decline, as well as with Thomas Brush and William Mass on organization and technology in the cotton textile industry. From these collective research efforts emerged the historical and theoretical foundations for many of the arguments in this book.

In addition, beginning in the early 1980s, I came into close contact with Alfred D. Chandler, Jr., of the Harvard Business School, an innovative and open-minded scholar whose work over four decades has made business history relevant, and in my view central, to the social sciences. Between 1984 and 1986, I had the good fortune of spending two years on research fellowships "across the river" at the Harvard Business School. As the Harvard–Newcomen Business History Fellow in 1984–5, I was part of the "business history group" that included Alfred Chandler, Robert Cuff, Leslie Hannah, Thomas McCraw, Richard Tedlow, and Richard Vietor. All of these scholars have in one way or another helped to shape and direct my ideas. Even after I began to teach at Barnard College of Columbia University in 1986, the Division of Research of the Harvard Business School generously funded frequent visits to Boston so that I could continue to participate in the school's Business History Seminar. I have also benefited from the suggestions and criticisms of commentators and other participants in the Business History Seminar, including Alice Amsden, Barbara Ankeny, Kim Clark, Herman Daems, Takashi Hikino, Patricia O'Brien, Michael Porter, Richard Rosenbloom, Richard Schmalensee, Bruce Scott, and Steven Tolliday. Although I absolve the Harvard Business School and anyone connected with it of any responsibility for the views expressed in this book, the fact is that these essays would not have been written without the stimuli and resources that HBS is uniquely equipped to provide.

Finally, at Barnard College, I had the good fortune of working in a likeminded economics department, where I enjoyed innumerable discussions with Duncan Foley and Perry Mehrling on themes that are taken up in this book. An unexpected bonus was the arrival of Richard R. Nelson at Columbia the same year that I began to teach there. We subsequently collaborated in a seminar on institutions and technological change in which the ideas in this book were further developed.

Besides the major intellectual influences on my work that I have already mentioned, I have received useful comments and criticisms from many scholars in a number of places over the past few years. The historical synthesis in Chapter 1 went through many revisions. I presented earlier versions to the Business History Seminar at the Harvard Business School in February 1987; the Second International Conference on the History of Enterprise, Terni, Italy, October 1–4, 1987; the Second International Joseph A. Schumpeter Conference, Siena, Italy, May 23–7, 1988; a symposium at the Center for Social Theory and Comparative History at UCLA, February 27, 1989; the Warwick Summer Research Workshop, University of Warwick, July 21, 1989; and the Social Science Seminar at the Institute for Advanced Study, Princeton, October 5, 1989. Versions of this chapter appear in G. Dosi, R. Giannetti, and P. A. Toninelli, eds., *Technology and Enterprise in a Historical Perspective* (Oxford University Press, forthcoming); and in Arnold Heertje and Mark Perlman, eds., *Evolving Technology and Market Structure* (Ann Arbor: University of Michigan Press, 1991), 77–98. Chapter 2 was presented to the Business History Seminar at the Harvard Business School in February 1986 and then to the International Symposium on Property Rights, Organizational Forms, and Economic Behaviour, Friiberghs Herrgård, Sweden, June 2–5, 1986. A version of this chapter can be found in Bo Gustafsson, ed., *Power and Economic Institutions: Reinterpretations in Economic History* (London: Elgar, 1991), 253–301. Elements of Chapter 3 were presented orally to the Conference on the Process of Technological Change at the New School for Social Research, November 10–11, 1989. Chapter 4 is adapted from a paper written for a conference in honor of David Landes that met at the Villa Serbelloni, Bellagio, Italy, August 30 to September

4, 1987. The original paper will appear in Patrice Higgonet and Henry Rosovsky, eds., *Technological Constraints and Entrepreneurial Responses: Essays in Modern and Contemporary Economic History* (Cambridge, Mass.: Harvard University Press, forthcoming). Chapter 5 is part of a paper, "Beyond the Market Mentality," that I presented to the Business History Seminar at the Harvard Business School in March 1986. Chapters 6 and 7 were originally written as a review essay of Oliver Williamson's *The Economic Institutions of Capitalism* to appear in *Business History Review*. In its length and content, however, the essay outgrew the bounds of the original mandate given to me by the editor of the *Review*. Under the title "The Causes and Consequences of the Modern Corporation: Innovation and Adaptation in the Theory of the Firm," a version of Chapter 6 was presented to the Conference on New Directions in Business History: Industrial Performance and Enterprise, University of California, Santa Cruz, April 29 to May 1, 1988, with Oliver E. Williamson as a commentator.

I have received helpful comments on various parts of this book from Michael Bernstein, Samuel Bowles, Andre Burgstaller, Bernard Elbaum, Lou Ferleger, Duncan Foley, Louis Galambos, Howard Gospel, Chris Green, Susan Helper, Stephen Marglin, William Mass, Perry Mehrling, and Richard Nelson. I am particularly grateful to Carol Heim for extensive and incisive comments on an earlier version of the manuscript, to Thomas McCraw for his suggestions on the organization of the manuscript, to Bo Gustafsson for his comments on Chapter 2, to Duncan Foley for discussions of Chapter 3, and to Lou Ferleger and William Mass for suggestions on the form and content of Chapter 9. I am also pleased that the Associazione di Storia e Studi Sull'impresa (ASSI) has deemed it worthwhile to translate this work into Italian, with Renato Giannetti as the translator and Il Mulino as the publisher. Economics as a social science is so fraught with errors and omissions that none of these people could possibly bear responsibility for any that remain in this book.

Besides general research funds that I received from the Division of Research, Harvard Business School, my second year as a research fellow at the Harvard Business School was financed by fellowships from the German Marshall Fund of the United States and the National Science Foundation, Program on the History and Philosophy of Science. The book took its final form while I was a Visiting Member of the School of Social Science, Institute for Advanced Study. Constrained as I was by my obsolete word processing technology, I am grateful that Ruthe Foster had the time and energy to reprocess the manuscript during my stay at the institute. Robert O'Connor helped with final revisions. Mary and Robert Racine copyedited the manuscript for Cambridge University Press, while Marko

Ahtisaari assisted me in last-stage editing in New York and John Bois proofread in Cambridge, Mass. I would also like to thank Frank Smith of Cambridge University Press for seeing the project through.

Finally, I thank Kathy Cannings for sharing all aspects of my intellectual life and family life as the ideas and then the words in this book took form. To her, this book is dedicated.

Introduction: the wealth of three nations

Historical foundations for the "invisible hand"

In 1975 the noted institutional economist Robert A. Gordon entitled his American Economic Association presidential address "Rigor and Relevance in a Changing Institutional Setting." Gordon argued that "the mainstream of economic theory sacrifices far too much relevance in its insistent pursuit of ever increasing rigor." "We economists," he complained, "pay too little attention to the _changing_ institutional environment that conditions economic behavior." Gordon continued, "We do not often enough reexamine our basic postulates in light of changes in this environment, and, perhaps more important, we shy away from the big questions about how and why the institutional structure is changing – and where it is taking us."[1]

In the history of economic thought, economists have not always ignored the "big questions." Indeed the attempt to relate economic institutions to economic development was first taken up in a serious way in the late eighteenth century when Adam Smith inquired into the "nature and causes of the wealth of nations." Writing on the eve of the world's first industrial revolution in an era when ownership and control of the manufacturing enterprise were a proprietary affair, Smith emphasized how the growth of economic individualism would benefit the growth of the economy. And, indeed, as I shall outline in Chapter 1, Britain's rise to its position of industrial leadership in the nineteenth century did rely on highly specialized proprietary firms, the activities of which were coordinated by market relations. Yet a closer look at the content of Smith's own ideas as well as the longer-run historical causes of the wealth of the British nation reveal that the link between individualistic institutions and Britain's rise to economic dominance can be overdrawn.[2]

Smith encapsulated his theory of economic development in the dictum

---

[1] Robert A. Gordon, "Rigor and Relevance in a Changing Institutional Setting," _American Economic Review_, 66 (March 1976), 1–14, quoted at 1.

[2] For an extended version of the following argument, see William Lazonick, "El capitalismo moderno" [Modern capitalism], paper presented at the colloquium entitled "Ideology, Enterprise, and Development," sponsored by Instituto de Investigacion para el Desarrollo Economico Nacional (IDIDEN), Lima, Peru, June 19–21, 1990.

"Division of labor is limited by the extent of the market."[3] The more extensive the demand that a firm, industry, or national economy faces, the more extensive the specialized division of labor that the firm, industry, or national economy can put in place. And for Smith, the more specialized the division of labor, the greater the productive powers of labor.

Smith did not argue that this specialized division of labor itself had to be coordinated by the market. Indeed, in Smith's famous example of the division of labor in pin manufacture a capitalist employer, not the market, coordinated the specialized division of labor.[4] Rather, Smith's arguments for laissez-faire had to do with eradicating legislated barriers to the mobility of capital into those uses in which its owners deemed it most profitable to employ it – that is, into those uses that offered the most scope for specialized divisions of labor. If the barriers to entry into productive activity and product markets were broken down, Smith argued, the invisible hand of self-interest would guide capital into those uses in which the division of labor could be carried the furthest.[5]

In making these arguments, Smith was proposing institutional change. In the British context of the 1770s, the political purpose of the *Wealth of Nations* was to attack the mercantilist institutions that the British economy had built up over the previous two hundred years. Yet in proposing institutional change, Smith lacked a dynamic historical analysis. In his assault on these institutions, Smith might have asked why the extent of the world market available to Britain in the late eighteenth century was *so uniquely under British control.* If Smith had asked this "big question," he might have been forced to grant credit for Britain's extent of the world market to the very mercantilist institutions he was attacking.

In particular, Smith might have recognized the importance of the joint-stock trading companies such as the East India Company and the Royal Africa Company, chartered by the British monarchy, in opening up new markets around the world to British goods, particularly yarn and cloth exports. In turn, these companies, with their organizations abroad and their armed merchant fleets, became the bulwarks of British international political and military power.[6]

---

[3] Adam Smith, *An Inquiry into the Nature and Causes of the Wealth of Nations* (New York: Modern Library, 1937), Bk. 1, ch. 3.

[4] See Chapter 8.

[5] See Smith, *Wealth of Nations*, 423, for the reference to the "invisible hand."

[6] See, e.g., Ramkrishna Mukherjee, *The Rise and Fall of the East India Company* (New York: Monthly Review Press, 1974); K. G. Davies, *The Royal African Company* (London: Longman Group, 1957); Alfred C. Wood, *A History of the Levant Company* (Oxford: Oxford University Press, 1935). More generally, see G. D. Ramsay, *English Overseas Trade During the Centuries of Emergence* (London: Macmillan Press, 1957); Theodore K. Rabb, *Enterprise & Empire: Merchant and Gentry Investment in the Expansion of England, 1575–1630* (Cambridge, Mass.: Harvard University Press, 1967); Robert Brenner,

Smith might then have mentioned Britain's use of its political power to stifle the growth of the textile industries of Portugal and Ireland in the eighteenth century, thus leaving the extent of the market for these tradable goods to be supplied by British manufacturers. He might also have emphasized how Britain's victorious wars against the Spanish in the sixteenth century, the Dutch in the seventeenth century, and the French in the eighteenth century helped to ensure that British ships would be free to trade where and when they pleased. Smith might have conceded that, from the late seventeenth century, Britain's growing extent of the market depended on its national power, exercised both militarily and diplomatically, to impose and enforce the Navigation Laws. These laws, which endured well into the nineteenth century, secured Britain's position as the entrepôt of the world and effectively protected British manufactures from foreign competition in the home market. In short, Smith might have recognized the integral relation between economic and political power in the rise of Britain to international dominance.[7]

With his focus on division of labor as the source of economic development, Smith also oversimplified the transformations that enabled British industry to supply the growing extent of the market. History shows that Britain's supply-side response was not simply a more specialized division of labor, as depicted in Smith's example of pin manufacture. More profoundly, this response entailed a reorganization of the ways in which productive labor was performed in both agriculture and industry.

In agriculture, the emergence and growth of market opportunities to sell wool and grain – opportunities that were opened up by mercantile ventures supported by the power of the state – created incentives to reallocate the use of land from traditional subsistence crops to the production of these tradable commodities. The reorganization of agricultural land, which went forward in Britain from the sixteenth century under what has become known as the enclosure movement, inevitably undermined the viability of traditional peasant agriculture. While the enclosure movement permitted British agriculture to take advantage of new opportunities for commercial farming, it also created a sizable labor force of disinherited peasants with only tenuous attachments to the land. To earn a living, many of these peasants turned to "domestic industry" – the production of goods in their cottages. The most important branches of domestic industry were textiles – at first woolens, using the homegrown raw

"The Social Basis of English Commercial Expansion, 1550–1650," *Journal of Economic History*, 32 (March 1972), 361–84.

[7] See C. H. Wilson, *England's Apprenticeship, 1603–1763* (London: Longman Group, 1965); Ralph Davis, *The Rise of the Atlantic Economies* (Ithaca, N.Y.: Cornell University Press, 1973); John Brewer, *Sinews of Power: War, Money, and the English State, 1688–1783* (Cambridge, Mass.: Harvard University Press, 1990).

material, but increasingly from the eighteenth century, cottons, using the raw material imported into Britain on the third leg of the triangular trade with Africa and the Americas.[8]

It was the eighteenth-century expansion of domestic industry, with capital flowing to workers in the English countryside, that laid the basis for the British Industrial Revolution. The emergence of labor-saving machine technologies in the later decades of the eighteenth century transformed the productive potential of textile manufacture. Increasingly, the technologies were housed in factories, but during the Industrial Revolution domestic industry based on handloom weaving expanded to service the factory system based on mechanized spinning. Ultimately, as the nineteenth century progressed and as the textile industries became increasingly more export oriented, mechanization ousted hand methods, and the factory replaced the family home as the predominant site of production.[9]

The rise of the factory represented a dramatic social change in the way in which workers sought to earn a living. Yet even with the coming of this more collectivized mode of production, the ownership and management of firms remained under the control of individual proprietors or close partnerships. As I shall outline in Chapter 1, beyond the well-known entrepreneurs of the early Industrial Revolution such as Arkwright and Peel, the capitalist-employers who ran the British factories of the nineteenth century tended to possess relatively narrow managerial skills and limited financial capital. Hence, they generally chose to set up shop in narrowly specialized branches of industry and in geographic locations that already possessed ample supplies of key resources, particularly skilled workers (themselves the legacy of the prior prevalence of domestic industry) who could keep imperfect machines running and goods in process on the shop floor. Vertical specialization and industrial localization spawned horizontal fragmentation. As a result, there emerged structures of industrial organization internal to Britain's major industries in which the market coordination of economic activity played a dominant role.[10]

---

[8] For a critical survey of the impact of the enclosure movement, see William Lazonick, "Karl Marx and Enclosures in England," *Review of Radical Political Economics*, 6 (Summer 1974), 1–32; see also Michael Turner, *Enclosures in England, 1750–1830* (London: Macmillan Press, 1984). On domestic industry, see Maxine Berg, Pat Hudson, and Michael Sonenscher, eds., *Manufacture in Town and Country before the Factory* (Cambridge University Press, 1983); G. D. Ramsay, *The English Woolen Industry, 1500–1750* (London: Macmillan Press, 1984); L. A. Clarkson, *Proto-Industrialization: The First Phase of Industrialization?* (London: Macmillan Press, 1985); Maxine Berg, *The Age of Manufactures, 1700–1820* (London: Fontana, 1985).

[9] On the often complementary coexistence of hand methods and machine methods, see Berg, *Age of Manufactures*; Raphael Samuel, "Workshop of the World: Steam Power and Hand Technology in Mid-Victorian Britain," *History Workshop*, 3 (1977), 6–72; Royden Harrison and Jonathan Zeitlin, eds., *Divisions of Labour: Skilled Workers and Technological Change in Nineteenth Century England* (Sussex: Harvester Press, 1985).

[10] See Chapter 1.

It was the emergence of these highly individualistic structures of industrial organization in the nineteenth century that lent credibility to the idea of the efficacious running of the economy by an "invisible hand." Given the competitive advantages in international competition that British industry had attained as a result of the Industrial Revolution, British manufacturing interests also saw fit to make the argument that unfettered market forces should operate in the international economy as a whole. The nineteenth-century British advocated laissez-faire because, given the advanced economic development that their industries had already achieved, they thought that their firms could withstand open competition from foreigners. The ideological goal of the British manufacturing interests was to convince other nations that they would be better off if they opened up their markets to British goods.

The argument for laissez-faire in international trade found theoretical justification in David Ricardo's theory of comparative advantage – a set of propositions that still appears in economics textbooks and that in retrospect marks the beginning of static analysis as a methodological feature of Anglo-American economics.[11] What the British advocates of laissez-faire neglected to talk about was the role that a system of national power had played in creating conditions for Britain to embark on its dynamic development path. In the last half of the nineteenth century, the proponents of the unfettered operation of international markets accepted as a natural fact of life Britain's dominant position as the "workshop of the world." They did not bother to ask how Britain had attained that position, while they conveniently ignored the ongoing system of national power – the British Empire – that even at the beginning of the twentieth century continued to support Britain's position of international economic leadership.

But the ultimate critique of nineteenth-century laissez-faire ideology is *not* that it ignored the role of national power in Britain's past and present. Rather, the ultimate critique is that laissez-faire failed to comprehend Britain's economic future – a future in which, confronted by far more powerful systems of national capitalism, the British economy would enter into a long-run relative decline from which it has yet to recover.[12] In contrast to the message of those who propound what I call the myth of the market economy, Britain's problem in the twentieth century was not that it relied too little, but that it relied too much, on market coordination

---

[11] David Ricardo, *The Principles of Political Economy and Taxation* (Harmondsworth: Penguin Books, 1971), ch. 7. For a critique of the theory of comparative advantage as a determinant of British exports and imports in the late nineteenth and early twentieth centuries, see Bernard Elbaum, "Cumulative or Comparative Advantage? British Competitiveness in the Early Twentieth Century," *World Development*, 18 (September 1990), 1255–72.

[12] See Bernard Elbaum and William Lazonick, eds., *The Decline of the British Economy* (Oxford: Clarendon Press, 1986).

of its economic activities. Moreover, Britain's problem lay less in an inadequate involvement of the state in the economy than in an inability of
its business organizations to engage in the planned coordination of the
specialized divisions of labor that were coming to characterize the ascen-
dent capitalist economies abroad.

Modern capitalism: mythology and reality

In Chapter 8, I shall show how some twentieth-century economists, namely,
Allyn Young and George Stigler, have misused Adam Smith's notion that
the division of labor is limited by the extent of the market by assuming
that the supply-side response – the specialized division of labor – would
be coordinated by markets.[13] Such ideological preconceptions have both
sustained the myth of the market economy and enabled modern economists to avoid asking what Gordon called the "big questions."

Gordon specifically identified Stigler as a modern economist who took
refuge in conventional economic theory to avoid confronting the issue of
the evolving relation between theory and reality. In typical neoclassical
fashion, Stigler used conventional theory to evaluate reality rather than
vice versa. Gordon quoted Stigler's defense of this mainstream methodology:

> The dominant influence upon the working range of economic theorists is the set
> of internal values and pressures of the discipline. The subjects of study are posed
> by the unfolding course of scientific developments. . . . This is not to say that the
> environment is without influence [in determining the questions that economic
> theorists ask]. [But] whether a fact or development is significant depends primar-
> ily on its relevance to current economic theory.[14]

Gordon aptly remarked on Stigler's statement: "What a curious relating
of rigor to relevance! Whether the real world matters depends presumably on 'its relevance to current economic theory.' Many if not most of
today's economic theorists seem to agree with this ordering of priorities."[15]

There are undoubtedly mainstream economic theorists who, disagree-
ing with Gordon, would argue that they have always been asking the "big
questions": What is the optimal allocation of scarce resources and how
can it be achieved? To such economists, I would respond that the focus
on the "optimal allocation of scarce resources" cannot generate answers

---

[13] Allyn Young, "Increasing Returns and Economic Progress," *Economic Journal*, 38 (December 1928), 527–42; George Stigler, "The Division of Labor Is Limited by the Extent
of the Market," *Journal of Political Economy*, 59 (June 1951), 185–93. See also Chapter 8.
[14] Gordon, "Rigor and Relevance," 2.   [15] Ibid.

to the questions I shall pose in this book: How are productive resources developed and, once developed, what determines the extent of their utilization? Neoclassical economists begin their analyses of the "optimal" allocation of scarce resources by assuming a given endowment of productive resources. They simply do not ask how a society overcomes scarcity by changing the quality and quantity of productive resources that it uses – that is, by developing and utilizing its productive resources.

I would argue, moreover, that the propensity of mainstream economists to look first and foremost to market coordination to allocate resources serves as an intellectual barrier to perceiving the changing institutional reality of successful capitalist development; for as history shows, this changing institutional reality is characterized by the growing importance of planned coordination within the business organization and the growing dominance of the business organization over the determination of economic outcomes. Through the process of innovation, particular business organizations gain competitive advantage, thus driving the development process. Mainstream economics contains no theory of innovation and no theory of competitive advantage.

Some of today's mainstream economists might well agree with Gordon's perspective on the narrowness of conventional economic theory as it existed in the mid-1970s but contend that, since then, neoclassically trained economists have by no means been impervious to the existence of "imperfect markets" in the real-world economy.[16] In general, however, the explanatory power of these explorations of market imperfections remains constrained by the static methodology and individualist ideology of conventional economics. Despite the broadened scope of their inquiry, economists who remain bound by these intellectual constraints fail to address, let alone provide answers to, the question of how successful capitalist development occurs.

The modern theorists of "imperfect markets" continue to view a perfectly competitive market economy as the ideal, even if unattainable in practice, against which the phenomena that they study must be judged. Their obsession with equilibrium means, moreover, that their conception of this ideal is static. The theory of the market economy, as it has been elaborated in the twentieth century, contains no theory of economic development, and hence no conception of "ideal" economic outcomes that

---

[16] See, e.g., George Akerlof and Janet L. Yellen, eds., *Efficiency Wage Models of the Labor Market* (Cambridge University Press, 1986); George A. Akerlof, *An Economic Theorist's Book of Tales* (Cambridge University Press, 1984); Joseph E. Stiglitz, "Credit Markets and the Control of Capital," *Journal of Money, Credit, and Banking*, 17 (May 1985), 133–52; idem, "Theory of Competition, Incentives, and Risk," in Joseph E. Stiglitz and Frank Mathewson, eds., *New Developments in the Analysis of Market Structure* (Cambridge, Mass.: MIT Press, 1986), 399–446.

are themselves subject to continual change. History shows that the driving force of successful capitalist development is not the perfection of the market mechanism but the building of organizational capabilities.

Indeed, as I shall argue in my critique of the transaction cost approach of Oliver Williamson, what mainstream economists view as "market failures" I view as "organizational successes." They have difficulty comprehending the increasingly important role of the planned coordination of specialized divisions of labor in generating successful capitalist development. Their modeling techniques are much more sophisticated than economists such as Joan Robinson and Edward Chamberlin used over a half-century ago to analyze "imperfect competition."[17] But by their very proficiency in utilizing their training in the static methodology of mainstream economic theory and by their unquestioning acceptance of the ideology that views the perfection of market coordination as an economic ideal, the new theorists of "imperfect markets" have become intellectual captives of the myth of the market economy.

In contrast to the vision of the efficacy of market-coordinated individualism inherent in the theory of the market economy, let me summarize my general arguments concerning the changing institutional foundations of successful capitalist development. The superior development and utilization of productive resources increasingly requires that business organizations have privileged access to productive resources. Inherent in such privileged access is the supersession of market coordination to some degree. The shift from market coordination to planned coordination within business organizations has become an increasingly central characteristic of a successful capitalist economy.

In the past a prime locus of superseded markets was the business *firm*. But for some time the locus of superseded markets has been shifting from the business firm itself to the business *organization* that links business firms engaged in interrelated productive activities. In today's most successful capitalist economies – Japan in particular – formal ownership of the assets of specific firms does not constrain cooperation among firms that have common interests.

This cooperation, moreover, is aimed less at maintaining high prices or creating barriers to entry than at enhancing the capabilities of the participating enterprises to develop and utilize their productive resources. This is not to say that Japanese business enterprises do not compete with one another. As Michael Porter has shown, by international standards leading Japanese industries have a relatively large number of competi-

---

[17] Joan Robinson, *The Economics of Imperfect Competition* (London: Macmillan Press, 1933); Edward Chamberlin, *The Theory of Monopolistic Competition* (Cambridge, Mass.: Harvard University Press, 1933).

tors, and these enterprises compete for market share. At the same time, however, these enterprises recognize the importance of sharing basic technical information for the sake of developing the national industry as a whole.[18]

As I shall argue in this book, privileged access to finance, labor, and technology by firms and industries may be critical to the process of industrial innovation writ small and the process of economic development writ large. A theory of economic activity that assumes from the outset that the absence of market coordination represents a failure in the economic system cannot grasp the growing importance of planned coordination for generating economic growth.

Business organization and economic theory

The main objective of this book is to demonstrate the need for an alternative conception of the capitalist economy that can account for shifts in international industrial leadership and that can make the discipline of economics relevant to what were once considered the big questions: the nature and causes of the innovative enterprise in which the dynamic interaction between business organization and technological change is central. The theoretical framework that I shall present builds on basic cost concepts that can be found in any economics textbook. But whereas the textbooks ask how strategic decision makers in the firm optimize subject to given cost structures, I ask how the business organization can attain and sustain competitive advantage by contributing to the generation of new cost structures.

By summarizing the comparative history of capitalist development in Britain, the United States, and Japan – three national economies that have been world leaders in industry over the past century – I shall show the growing importance of planned coordination for attaining and sustaining competitive advantage. I shall also provide a conceptual outline of the

[18] See Michael E. Porter, *The Competitive Advantage of Nations* (New York: Free Press, 1990). For Japanese cooperation, see Ronald Dore, *Taking Japan Seriously: A Confucian Perspective on Leading Economic Issues* (Stanford, Calif.: Stanford University Press, 1987), ch. 10; Christopher Freeman, *Technology Policy and Economic Performance: Lessons from Japan* (London: Pinter, 1987), chs. 2–3; Michael Best, *The New Competition: Institutions of Industrial Restructuring* (Cambridge, Mass.: Harvard University Press, 1990), ch. 6; Marie Anchordoguy, *Computers Inc.: Japan's Challenge to IBM* (Cambridge, Mass.: Harvard University Press, 1989); Martin Fransman, *The Market and Beyond: Cooperation and Competition in Information Technology in the Japanese System* (Cambridge University Press, 1990). On cooperation with suppliers, see Susan Helper, "Comparative Supplier Relations in the U.S. and Japanese Auto Industries: An Exit/Voice Approach," *Business and Economic History*, 2d ser., 19 (1990), 153–62; Michael J. Smitka, "The Invisible Handshake: The Development of the Japanese Automotive Parts Industry," *Business and Economic History*, 2d ser., 19 (1990), 163–71.

related roles that organizations and markets play in a modern capitalist economy, with a particular focus on how people as individual economic actors try to make use of organizations and markets in pursuit of their own economic strategies.

Through the critical evaluation of the theories of economic development put forth by three leading economists, Karl Marx, Joseph Schumpeter, and Alfred Marshall, I shall show that the failure of modern mainstream economists to construct a relevant theory of capitalist development cannot be attributed to a lack of relevant theory in the history of economic thought. Marx with his focus on the utilization of productive resources, Schumpeter with his focus on the development of productive resources, and Marshall with his focus on planned versus market coordination in the generation of cost reductions all provided theoretical arguments that constitute points of departure for a theory of capitalist development that is of use today. We need not accept all of the conclusions reached by Marx, Schumpeter, or Marshall to recognize the importance of their major insights into the process of capitalist development. Indeed, it should be possible to integrate their insights into a theoretical structure that, in terms of understanding the dynamics of capitalist development, offers more than the sum of these three major contributions taken separately.

Beyond merely asserting that mainstream economics has ignored key contributions in its own intellectual tradition, I shall also trace the manner in which, over the course of the twentieth century, this neglect of both the history of economics and the history of capitalist economies has occurred. Since the late nineteenth century, a defining characteristic of mainstream economic theory has been an obsession with finding equilibrium solutions – that is, with finding the relationship among economic variables in situations where change does not occur. To this intellectual endeavor, the big questions that Marx, Schumpeter, and Marshall posed concerning the process of economic change were anathema. Given the nature of the questions that mainstream economists ask, it is by no means inappropriate that conventional economic theory assumed the label "marginalist."

To make the search for equilibrium solutions the end of economic science is to ignore the process of capitalist development. At issue is not the logic of marginalist thinking; it can be employed by a number of theoretical frameworks, including those of Marx and Keynes.[19] But it is only because neoclassical economics ignores the process of economic development that marginalist logic can be central to its methodology. In contrast, this logic plays a trivial role in a theoretical framework that seeks to comprehend the process of economic development.

It is not, however, just its static methodology, and its consequent focus

---

[19] Stephen A. Marglin, *Growth, Distribution, and Prices* (Cambridge, Mass.: Harvard University Press, 1985), ch. 10.

on equilibrium solutions, that renders neoclassical economic theory irrelevant. It is also its assumption that, in a well-functioning capitalist economy, it is market coordination that determines the allocation of productive resources, with business enterprises adapting to changes in market prices subject to given technological constraints. This assumption accords well with individualist ideology. It does not accord well with the realities of successful capitalist development.

It was by combining a methodological obsession with equilibrium and an ideological obsession with market coordination that mainstream economic theory lost touch with the realities of successful capitalist development and its practitioners became intellectually bound by the myth of the market economy. As I shall detail in Chapters 6 and 7, even an economist such as Oliver Williamson, who has sought to comprehend the "nature of the firm" in order to elaborate a theory of the relation between markets and hierarchies in the capitalist economy, has constrained the scope of his inquiry by his adherence to the myth of the market economy. In particular, Williamson portrays the nature of the firm very differently than does the great business historian Alfred Chandler. Ideologically smitten by the "marvels of the market," Williamson has failed to recognize the organizational success wrought by the "visible hand."

Fortunately, not all major economists of the last half of the twentieth century have been intellectually constrained by static methodology and individualistic ideology. As I shall summarize in Chapter 8, over the course of the twentieth century some prominent economists, seeking to comprehend the dynamics of capitalist development, have built on the insights of Marx, Schumpeter, and Marshall. Fortunately as well, these lines of inquiry are still in progress and their intellectual momentum may even be gathering force.

The rise of Japanese industry to a position of international leadership, moreover, has begun to open some conventional economic eyes. In his *Business Week* column dated October 8, 1990, Alan Blinder, a well-known Keynesian economist, observed:

Much has been written about Japan's formidable challenge to American industrial preeminence. But the amazing Japanese economy poses another challenge – one that has been barely noticed. I refer to Japan's challenge to received economic doctrine. Stated briefly and far too boldly, the Japanese have succeeded by doing everything wrong (according to standard economic theory). That should make economic theorists squirm.[20]

After citing a host of "market imperfections" in the operation of the Japanese economy – everything from cartels to permanent employment – Blinder commented:

[20] Alan Blinder, "There Are Capitalists, Then There Are the Japanese," *Business Week*, October 8, 1990, 21.

All in all, economists weaned on Western economic thought must conclude that Japan does almost everything wrong. Such a litany of errors should cost them dearly. Yet Japan's economy is a dynamo. How do they do it?

Blinder continued:

American capitalism rests on a grand theory begun by Adam Smith. There is no comparable theory of Japanese capitalism, but we need one if we are to formulate an intelligent economic policy toward Japan. The Japanese themselves seem less concerned with conceptualizations than with results. So, we may have to produce that theory ourselves.[21]

Blinder's conventional eyes are only partly opened. Before U.S. economists take up the challenge of producing a theory of Japanese capitalism that will permit us "to formulate an intelligent economic policy toward Japan," we must produce a theory that can comprehend the rise and decline of *U.S.* managerial capitalism. Only then can we, to paraphrase Blinder, formulate an intelligent economic policy toward the United States; for as I shall argue in this book, not only is the standard economic theory to which Blinder refers wrong for Japan, it is wrong for the United States. Indeed, when the histories of capitalist development in both the United States and Japan are properly understood, the institutions of planned coordination that have been responsible for Japan's rise to international industrial leadership will be seen to represent not so much a departure from U.S. experience as a more thoroughgoing elaboration of the institutions of planned coordination that had previously brought leadership to the United States.

Lessons of history

Economic dominance, once attained, does not last forever. With the culmination of the postwar Japanese "miracle" over the past two decades, U.S. industrialists, politicians, and academics have begun to learn this lesson of history. Indeed, it is a lesson that the British had learned before World War II. Yet there is scarcely a consensus concerning the means to restore the industrial competitiveness of once-dominant economies such as Britain and the United States, in large part because there are deep disagreements concerning the sources of Japanese success and the causes of national economic decline.

The conventional wisdom has it that the erosion of national competitiveness is simply the result of a maladjustment of market forces that can

---

[21] Ibid. For an important book on successful capitalist development that shows how South Korea "got prices wrong," see Alice H. Amsden, *Asia's Next Giant* (New York: Oxford University Press, 1989).

be corrected by changes in relative wages, exchange rates, and the elimination of unfair trade practices. The economies of Britain and the United States are, after all, "market economies." Let the market work to equilibrate supply and demand and "get prices right."

So mainstream Anglo-American economists tell us. But the history of modern capitalism tells a different story – one that challenges beliefs that letting the market work will either generate industrial success or reverse competitive decline. Since the late nineteenth century, the most successful capitalist economies have moved away from market coordination toward the planned coordination of their productive activities. The movement to planned coordination has not occurred solely, or even primarily, at the level of the state, but at the level of the business organization. Far from economic prosperity requiring a "perfection" of the market mechanism, the experience of the twentieth century has shown that the wealth of different nations has become increasingly dependent on the planned coordination that takes place within business organizations.

There was a time and place when market coordination sufficed in international economic competition. The time was the late nineteenth century, the place was Britain, the world's first industrial nation. The institutional basis for market coordination was the proprietary firm – an enterprise owned and managed by family members or a closed partnership for their own benefit. Constrained by limited managerial and financial resources, the proprietary firm tended to be a single-plant operation that specialized in a narrow range of activities. It therefore had to rely extensively on market relations to supply its various inputs as well as to distribute its products. The state maintained internal law and order, undertook essential welfare programs, provided elementary education, and ensured the defense of the realm. But in the coordination of economic activity, industry was left to react to the unregulated forces of supply and demand.

By the 1870s market-coordinated proprietary capitalism had made Britain the "workshop of the world." In 1870 labor productivity was higher in Britain than in the United States – 14 percent higher by one estimate.[22] In the early 1880s Britain had more than 40 percent of world manufactured exports and the United States only 6 percent.[23]

The following decades, however, saw a reversal in the relative productivity levels of the two nations and dramatic changes in their export market shares. U.S. productivity had caught up to the British level by 1890, if not before, and on the eve of World War I was at least 20 percent

---

[22] Angus Maddison, *Phases of Capitalist Development* (New York: Oxford University Press, 1982), 98.
[23] R. C. O. Matthews, C. H. Feinstein, and J. C. Odling-Smee, *British Economic Growth, 1856–1973* (Stanford, Calif.: Stanford University Press, 1982), 435.

greater. From the 1890s the British share of manufactured exports steadily eroded while the U.S. share steadily increased, until by 1929 Britain
exported 24 percent of the world's manufactures and the United States
22 percent.[24] Britain remained an advanced industrial economy in the
twentieth century, but continually lost ground not only to the United
States but also to nations such as Germany and Japan.

In the passing of industrial leadership from Britain to the United States,
the institutional character of capitalism changed dramatically. In contrast
to the small, vertically specialized proprietary firms that had characterized Britain's rise to economic dominance, U.S. competitive advantage
came from managerial enterprises that operated a number of geographi-
cally dispersed plants and offices and that integrated a number of vertically related activities.

Internally generated funds financed the expansion of U.S. managerial
enterprises. If necessary for further industrial expansion, successful industrial firms were able to draw on the services of Wall Street investment
bankers to supplement retained earnings with long-term bond finance.
The growth of managerial enterprises also created a need for a large number of qualified line and staff personnel. In response, large-scale infusions
of business and public funding transformed the educational system to meet
the demand for "organization men" (and much later "organization women").

Besides its critical role in the expansion of higher education, the U.S.
government stood ready to provide tariff protection to industry. But it
was the rise of planned coordination within, by, and for the private-sector
economy that marked the rise of U.S. managerial capitalism. By the first
decades of the twentieth century, managerial capitalism with its planned
coordination had replaced proprietary capitalism with its market coordination as the most powerful generator of economic growth.

The recent emergence of Japan as an economic power does not signal a
reversion to proprietary capitalism, despite the number and importance
of proprietary firms in the present-day Japanese economy. The vast majority of proprietary firms in Japan are integral elements of networks of
enterprises, each group dominated by powerful industrial, commercial,
and financial firms. Far from turning toward market coordination, the
basis of Japanese economic success over the past decades has been a more
far-reaching elaboration of the institutions of managerial capitalism that
underlay U.S. international competitive advantage in the first six decades
of this century. Through Japan's enterprise group system, planned coordination extends across legally distinct firms to ensure that their various

---

[24] Maddison, *Phases of Capitalist Development*, 252–4; Matthews et al., *British Economic
Growth*, 435.

activities coalesce in the pursuit of common goals. Within the dominant Japanese firm, planned coordination extends further down the organizational hierarchy to include male blue-collar workers as members of the business organization, thus facilitating the managerial function of ensuring that shop-floor activities further organizational goals.

Much more than was the case with the rise of managerial capitalism in the United States, the Japanese state has played an important role in preserving the home market for Japanese firms. By influencing the distribution of income, the organization of industry, the availability of finance, the education of labor, and even the patterns of consumer demand, the Japanese government has gone much further in creating conditions supportive of economic development. Yet ultimately the Japanese economy relies on the strategies and structures of private-sector enterprises to generate the high-quality products at low unit costs that have enabled Japanese industry to capture major shares of world markets.

Underlying the phenomenal success of the Japanese economy since the 1950s, therefore, have been the willingness and ability of its corporate enterprises to extend the principle of planned coordination – a principle that served American corporations so well in the rise of managerial capitalism – across firms, within firms, and to business–government relations. The Japanese have not rejected managerial capitalism, but have elaborated it into a set of institutional relationships that I call collective capitalism.

What was it about managerial capitalism that enabled U.S. industry to gain competitive advantage over the market-coordinated British economy in the first decades of this century? And what is it about collective capitalism that has enabled Japan to outcompete the United States more recently? More generally, what is the relation between economic institutions and economic performance, and how have the economic institutions of the most successful capitalist economies changed over the past century?

The answers to these questions require an understanding of the value-creating capabilities of different modes of economic organization in different social contexts. The first and fundamental step is to comprehend how, in general, a capitalist economy creates *value* – products that people desire at prices they can afford. Because capitalist economies ultimately rely on the strategies and structures of business enterprises to create value, the analysis of the process of value creation requires an explicit conception of the value-creating business organization. The analysis must then explore why specific modes of coordination of the activities of business enterprises have possessed superior value-creating capabilities in particular times and places. Finally, the analysis must ask why those national economies that had gained international dominance on the basis of one mode˙of economic coordination – for example, Britain on the basis of proprietary capitalism and the United States on the basis of managerial capitalism – have had difficulty responding to the new competition based on more highly organized institutional structures.

This book does not provide all the answers to these historical questions. Rather, its goal is to provide economists and historians with the intellectual orientation that is critical to historical analysis. In explicating this intellectual orientation, this book also confronts conventional academic views about the relation between economic institutions and economic prosperity. The ideology that rules the thinking of mainstream economics, in the English-speaking world at least, is that well-functioning *capitalist* economy is a *market* economy. Although mainstream thinking has shown great ingenuity in considering the nature of "imperfect" markets and their impacts on economic outcomes, the unquestioned underlying assumption is always that the perfection of markets, if only attainable, would result in the most efficient economic outcomes.

I call this misguided assumption the "myth of the market economy" because it is contradicted by the reality of *successful* capitalist development in the twentieth century. In its seemingly endless search for solutions, both theoretical and political, to remedy the "disabilities" of imperfect markets, mainstream economics has failed to recognize the growing importance of business organization relative to market exchange for generating economic development. In particular, the neoclassical perspective on the operation of the "market economy" that fills economics textbooks, classroom lectures, and academic journals contains no theory of the *innovative* business organization – an organization that generates the higher-quality products at lower unit costs that are the essence of the process of economic development. In this book, I shall outline a theory of the innovative business organization that provides the foundations for explaining shifts in international industrial leadership and changes in the wealth of capitalist nations. The elaboration of such a historically relevant theory is a worthwhile project in its own right. In the process, however, I also hope to explode the myth of the market economy, if only because it represents such a formidable ideological impediment, both within academia and in the world beyond, to understanding how we might shape social institutions to manage the economic future.

The ordering of the chapters is designed to emphasize the use of comparative historical methodology to develop dynamic theory and the use of historically relevant dynamic theory to critique static methodology and misinformed ideology. Synthesizing recent empirical research (including my own), Chapter 1 provides a historical analysis of the changing institutional foundations of international industrial leadership as it has moved from Britain to the United States to Japan over the past century. On the basis of this historical synthesis, Chapter 2 proposes a conceptual framework for understanding how and why organizations characterized by the planned coordination of specialized divisions of labor have increasingly superseded markets as the institutional basis for successful capitalist development. Drawing on the historical analysis and conceptual framework, Chapter 3 transforms the static theory of the firm of the conventional textbooks into a dynamic theory of the business organization as an engine of economic growth.

Just in case the reader finds my theoretical, historical, and conceptual arguments in the first three chapters novel, Chapter 4 outlines the influence on my approach of the work of two economists, Karl Marx and Joseph Schumpeter, and two historians, Alfred Chandler and David Landes. My purpose is not to render praise unto these scholars, but to provide accessible critical evaluations of their work so that economists might build relevant intellectual traditions without, as is so often the case, having to reinvent the intellectual wheel.

The importance of building on relevant intellectual traditions, and of using intellectual traditions in a relevant way, should become apparent in Chapter 5. Here I show how the work of Alfred Marshall could have contributed to the analysis of business organization and economic development. I argue that the application of his concept of internal economies of scale to the analysis of capitalist development could have long since dispelled the myth of the market economy. I recount how, from the turn of the century, mainstream economists managed to miss the significance of both the advent of managerial capitalism and Marshall's framework for analyzing the sources of economic development. Instead, mainstream economists constructed a theory of the firm in equilibrium. I go on to illustrate how, during the 1960s and 1970s, some prominent economists – specifically Gary Becker, Harvey Leibenstein, and the team of Armen Alchian and Harold Demsetz – whose work raised important issues concerning the origins, operations, and impacts of the modern business enterprise, nevertheless remained prisoners of an outmoded market mentality.

Chapter 6 develops the theory of the innovative organization and uses it to critique the transaction cost approach of Oliver E. Williamson. Transaction cost theory permits Williamson to recognize the empirical importance of administrative coordination in economic activity while still extolling (as he put it) "the marvels of the market." I characterize his approach as a theory of the "adaptive" organization, in contrast to the theory of the "innovative" organization – a theory that I argue has become central to any analysis of the dynamics of economic development in the advanced capitalist nations.

In Chapter 7, I take the critique of Williamson's transaction cost approach further by showing how, for lack of a theory of the innovative organization, Williamson misinterprets critical institutional transformations in U.S. business history as documented by Alfred Chandler. One purpose of this chapter is to show how an ill-suited, preconceived theory can result in the misuse of history, as (whether consciously or not) the "facts" are made to fit the theory. Another purpose of this chapter is to provide the reader with a summary of what Chandler really said in his path-breaking book *The Visible Hand*. A final purpose of the chapter is to debunk a common view that the economist Williamson and the historian Chandler are simply making the same arguments from different disciplinary perspectives. They are not. Although both deal with the relation between business organizations and market exchange in advanced capitalist economies, one has succumbed to the myth of the market economy, while the other has not.

I conclude the book with two chapters that aim to help overcome the intellectual constraints that render mainstream economics largely irrelevant for comprehending the process of capitalist development and shifts in international competitive advantage. In Chapter 8, I outline how the Marxian, Schumpeterian, and Marshallian theories of capitalist development must be revised in order to capture the essential features of the relation between economic institutions and economic performance in leading capitalist economies. Indeed, I review the ways in which, over the past few decades, leading neo-Marxians, neo-Schumpeterians, and neo-Marshallians have undertaken such revisions. I critically evaluate the extent to which these revisions of the three lines of theoretical inquiry provide foundations for future research into the historical dynamics of economic development in the advanced capitalist world.

To overcome prevailing intellectual constraints, however, relevant theory is not enough. Precisely because we are analyzing the process of change, theory is only a guide to ongoing empirical analysis, and not (as is generally the case among mainstream economists) a substitute for it. It is on the basis of rigorous historical analyses, brought up to the present, that one can continually reassess the relevance of existing theory for guiding political intervention into the process of change. To do rigorous historical analysis requires not only a relevant theoretical framework, but also an appropriate historical methodology. For understanding the dynamics of capitalist development in the late twentieth century and beyond, mainstream economics is constrained by its adherence not only to the theory of the market economy, but also to the methodology of constrained optimization. Chapter 9 explains the intellectual constraints inherent in an exclusive reliance on the constrained optimization methodology and then,

by considering the work of economic historians and institutional economists in the United States, seeks to provide methodological content to
the intellectual phenomenon that Joseph A. Schumpeter called "historical
experience."[25]

[25] Joseph A. Schumpeter, *History of Economic Analysis* (New York: Oxford University Press, 1954), 13.

PART I

Economic institutions and economic performance

1

Institutional foundations of industrial dominance and decline

Capitalism: proprietary, managerial, and collective

What were the characteristics of the business institutions that underlay the shifts in international industrial dominance from Britain in the late nineteenth century to the United States in the early twentieth century to Japan more recently? What were the sources of economies, internal and external to business enterprises in these three nations, that formed the bases for international competitive advantage during their eras of dominance? And how and to what extent did the very different strategies and structures of business organizations that brought first Britain and then the United States to international dominance persist as impediments to organizational and technological transformation in subsequent eras when more powerful modes of business organization had appeared on the international economic scene? Drawing on a large and rapidly growing body of relevant empirical research, I shall attempt in this chapter to answer these questions.

Of necessity, the answers will be summary – succinct, but at times cryptic (particularly for the historically uninformed). My purpose here is to make the case for the growing importance of planned coordination relative to market coordination in the conduct of business activities in the most successful capitalist economies. Further elaboration and proof of the case – of the movement from proprietary to managerial to collective capitalism as the organizational foundations for industrial dominance – is a subject for ongoing research, for which the historical perspective presented here provides a general framework. For the sake of presenting this framework in as clear a manner as possible, I make reference in this chapter only to those secondary works (a number of my own contributions among them) that both present and document the key historical arguments. The interested reader should consult these works for more details and further references.

Whether proprietary, managerial, or collective, capitalist development by definition depends on private-sector enterprise to make investments in productive resources and to develop and utilize those resources in order to generate useful products at affordable costs. In a capitalist econ-

23

omy, the strategies and structures of private enterprise are the prime determinants of the levels of employment, productivity, output, and income.

The distinguishing feature of proprietary capitalism is the integration of asset ownership with managerial control, this integration placing financial and administrative constraints on the growth of the firm. The distinguishing feature of managerial capitalism is the separation of ownership from control, made possible by investments in managerial structures. The distinguishing features of collective capitalism are (1) the organizational integration of a number of distinct firms (i.e., units of financial control) in pursuit of a common investment strategy, (2) the long-term integration into the enterprise of personnel below the managerial level, and (3) the cooperation of the state in shaping the social environment to reduce the uncertainty facing private-sector investments.

The evolution of capitalism from the proprietary to the managerial to the collective eras has occurred across national economies as well as over time. Before the late nineteenth century, managerial capitalism did not yet exist. In the last half of the nineteenth century, proprietary capitalism formed the institutional basis for British dominance of the international economy. By the early decades of the twentieth century, managerial capitalism had emerged, particularly in the United States, to pose a formidable competitive challenge to proprietary capitalism. More recently, Japan has elaborated the managerial model, particularly as developed in the United States, into the potent economic force that I call collective capitalism.

Over the long run, managerial capitalism has proved itself more powerful than proprietary capitalism in the development and utilization of productive resources. Similarly, collective capitalism has proved itself more powerful than managerial capitalism. But, as we shall see, capitalist economies that have risen to positions of international industrial leadership on the basis of an earlier mode of business organization – proprietary or managerial, as the case may be – do not necessarily or easily make the transition to the more powerful mode of business organization. Because of vested interests and the ability to compete by making adaptive responses using traditional technologies and organizations, the very business institutions that formed the foundations for the rise to industrial leadership in one era can and do persist to pose barriers to industrial transformation within the once-dominant economies. Therefore, after outlining the relation between economic institutions and economic performance in the rise of Britain, the United States, and Japan to international industrial dominance, I shall discuss the constraints on the value-creation process that the legacy of proprietary capitalism has imposed on the British economy and that the legacy of managerial capitalism has imposed on the U.S. economy.

Proprietary capitalism

Enterprise management was important to the success of the pioneering factories in the early stages of the British Industrial Revolution. Yet as the nineteenth century progressed, firms came to rely more on the external environment than on internal planning and coordination to ensure access to the productive resources required to generate (what were by the standards of the time) high-quality products at low unit costs. The most important external resource that became available to British manufacturing firms in the nineteenth century was an ample supply of highly skilled and well-disciplined labor. Senior workers – who eventually came to be known collectively as the "aristocracy of labor" – not only provided their own skills to the building and operation of machinery but also recruited junior workers whom they trained and supervised on the shop floor. As reflected in the widespread use of piece-rate payments to senior workers, however, the employment relation between capitalist and worker was basically a market relation: pay in proportion to output produced.[1]

Capitalists' reliance on skilled labor to organize work and reproduce the labor force had the advantage of low fixed costs not only for individual firms but also for the British economy as a whole. The progress of the British Industrial Revolution did not rely to any significant extent on state-supported or industry-supported education. The reproduction of an abundant and skilled labor force, effected as it was by worker-run, on-the-job training, required little, if any, expense to either employers or the state. Eager to gain entry into the aristocracy of labor, younger workers were motivated to work hard by the prospect of promotion. The older workers, generally protected by union bargains that assured them shares of daily or weekly revenues, were themselves not averse to long and steady labor. In addition, the skilled workers' intimate practical knowledge of production methods meant that, as by-products of shop-floor experience, they were able to keep imperfect machinery running steadily and contribute to minor technological improvements.

The reproduction and expansion of a labor force with particular indus-

---

[1] E. J. Hobsbawn, *Labouring Men* (London: Weidenfeld & Nicolson, 1968); idem, *Workers: Worlds of Labor* (New York: Pantheon, 1984); Keith Burgess, *The Origins of British Industrial Relations* (London: Croom Helm, 1975); Royden Harrison and Jonathan Zeitlin, eds., *Divisions of Labour: Skilled Workers and Technological Change in Nineteenth Century Britain* (Sussex: Harvester, 1985); William Lazonick, *Competitive Advantage on the Shop Floor* (Cambridge, Mass.: Harvard University Press, 1990), chs. 3–6. For these and the following arguments more generally, see Bernard Elbaum and William Lazonick, eds., *The Decline of the British Economy* (Oxford: Clarendon Press, 1986). For an industry case study, see William Mass and William Lazonick, "The British Cotton Industry and International Competitive Advantage: The State of the Debates," *Business History*, 32 (October 1990), 9–65.

trial skills was a community-based phenomenon. As older workers trained younger workers, supplies of specialized labor expanded in certain localities during the nineteenth century. Given an industrialist's choice of business (itself typically a function of his own specialized training in a particular locality), he would tend to invest where labor with the necessary specialized skills was in relatively abundant supply. As a consequence, particular industries became increasingly concentrated in particular regions of Britain during the nineteenth century. The regional concentration of specific British industries meant that employers had access not only to large supplies of labor with the requisite skills, but also to communication and distribution networks that supplied a regional industry with its basic inputs, enabled work in progress to flow through its vertically specialized branches, and marketed its output. As the extent of the market for a regionally concentrated industry expanded, all the firms in the industry experienced external economies as the fixed costs of infrastructural investments in communications and distribution networks were spread over a larger industry output.

The growth of a regionally concentrated industry facilitated the vertical specialization of constituent firms in a narrow range of activities, these firms relying on other firms both to supply them with the necessary inputs and to purchase their outputs for resale downstream. The tendency toward vertical specialization was self-reinforcing because the growing availability of suppliers and buyers for intermediate products made it all the more easy for new firms to set up as specialists. Hence, the growth of a regionally concentrated industry was characterized more by the entry of new firms than by the growth of existing firms. Vertically specialized industries became horizontally fragmented industries.

The evolution of industry structures characterized by regional concentration, vertical specialization, and horizontal fragmentation as well as employers' ongoing reliance on skilled labor to organize work on the shop floor diminished the need for business firms to invest in the development of managerial structures and organizational capabilities. The lack of managerial organization in turn reinforced the tendency for industrial structures to be fragmented and specialized. Limited in their managerial capabilities, proprietary firms tended to confine themselves to single-plant operations, thus facilitating the entry of new firms into vertical specialties, and hence increasing the extent of horizontal as well as vertical fragmentation of industrial sectors.

The result was the rise during the nineteenth century of a market-coordinated industrial economy. By reducing the managerial as well as financial resources necessary to run a business, the vertically specialized and horizontally fragmented structure of industry permitted capitalist families to avoid the separation of capital ownership from managerial control; their firms remained proprietary. Market coordination and proprietary capitalism – both expressions of the dominance of individualism in the coordination of economic activity – went hand in hand.

Relying more on markets than managers to coordinate industrial activity, and hence more on external than internal economies to cut costs over time, British industry gained international competitive advantage. It was the institutions of market-coordinated proprietary capitalism, including heavy reliance on a self-reproducing supply of skilled labor to coordinate as well as execute work, that permitted British manufacturing to dominate world markets in the late nineteenth century. Britain's rise to industrial dominance occurred without significant investments in managerial structures that could develop firm-specific organizational capabilities. If the coordination of industrial activity by markets could ever lay claim to generating superior industrial performance, it was in Britain in the late nineteenth century.

Managerial capitalism

During the first decades of the twentieth century, proprietary capitalism gave way to managerial capitalism as the dominant engine of industrial development. Using managerial structures to plan and coordinate mechanized production processes and to apply scientific knowledge to industry, U.S. corporations had by the 1920s generated a Second Industrial Revolution. Proprietary capitalism proved inadequate to deal with the technological complexities and the attendant high fixed costs of the new industrial era.

In the first half of the nineteenth century, a scarcity of skilled labor available to capitalist firms induced the development of skill-displacing mechanical technologies in the United States. In a sparsely populated country with as yet a rudimentary transportation system, a manufacturing enterprise had to organize more activities internally to supply inputs and sell outputs. The reliance on mechanized technologies tended by unskilled labor along with high degrees of vertical integration necessitated investment in, and the development of, managerial organization to transform high fixed costs into low unit costs. Combined investments in technology and organization resulted in the emergence of innovative firms in the woodworking and metalworking industries, giving rise to what came to be known as the "American system of manufactures." Analogous developments occurred in the Lowell system of cotton textile production, the investments in organization and technology rendering the early U.S. factory system more capital intensive and reliant on managerial coordination than the textile manufacturing system that was central to the British Industrial Revolution.[2]

Critical for opening up new opportunities for innovative firms in the United States was the development in the middle decades of the century of a national communications network based on the railroad and telegraph. In addition to providing manufacturing firms with better access to raw materials and product markets, improved communications facilitated the rapid population of the nation's vast spaces, thus greatly augmenting the supplies of labor with various skills available to capitalist firms while fostering the rapid growth of aggregate demand.

In principle, these infrastructural developments could have generated external economies that could have encouraged the growth of fragmented and specialized industrial structures as in Britain. To some extent, market coordination of the U.S. economy did become more pronounced in the late nineteenth century as wage labor, as distinct from self-employment, became more widespread and as obstacles to interregional trade and capital flows were overcome. At the same time, however, some U.S. manufacturing firms seized the opportunity created by expanding national markets to make innovative investments in production and distribution facilities. They built organizational structures that would enable them to capture large shares of the national markets and transform the high fixed costs of an innovative strategy into low unit costs.[3]

In the more capital-intensive industries, innovative firms such as Carnegie in steel, Rockefeller in oil refining, Singer in sewing machines, Du Pont in chemicals, General Electric in electrical equipment, Ford and then General Motors in automobiles (to name a few) were able to generate sufficient internal economies to leap ahead of their rivals and become dominant firms; indeed, so much so that by the 1920s oligopoly characterized much of U.S. manufacturing.[4] By the middle of the twentieth century some dominant corporations had even emerged in the relatively labor-intensive U.S. textile industry.[5]

Underlying the growth of these dominant corporations was the planned coordination of their specialized divisions of labor – what Alfred D. Chan-

[2] Nathan Rosenberg, *Perspectives on Technology* (Cambridge University Press, 1976), chs. 1 and 2; David A. Hounshell, *From the American System to Mass Production, 1800–1932* (Baltimore, Md.: Johns Hopkins University Press, 1984), ch. 1; Steve Dunwell, *Run of the Mill* (Boston: Godine, 1978), chs. 1 and 2.

[3] Alfred D. Chandler, Jr., *The Visible Hand: The Managerial Revolution in American Business* (Cambridge, Mass.: Harvard University Press, 1977).

[4] Alfred D. Chandler, Jr., *Scale and Scope: The Dynamics of Industrial Capitalism* (Cambridge, Mass.: Harvard University Press, 1990), pt. 2.

[5] Solomon Barkin, "The Regional Significance of the Integration Movement in the Southern Textile Industry," *Southern Economic Journal*, 15 (April 1949), 395–411; Jesse Markham, "Integration in the Textile Industry," *Harvard Business Review* 28 (January–February 1950), 74–88.

dler, Jr., has aptly described as the "visible hand."[6] Through managerial coordination, industrial corporations were able to develop the combined productive capabilities of human and physical resources in ways that market coordination, with its unplanned interaction of specialized producers, was unable to do. The more technologically complex the process or product and the less it relied on existing external resources, the greater the corporation's need for the organizational capability to plan and coordinate in order to generate returns.

The innovative enterprise had to invest in its own research and development facilities as well as provide customers with necessary product information, credit, and after-sales service. The business organization then had to plan and coordinate the interaction of production, marketing, and R&D to generate the types of products that buyers wanted at prices they could afford. The internalization of the innovation process made the enterprise all the more capital intensive. Hence, the generation of internal economies depended all the more on the achievement of high levels of organization-specific resource utilization from initial process to sold product.

The planned coordination of a vertically related division of labor enabled the enterprise to achieve higher levels of resource utilization than if the flow of materials through the same processes had been coordinated by market relations. Shortages at any given vertical stage could be foreseen before they actually occurred, and systems of rewards and punishments could be put in place to induce employees to exert the effort required to maintain the work flows. In addition, by integrating forward into distribution, the enterprise gained greater certainty over the extent of its ongoing market share, thereby permitting it to produce in anticipation of demand and thus enhancing its control over the utilization of its productive capacity.

An enterprise that had used managerial coordination to attain competitive advantage could cumulate its advantage by exercising control over input and output markets in ways that its competitors with less organizational capability could not. Employees were less apt to leave the dominant corporation, thereby increasing the incentive for the enterprise to invest in the development of the capabilities of its personnel. External suppliers were more dependent on keeping the business of the dominant corporation. Indeed, the regular demand for goods and services from a dominant corporation provided a basis for suppliers to achieve higher levels of utilization of *their* fixed resources. A portion of the resultant value gains were passed along from the supplier to the dominant buyer in the forms of privileged access to inputs and specially low prices in order to secure present, and ensure future, business.

---

[6] Chandler, *The Visible Hand.*

Superior organizational capability gave enterprises privileged access not only to physical and human resources, but also to financial resources that could be allocated to long-run value-creating investments. The turn-of-the-century merger movement in effect created a market in industrial securities, particularly for the issues of dominant corporations that were listed on, and hence endorsed by, the New York Stock Exchange. The owner-managers who, especially in the expansionary post-Civil War decades, had transformed their firms from new ventures into going concerns could now monetize the value of the assets that their enterprises had accumulated over the years by floating securities to the wealthholding public. In most cases, the old entrepreneurs used the fortunes acquired from the public offering of their enterprises to retire from the industrial scene. Left in control of the long-run investment strategies of these dominant corporations were career managers whose skills and efforts had enabled the founding entrepreneurs to implement their innovative strategies and their firms to gain sustained competitive advantage.[7]

The new owners of these public corporations had neither the incentive nor ability to assume strategic direction of the companies whose shares they had bought. The market for industrial securities that was essentially created by the merger movement and continued to grow thereafter resulted in the widespread distribution, and hence fragmentation, of shareholding in the dominant corporations. Despite their voting rights, investors in common stock were powerless to exercise control over the allocation of the surpluses of the corporations that they collectively owned. Rather, control over the surpluses was left in the hands of the professional managers who increasingly replaced the original entrepreneurs as strategic managers of the dominant corporations. In contrast to the new owners who, as portfolio investors, typically knew next to nothing about the products and processes of the companies in which they held shares, the career managers possessed intimate organization-specific knowledge that made them ideally suited to plot the long-run investment strategies of the enterprises that they now effectively controlled.[8]

Unencumbered by either the old or the new owners, corporate managers were able to use retained earnings as the financial foundation for the high-fixed-cost investments that were essential for continued innovation and dominance. The sources of finance for further enterprise expan-

---

[7] Thomas Navin and Marion Sears, "The Rise of a Market for Industrial Securities, 1887–1902," *Business History Review* 24 (June 1955), 105–38.

[8] William Lazonick, "Financial Commitment and Economic Performance: Ownership and Control in the American Corporation," *Business and Economic History*, 2d ser., 17 (1988), 115–28; idem, "Controlling the Market for Corporate Control: The Historical Significance of Managerial Capitalism," paper presented to the meetings of the Third International Joseph A. Schumpeter Society, Airlie, Va., June 3–5, 1990.

sion were retained earnings first, bonded debt second, and new stock issues hardly at all. Underpinned by retained earnings and endorsed by Wall Street institutions such as Standard and Poor's, corporate debt represented a relatively inexpensive source of long-term funds.

Managerial capitalism had arrived. Its continued success depended on the building of managerial structures that could plan and coordinate ever more complex specialized divisions of labor. The growth of managerial capitalism required new and greatly expanded supplies of highly trained and properly socialized managerial personnel. Funded by the federal government and the private philanthropic foundations based on the industrial fortunes of late-nineteenth-century entrepreneurs such as Carnegie and Rockefeller, the social system responded. It was these public and private organizations, not autonomous market forces, that planned and coordinated the transformation of the U.S. educational system. The widespread and prolonged economic success of U.S. industrial corporations in the first decades of the twentieth century would not have been possible without the massive transformation of the system of higher education that occurred between the 1890s and 1920s to service the personnel requirements of managerial capitalism.[9]

Ironically, the critical changes that made U.S. higher education integral to managerial capitalism occurred in the land-grant colleges founded in the 1860s to enhance the social positions of the artisan and farmer as the bulwarks of Jeffersonian democracy. Farmers themselves had little use for four-year college degrees. But with the growth of U.S. agricultural exports in the late nineteenth century and the consequent founding of the United States Department of Agriculture in the 1880s, the colleges began to receive large amounts of resources, mostly public, but also some private, to research, develop, and diffuse agricultural innovations to the farmers. After the turn of the century, private foundations, banks, mail-order firms, and agricultural machinery manufacturers supported the state-coordinated effort to make the high-fixed-cost investments in the development of agricultural inputs that the millions of family farmers could never have undertaken themselves.[10]

From the 1890s large sums of business money began to support the development of engineering education, particularly at land-grant institutions such as MIT and Purdue. The growing prosperity of these new educational institutions in turn pressured the elite classical colleges such as

[9] David Noble, *America by Design* (New York: Oxford University Press, 1977); William Lazonick, "Strategy, Structure and Management Development in the United States and Britain," in Kesaji Kobayashi and Hidemasa Morikawa, eds., *Development of Managerial Enterprise* (Tokyo: University of Tokyo Press, 1986), 101–46.

[10] Lou Ferleger and William Lazonick, "The Industrial District and the Developmental State: The Case of U.S. Agriculture," photocopy, Harvard University, 1991.

Harvard and Yale to adapt their curricula to cater to business needs, often against the wishes of their leading educators. In the first decades of the century, leading businessmen, with the cooperation of the professional engineering societies, transformed and designed engineering education to serve corporate needs for managerial and technical personnel. Once this system of higher education was in place – and it essentially had taken on its current form by the 1920s – corporate employers were able to take it for granted that recruits to the managerial bureaucracy would possess the technical competency and social outlook necessary for effective performance within the business organization.

Within the corporations themselves, management development programs designed to shape social behavior and cognitive abilities to meet firm-specific needs could build on adequate and appropriate preemployment educational foundations. The most important type of management development was, and remains, the transformation of line and staff specialists into generalists who, by delegating authority without losing control, can effectively plan and coordinate extensive and complex divisions of labor. The ability to integrate technical specialists into the organization and transform some of them into general managers is the key to the success of the multidivisional organizational structure that emerged in the 1920s and diffused rapidly in the 1930s and 1940s across dominant firms in U.S. industry.[11]

The multidivisional structure grew out of the need for the already dominant firm, laden with fixed costs, to move into new product lines and regional markets in order to continue to transform the high fixed costs inherent in its past investments into low unit costs as old product lines and markets became saturated or outmoded. But to move into new products and regions required even more fixed costs for ongoing research and development facilities as well as for the plant, equipment, and personnel required to produce the new products and service the new markets.[12] The multidivisional structure, designed to ensure the success of continued innovation, itself added to the firm's fixed costs by requiring a more complex managerial organization. These higher fixed costs in turn increased the need for the business organization to achieve large shares in its various product and regional markets to drive down unit costs in all of them.

By enhancing the capability of top management to plan and coordinate the specialized division of labor, the multidivisional structure enabled the

[11] Lazonick, "Strategy, Structure and Management Development."

[12] Alfred D. Chandler, Jr., *Strategy and Structure: Chapters in the History of the American Industrial Enterprise* (Cambridge, Mass.: MIT Press, 1962); David Hounshell and John Kenly Smith, Jr., *Science and Corporate Strategy: Du Pont R&D, 1902–1980* (Cambridge University Press, 1988).

corporation to augment its organizational capability for the purpose of expanding the scope of its activities to a wider range of product lines and more distant market locations. By separating strategic from operational decision making, top management could (potentially but not necessarily) focus all its attention on planning long-run investment strategies. But in focusing on strategic decision making, top managers had to ensure that the operating divisions would respond to the overall goals of the enterprise. To do so, top managers had to delegate authority to middle managers without losing control. Essential to the superior performance of the enterprise that adopted the multidivisional structure was the *organizational integration* of the managerial structure through the training and motivation of salaried personnel. By harmonizing the goals of junior and middle managers with the goals of the enterprise, organizational integration permitted the modern industrial corporation to realize the productive potential of its investments.

Centralized control facilitated the planning and coordination of management development programs that fostered organizational integration. An important element of long-run planning was management development that was not confined to particular functional activities, product divisions, or geographic regions of the corporation. In terms of training, enterprise-wide management development programs made it possible to install job-rotation systems that were part of a continuous process of transforming promising specialists into generalists. These systems often involved the movement of people not only between divisions but also from divisions to centralized staff functions. In terms of incentives, enterprise-wide management development programs expanded the potential for advancement within the organization, while encouraging junior and middle managers to conform to overall enterprise goals, rather than simply to the goals of particular workgroups, specialist activities, divisions, or regions.[13] Given the dependence of top management on employees to whom it had delegated considerable authority, positive incentives of advancement were much more powerful inducements to securing superior performance than were negative sanctions of demotion or dismissal.

Given centralized control, therefore, the key to the success of the multidivisional structure in the United States was the delegation of authority over operational decision making without loss of control by top management over the implementation of enterprise strategy. The setting up of divisional profit centers and the monitoring of the performance of the divisions did not in and of themselves create effective middle management. In terms of training, if middle managers were to be capable of directing the day-to-day operations of divisions along profitable lines, they

---

[13] Lazonick, "Strategy, Structure and Management Development."

themselves had to be capable of coordinating and monitoring specialized divisions of labor within their prescribed domains. The development of this generalist capability required the development of specialists who were more or less continuously in the process of becoming generalists. Such training programs required that the delegation of decision-making authority descend well down the managerial hierarchy, with the scope for planning and coordination increasing as managers climbed the organizational ladder.

Just as the delegation of authority extended decision-making responsibility down the organization's hierarchy, so did open lines of promotion help to ensure that the loyalty of managerial personnel would extend up the hierarchy. Moreover, the very possibility of moving up the hierarchy made middle managers willing to pass on information and delegate authority to subordinates who might one day take their places, thus extending appropriate training and positive incentives further down the organizational structure. At the same time, by separating control of key staff functions from the divisions, top management ensured that critical information would not become the property of self-serving entities within the organization.

By achieving organizational integration on the basis of the multidivisional structure, U.S. corporations developed sufficient managerial capabilities to enable their version of managerial capitalism to dominate the international economy from the 1920s into the 1960s. Ultimately, however, within the business organization the transformation of the high fixed costs of mass-production technology and managerial organization into low unit costs depended on the achievement of high throughput on the shop floor. From the 1880s a prime function of the development of managerial structures in U.S. manufacturing industry was to take control of work organization off the shop floor, where, although to a lesser degree than in Britain, U.S. employers had remained reliant on skilled workers to plan and coordinate the flow of work in an age of less mechanized technology. With the help of skill-displacing technological innovation and a successful attack on craft unionism in the more capital-intensive industries, management assumed control of the planning and coordination of the shop-floor division of labor. In the process, the work of the operative became not only stripped of skill but also virtually devoid of intrinsic appeal. Work for blue-collar workers in most dominant U.S. corporations was reduced to simply a means to material ends.[14]

Even as shop-floor work became more alienating, however, the large-scale investments in high-throughput technologies rendered management all the more dependent on the supply of effort forthcoming from

[14] Lazonick, *Competitive Advantage*, ch. 7.

workers. Because the productivity of physical capital was dependent on the supply of effort by workers, the quantity of effort forthcoming affected not only unit labor costs but also unit capital costs. In addition, and often of great economic significance, the considerable damage that disloyal or inattentive workers could do to expensive capital equipment, materials, and work in progress meant that management had to be concerned about the quality of workers' effort. Workers could apply their effort to sabotaging rather than maintaining the flow of work.

In eliciting effort from workers for whom work had become simply a means to an end, corporate management found that it was not enough merely to offer higher wages. Shop-floor experience taught workers that, without the support of strong craft unions, greater individual effort could often result in higher manning ratios and reductions in the company's workforce, and that higher wages were often short-lived managerial inducements that only culminated in higher effort norms. To protect their jobs and conserve their energy, therefore, workers would quite rationally, and typically collectively, restrict output even when offered wage incentives. Demonstrating that their planning horizons went beyond today's pay, workers tended to be less interested in short-run wage gains than in longer-run employment stability and improvements in work conditions.

To overcome restrictions of output and encourage workers to apply their effort to further the goals of the enterprise, employers had to assure the workers that promises of higher wages, better work conditions, and employment stability would be kept. Most capable of keeping such promises were those corporations that had already attained competitive advantage in their product markets. It was these corporations that were already generating value gains that could be shared with workers to an extent that other, less advantaged corporations could not. The most effective way to implement these incentives was by promising hard-working, loyal workers long-term employment security and a rising standard of living both on and off the job. Hard and reliable work today would be rewarded by higher pay, more employment security, and better work conditions tomorrow.[15]

Insofar as a company could make good on its promises of employment security and rising living standards, a degree of organizational integration could be achieved even on the shop floor. The dominant U.S. mass producers began to use this labor-relations strategy in the boom years of the 1920s. But during the depression of the 1930s, with a few exceptions like IBM, which kept its workforce fully employed by selling business machines to New Deal governments, most of the dominant mass producers

[15] Ibid.

could not or would not sustain the practice of long-term attachment and internal advancement for their shop-floor workers. Workers turned to unions to demand that employers provide them with employment security.

In the renewed prosperity of the 1940s, dominant mass producers were able once again to offer their shop-floor workers employment security and standards of living that were superior to those in the more competitive sectors of the economy. But the failure of the corporations to live up to these promises in the 1930s meant that they had to bargain with the new industrial unions to gain the cooperation of workers. The unions did not challenge the *principle* of management's right to plan and coordinate the shop-floor division of labor. In practice, however, the quid pro quo for union cooperation was that seniority be a prime criterion for promotion along well-defined, and ever more elaborate, job structures, thereby giving older workers best access to a hierarchical succession of jobs paying gradually rising hourly wages. In return, union leadership sought to ensure orderly collective bargaining, including the suppression of illegal work stoppages.[16]

From the 1940s into the mid-1960s union–management cooperation in the coordination of shop-floor relations permitted high enough throughput to sustain competitive advantage, despite the failure of the dominant mass producers to address the issue of deskilled, monotonous, and hence alienating work. By sharing some of the gains that came with dominance, U.S. mass producers exercised a degree of control over – even if they did not gain the loyalty of – their blue-collar workers. But as will be evident from a consideration of the institutional bases for Japan's rise to industrial dominance, the labor–management relations that prevailed in the era of U.S. economic dominance would prove problematic in a later era when, faced by more powerful organizational capabilities abroad, U.S. competitive advantage could no longer be sustained.

Collective capitalism

Over the past two decades, Japanese manufacturing has outperformed U.S. manufacturing in the mass production of consumer durables, particularly in automobiles and electronic equipment. These are the industries in which the United States had its greatest international competitive advantages in the first six decades of this century. Japanese manufacturing has also made great progress in vertically related capital-goods industries: steel, machine tools, electrical machinery, and semiconductors. Entering

[16] David Brody, *Workers in Industrial America* (New York: Oxford University Press, 1980), chs. 3–6; Lazonick, *Competitive Advantage*, ch. 9.

the 1990s, there is no doubt that Japanese manufacturing has taken the leading role in the microelectronics-based Third Industrial Revolution.

As was the case historically in the United States, the Japanese state has played an important role in protecting the home market to permit business organizations to develop and utilize their productive resources to the point where they could attain competitive advantage in open international competition. But the Japanese state has also gone further. It has maintained a stable macroeconomic environment, including high levels of employment and a relatively equal distribution of income across sectors, thus enlarging the extent of the Japanese market for manufactured goods. It has created incentives for consumers and businesses to purchase goods (e.g., televisions and computers) that embody state-of-the-art technologies. It has sought to limit the number of enterprises competing in major manufacturing industries, thus creating incentives for these companies to incur the high fixed costs necessary to attain competitive advantage. It has promoted cooperative research and development among major Japanese competitors. It has ensured manufacturing corporations access to inexpensive finance. And the Japanese state has provided industry with a highly educated labor force to fill blue-collar, white-collar, and managerial positions.[17]

But however important the role of the Japanese state in shaping an environment conducive to economic development, the formulation of investment strategies and the building of organizational structures to carry them out has been left to private-sector enterprises. Over the long run these organizations have outperformed, and in my view will continue to outperform, their U.S. counterparts because of organizational integration that extends beyond the limits of the planned coordination of the specialized division of labor as practiced under U.S. managerial capitalism. First, organizational integration in Japan extends across vertically related companies to a much greater extent than in the United States so that planned coordination spans units of financial control. Second, within the dominant Japanese enterprise, organizational integration extends further down the corporate hierarchy to include male blue-collar workers. Both extensions of organizational integration significantly enhance the organizational capability available to Japanese enterprises.[18]

The combination of far-reaching organizational integration within pri-

---

[17] Thomas K. McCraw, ed., *America versus Japan* (Boston: Harvard Business School Press, 1986); Lazonick, *Competitive Advantage*, ch. 9; Michael Best, *The New Competition: Institutions of Industrial Restructuring* (Cambridge, Mass.: Harvard University Press, 1990), ch. 6. For a case study, see Marie Anchordoguy, *Computers, Inc.: Japan's Challenge to IBM* (Cambridge, Mass.: Harvard University Press, 1989).

[18] James C. Abegglen and George Stalk, Jr., *Kaisha: The Japanese Corporation* (New York: Basic, 1985).

vate-sector manufacturing and the activist role of the state in creating an economic and social environment conducive to the emergence of innovative business enterprises represents a qualitatively new mode of business organization in the evolution of capitalism. The extent of collectivization of interests under Japanese capitalism contrasts with the more limited planned coordination of the specialized division of labor under U.S. managerial capitalism and the virtual lack of planned coordination that existed during the days of British proprietary capitalism.

A fundamental institution of collective capitalism is the enterprise group. The original enterprise groups in modern Japan were the family-controlled *zaibatsu* that led the development of heavy industry – particularly iron and steel and shipbuilding – from the turn of the century until World War II. Since the war, the largest of these corporate entities – Mitsubishi, Mitsui, and Sumitomo – shorn of family control, have remained powerful corporate actors in the Japanese economy, along with a few other large groups built up either by powerful banks or by industrial enterprises such as Toyota and Sony that have emerged as dominant in the automobile and electronics industries. The abolition of *zaibatsu* control ultimately left the enterprise groups intact. But shareholding of individual enterprises was distributed across industrial and financial companies, both within and across groups.[19]

Central to the success of enterprise groups has been the emergence of one or more dominant enterprises as "core" companies that can take the lead in the planned coordination of group activities, including the setting up of new vertically related enterprises as the need arises. Enterprise groups permit the core companies to enjoy the advantages that the vertical integration of production and distribution creates for the borrowing of technology and the implementation of process and product innovation, without enduring the disadvantages of unmanageable bureaucracies that stifle technological and organizational change. By circumventing the intrafirm organizational structure through subcontracting arrangements with satellite enterprises, the core company can pursue new investment strategies that require entrepreneurial initiative and leaps in technological capability.[20]

The growth of enterprise groups provides core companies with the op-

[19] J. Hirschmeier and T. Yui, *The Development of Japanese Business*, 2d ed. (London: Allen & Unwin, 1981), chs. 3–4; Robert Ballon and Iwao Tomita, *The Financial Behavior of Japanese Corporations* (Tokyo: Kodansha International, 1988).

[20] P. Sheard, *Auto Production Systems in Japan* (Papers of the Japanese Study Centre, no. 8), Monash University, 1983; Ronald Dore, *Flexible Rigidities: Industrial Policy and Structural Adjustment in the Japanese Economy, 1970–1980* (Stanford, Calif.: Stanford University Press, 1986); Best, *The New Competition*, ch. 5; Michael J. Smitka, "The Invisible Handshake: The Development of the Japanese Automotive Parts Industry," *Business and Economic History*, 2d ser., 19 (1990), 163–71.

portunity for strategically locating more labor-intensive activities in smaller firms in which the top managers have direct proprietary interests in enterprise performance and in which control of the terms of employment and work conditions need not be shared with the enterprise unions that have become central to labor–management relations in the dominant companies. Although as subcontractors for the core enterprise, the satellite firms can in principle act independently, in practice the very success of the innovative strategies of the dominant companies and their commitment to maintaining long-term relations with their subcontractors leads the smaller firms to view themselves as members of an integrated organizational structure.

Over time some of these "satellites," if successful, can take on lives of their own, as in the case of Fanuc, the company set up by Fujitsu to develop numerical control units for machine tools. Even then, the very fact that one strong vertically related enterprise has emerged out of the development of another creates a continuing basis for cooperative investment policies while each builds its own internal organization. The organizational capability developed through interenterprise cooperation within groups undoubtedly enhances the ability of enterprises from different groups to engage in cooperative research and development projects, as has been the case in the emergence of an internationally competitive Japanese computer industry.[21]

The ability to organize cooperative investment strategies *across* enterprises is enhanced by the structure of managerial decision making *within* enterprises. Consensus decision making – the *ringi* system – emphasizes the two-way flow of ideas and information up and down the corporate hierarchy. Consensus decision making grew out of the need of the rapidly growing *zaibatsu* of the early twentieth century to lure college graduates – products of a concerted effort by the state to create an educated elite – away from prestigious government posts. Considerable technical information was required from, and considerable authority had to be delegated to, these professional managers. Even in the cotton textile industry, which in Japan as in Britain and the United States played a major role in early industrialization, the recruitment of college graduates to serve as technical specialists was important to develop technology and increase throughput on the basis of inexpensive cotton and unskilled labor.[22]

---

[21] David J. Collis, "The Machine Tool Industry and Industrial Policy, 1955–82," in A. Michael Spence and Heather A. Hazard, eds., *International Competitiveness* (Cambridge, Mass.: Ballinger, 1986), 75–114; Anchordoguy, *Computers Inc.*

[22] Shin'ichi Yonekawa, "University Graduates in Japanese Enterprises before the Second World War," *Business History* 26 (July 1984), 193–218; Hidemasa Morikawa, "The Increasing Power of Salaried Managers in Japan's Large Corporations," in William D. Wray, ed., *Managing Industrial Enterprise: Cases from Japan's Prewar Experience* (Cam-

Ringi permits the knowledge and outlooks of the various division and department heads to become integral to the planning process itself. By formalizing a system of gathering input and approval from the various individuals who will be responsible for overseeing the implementation of strategic decisions, *ringi* permits the identification, and if need be accommodation, within the organization of potential obstacles to the success of a strategy before strategic commitments have already been made. When operating effectively so that individual managers cannot circumvent the group process, consensus decision making eliminates competing centers of decision-making power within the organization that might otherwise undertake investments that have conflicting objectives. In effect, investment strategy and managerial structure are organizationally integrated.

At the same time, the process of consensus decision making not only provides a valuable source of information from below for top executives but also helps to ensure that a large number of more specialized managers on their way up the hierarchy are developing a general conception of organizational needs and capabilities. By promoting the transformation of technical specialists into general managers, consensus decision making enhances organizational integration.

The institutional basis for the devolution of decision-making power from chief executives to a wider group that extends further down the formal hierarchy is permanent, or lifetime, employment. Japanese managers typically rise out of the ranks of "white-collar workers" who enter the company after graduating from college. Like consensus decision making, the policy of permanent employment was extended to professional managerial personnel in the early twentieth century in order to attract them away from government service and to create the long-term attachments that would make it worthwhile for the business enterprises to invest further in the training of the recruits.[23]

Over time, however, the offer of permanent employment has been extended further down the organizational hierarchy. Before World War II, permanent employment was used as a strategy to transform "key" skilled workers (*oyakata*), previously highly mobile labor contractors who recruited, trained, and supervised shop-floor labor, into permanently employed foremen who now performed the same functions, but with a long-term commitment to one particular company. In the early 1950s a strategy of substituting cooperative enterprise unions for the militant industrial unions that had arisen after World War II resulted in the exten-

bridge, Mass.: Council on East Asian Studies, 1989), 27–51. See also Mass and Lazonick, "The British Cotton Industry."

[23] E. Daito, "Recruitment and Training of Middle Managers in Japan, 1900–1930," in Kobayashi and Morikawa, eds., *Development of Managerial Enterprise*, 151–79.

sion of permanent employment status to all male blue-collar workers in the larger enterprises.[24]

Some argue that permanent employment is not a *critical* economic institution in Japan because "only" some 30 percent of the Japanese labor force have permanent employment status. But this figure, derived from the present proportion of the Japanese labor force that is unionized, includes virtually all males working for the dominant industrial enterprises, whether as blue-collar or white-collar employees. Within these dominant industrial enterprises, the most prevalent form of labor-force segmentation is between women, who are generally excluded from permanent employment (although in recent years some university-educated women have gained access to it), and men. Moreover, many male industrial workers who do not have permanent employment status enjoy substantial employment security often amounting to de facto permanent employment because the smaller-sized enterprises for which they work have long-term organizational ties with core companies that in part owe their organizational integration and dominance to the institution of permanent employment.[25] The phenomenal success of these dominant business enterprises has in turn made it economically viable for the government to implement policies that provide employment stability in small-scale enterprises in agriculture and retailing, even though the workers in these sectors would not be counted among the ranks of "permanent employees."[26] In dynamic historical perspective, permanent employment in what have emerged as the dominant business enterprises has been central to generating the organizational integration that is the essence of the Japanese economic "miracle."

Japanese permanent employment functions both as a training system that develops the skills of employees in a planned and coordinated way and as an incentive system that elicits effort of high quality and quantity from individuals. During the first decade of an employee's career, pro-

---

[24] Reiko Okayama, "Japanese Employer Policy: The Heavy Engineering Industry, 1900–1930," in Howard Gospel and Craig Littler, eds., *Managerial Strategies and Industrial Relations* (London: Heinemann, 1983), 157–70; Andrew Gordon, *The Evolution of Labor Relations in Japan: Heavy Industry, 1853–1955* (Cambridge, Mass.: Harvard University Press, 1985); Michael Cusumano, *The Japanese Automobile Industry* (Cambridge, Mass.: Harvard University Press, 1985), ch. 3.

[25] For a survey of the structure of the Japanese labor force, see William Lazonick, "Cooperative Employment Relations and Japanese Economic Growth," photocopy, Institute for Advanced Study (May 1990). See also Kazuo Koike, *Understanding Industrial Relations in Modern Japan* (New York: St. Martin's, 1988).

[26] Thomas K. McCraw and Patricia O'Brien, "Production and Distribution: Competition Policy and Industry Structure," and Michael R. Reich, Yasuo Endo, and C. Peter Timmer, "Agriculture: The Political Economy of Structural Change," in McCraw, ed., *America versus Japan*, 77–116, 151–92.

motion and pay increases occur by gradual steps and by seniority – "fast tracks" have been rare in the Japanese corporate enterprise. During this initial period, the company invests in considerable specialist training of its permanently employed personnel. In contrast to the U.S. practice of applying the terms "unskilled," "semiskilled," and "skilled" to different types of jobs to be filled by different types of workers, the Japanese have used these terms to apply to the stages through which a particular worker passes during the first ten years of employment. The company also provides more general training by the rotation of employees to different technical specialties within the enterprise and, at times, even within the enterprise group. When qualitatively new investment strategies require qualitatively new skills, the permanent employment system gives Japanese companies the incentive to invest in the retraining of midcareer personnel.[27]

The existence of permanent employment and the emphasis on seniority in promotion and rewards, particularly in the early years of an employee's career, encourage personnel to cooperate with one another in pursuit of the goals of the business organization. It is only in midcareer that promotion on the basis of individual performance becomes important, although even then seniority continues to have some influence on promotion decisions and remains the predominant determinant of salary increases. To encourage individual creativity and initiative, non-seniority-based incentives are also used, in particular the possibility of retaining an influential position in the company after the normal retirement age. But individual incentives are not the only, or necessarily even the best, means of motivating employees. In a corporate environment, economic success depends on not only individual initiative but also cooperative effort, and collective rewards may provide the appropriate incentive mechanism. Backed by the bargaining power of enterprise unions, all permanent employees receive semiannual bonuses, which typically constitute one-third of an individual's annual earnings but are adjusted according to the profitability of the enterprise and hence its ability to pay.[28]

Through the organizational commitments inherent in permanent employment, the skills and efforts of male blue-collar workers have been made integral to the organizational capabilities of their companies, thus enabling the Japanese to take the lead in innovative production systems such as just-in-time inventory control, statistical quality control, and flexible manufacturing. Critical to the functioning of these production sys-

[27] Kazuo Koike, "Human Resource Management and Labor–Management Relations," in Kozo Yamamura and Yasukichi Yasuba, eds., *The Political Economy of Japan* (Stanford, Calif.: Stanford University Press, 1987), 1: 289–330.
[28] Abegglen and Stalk, *Kaisha*, ch. 8; Ronald Dore, *Taking Japan Seriously* (Stanford, Calif.: Stanford University Press, 1987), ch. 4.

tems is the willingness of Japanese managers to leave skills and initiative with workers on the shop floor. Indeed, the recent success of Japanese mass producers in introducing flexible manufacturing systems owes much to the fact that, for decades before the introduction of the new automated technologies, blue-collar workers were granted considerable discretion to monitor and adjust the flow and quality of work on the shop floor.[29]

Japanese practice is in marked contrast to the U.S. managerial concern with using technology to take skills and the exercise of initiative *off* the shop floor, a practice that goes back to the late nineteenth century when the success of U.S. mass production was dependent on breaking the power of craft workers and transferring to management the sole right to plan and coordinate the flow of work. Despite the existence of militant unionism in Japan at various points in the first half of the twentieth century, there was never any attempt by Japanese workers or their organizations to establish *craft control* on the shop floor.[30] As a result, Japanese employers never had to confront established craft positions of workers, as was the case with U.S. manufacturers around the turn of the century, nor did they have to resign themselves simply to leaving skills on the shop floor in the hands of autonomous craftsmen, as was the case in Britain.

Historically, the problem facing Japanese capitalists was not to rid themselves of skilled workers who might use their scarce skills to establish craft autonomy on the shop floor. Rather, their problem coming into the twentieth century was the absence of a self-generating supply of workers with industrial skills. To overcome this constraint, industrial capitalist employers had to make the investments that would transform unskilled workers into skilled workers and then retain them by integrating them into the organization. To be sure, the same employers generally accepted the institutionalization of permanent employment, enforced by enterprise unions, only when compelled to do so by the threat of militant unionism after World War II. In practice, however, out of the exigencies of developing and utilizing workers with industrial skills, the social foundations for the current permanent employment system were laid in Japan decades before the long-term attachment of the blue-collar worker to the company became a recognized institutional feature of Japanese industry.

Organizational integration and segmentation

In the post-World War II decades, permanent employment and enterprise unionism have promoted the organizational integration of male white-collar and blue-collar workers in Japan with beneficial impacts on the

---

[29] Cusumano, *The Japanese Automobile Industry*, chs. 5 and 6.
[30] Gordon, *The Evolution of Labor Relations in Japan*, pt. 1.

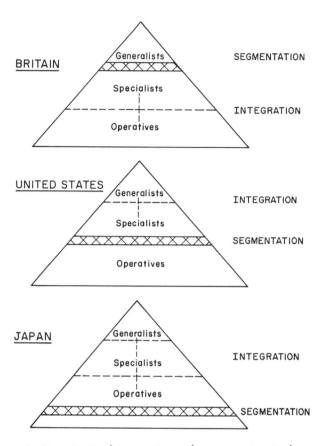

Figure 1. Organizational integration and segmentation in three social environments.

transformation of high fixed costs into low unit costs. Figure 1 illustrates the basic differences in organizational integration across large British, U.S., and Japanese industrial enterprises in recent decades. In each national economy, the industrial enterprise is depicted as a hierarchical triangle, stratified into a small layer of managerial *generalists* at the top, a larger layer of line and staff *specialists* in the middle, and an even larger layer of shop-floor *operatives* at the bottom.

In the British enterprise, organizational segmentation occurs between the generalists and specialists because of (as outlined later) the failure of British management to take control of work organization off the shop floor, top management's quest for elite status, and the consequent formation of specialist standards from the bottom up rather than from the top down.

In the U.S. enterprise, organizational segmentation occurs further down the hierarchy, with specialists divided from operatives. With the help of the national educational system, generalists in the United States have created an integrated line and staff bureaucracy, while they have refused to consider "hourly" blue-collar wage earners members of the corporation, despite the fact that they often experience long-term attachment to the firm. In the Japanese company, organizational segmentation, if it occurs at all within the company itself, as distinct from its satellites, can be found only at the lower levels of the operative ranks because of the policies of consensus decision making and permanent employment, as well as the historic triumph of company unionism, which combines specialists and operatives, over independent blue-collar unionism.

These cross-national differences in organizational integration manifest the central institutional rigidities that have long faced British business organizations in restructuring their economic institutions to respond to the economic superiority of U.S. managerial capitalism, and the institutional rigidities now facing U.S. business organizations in restructuring their economic institutions to respond to the economic superiority of Japanese collective capitalism. The British case manifests the long-term impacts of the institutions of proprietary capitalism even in an age of the demise of managerial capitalism. The U.S. case manifests the long-term impacts of the institutions of managerial capitalism in the new age of collective capitalism. Understanding the nature and persistence of these institutional rigidities is the key to explaining the international competitive declines of first the British economy and then also the U.S. economy in the twentieth century.

The limits of proprietary capitalism

The case of Japan demonstrates how collective capitalism has replaced managerial capitalism in providing the institutional foundations for the creation of value. In contrast, the case of Britain shows how the institutions of proprietary capitalism that had formed the basis of British dominance could become formidable obstacles to institutional transformation and become central to the problem of long-run economic decline. The sources of the institutional rigidities facing British capitalism in the twentieth century were the vested interests and limited abilities of those who participated in, and contributed to, the nation's prior success. Yet the impediments to institutional change far outlived the generation of individuals who had been involved with the organizations and technologies that had secured the economic domination of Britain in the third quarter of the nineteenth century. Even new industries and new movements for institutional change succumbed to overwhelming incentives to achieve their objectives by relying on existing productive resources and social institutions rather than undertaking the massive and concentrated investments to generate technologies with more productive potential and organizations with more capability to plan and coordinate.[31]

Put simply, the origins of twentieth-century institutional rigidity in Britain can be found in the nature of industry and enterprise structures that characterized Britain's rise to economic power. On the one hand, the horizontal and vertical fragmentation of firms – itself a consequence of the reliance of British industrialists on external economies, including the ready availability of large supplies of skilled labor in certain localities – made it unnecessary to develop managerial structures that could generate economies internal to the enterprise. In the staple industries – iron and steel, shipbuilding, mechanical engineering, and textiles – that had brought Britain to economic supremacy, more organizational capability resided in craft control on the shop floor than in the underdeveloped managerial structures.

Insofar as British craft workers continued to cooperate with their employers in the twentieth century, it was typically by squeezing as much productivity as possible out of the *existing* technologies (often by failing, within limits, to maintain the quality of the product), driving their shop-floor assistants as well as themselves to supply more effort, and, as it became necessary in order to retain their jobs, accepting lower wages. Immobile because of their highly specialized skills, both workers and employers had the incentive to ensure the survival of the firms through which they gained their livelihoods. Many British firms in the staple industries were able to survive for decades by living off the plant, equipment, and infrastructures accumulated in the heyday of proprietary capitalism.

In some industries (mechanical engineering in particular), employers tried to use their collective power to break craft control over the organization of work and the determination of remuneration. Even when employers rolled back prior union gains, however, craft control was not eliminated, in large part because proprietary capitalists had no organizational alternative to put in its place. What is more, even in *new* machine-based industries such as automobile manufacture, in which the craft unions were not already ensconced, craft-like organization of production emerged in the first decades of the twentieth century as the automobile manufacturers tended to rely on craft workers to plan and coordinate the flow of work on the shop floor.[32]

---

[31] The following arguments are based on Leslie Hannah, *The Rise of the Corporate Economy: The British Experience*, 2d ed. (London: Methuen, 1983); Elbaum and Lazonick, eds., *The Decline of the British Economy*; Lazonick, "Strategy, Structure and Management Development"; idem, *Competitive Advantage*, ch. 6; Chandler, *Scale and Scope*, pt. 3.

[32] Jonathan Zeitlin, "The Labour Strategies of British Engineering Employers, 1890–1922,"

Reliance on shop-floor workers to perform what we would consider to be managerial functions continued during the interwar period, even in firms such as Austin and Morris that were becoming dominant mass producers in the British market. In the 1940s and 1950s, under conditions of tight labor markets combined with the limited opportunities for firms that relied on labor-intensive technologies to generate new sources of productivity, these workers took advantage of the shop-floor organizational responsibilities that had been delegated to them to form strong specialized craft unions. The result was that by the 1960s one could find scores of separate craft agreements in place at any point in time in any one automobile plant, thereby placing severe constraints on the planned coordination of the specialized division of labor.

Yet the British automobile industry remained viable in international competition until the 1960s because of its low fixed costs (including the almost complete neglect of R&D) as well as the acceptance of relatively low returns by workers, managers, and owners. The 1960s and 1970s revealed, however, that like the staple industries of the nineteenth century, the British automobile industry had reached the technical and social limits of the utilization of its resources. Facing the continued development of the Continental producers as well as the rise of the Japanese automobile manufacturers, the economic viability of the British industry could no longer be sustained.

The development of organizational capability was somewhat different in the science-based industries of the Second Industrial Revolution – chemicals, rubber, electrical equipment and appliances – in which it was impossible to enter into competition on the basis of technological capabilities inherited from the past. Largely through the efforts of dedicated and aggressive entrepreneurs (typically, although not always, owners as well as managers) who either developed new technologies or controlled foreign patents, a number of British firms such as Lever Brothers, Pilkington Brothers, Dunlop, Courtaulds, Crosfield's, Nobel's, and Brunner, Mond were able to become serious competitors in the late nineteenth and early twentieth centuries.[33]

in Gospel and Littler, eds., *Managerial Strategies and Industrial Relations*, 25–54; Steven Tolliday and Jonathan Zeitlin, eds., *Shopfloor Bargaining and the State: Historical and Comparative Perspectives* (Cambridge University Press, 1985); Wayne Lewchuk, *American Technology and the British Vehicle Industry* (Cambridge University Press, 1987).

[33] Charles Wilson, *The History of Unilever* (Cambridge University Press, 1984), vol. 1; T. C. Barker, *The Glassmakers: Pilkington–The Rise of an International Company, 1826–1976* (London: Weidenfeld & Nicolson, 1977); Geoffrey Jones, "The Growth and Performance of British Multinational Firms before 1939: The Case of Dunlop," *Economic History Review*, 2d ser., 37 (February 1984), 35–53; D. C. Coleman, *Courtaulds: An Economic and Social History* (Oxford: Clarendon Press, 1969), vol. 1; A. E. Musson, *Enterprise in Soap and Chemicals* (Manchester: Manchester University Press, 1965); William J. Reader, *Imperial Chemical Industries* (Oxford University Press, 1975), vol. 1.

Nevertheless, after the turn of the century, the largest British enterprises were not only much smaller than the largest U.S. enterprises, but also much more under the control of family ownership. The British practice of passing on managerial control of the firm to family members from generation to generation, regardless of relevant career credentials, stifled the growth of the enterprise and the development of organizational capability. The family firm often adopted a nonexpansionary strategy in order to avoid becoming dependent on outside creditors or shareholders who might threaten loss of control or to avoid becoming reliant on, and potentially subservient to, a bureaucracy of technical specialists and middle managers.

During the interwar period, an increasingly common route to growth for British firms was amalgamation. But this type of enterprise growth was the result of a strictly adaptive response that represented attempts by competitive firms to combine to control product prices rather than rationalize operations. Such amalgamations tended to leave previous family owners with their autonomy intact within the amalgamated structures.[34]

The persistence of family control meant that at the higher managerial levels recruitment was from within a fairly closed circle. The heads of the most successful firms, themselves typically of middle-class origin, sought to have their sons educated at the elite public schools and at Oxford and Cambridge – institutions that remained firmly under the control of the aristocracy of landowners and financiers who had little use for industry or technology. When the largest enterprises recruited potential top managers from outside the family, an Oxbridge education was the most highly preferred credential. As a result, and in contrast to the dramatic transformation of the U.S. system of higher education early in the century, there was little pressure on the British educational system to offer technical and managerial training to the future captains of industry until the 1960s and 1970s, when the British finally began to take cognizance of their long-term relative decline.[35]

The ultimate impact of the pursuit of aristocratic status by industrialists was to legitimize and reinforce the closed circle of managerial succession by constituting higher management as a separate social class within the enterprise. The relatively closed ranks at the higher management levels in effect segmented general management from technical specialists and lower-level line managers. As British companies grew in size in the inter-

---

[34] Hannah, *The Rise of the Corporate Economy*, ch. 6; Lazonick, "Strategy, Structure and Management Development"; Chandler, *Scale and Scope*, ch. 7.

[35] Michael Sanderson, *The Universities and British Industry, 1850–1970* (London: Routledge & Kegan Paul, 1972); Lazonick, "Strategy, Structure and Management Development."

war period, organizational segmentation between top management and the rest of the employees became the norm and remained characteristic of British managerial structures even into the 1960s and 1970s. Again, we see a sharp contrast with the United States. Although U.S. managerial personnel were an elite relative to white-collar and blue-collar workers, higher education and internal promotion policies integrated specialists and lower-level managers into this elite rather than excluding them, as was the case in Britain.

Throughout the twentieth century, organizational segmentation *has* been present in the United States, but it divides shop-floor and clerical workers from professional, managerial, and technical workers, with educational credentials serving as means of allocating people to hierarchical segments and legitimizing the segmentation. As a general rule, however, U.S. *managerial* structures have been characterized by organizational integration. Conversely, in terms of training and promotion in British industrial hierarchies, highly trained technical specialists tended to be more closely integrated with shop-floor workers below than with general managers above.[36] Within what we have come to think of as the corporate managerial structure, organizational segmentation remained widespread in Britain well into the second half of the twentieth century, this segmentation between top management and enterprise employees thwarting the development of organizational capability in British industrial enterprises.

The limits of managerial capitalism

Yet just as from the turn of the century British firms had difficulty transforming their social environment to respond to the U.S. challenge, so too have U.S. business enterprises faced social obstacles in responding to the rise of the Japanese. Confronted by formidable foreign competition, many U.S. companies turned during the post–World War II decades to adaptive responses – living off value-creating capabilities created in the past – rather than confronting the uncertainties inherent in innovative investment strategies that could generate new value-creating capabilities for the future.

In the process, the organizational structures of these companies conformed to their adaptive strategies. Until recently at least, U.S. industrial corporations continued, by and large, to promote from within the managerial hierarchy. But in the adaptive organization, the most successful middle managers became those who cut costs on the basis of existing technologies, as distinct from those who could contribute to process and

---

[36] Geoffrey Crockett and Peter Elias, "British Managers: A Study of Their Education, Training, Mobility, and Earnings," *British Journal of Industrial Relations* 22 (March 1984), 34–46; Lazonick, *Competitive Advantage*, ch. 6.

product innovation. In the transition from an innovative to an adaptive strategy, the specialist skills of those who came to occupy top decision-making positions changed from a production to a financial orientation, while their generalist outlook shifted from long-run development to short-run profit maximization. In addition, the compensation of top executives became increasingly tied to short-term performance, including the market value of stock options, which, along with mandatory retirement, reinforced the conservative time horizons of strategic decision makers and their subjective evaluations of the uncertainties inherent in an innovative strategy.[37] These changes in organizational capability made it all the more difficult to revert to innovation once the economic viability of adaptation had been exhausted.

Even when top executives in U.S. companies were inclined to engage in innovation, they faced increasing uncertainty that their mature organizational structures would be equal to the task. Just because the organizational capabilities of U.S. enterprises had in effect *created* the productive and competitive challenges of the Second Industrial Revolution did not mean that these capabilities could cope with the technological and organizational complexities of the Third Industrial Revolution. Compared with Japanese business practice, in most U.S. industrial corporations the long-term commitments of the organization to its personnel, and of personnel to the organization, are too limited. In U.S. corporations, explicit guarantees of permanent employment even at the managerial level are the exception rather than the rule.

To be sure, the widespread firing of managers with considerable seniority in a particular U.S. corporation sends a signal down the organizational hierarchy that the company is not one in which younger specialists should stake their hopes for employment security, personal development, and social mobility. Mass layoffs of managers make it difficult to attract good recruits and undermine the organizational commitment of those managerial personnel who are already there. Nevertheless, the readiness of most U.S. corporations to terminate the employment of any particular manager remains. In such organizations, each manager has an incentive to resist the implementation of investment strategies that might make his or her particular skills expendable and to advocate the continuation of those strategies that do not.

By the same token, in U.S. business organizations the possibility exists for any particular manager to quit when a better career opportunity arises. Because virtually all large U.S. corporations maintain only partial and

[37] Robert Hayes and William Abernathy, "Managing Our Way to Economic Decline," *Harvard Business Review* 58 (July–August 1980), 67–77; Lazonick, "Controlling the Market for Corporate Control."

conditional commitments to permanent employment, interfirm competition for the best midcareer managers always remains a possibility and is typically quite vigorous. As a result, despite the expectation that a significant number of managers will complete their careers with a particular business organization, the current employer does not have an unambiguous incentive to ensure that the capabilities of personnel, and particularly the most talented personnel, are developed to their full potential. Despite the importance of internal career ladders for ensuring that the long-term goals of individual managers are consistent with the investment strategies of the organization, the possibility is always present that some managerial employees, and even those in positions of considerable decision-making power, will view their long-term attachment to the organization as tenuous and opt to pursue personal goals that undermine the successful implementation of the enterprise's investment strategies.

The lack of complete commitment of organizations to individuals and of individuals to organizations is likely to be most problematic when the enterprise is experiencing a crisis because its old investment strategies can no longer sustain the economic viability of the company. Historically, structural reorganizations to implement new investment strategies tend to follow periods of crisis.[38] Retaining and retraining committed personnel are critical for ensuring the organizational capability to transform crisis into renewed growth.

If the organizational cohesion of U.S. business enterprises has become inadequate within the managerial structure, the problems are even greater on the shop floor, where wages rather than salaries are the rule. During the period of consolidation of their market power in the 1920s, many of the U.S. oligopolies attempted with some success to integrate blue-collar workers into their organizational structures by the promise (often implicit, but in some cases more formal) of long-term employment security. In boom conditions, the industrial relations strategy worked. But amidst the depressed conditions of the 1930s, which even the corporate giants could not control, the response of the industrial mass producers was to cut back production and employment dramatically. The promise of employment security could not be kept. It became apparent that, whatever the expectations for employment security harbored by the mass of industrial workers, when push came to shove they were nothing more than wage laborers, paid an hourly rate to do a particular job when work was available.

The industrial workers organized, and the state intervened with legislation to aid their efforts at gaining bargaining power. In the late 1930s and 1940s, attempts by the more radical elements in the newly recog-

---

[38] Chandler, *Strategy and Structure*.

nized unions to gain measures of control over shop-floor work organization and enterprise investment strategies met with failure. Indeed, with issues of work organization and investment policies excluded from the scope of collective bargaining, post-World War II union leaders often found themselves in the position of defending the prerogatives of management against the demands and actions of their own rank and file.[39]

What the unionized workers in the mass-production corporations did gain was seniority protection as well as the right to bargain over wage levels and differentials for internal job structures. The newly acquired union prerogatives meshed well with the managerial strategy of offering employment security and rising living standards to create loyal workers that many of the very same corporations had been pursuing, however tentatively, in the nonunion era before the Great Depression. The strategy once again became viable in the 1940s, 1950s, and 1960s as the U.S. economy entered a long boom characterized by expansion and diversification of the large corporations and U.S. domination of world markets. Ironically, however, the more senior workers attained de facto "permanent employment" with the corporation, even though as workers who were paid an hourly rate depending on the job they were currently performing, their long-term attachment to the firm was never formally acknowledged. With their dominant and expanding market shares, the managers of U.S. oligopolistic enterprises could accede to the demands of workers for higher wages and job security, but they would not grant them membership in the corporate collectivity.[40]

When the new international competition began to be felt from the late 1950s, many of the U.S. giants found themselves vulnerable. In industries such as steel and automobiles that were dominated by adaptive oligopolists, the costs of the accord with labor began to outstrip productivity gains. As long as there was no serious foreign competition and the U.S. national enterprises in an industry did not engage in significant price competition among themselves, U.S. corporations were able to pass off higher labor costs to consumers in the form of higher prices. By the late 1960s, however, the limits of the adaptive strategy had been reached as domestic inflation eroded U.S. international competitive advantage.

The problem of U.S. competitiveness was not only one of higher wages but also one of lagging productivity. High wages, tight labor markets, and the availability of unemployment benefits had weakened managerial con-

[39] Brody, *Workers in Industrial America*, chs. 5–6; Howell John Harris, *The Right to Manage: Industrial Relations Policies of American Business in the 1940s* (Madison: University of Wisconsin Press, 1982); Nelson Lichtenstein, "UAW Bargaining Strategy and Shop-Floor Conflict," *Industrial Relations* 24 (Fall 1985), 360–81.

[40] Michael J. Piore and Charles F. Sabel, *The Second Industrial Divide: Possibilities for Prosperity* (New York: Basic, 1984), ch. 9; Lazonick, *Competitive Advantage*, ch. 9.

trol over the production process. Alienated in any case by the routine nature of their work and without any formal power to influence the nature of the work environment, blue-collar workers sought to control their expenditure of effort by unauthorized work stoppages, work to rule, and absenteeism, all of which had adverse consequences for productivity.

In the 1970s many observers of U.S. industry pointed to the alienated shop-floor workers as an explanation of the slowdown in the growth of labor productivity in U.S. manufacturing that had begun in the mid-1960s. In many plants around the country, experiments in job enlargement and job enrichment were undertaken to try to elicit more and better effort from workers. Although the initial impact of these programs was generally positive, many of the experiments in the early 1970s were cut short when the workers whose jobs had been enriched and enlarged began questioning traditional managerial prerogatives inherent in the bureaucratically segmented organizational structure. In the long run, attempts such as these at piecemeal transformation of the organizational structure may well have reduced rather than enhanced organizational capability by creating expectations for more meaningful work that in the end were not fulfilled.[41]

The transition from a structure of work organization based on control to one based on commitment that can effect the organizational integration of shop-floor workers requires transformations in the traditional division of labor between managers and workers as well as the skills and attitudes of workers themselves.[42] To effect these transformations, institutional rigidities in the U.S. educational system must be confronted. In the early twentieth century, when vocational schooling entered the U.S. secondary education system to track youths away from college and into the blue-collar labor force, the resultant segmentation of the labor force was consistent with the social division of labor between managers and workers in the world of work.[43] But as the expansion of community colleges during the post-World War II decades extended the tracking of managers and workers into higher education, the U.S. educational system began to lose

---

[41] United States Department of Health, Education, and Welfare, *Work in America* (Cambridge, Mass.: MIT Press, 1972); Andrew Zimbalist, "The Limits of Work Humanization," *Review of Radical Political Economics*, 7 (Summer 1975), 50–9; Stephen Marglin, "Catching Flies with Honey: An Inquiry into Management Initiatives to Humanize Work," *Economic Analysis and Workers' Management*, 13 (1979), 473–88.

[42] Richard E. Walton, "From Control to Commitment: Transforming Work Force Management in the United States," in Kim B. Clark, Robert H. Hayes, and Christopher Lorenz, eds., *The Uneasy Alliance: Managing the Productivity–Technology Dilemma* (Boston: Harvard Business School Press, 1985), 237–65; Thomas A. Kochan, Harry C. Katz, and Robert B. McKersie, *The Transformation of American Industrial Relations* (New York: Basic, 1986).

[43] Samuel Bowles and Herbert Gintis, *Schooling in Capitalist America* (New York: Basic, 1976), chs. 6–7.

touch with the changing human resource needs of the Third Industrial Revolution, especially on the shop floor.

What was needed was an educational system that would reject the conception of the worker as a mere appendage of the machine and prepare future workers for active involvement in speeding the flow of work while maintaining its quality in the "flexible" factory. There is no point, however, in building new organizational structures and educational systems if those who run the largest corporations eschew innovative investment strategies.

To be innovative in the Third Industrial Revolution requires not only appropriate human resource development and far-reaching organizational integration, but also massive *financial commitments* in the face of returns that are more uncertain than ever. In general, financial commitment means that those employees, creditors, or owners who can lay claim to the revenues of the corporation will not enforce those claims in ways that undermine the ability of the enterprise to develop and utilize its productive resources.[44]

In the private-sector enterprise, financial commitment generally means the retention of earnings for the sake of developing the resources of the firm. High degrees of financial commitment characterize those industrial enterprises in Japan and Germany that are the major international competitors in the late twentieth century. In international competition, financial commitment has become ever more critical to the development and utilization of organizational capabilities. Yet since the 1950s a number of forces in the U.S. economy have been eroding financial commitment.

The erosion began within the industrial enterprise itself.[45] During the first half of the century, when the major U.S. industrial corporations rose to international dominance, ownership was increasingly separated from control. Stockholding was widely dispersed among portfolio investors who, by virtue of the fragmentation of ownership, ceded to professional managers the right to determine the allocation of the corporation's financial resources. The interests of these top managers were bound up with the interests of their managerial organizations. They had typically pursued their careers with the organizations that they now ran. As salaried managers, moreover, their only claims to higher levels of remuneration derived from the long-run competitive performance of the enterprise.

During the 1950s, however, top managers ceased to be merely salaried employees. Through stock-based compensation systems, they became substantial owners, and hence the beneficiaries of the prolonged run up in stock prices that ended only at the close of the 1960s. During the 1950s

---

[44] Lazonick, "Controlling the Market for Corporate Control."
[45] The following arguments are elaborated in ibid.

and 1960s, the incentives increased for top managers of the major corporations to identify with the short-run market performance of their companies' stocks. The methods for improving short-run financial performance often conflicted with the long-term financial requirements for building organizational capability for the sake of sustained innovation.

By the same token, top managers now had vastly more scope than previously to use their positions of strategic management as the basis for their own individual aggrandizement rather than for the development of the organizational capabilities of their enterprises. Hence, as an alternative to engaging in innovative investment strategies in their current or technologically related lines of business, many top managers of the 1960s became conglomerateurs, each one with financial control over a multitude of industrial enterprises in which he had neither organizational roots nor technological expertise. These conglomerate managers controlled the financial resources required to undertake innovative investment strategies. But the planning and coordination of these strategies were the tasks of the new "middle" managers – often (initially at least) the former top managers of the acquired companies who now headed the conglomerate divisions and who had the requisite understanding of the division's organizational capabilities to manage the innovation process.

Besides knowledge of products, processes, and people, however, the management of innovation requires financial commitment – and more specifically control over the allocation of enterprise earnings – which is precisely what the new middle managers whose role it was to manage innovation no longer had the power to provide. Moreover, evaluated by the head office on the basis of their short-term performance, the divisional heads who indeed pursued innovative investment strategies quickly learned (if they were still around to make use of their knowledge) that adaptive behavior – managerial behavior that did not make large and sustained demands on enterprise earnings – got a better reception from the conglomerate bosses.

Although the conglomerate movement abated and indeed reversed itself somewhat in the 1970s as many ill-managed divisions were sold off, considerable damage to the organizational capability of many U.S. industrial corporations had been done. At the same time, increasingly powerful international competitive challenges made the top managers of U.S. industrial enterprises think twice about committing corporate resources to long-run innovative strategies. Instead, the tendency was for these companies to try to adapt on the basis of their successful investments of the past. In this adaptive mode, the rewards of promotion to top management positions went to those who displayed the most talent for improving the "bottom line." We can conjecture that it was this type of top manager, driven by financial goals, who was most likely to cooperate with the raiders in the hostile takeover movement of the 1980s. The popularity of "golden parachutes" and other compensation schemes designed to bribe top management to make way for corporate raiders revealed that U.S. industrial leaders could pursue their own individual ends not only through the medium of the securities markets, but also by selling their very offices of managerial control.

The use of securities markets to buy and sell industrial enterprises for the sake of individual gain has often torn apart U.S. organizational capabilities without creating the conditions for putting more powerful organizational capabilities in their place. The problem is not mergers and acquisitions per se, but the purposes for which, and the conditions under which, they are undertaken. It may make strategic sense for an innovative enterprise to acquire or merge with other existing enterprises that have already developed unique capabilities, rather than adopt the much slower and more uncertain strategy of developing these operations from the ground up.

The success of such mergers and acquisitions in permitting the production of higher-quality goods at lower unit costs depends on the willingness and the ability of the previously distinct and separate enterprises to integrate their capabilities so as to join forces in the pursuit of a common organizational goal. As demonstrated by the history of British economic decline, the simple vertical or horizontal amalgamation of firms or operations without organizational integration does not result in sustained competitive advantage – a lesson that was repeated in the United States with the rise and fall of the conglomerate movement in the 1960s and 1970s.[46] Financial integration does not imply organizational integration. And as demonstrated by the organizational advantages of the Japanese system of enterprise groups, organizational integration can occur across units of distinct financial control.

The roots of the declining international competitiveness of the U.S. economy can be found in the complacency of many (although by no means all) dominant U.S. business enterprises with their prior successes in the face of the emergence of superior organizational capability backed by greater financial commitment abroad. Those who seek to accumulate wealth without making financial commitments to the rebuilding of organizational capabilities are simply exploiting the vulnerability of U.S. industry. There is no doubt that, in many adaptive companies in many older industries, there is an urgent need to change strategic managers and restructure organizations. But those managers and financiers who spent the 1980s bat-

---

[46] David J. Ravenscraft and F. M. Scherer, *Mergers, Sell-Offs, and Economic Efficiency* (Washington, D.C., Brookings Institution, 1987). For a case study, see Max Holland, *When the Machine Stopped* (Boston: Harvard Business School Press, 1989).

tling it out in the "market for corporate control" generally lacked either the incentive or ability (and often both) to regenerate the organizational capabilities of the dominant enterprises to meet the competitive standards of late-twentieth-century collective capitalism.

American business is losing competitive advantage not only in the "mature" industries of the Second Industrial Revolution, but also in the high-technology industries of the Third Industrial Revolution.[47] Among the major electronic equipment companies, the formation of Sematech to combine resources in the research and development of semiconductors was a step in the direction of a more collective capitalism, although the attainment of competitive advantage requires several more steps toward organizational integration of the industry's productive capabilities. As for new enterprises, it was not that many years ago when financial commitment by venture capitalists was key to building the U.S. business organizations that indeed gained competitive advantage in the high-technology fields. Yet in the 1980s venture capitalists often became what some journalists have called "vulture capitalists"; they sought to generate returns by raiding whole teams of managerial and technical personnel from the very organizations that venture capital created and by taking the new companies public before they had developed their investments enough to withstand the inevitable pressures from portfolio investors for short-term gains.[48]

If there is one lesson to be learned from the comparative history of three industrial revolutions, it is that, now more than ever, industrial innovation requires the long-term commitment of resources to organizations that can plan and coordinate the development and utilization of productive capabilities. In developed capitalist economies, however, those who control wealth can choose to live off the past rather than invest in the future. A necessary condition for continued investment in innovation is that such adaptive behavior be constrained. A sufficient condition is that the economic uncertainty inherent in innovative investment be reduced by means of policies that educate the labor force, mobilize committed financial resources, and coordinate interdependent innovative efforts.

If, in a particular social environment, private enterprise cannot itself create the organizational conditions for the appropriate education, mobilization, and coordination to occur, then public intervention is required.

[47] Stephen S. Cohen and John Zysman, *Manufacturing Matters* (New York: Basic, 1987), pt. 1; Michael L. Dertouzos, Richard K. Lester, and Robert M. Solow, *Made in America: Regaining the Productive Edge* (Cambridge, Mass.: MIT Press, 1989).
[48] John W. Wilson, *The New Venturers: Inside the High-Stakes World of Venture Capital* (Reading, Mass.: Addison-Wesley, 1986), ch. 13; Richard Florida and Martin Kenney, *The Break-Through Illusion* (New York: Basic, 1990), chs. 4 and 5.

Proprietary capitalism has long since vanished, and managerial capitalism can no longer compete. Almost a half century ago, the economist Joseph A. Schumpeter emphasized in *Capitalism, Socialism, and Democracy:* "We shall see that gradual socialization *within the framework of capitalism* is not only possible but even the most obvious thing to expect."[49] Anyone interested in understanding the nature and causes of the wealth of capitalist nations in the late twentieth century must grasp the enormous, and apparently growing, economic power of collective capitalism.

[49] Joseph A. Schumpeter, *Capitalism, Socialism, and Democracy,* 3d ed. (New York: Harper, 1950), 227, emphasis in original.

2

Organizations and markets in capitalist development

Organizations and markets

The historical experience of capitalist development demonstrates the growing importance of *organizational coordination* relative to *market coordination* in the value-creation process. To be sure, market exchange remains a distinctive feature of advanced capitalist economies. But to construct a historically relevant theory of the capitalist economy requires an analysis of the evolution of the relation between organizations and markets in particular historical contexts and identification of the impacts of the organization–market relation on national value-creating capabilities. Given the underdeveloped state of current debate on the microeconomic institutions that promote economic growth, the analysis must begin with basics.

What is it that distinguishes a *market* from an *organization?* The defining social characteristic of a market is the impersonal relation between buyer and seller. Both sides pursue their self-interests independently of one another, both in specifying their goals and in engaging in activities to achieve those goals. The impersonality of the market is manifested by the willingness of sellers of goods and services to enter into exchange with the highest bidders. As long as a buyer has the purchasing power to pay the highest price, his or her identity is of no concern to the seller.

A seller's identity is of concern to the buyer only insofar as the personal (or "firm-specific") capabilities of the seller in some way enter into the use-value of the good or service to be bought. Even then, in a market process, buyers have no ongoing commitments to purchase from particular sellers. Rather, buyers stand ready to shift their "custom" to whomever can offer the greatest use-value per unit of purchasing power.

For market relations between buyers and sellers to persist over time, moreover, the provision of goods or services to the highest bidders at one point in time must not preclude sellers from offering goods and services to (possibly different) highest bidders at later points in time. *Market exchange* does not exist, that is, if particular buyers have *privileged access* to the goods and services of particular sellers, or vice versa. By definition, the existence of market exchange requires that buyers have *equal access* to the resources of sellers. According to this definition, a long-term contract, once entered into, ostensibly precludes market exchange for the duration of the term.

Note that this definition of a market is consistent with either the buyer or the seller, or both of them, being a highly organized collectivity of individuals. The degrees to which buyers and sellers are organized among themselves are determinants of the relative power of the two sides in market exchange. But the existence of organized buyers or organized sellers does not preclude the existence of markets that mediate their transactions. Even with highly organized entities on both sides of the market, the interaction between buyers and sellers can be on a purely impersonal basis.

In a *perfectly competitive* market, as idealized by neoclassical economists, there is no organization among or between buyers and sellers. In the pursuit of their own self-interests, buyers compete among themselves for access to marketed goods and services, while sellers compete among themselves for access to the currency of buyers. But whether markets are characterized by perfect competition or bilateral monopoly, the necessary and sufficient condition for the existence of a market is the impersonal relation between buyer and seller.

In contrast, the defining characteristic of a business organization is the *planned coordination* of the activities of groups of individuals who participate in hierarchical and functional divisions of labor. Unlike participation in the market, where each individual determines his or her goals and activities autonomously, those who wish to participate as members of an organization are expected to conform to *collectively specified* goals and activities. In markets, collective goals are not specified, and the planned coordination of the activities of individuals does not take place.

Within an organization, individuals are related to one another through a specialized and hierarchical division of labor. Lines of hierarchical authority coordinate the functional division of labor in order to ensure that the workplace activities of those who participate in the organization further the organization's strategic goals. In and of itself, hierarchical planning tends to make bureaucracies impersonal – those who play no role in the planning process are expected to act in accordance with a predetermined and imposed set of rules. But the successful coordination of the activities of the large number of individuals who participate in an organization to achieve strategic goals must somehow secure the personal involvement of those individuals in the performance of work that furthers organizational goals.

If anything, it is when an organization relies predominantly on the threat of throwing employees back on the market to secure conformity to its goals that the impersonality of the enterprise is most marked. In practice, if the corporation is to induce employees to identify with organizational goals, it cannot rely primarily on the threat of dismissal as an incentive mechanism but must cater to the goals of employees by offering them relevant rewards for the work they perform.

Economic performance

The relations between organizations and markets that characterize a national economy can have profound implications for the development and utilization of a nation's productive resources. The planned coordination of a specialized division of labor that is the characteristic feature of an organization generates a *potential* for the development and utilization of productive resources, and hence for the creation of value, that does not exist when the specialized division of labor is coordinated by market forces. I shall argue, moreover, that the *realization* of the value-creating potential of organizational coordination requires that business enterprises have privileged access to key productive resources and, what amounts to the same thing, that the owners of these resources commit their goods and services to the use of particular business organizations irrespective of currently available market opportunities to reap returns. For the sake of the creation of value, organizational coordination is continually superseding market coordination, and substituting privileged for equal access to resources, in key areas of economic activity.

The emphasis on the planned coordination of economic activity as the foundation for the value-creation process flies in the face of cherished notions of the efficacy of individualism that, from the time of Adam Smith and Britain's Industrial Revolution, have dominated economic thinking in the Western capitalist world. With the recent success of the Japanese economy on the basis of highly collectivized business organizations, however, Westerners have become more receptive to the notion that the internal organization of the business enterprise, or even groups of business enterprises, may be critical to an economy's value-creating capabilities.

The importance of internal organization for the performance of capitalist economies is, however, by no means a Japanese creation. Even in the nineteenth-century success of British capitalism, characterized as it was by high degrees of horizontal competition and vertical specialization, large mercantile corporations and the factory system played important developmental roles. What has changed dramatically over the past two centuries is the relation between organizational and market coordination that is required to attain and sustain competitive advantage.[1] Since the late

---

[1] For a contemporary analysis that is consistent with these arguments, see Michael E. Porter, *Competitive Advantage* (New York: Free Press, 1985).

nineteenth century, the planned coordination of the specialized division of labor has been central to the successes of Western capitalist economies, including the United States.

In historical perspective, the Japanese model of business organization that has attracted so much attention recently is an elaboration of the corporate enterprise that brought the U.S. economy to dominance a half-century or so earlier. The advantage of Japanese organization over American organization is not that it is fundamentally different in its conception of planned coordination, but that it is able to put that conception into operation subject to many fewer individualistic political and cultural constraints.

The theory of the market economy

The prominence of internal organization in the development and operation of the economy runs directly counter to the vision that most economists have of the way in which successful capitalist economies operate. In modern economic thinking, it is the analysis of markets, not organizations, that holds center stage. Orthodoxy in economics argues that a well-functioning capitalist economy is a market-coordinated economy. The ability of an organization to influence the allocation of resources and distribution of income is an undesirable abnormality – a "market imperfection." Economic success is supposed to occur when resources are highly mobile via markets rather than when they have been captured by particular firms. According to economic orthodoxy, the optimal economy is one in which market forces determine the nature of organizations, not one in which organizations determine the nature of markets.

Even as large-scale business organization has become ever more prominent over the past century, economists have elaborated a theory of market exchange that accords scant attention to the internal organization of the business enterprise and its impact on the operation and performance of the capitalist economy. What has become known as neoclassical economics – essentially the theory of a market economy – maintains a powerful intellectual presence within the academic discipline.

To be sure, most economists regard the textbook version of the perfectly competitive market economy as an ideal type rather than an accurate depiction of economic reality. Nevertheless, economists insist on theoretical rigor, and insofar as they have a *systematic* view of the economic world that permits them to analyze and assess the impact of existing institutional arrangements on economic performance, it is the theory of the market economy that guides their thinking.

The defining feature of a neoclassical view of the world is that households rather than firms make all the critical decisions that direct economic activity. So far as the theory is concerned, households are synonymous with individuals – hence current notions that husbands and wives interact as individuals through a "marriage market," taking the place of the now unfashionable notion that (as the British legal commentator Blackstone put it) "in marriage husband and wife are as one, and that one is the husband." Households own productive resources and sell some of them on capital, labor, and land markets in order to obtain the income to purchase desired goods and services. Directed by market prices and constrained by available technology, firms combine productive resources that are purchased on various markets to produce goods and services that households want to buy.

Each acting independently, millions of households decide how much of their labor they prefer to supply to firms in exchange for wages, what marketable commodities they prefer to buy with their available financial resources, and how much of their current income they prefer to save. Backed by productive resources or purchasing power, all these preferences are aggregated on markets for labor, goods and services, and finance, these markets allocating "as if by an invisible hand" society's resources at a point in time and over time. It is the atomistic nature of household decision making and action combined with the propensity of households to organize their consumption through exchange that gives rise to the market economy in which individualism has free rein.

As buyers of inputs and sellers of outputs, firms play a decidedly secondary, and indeed passive, role in a neoclassical economy. Constrained by the impersonal dictates of input and output markets as well as by available technology, the business enterprise enters the theory of the market economy, not as a *social* organization that takes an active role in managing its productive investments, but only as a "production function" that puts *technical* limits on how productive resources can be transformed into the products that consumers demand. According to this vision, the firm has no independent power to determine what is produced, how it is produced, or how income is distributed. Forever facing extinction by market competition, the firm merely reacts to the pushes and pulls of market forces that are themselves derivative of the aggregated decisions of millions of isolated, and hence powerless, households.

As elaborated during the two hundred years since Adam Smith described the action of these impersonal market forces as the "invisible hand," the theory of the market economy has a message that is both political and economic. The political message is that the exercise of social power plays no role in the operation of the capitalist economy because control over the allocation of resources is so widely dispersed among households. In a

market economy, individuals are free from inherent personal commitment and dependence on the will of others. They are, as Milton and Rose
Friedman have put it, "free to choose."[2]

The economic message is that the invisible hand of the market will
ensure that resources are allocated to their most productive uses, with
the net satisfaction, or utility, that individuals derive from producing and
consuming marketable commodities serving as the ultimate measure of
productivity. If we let impersonal market forces direct the allocation of
resources and the distribution of income, so the story goes, individual
freedom and economic well-being will go hand in hand.[3]

The prime sources of so-called imperfections in the market economy
are firms that have privileged access to resources or buyers. Evaluated in
terms of the aggregate utility of the millions of individuals for whom the
economy is supposed to operate impersonally and impartially, the exercise of market power can supposedly yield only negative results. On the
one hand, managers of privileged firms are not compelled by market forces
to serve the aggregated interests of households by minimizing costs. On
the other hand, the free flow of resources into the production of the types
of goods and services demanded by households is restricted. As a result
of imperfect markets, production does not fully serve consumption, and
aggregate social utility is not maximized. The corollary to this conclusion
is the belief that the invisible hand of the market – and the flourishing
individualism that it encourages – can claim primary responsibility for
the successful development of the Western capitalist economies over (at
a minimum) the past two hundred years.

The "market economy" and capitalist development

The theory of the market economy may have ideological appeal for those
who wish to argue that individualism remains a viable alternative to collectivism in the conduct of economic affairs. But in providing an elaborate
rationale for the efficacy of autonomous decision making and activity, the
theory of the market economy fails to address the central problem of economic development: the growth of value-creating capabilities that result
in higher-quality products at lower unit costs.

What distinguishes neoclassical economics as a school of economic
thought is not just its market-oriented depiction of economic activity, but
also its definition of the nature of the economic problem. For neoclassical
economists, the most efficient economy is one that achieves the optimal
allocation of *scarce* resources among competing ends, where efficiency

---

[2] Milton Friedman and Rose Friedman, *Free to Choose* (New York: Avon, 1981).
[3] Milton Friedman, *Capitalism and Freedom* (Chicago: University of Chicago Press, 1962).

and optimality are assessed in terms of the aggregated maximization of the utility of the individuals who participate in the economy. In defining the economic problem as the allocation of scarce resources, neoclassical economics ignores the analysis of how individuals, firms, and economies create more value with the same amount of human and physical resources, and thereby overcome scarcity. In short, neoclassical economics has a theory of value *allocation*, but it lacks a theory of value *creation*.

The astute neoclassical economist might contend that the theory of the market economy has a quite adequate theory of the creation of value. The more individuals choose to save for the future rather than consume now, the more scarce resources are available for investment, and the more value will grow. The response is inadequate. As Keynesians have argued, the quantity of investment demand may be deficient because the market may not be able to coordinate the supply of savings and the demand for investment to maintain full employment of resources. It is business organizations, not individual households, that make the most important investment decisions, and in so doing they are influenced by factors besides the market rate of interest. One factor is the expected net value of an investment – an outcome that may be determined more by the organizational capability of the investing firm to develop technology and enhance productivity than by the configuration of market prices that the firm takes as given.

It follows that, in addition to the issue of the locus of investment decision making raised by John Maynard Keynes, what remains to be explained is why, under what conditions, and to what extent "investment" results in the creation of value. Understanding the evolving relation between organizations and markets is central to analyzing the value-creating potential of investments in productive resources. A theory that simply assumes that the greatest economic prosperity is achieved when organizations are subservient to market forces, as neoclassicists argue, cannot comprehend the changes in the ways in which invested resources have been transformed into higher-quality products at lower unit costs over the past two centuries of capitalist development.

Notwithstanding the dogmatic and static neoclassical perspective, attempts to analyze the evolving relation between organizations and markets are not entirely new to economic thinking (as I shall elaborate in Chapters 4 and 5). More than one hundred years ago, Karl Marx sought to show that the key to understanding the capitalist economy was to be found in the analysis of the evolution of the production process rather than by focusing solely on the balancing of supply and demand in the process of market exchange.[4] His methodological approach, which stressed

---

[4] Karl Marx, *Capital* (New York: Vintage, 1977), vol. 1.

the interaction of relations and forces of production, his distinction between productive capability and productive performance, and his conceptual framework for analyzing the relation between machinery and human productive capabilities in the development process remain central to a theory of capitalist development.[5]

A generation after Marx, Alfred Marshall established himself as Britain's leading economist through his synthesis of the neoclassical analyses of the role of the market mechanism in the allocation of scarce resources.[6] But unlike other pioneering neoclassical economists, such as Leon Walras in Switzerland and J. B. Clark in the United States, who sought to construct a full-blown theory of the market economy, Marshall imbedded his analysis of marginal adaptation in response to market forces within an evolutionary institutional framework in which business organization was central. Indeed, he spent the last decades of his life grappling with the issue of the relative importance for national economic performance of internal and external economies of scale.[7] Internal economies of scale result from organizational coordination of productive resources within the firm that spreads the fixed costs of that *specific firm* over more output, thus lowering unit costs. External economies of scale result from market coordination within a specific region (perhaps a national economy) that spreads the fixed costs of investments *within that specific region* over more output, thus lowering unit costs. In the one case, organizational coordination fosters economic development; in the other case, market coordination does so.[8]

Meanwhile, influenced by Marx's historical method, although not by his theory of production, Joseph Schumpeter put forth the proposition that the process of economic development could not be understood within the confines of the theory of the market economy.[9] His intellectual innovation was to distinguish entrepreneurial activity that results in organizational and technological innovation and drives the development process from managerial adaptation to changes in the balance of supply and demand, taking productive capabilities as given. "The essential point to grasp," Schumpeter argued in *Capitalism, Socialism, and Democracy,*

is that in dealing with capitalism we are dealing with an evolutionary process. It may seem strange that anyone can fail to see so obvious a fact which moreover

---

[5] William Lazonick, *Competitive Advantage on the Shop Floor* (Cambridge, Mass.: Harvard University Press, 1990), ch. 1.

[6] Alfred Marshall, *Principles of Economics*, 9th (variorum) ed. (London: Macmillan Press, 1961), vol. 1 (text).

[7] Alfred Marshall, *Industry and Trade* (London: Macmillan Press, 1919).

[8] Marshall, *Principles of Economics*, bk. 4, ch. 4; see also Chapters 3 and 5, this volume.

[9] Joseph Schumpeter, *The Theory of Economic Development* (New York: Oxford University Press, 1961).

was long ago emphasized by Karl Marx. Yet that fragmentary analysis which yields the bulk of our propositions about the functioning of modern capitalism persistently neglects it.[10]

In elaborating the "process of Creative Destruction" that is capitalism's engine of growth and in mounting a devastating critique of the way in which neoclassical economists pose the economic problem, Schumpeter contrasted an economy that optimizes subject to given constraints with an economy that develops its productive capabilities:

> Since we are dealing with a process whose every element takes considerable time in revealing its true features and ultimate effects, there is no point in appraising the performance of the process *ex visu* of a given point of time; we must judge its performance over time, as it unfolds through decades or centuries. A system – any system, economic or other – that at *every* given point of time fully utilizes its possibilities to the best advantage may yet in the long run be inferior to a system that does so at *no* given point of time, because the latter's failure to do so may be a condition for the level or speed of long-run performance.[11]

Neither Marx, nor Marshall, nor Schumpeter developed an adequate conception of the capitalist economy as a whole. All of them stressed, however, that a theory of economic development had to be based on a sound understanding of historical experience. The Marxian dialectic of relations and forces of production, the Marshallian distinction between external and internal economies, the Schumpeterian demonstration that innovation rather than adaptation lies at the heart of the development process – these fundamental insights into the nature of value creation under capitalism all remain relevant today.

Neoclassical economists have chosen not to build on these insights, primarily because they have not been especially concerned with discovering how individuals, firms, and economies overcome scarcity by creating value. Despite the fact that the ever-changing character of capitalist institutions was, as Schumpeter put it, "long ago emphasized by Karl Marx," neoclassical economists have failed "to grasp that in dealing with capitalism we are dealing with an evolutionary process."

In the midst of the profound economic crisis of the 1930s, prominent neoclassical economists explicitly argued that the analysis of economic development lay beyond the boundaries of conventional economic theorizing. Lionel Robbins, a distinctly conservative influence in British economics, excluded the analysis of economic development from his definition of "Economics." "Whatever Economics is concerned with," Robbins wrote, "it is *not* concerned with the causes of material welfare as such."

---

[10] Joseph Schumpeter, *Capitalism, Socialism, and Democracy*, 3d ed. (New York: Harper, 1950), 82.
[11] Ibid., 83.

Rather he went on to argue that "Economics is the science which studies human behavior as a relationship between ends and scarce means which have alternative uses" and that "the technical arts of production are simply to be grouped among the *given* factors influencing the relative scarcity of different economic goods."[12]

Liberal British economists were more impressed by the gravity of the "Great Slump" of the early 1930s. But despite an emphasis on the role of the "animal spirits" of businessmen in the determination of investment demand, even John Maynard Keynes managed to restore the theory of the market economy to its central analytical position, provided only that the government would step in to ensure full-employment levels of aggregate demand. As Keynes asserted toward the end of his classic book *The General Theory of Employment, Interest, and Money:*

> If central controls succeed in establishing an aggregate volume of output corresponding to full employment as nearly as is practicable, the classical theory [of the market economy] comes into its own again from this point onwards. If we suppose the volume of output to be given, i.e., *to be determined by forces outside the classical scheme of thought*, then there is no objection to be raised against the classical analysis of the manner in which private self-interest will determine what in particular is produced, in what proportions the factors of production will be combined to produce it, and how the value of the final product will be distributed between them.[13]

Whatever Keynes's genuine insights into the economic problems of his era, his acceptance of the theory of the market economy as an adequate depiction of supply-side processes meant that his "general theory" would have little to say about the role of business organizations in the process of economic development.

In the United States, some eminent neoclassical economists recognized the limited scope of prevailing economic theory. For example, Frank Knight, a founding father of the Chicago school of economics, concluded an essay on statics and dynamics in economics:

> Always history is being made; opinions, attitudes, and institutions change, and there is evolution in the nature of capitalism. . . . Such social evolution is rather beyond the province of the economic theorist, but it is pertinent to call attention to the utter inapplicability to such changes, i.e., to history in the large, of the notion of tendency toward a price equilibrium. Probably we must go further and reject entirely the use of the mechanical analogy, the categories of force, resistance, and movement, in discussing basic historical changes.[14]

---

[12] Lionel Robbins, *The Nature and Significance of Economic Science* (London: Macmillan Press, 1932), 9, 16, 33.

[13] John Maynard Keynes, *The General Theory of Employment, Interest, and Money* (New York: Harcourt, Brace & World, 1936), 378–9, my emphasis.

[14] Frank Knight, *The Ethics of Competition* (New York: Harper, 1935), 184, 185.

In his *Foundations of Economic Analysis* (written in the late 1930s, but first published in 1945), Paul Samuelson wrote that "often the economist takes as data certain traditionally noneconomic variables such as technology, tastes, social and institutional conditions, etc.; although to the students of other disciplines these are processes to be explained and analyzed, and are not merely history."[15] In the last sentence of his book, Samuelson voiced the hope that sometime in the future analytical economics would confront the "majestic problems of economic development."[16] But his own practice of economics – most notably his "grand neoclassical synthesis" of Keynesian macroeconomics into the theory of the market economy – contributed substantially to an intellectual environment in which successive generations of well-trained economists would be unwilling and increasingly unable to comprehend the nature and causes of the wealth of nations.

Over the past fifty years, capitalist development has hardly stood still. Yet economic thought continues to be dominated by the myth of the market economy. The mainstream of the economics profession has paid little heed even to warnings from within, such as that of Knight just cited, that economists must shed their peculiar obsession with equilibrating market forces if they want to understand historical change. On the contrary, over the past fifty years, the theory of the market economy has become ever more entrenched as the dominant economics paradigm in the Western world. Reared on this ideology of the efficacy of individualism, the current proponents of the neoclassical vision are much less conscious than their teachers of the limits of their perspective.

It is true that many mainstream economists depart from the theory of the market economy in their attempts to analyze this or that slice of reality. The problem is that, in doing so, they are typically unaware – and if aware, apparently unconcerned – about the disjuncture between empirical insights garnered from the observation of the real world and the overriding theoretical vision that they call on to systematize these insights. With their intellectual visions limited by the theory of the market economy, mainstream economists have made little if any attempt to formulate a theory of capitalist development.

Contrary to Lionel Robbins, economic analysis must be concerned with the "causes of material welfare" if it is to illuminate more than it obscures. It makes no sense for economists to concern themselves with the "optimal" way to slice a "scarce" economic pie if they have no understanding of what determines the changing size of the pie. Indeed, the history of

---

[15] Paul Samuelson, *Foundations of Economic Analysis*, enlarged ed. (Cambridge, Mass.: Harvard University Press, 1983), 318–19.
[16] Ibid., 355.

capitalist development suggests that the way in which the pie is sliced – the way in which resources are allocated and goods and services distributed – has a significant impact on how rapidly the pie grows. A major role of well-functioning business organizations is to structure the distribution of income among their participants – workers, managers, owners, suppliers, buyers – in ways that augment the creation of value.

For those concerned with the wealth and welfare of nations, there is a need to reconceptualize economic theory in terms of a dynamic developmental process. In the remainder of this chapter, I shall lay out a general conceptual framework for analyzing the relation between organizations and markets in capitalist development that is consistent with the comparative historical analysis presented in Chapter 1. In later chapters I shall use this conceptual framework and the comparative historical experience on which it draws to evaluate the Marxian, Schumpeterian, and Marshallian theoretical contributions to our understanding of the role of business organizations in twentieth-century capitalist development as well as to critique the economics mainstream for its persistent adherence to the myth of the market economy.

The value-creating economy

As in the theory of the market economy, my conception of capitalism as a value-creating economy begins with the individual. But unlike the theory of the market economy, my approach focuses not on how individuals allocate their *scarce* resources, but on how individuals attempt to *overcome* scarcity by developing and utilizing their value-creating capabilities.

In particular, I explore how individuals make use of organizations and markets in their pursuit of stable and remunerative employment. From this developmental perspective, I then focus on business enterprises as organizations that rely on privileged access to resources to create value so as to achieve competitive advantage. The conceptual framework enables us to understand the emergence of the dominant business enterprise as well as to analyze the potentially positive and negative roles that it can play in a national process of economic development.

Conceptually, we can distinguish two interrelated sources of value creation. One is the *development* of the productive capabilities of human and physical resources. The other is the more complete *utilization* of resources, given their productive capabilities. A theory of economic development requires a systematic analysis of how the development and utilization of productive resources occur. A theory of *capitalist* development requires an analysis of the impacts of private enterprise and market exchange on the development and utilization of productive forces.

The development and utilization of *human* resources determine the value of all other resources, as people master nature and plan investments in productive capabilities in order to produce goods and services that meet human needs and wants. The development of the considerable productive capability that becomes embodied in plant, equipment, and materials originates in human creativity, investment decisions, and work effort. Moreover, the utilization of the productive capability of physical capital – the transformation of latent into effective productive forces – requires human initiative and social organization.

Even though the development and utilization of productive resources may take place in organizations that collectivize the activities of a large number of people, it is individuals (or, in earlier years, their guardians) who ultimately have the power to decide how to develop and utilize their own productive resources. To understand how individuals are integrated into value-creating economic activity requires an analysis of how and to what effect individuals use markets and organizations to develop and utilize their productive capabilities. Once one understands the relations between individuals and economic institutions and the impact of these relations on the creation of value, one is in a position to analyze the impact of prevailing economic institutions on national economic performance.

The development of human resources

When an individual invests in the development of his or her productive capabilities, he or she may expect to reap returns in the form of stable and remunerative employment that will permit a decent standard of living over a period of some forty to fifty years. For many individuals, such economic security represents the foundation for the achievement of other goals such as work satisfaction, luxury consumption, and social mobility for themselves or their children. Through inheritance, gambling, theft, extortion, speculation, and so on, individuals can reap where they have not sown. But for most people in a capitalist society, the development of productive capabilities is a prerequisite to stable and remunerative employment, which is in turn the primary means to achieve personal goals.

The ability to make a living depends on a lengthy process of investment in "human capital" that extends from childhood nurturing and schooling through on-the-job experience in one's occupation or career. As prevailing technological practices as well as the social settings in which the technologies are transformed into productive forces become more complex, even those individuals whose only ambition is to get a job and earn a living wage may have to spend a substantial part of their lives acquiring productive capabilities, such as basic communication skills, before they actually become productive agents who can reap returns from their investments in their own capabilities.

For the first fifteen to twenty-five years of life, individuals are protected from market forces by family structures and educational systems so that they may acquire the general cognitive and behavioral equipment required for the world of work. Indeed, those individuals who take early leave of the personalized and organized environment provided by family and school to enter the labor market are more likely to find themselves relatively handicapped for the rest of their lives in their abilities to hold stable and remunerative employment. Those who enter the labor market earlier seek their livelihoods through highly competitive markets for unskilled labor, in which the duration of jobs is only short term and the content of jobs does little to develop one's productive capabilities. Certainly, such workers make ample use of labor markets over their lifetimes as they switch from employer to employer. But mobility via the market is their problem, not their salvation. They are free to choose employers – if they can find them. And when they do find employment, they do not have much in the way of productive capabilities to sell or rewards to reap.

Individuals with loftier aspirations and stronger familial or institutional support stay within the organized educational system longer in an attempt to develop specialist capabilities that will enable them to avoid exposure to the impersonal labor market. The least capable and least affluent of this group will choose to buy higher-education services on a relatively impersonal college market, while the more capable and more affluent will find that they have access to elite training, credentials, and social connections that promise to shield them from exposure to the labor market for the rest of their lives. Much more than the use of impersonal markets, it is the ability of individuals to remain attached to and supported by familial and educational organizations that enhances their freedom to choose not only careers and employers but also consumption and saving patterns.

Careers and entrepreneurs

Once they enter the world of work, there are two ways that individuals can protect themselves from market forces as they pursue their personal goals. One way – which I shall call the *career strategy* – is to work for an organization that has an entrenched product-market position, including not only dominant capitalist enterprises but also nonprofit institutions such as the civil service, the armed forces, and the educational system. Possessing considerable market power, these institutions can hold out to the individual the expectation of stable employment and possibilities for advancement in social position, responsibility, and pay. The other way – which I shall call the *entrepreneurial strategy* – is to invest in one's own business and become one's own boss.

In pursuing the career strategy, individuals are permitted by the labor market to seek out organizations that offer the best prospects for achieving personal goals. In practice, however, the employment policies of organizations constrain most employees to use the labor market sparingly during the forty to fifty years of their careers. Organizations are willing to establish long-term employment relations, including internal promotion policies, first to attract individuals with requisite aptitudes and skills, then to give the organization the incentive to invest in the further development of productive capabilities of these individuals, and finally to motivate employees to put forth the effort that ensures high levels of utilization of those capabilities. Most individuals pursuing the career strategy tend, therefore, to see their future employment prospects in terms of the particular organizations that they entered when they were relatively young. Over time, individuals develop an interest in the performance of the particular organizations that provide them with employment security, if only because of the fear that the relative decline of the organization might throw them back on the labor market. When career-oriented individuals *choose* to use the market to change employers, they do so strategically, with due regard for the organizational capabilities of current and prospective employers, and hence the relative prospects for stable and remunerative employment.

Not all individuals are content to pursue their personal goals by climbing around and up one or more organizations. The other employment strategy to achieve personal goals is to create one's own firm. Would-be entrepreneurs have to acquire relevant productive capabilities, typically by attaching themselves at an early stage to the same public and private organizations as those individuals who are pursuing careers. In addition, however, the entrepreneur must gain access to the capital necessary to finance investments in plant, equipment, materials, and managerial organization, the productive capabilities of which will typically require a long period before they are sufficiently developed and utilized to yield returns.

A new entrepreneurial venture is by nature highly uncertain. The initial stake for the enterprise, therefore, generally comes from inherited wealth, personal savings, or friends, relatives, and business associates who have faith in the entrepreneur's capabilities. Personal knowledge of the integrity, resolve, and energy of the entrepreneur does not guarantee that the new venture will be a success. Such knowledge nevertheless provides the only rational basis on which those who possess finance can make the decision to commit their resources to a new and uncertain project.

The more uncertain the venture and the less confidence that financiers have in the entrepreneur, the more will they demand substantial decision-making power over the allocation of enterprise resources – power that is typically secured by taking substantial equity positions in the firm. There are limits, however, to the willingness of the entrepreneurial individual to accede to these demands because the sharing of property rights and managerial power in the enterprise can jeopardize the ability to be one's own boss. For this reason, entrepreneurs are wary of going to impersonal capital markets to finance long-term investment, just as financiers are wary of making long-term loans to individuals with whom they have no ongoing personal relations.

The vision, capability, and energy of the entrepreneur, or of a group of entrepreneurial associates acting in concert, are critical for the initial success of the enterprise, especially when new products or processes and large fixed-capital investments are involved. Even more so than for career-oriented employees, who invest only in themselves and not in the employing enterprise, the future of self-employed entrepreneurs depends on the creation of value – the development and utilization of productive resources – within their particular business organizations.

The growth of the entrepreneurial firm

A business enterprise can grow by pursuing a strategy of horizontal expansion or one of vertical integration. Either strategy requires managerial capability, so that the growth of the entrepreneurial firm is limited by the scale and scope of the value-creating activities that the entrepreneur can properly manage – limits that organizational theorists have referred to as "bounded rationality."[17] The viability of horizontal enterprise expansion assumes the availability of greater supplies of the requisite vertically related inputs as well as greater demand for the firm's outputs. In other words, successful horizontal expansion on a vertically specialized basis assumes the existence of the necessary vertically related markets. Conversely, high degrees of vertical specialization and horizontal competition tend to go hand in hand. Easy access to input and output markets as well as the relatively low demands on managerial and financial resources facilitate entry into a vertical specialty, thus increasing the number of competitors within it.

Readily accessible markets for purchasing inputs and selling outputs save the vertically specialized firm the fixed costs of not only vertically related technology but also the managerial organization to plan the development and coordinate the utilization of vertically related productive activities. By the same token, however, not having invested in firm-specific organizational capabilities that can develop and utilize productive re-

---

[17] Oliver Williamson, *The Economic Institutions of Capitalism* (New York: Free Press, 1985); see also Chapter 6, this volume.

sources, the firm cannot expect to generate internal economies that will give it competitive advantage over other firms in the industry. Rather, by relying on external, market-supplied resources to which all firms in the industry have equal access, the firm will tend to operate subject to the same cost and revenue constraints as its competitors. All firms in a regional industry may benefit from external economies because of more complete utilization of productive resources on which the industry relies.

But because impersonal market forces impose similar constraints on the activities of all firms in the industry, each firm will find itself stuck in "competitive equilibrium." Under competitive equilibrium, there is no firm that has the privileged access to superior productive resources, either organizational or technological, that could enable it to generate internal economies that would destroy the old equilibrium and permit the firm to gain competitive advantage over its rivals. To understand the processes of value creation and economic development requires a conceptual framework that explores how some enterprises manage to *escape* from competitive equilibrium by generating higher-quality products at lower unit costs than their rivals. One cannot understand capitalist development if, as in neoclassical analyses, the prime analytical issue is to determine how through market coordination and equal access to resources, business enterprises become entrapped in competitive equilibrium.[18]

Attaining competitive advantage

For a particular enterprise, the means of escape from competitive equilibrium are the generation of internal economies that enable it to provide a good or service of given quality at lower unit cost than competitors, or a higher-quality good or service at the same unit cost, or both. The more complex an industry's technologies and the more extensive the demands of an industry's buyers, the greater are the opportunities for a "first-mover" enterprise to differentiate itself from other enterprises in the industry. An enterprise that differentiates itself from its rivals, and thereby attains competitive advantage, does so by means of internal economies that manifest its superior value-creating capabilities.

If the resources that yield internal economies are quickly diffused to other enterprises in the industry, however, the competitive advantage will be short lived. Indeed, as the enterprise loses privileged access to the resource that gave it competitive advantage, a market in that resource comes into being, and what was a source of internal economies to the particular enterprise becomes a potential external economy available to any entrepreneur who wants to participate in the industry. As we have

---

[18] See Chapter 5.

seen, external economies result from the existence of markets that give all enterprises access to financial, human, and physical resources on the same terms. In contrast, internal economies result from the ability of particular enterprises to gain privileged access to resources, be they financial, human, or physical.

Privileged access to resources means that some enterprises can obtain particular productive services at lower unit costs than other enterprises. But how might an enterprise gain such a competitive advantage in a society where all owners of productive resources are ostensibly free to use the market to sell the services of their property to the highest bidder? Why might the owner of a productive resource withhold it from the market by granting privileged access to a particular enterprise rather than extract the highest market price that the resource will currently command?

Individuals grant an enterprise privileged access to their resources when they expect that their personal goals will be better attained by long-term attachment to the particular enterprise rather than by reallocating their resources from one business to another via the market. For example, an individual might give privileged access to his or her resources to an enterprise in which he or she can exercise some control over work conditions and can interact with people with whom he or she has a common philosophical outlook, familial ties, or other personal bonds. These conditions are characteristic of household (peasant and "mom and pop") enterprises in which the size of the firm is limited by an unwillingness to undertake an expansion of the enterprise that would require the substantial delegation of authority to employees who are not part of the family unit and would expose the proprietors to external financial control. Such conditions are also characteristic of communal enterprises in which the opportunities that the market offers for individual gain are explicitly eschewed for the sake of working as part of a specific group. In both cases, control over work and access to a desired work environment are inextricably bound up with long-term attachment to a particular enterprise secured through familial or communal ownership.

As the creators of capitalist enterprises, entrepreneurs give their firms privileged access to their human and financial resources. They expect that over the long run the way in which the firm develops and utilizes its productive capabilities will make them better off than if these resources had been supplied to the highest bidder on the market. Ownership and control of their enterprises assure entrepreneurs that they will be able to appropriate returns if and when the firm achieves the necessary extent of the market to generate profits.

At the initial stages of an enterprise, an entrepreneur may also secure privileged access to financial resources from relatives, friends, and associates who expect that the business vision, managerial capability, and personal commitment of the entrepreneur will result in the generation of internal economies that will eventually yield returns to their financial stake that more than offset forgone market returns. Even some career-oriented individuals who do not hold shares in the enterprise might be willing to give the entrepreneur privileged access to their human resources because they expect that over the long run their personal goals will be better served by the growth of the particular entrepreneurial organization than by other employment opportunities currently available on the market.

These expectations may not be fulfilled. The success or failure of a new venture or the ability of unsecured participants to share in the gains of enterprise can only be known in retrospect. The initial competitive advantage inherent in privileged access to resources may not be sustained, either because of the rise of competitors with superior value-creating capabilities or because the privileged firm dissipates rather than develops the productive resources at its disposal. Even when competitive advantage is sustained, moreover, the firm's owners may renege on promises (implicit or explicit) to share value gains with unsecured "stakeholders."

Choosing the firm that will be a winner – that will attain and sustain competitive advantage – is a highly uncertain affair. If the enterprise cannot generate internal economies that enable the firm to pay returns to productive resources that are greater than those that could have been had by using the market, then, in strictly economic terms, the venture has failed (although it need not necessarily go out of business). The entrepreneur may regret that he or she used the firm rather than the market to seek a return to his or her resources. In retrospect, financiers as well may recognize that they misconstrued the breeding and track record of the entrepreneur on whom they placed their bets, and that they too would have been better off accepting a market rate of return on their resources. Reaping returns will be even more uncertain for employees who do not hold securities in the firm; they may have no legal basis for claiming returns to their investments of time and effort even if the firm does attain and sustain competitive advantage. The firm may win, but unsecured employees who contributed their productive resources to the success of the enterprise on the implicit promise of future returns may lose.

Sustaining competitive advantage

Even when privileged access to productive resources enables an enterprise to overturn the forces of competitive equilibrium and gain initial competitive advantage, it is the ongoing development and utilization of these resources to generate internal economies that enable it to sustain its competitive advantage. How might an enterprise that has gained an initial competitive advantage continue to escape the equalizing trap of competitive forces over the long run? The answer is *organizational capability*.[19] Once entrepreneurs, financiers, and careerists have committed their resources to a particular enterprise for the production of particular goods and services, an organizational structure must be put in place that can plan the development and coordinate the utilization of these resources. Finance buys plant, equipment, and material. Specialists within the enterprise develop and utilize physical capital to serve the process and product requirements of the enterprise strategy.

The essential role of the organizational structure is the planned coordination of a specialized division of labor that develops and utilizes the productive resources that have been committed to the enterprise. By developing and utilizing in a planned and coordinated fashion the productive capabilities of employees involved in the specialized division of labor, the enterprise builds organizational capability that can generate process and product innovation. To develop organizational capability, the enterprise must plan its human resource needs not only to facilitate the production and distribution of existing products, but also to generate new processes that will make existing products more competitive as well as new products that will permit the long-term stability and growth of the enterprise.

The planned coordination of a specialized division of labor has a hierarchical as well as functional dimension. With the creation of an organizational structure, the entrepreneur is transformed into a strategic manager. Like that of the entrepreneur, the role of the strategic manager is to choose the types of large-scale investments in processes and products that, when added to the enterprise's existing productive capabilities, are most likely to yield the greatest internal economies. But compared with the productive capabilities required to transform a new venture into a going concern, the human and physical resources that must be planned and coordinated by corporate management are much more complex.

The more technologically and socially complex the activities of the enterprise, the more must the strategic manager rely on a managerial structure to ensure that the activities of those involved in the specialized division of labor are consistent with strategic goals. The role of the managerial structure is to overcome the bounds on individual rationality by collectivizing the rationality of those involved in the organization.[20] To collectivize rationality, the strategic manager must delegate authority over opera-

[19] For the application of this concept, see William Lazonick, "Organizational Capabilities in American Industry: The Rise and Decline of Managerial Capitalism," *Business and Economic History*, 2d. ser., 19 (1990), 35–54.

[20] The seminal work is Chester Barnard, *The Functions of the Executive* (Cambridge, Mass.: Harvard University Press, 1938).

tional decision making to individuals who are uniquely qualified as well as motivated to make the decisions that are consistent with the goals of the enterprise.

But why might the planned coordination of a specialized division of labor result in sustained competitive advantage? Other things equal, the investment in a managerial structure *in addition to* investment in plant, equipment, materials, and personnel should put the organization at a competitive *disadvantage* compared with firms that rely less on internal coordination and more on market processes. What can organizational coordination do better than market coordination that enables the managerial enterprise to transform potential competitive disadvantage into actual competitive advantage?

Managerial coordination can develop and utilize productive resources in ways that market coordination cannot. The superior development of productive capabilities depends on *innovation*, while the superior utilization of productive capabilities of a given quality depends on *throughput*. Innovation can be defined as any new way of producing or designing a product that (in contrast to invention per se) the firm deems it profitable to introduce. Throughput can be defined as the speed at which given products are produced and distributed on the basis of given processes. *Economies of speed* occur when the decrease in unit costs that the firm achieves by spreading fixed production and distribution costs over more sold outputs more than outweighs the increase in unit costs because of investments in organization (including the R&D organization that may be necessary to generate innovations) and the sharing of productivity gains with employees as rewards necessary to secure the higher levels of throughput.[21]

Although conceptually distinct phenomena, in practice innovation and throughput are (as will be illustrated in Chapter 3) inextricably linked. The economic viability of a new process or product will depend on how the investment in the innovation is utilized once the change is introduced. Innovation will not occur unless strategic decision makers – those who allocate resources to the development of new products and processes – expect that the enterprise has the organizational capability to attain high enough levels of throughput on the basis of a new process or product to make the investment in the new productive forces profitable. The greater the fixed costs of the new process or product, the more important to the innovation decision are economies of speed.

But why might organizational coordination achieve innovation and

---

[21] See Alfred D. Chandler, Jr., *The Visible Hand: The Managerial Revolution in American Business* (Cambridge, Mass.: Harvard University Press, 1977); see also Chapter 3, this volume.

throughput so much better than market coordination that the higher fixed costs of internal organization are more than offset? Organizational coordination can be part of a planning process; market coordination cannot. Insofar as the productive activities of more than one individual enter into the development of a new process or product, the *planned* coordination of the activities of individuals with the requisite productive capabilities permits the conceptualization and implementation of changes in productive methods more effectively than the same individuals acting independently, coordinated only by the impersonal forces of supply and demand.

The planning of innovation, moreover, does not preclude those involved in the change from drawing on resources available on the market where and when they are needed. On the contrary, the development of the core elements of an innovation through planning facilitates the integration of knowledge available on the market into the further evolution of the innovation by subcontracting arrangements.

It may well be, moreover, that the most important R&D by subcontractors occurs *not* when they do their work with a view to selling only to the highest bidder (as in the definition of a market relation), but when an organization that has preconceptualized the desired process or product has invested in the subcontractor to develop new ways of doing things that fit into organizational plans. If the subcontractor is foreclosed from selling his or her products to other users and if the core organization makes an investment in the subcontracting enterprise in order to integrate it into the planning process, then the relation between the two parties can hardly be called a market relation. Indeed, with the development of capitalism one of the most potent forces for the creation of value is organizational integration across legally distinct enterprises.[22] Whether or not the enterprise itself as distinct from an enterprise group is the appropriate unit for analyzing the generation of *internal* economies depends on whether the productive relations between relevant enterprises are deemed to be organizational or market – committed or at arm's length.

It is hypothetically possible for innovation to occur through the sequential development of its components by individuals acting autonomously, with specialists at later stages securing the knowledge of those at earlier stages, perhaps through patent licenses. But particularly for technologically complex innovations, it is unlikely that such a method can compete with planned coordination. Specialists at later stages will not necessarily have the productive capabilities to readapt developments made at earlier stages in the light of new knowledge of process and product requirements. The use of market relations between vertically related specialists

---

[22] See Chapter 1.

is a cumbersome, and generally ineffectual, method for coordinating research and development.

Even if the enterprise (or enterprise group) has secured via the market all of the components that enter into an innovation, organizational coordination might still be better than market coordination in the achievement of high levels of throughput, and hence in achieving the high levels of utilization of the enterprise's existing productive capabilities required to transform high fixed costs into low unit costs. In effect, for any given set of vertically related activities, organizational coordination of production and distribution involves vertical integration, while market coordination involves vertical specialization. Organizational coordination of vertically integrated structures speeds up the flow of work because bottlenecks in vertically related processes can be better eliminated by the planning process than by market coordination. Within a planning process, shortages at any given vertical stage can be foreseen before they actually occur, and systems of rewards and punishments can be put in place to induce employees to provide the effort needed to maintain desired work flows.

In addition, through forward integration into the distribution of final goods and services, particular business organizations can attempt to control the extent of the market for their products. The resultant control over product markets in turn provides an informational basis superior to that available through market coordination (where the enterprise just gets whatever product demand happens to come its way) for determining the "optimal" scale of plant and equipment in which to invest in order to achieve high levels of capacity utilization and low unit costs. Both overinvestment and underinvestment in plant and equipment reduce economies of speed and increase unit costs – overinvestment by increasing the organization's fixed costs given the extent of the market, and underinvestment by limiting the extent of the market that the organization can supply given its fixed costs.

The most important resources that an enterprise develops and utilizes are not technologies embodied in processes and products but the specialists on whom the organization relies to develop and utilize its physical capital. To a certain extent, the organization finds specialists with the requisite productive capabilities readily available on the market, trained by the educational system. But as part of the planning process, the organization that seeks to sustain its competitive advantage will find it necessary to invest further in the development of more highly trained personnel so that they can contribute to innovation and throughput.

Given the existence of labor markets, the organization has no assurance that it will be able to reap the returns from any particular investments in the productive capabilities of its employees. Nevertheless, in an economy where the generation of internal economies has become important not only for competitive advantage but even for survival (because other enterprises are persistently using organizational coordination to leap ahead), any particular business organization will have no choice but to invest in its employees if it wants to remain in the competitive game.

In essence, the uncertainty surrounding the returns to investments in human resources is not different than the uncertainty surrounding all the precommitments of resources that the enterprise as a productive organization must make. Investment in the face of uncertain returns is the essence of capitalist enterprise.[23] In the presence of many successful enterprises that can market their securities, individuals who have nothing to do with productive activity but who do have access to financial resources can diversify their portfolios and (save for unforeseen events such as stock market crashes) transform uncertainty into calculable risk. Nevertheless, for any particular enterprise the uncertainty remains. Returns are not guaranteed to the enterprise but depend on how well the resources of the business organization are managed in relation to an evolving external environment.

Employees in whose productive capabilities the enterprise makes significant investments have to be managed by means of personnel policies such as internal promotion, profit sharing, and stock options that seek to ensure their long-term attachment to the enterprise. Because career-oriented individuals are concerned with employment stability, work satisfaction, and socioeconomic mobility, such personnel policies can be very effective in ensuring that the enterprise can utilize the human resources that it has developed.

To attain and sustain competitive advantage, however, the enterprise must not only develop and utilize productive resources, but also *appropriate* a share of the value gains. The business organization can then use its share of the value gains to give itself privileged access to financial resources that can be reinvested in the further development of the productive capabilities at its disposal. Alternatively, the organization can pass on the value gains to consumers in order to increase market share, which in turn increases the utilization of existing productive capabilities, thereby increasing the internal economies of scale.

But given the existence of markets in productive resources, how does the organization (as distinct from its various individual participants) capture the value gains? Even if resource owners do not actually use the market to remove their productive capabilities from the enterprise, why don't they use the *threat* of exit to appropriate all the value gains for themselves? If all resource owners who participate in the enterprise are

---

[23] See Chapter 6.

indeed able to capture all the gains from the development and utilization of their productive capabilities, the enterprise as an ongoing productive organization will no longer have *privileged* access to resources. Even when the enterprise has resources at its disposal that are superior to those of its competitors, if participants in the enterprise use the market (or the threat of using the market) to appropriate for themselves the resultant value created in the form of higher returns to their "factors of production," the organization will have costs that are no lower than its competitors, and hence no competitive advantage.

The conception of the nature of the business organization that I have just presented provides the basic answers to the question of appropriation. As in the case of the entrepreneurial firm, resource owners might be willing to grant the managerial organization privileged access to their productive capabilities because they expect that the enterprise will sustain its competitive advantage and that their shares in long-run gains of the enterprise will more than offset returns forgone by not using the market to withdraw returns as they become available in the short run. With the growth of the enterprise, however, it is no longer just the willingness of resource owners to give the organization privileged access to their productive capabilities that matters. The basis for the growth of the organization is the planned coordination of a specialized division of labor. The managerial organization succeeds because it collectivizes the interests and activities of key individual participants in the pursuit of the goals of the enterprise. The more successful the managerial organization, the more its resources create value *only as part of a collective structure*. It is the value-creating capability of this collective organizational structure – what I have called organizational as distinct from individual capability – that gives a particular business organization sustained competitive advantage.

As a result of the planned coordination of a specialized division of labor, the productive capabilities of resource owners become *organization specific*. Existing or potential rivals cannot secure the same level of productivity from any particular resource as the advantaged organization unless they replicate or surpass the organizational capability that the dominant enterprise has created. Superior organizational capability becomes a barrier to the entry of new firms into the industry. Lacking comparable organizational capability, no other enterprise can afford to reward these resources to the same extent. As a result, rivals who have not gone through the development process of building their organizational capability have no interest in using the market to bid piecemeal for productive resources.

Organization specificity occurs, therefore, because the productivity of any individual factor of production is not independent of the organizational capability of the particular enterprise that combines its productive services with those of other factors of production. As long as the advantaged organization uses its organizational capability to develop and utilize its productive resources better than its rivals, it can sustain its privileged access to resources and its competitive advantage.

Dominant business organizations

By enabling some business organizations to achieve sustained competitive advantage, the generation of internal economies changes the role and impact of existing market forces in the economy by constantly undermining any tendency toward a competitive equilibrium of enterprises in the relevant industry. The ultimate result is concentrated control of product markets, usually with a small number of dominant (typically called oligopolistic) organizations vying for market share.

There are two routes to dominance. Where, from the historical outset of a particular industry, the development and utilization of productive resources is complex and the services inherent in the product difficult to sell, the potential for organizational capability to reap internal economies may be great enough to result in the emergence of oligopoly, or even monopoly, without the industry going through a highly competitive phase. But in industries in which productive resources are easily sold, external economies will dominate and the potential for competitive advantage will be low. Such industries will be characterized by high levels of product-market competition.

If, however, changes in the nature of productive forces or product demand in a highly competitive industry provide the potential for organizational capability to reap internal economies, those organizations that are the first movers in creating effective organizational structures will disrupt tendencies to competitive equilibrium. Enterprises that continue to rely mainly on external economies will not necessarily be forced to close their doors in the face of the rise of managerial organizations within their industry. Rather, they may be able to remain competitive by cutting prices and living off their existing capital with no provision for replacement – that is, by means of the adaptive responses that give rise to the phenomenon of "cutthroat competition."

The rising managerial organizations will want to put an end to cutthroat competition. The most effective way to do so will be by merging their own interests and developing an even greater organizational capability that will limit further the economic viability of those enterprises that rely on external economies. The strategy will be successful, however, only if merger creates the possibility for the development and utilization of organizational capability that in turn results in the replacement of external economies by internal economies in the further evolution of the industry. The merger, that is, must result in a unified managerial structure that has the capability to plan and coordinate.

The dominant business organization has many potential advantages over its less dominant rivals in the pursuit of internal economies. Its dominant product-market position enables employees to place more credibility in promises that the organization can and will offer them employment stability, work satisfaction, and socioeconomic mobility – inducements that are critical to the creation of value and the generation of internal economies. The dominant organization has a greater incentive than its rivals to invest in in-house research and development because, even apart from patent protection, it has the organizational capability to transform new ideas into profitable innovations and to control the utilization of the improved productive resources.

With its secure market position in its existing product lines and geographical regions, the dominant organization can also look to the future and devote resources to the development of new product lines and entry into new regions. As the markets for existing product lines become saturated, product substitutes emerge, or consumer tastes change, the organization will possess the organizational capability to alter the geographic range and product diversity of its activities – changes in the *scope* of the enterprise that over the long run are essential for sustaining competitive advantage. When it does use the market to secure supplies of vertically related inputs, the dominant organization can use its significant purchasing power to gain better service and lower prices from suppliers than are available to other buyers who represent only small shares of the relevant demand.

The emergence of dominant organizations also permits the separation of asset ownership from managerial control, which in turn creates conditions conducive to sustaining competitive advantage. As was discussed in the case of a new entrepreneurial venture, any rational decision to commit financial resources to such an enterprise requires personal knowledge of the entrepreneur and the nature of his or her strategic plans. The existence of a dominant organization that, as manifested by its sustained competitive advantage, has already developed its organizational capability reduces the uncertainty for investors who know little or nothing about the relevant strategic managers or enterprise strategies. The uncertainty is reduced even further by the fact that, for the same reasons, a large number of other individuals stand ready to purchase shares in the organization, so that, for those with financial resources, investment in the organization becomes liquid. Once investors can choose a large number of dominant organizations in which to hold marketable securities, moreover, they can diversify their portfolios, thereby reducing uncertainty even further to (what they may consider to be) calculable risk.

As a result of its ability to market securities, the dominant organization gains privileged access to financial resources. Finance is much more readily available to it on the market than to less dominant enterprises because it already possesses the organizational capability to make use of the capital in ways that less well positioned (or potential) rivals cannot. The more dominant the business organization, the more acquiescent its shareholders are in forgoing immediate returns on their assets, as they make no attempt to challenge the propensity of strategic managers to retain a considerable proportion of the earnings of the organization to fund new investments. The lower the payout ratio, the more debt the organization can incur on the basis of a debt–equity ratio that will not jeopardize the financial viability of the organization's long-term investment strategies. The greater the expectations that investors have that the organization will sustain its competitive advantage, the lower its cost of capital.

Privileged access to retained earnings often occurs in organizations that have undergone a substantial separation of asset ownership from managerial control. This separation can enable the enterprise to overcome managerial as well as financial constraints. Specifically, the separation of ownership and control helps to overcome the constraints that entrepreneurial ownership puts on the continuity of the enterprise and managerial succession. By definition, when ownership is separated from control, the potential supply of top managers need not be restricted to members of the property-owning unit – the entrepreneur's family. Strategic management can be put in the hands of professional managers who have developed the capabilities for strategic decision making and the planned coordination of a specialized division of labor. Qualified members of the entrepreneurial family need not be excluded as candidates. But what is important for sustaining the competitive advantage of the enterprise – and what is ensured by sufficient fragmentation of shareholding – is that owners of the organization's assets will not exercise their legal rights to withdraw financial resources in ways that undermine the continued development and utilization of the organization's productive resources, and hence the ongoing value-creation process.

Competitive strategy and national policy

Once dominant organizations have come to characterize the structure of an industry, immense barriers to entry face potential competitors. Huge investments in plant, equipment, and personnel are needed. More important, the generation of internal economies, requiring as it does the development and utilization of productive resources *within* the organization, takes considerable time, particularly in the face of formidable incumbents. The organizational capability that forms the basis for privileged access to productive resources and internal economies in the managerial enterprise is not inherent in the initial investments in plant, equipment, and personnel, however massive such investments may be.

To generate organizational capability, the managerial enterprise must invest in the *development* of the productive capabilities of its personnel and then reap the returns to these investments by maintaining long-term access to the relevant resources. The generation of internal economies through the *utilization* of the firm's resources, moreover, requires that the new enterprise be able to capture market share comparable to the existing shares of the dominant incumbents – a feat that the new entrant cannot possibly accomplish until it has developed its organizational capability.

It is therefore one thing for a few business organizations to emerge as dominant in an industry that had been characterized by entrepreneurial firms and highly competitive conditions. It is quite another matter to break into an industry in which a few managerial enterprises have already developed the organizational capability to secure oligopolistic market power.

Hence, both *historical evolution* and *the exercise of national power* play important roles in the restructuring of global oligopolies. At any point in time, the historical evolution of powerful business organizations, themselves the products of particular economic, political, and cultural contexts, may pose formidable barriers for the newcomers to meet the competition for high-quality products at low unit costs. Historically, political strategies to develop national economies have provided critical protection and support to overcome these barriers to entry. In terms of the analytical framework presented earlier, the state can become involved in capitalist development by adopting strategies that seek to generate either external economies or internal economies – that is, economies that depend on either market coordination or organizational coordination.

By supporting the development of educational institutions, financial systems, communications networks, and public-sector R&D organizations, the state can help to bring into existence productive resources that are, by definition, available to any enterprise operating within the national environment that deems it worthwhile to make use of them. By implementing policies such as tariff protection, labor legislation, and investment subsidies (including changes in tax laws favorable to investment), the state can enable business enterprises to employ their productive resources at lower unit costs or reap higher prices for their products.

In a capitalist society that has an ideological commitment to make private property subservient to democracy, state intervention in the provision of resources or the creation of economic incentives will strive not to favor one enterprise in an industry over another, even though such intervention may well favor certain groups – for example, concentrated industries over fragmented industries, or capitalists over workers. If all of the business organizations in an industry have equal access to state-generated resources and subsidies, the resultant declines in unit costs (for a given quality of output) are external economies.

It is hypothetically possible that state promotion of external economies can generate enough economies for national firms to challenge existing dominant organizations abroad. In practice, however, the more dominant the existing organizations and the greater the capital investments required to enter the global industry, the more necessary will it be for a national strategy to give privileged access to public resources to those national business organizations that can best develop and utilize these resources. In effect, by enabling particular organizations to gain privileged access to productive resources, the state becomes committed to the success of those organizations as against other national enterprises that might compete for access to resources and market share.

Assume that a national strategy to overcome the competitive advantages of foreign business organizations in an already dominant national economy is successful, as evidenced by penetration into foreign markets and leadership in profiting from new products and new markets. How might the once-dominant foreign organizations react to the international challenge?

Whatever the past success of their enterprises, the strategic managers, both domestic and foreign, must continually assess whether further investments in productive resources will yield internal economies. In making investment decisions at any point in time, the strategic manager must consider both internal and external influences on future profitability. He or she must assess whether, in the light of its past growth and available resources, the enterprise is reaching the limits of its organizational capability. Will the more extensive division of labor required to plan and coordinate organizational expansion result in the breakdown of organizational integration, and hence a loss of organizational control? The strategic manager must also assess whether the development and utilization of productive resources by existing or potential competitors will undercut expected returns over the relevant time frame for a projected investment. Whatever its past success, in other words, the future growth of the enterprise depends on how the expected evolution of its own organizational capability compares with that of its national and international competitors.

When faced with the international challenge, the substantial productive resources that the dominant organization has at its disposal enables it to choose from two broad, and very distinct, competitive strategies – one innovative and the other adaptive. The innovative strategy is to plan, invest in, and create more powerful organizational and technological capabilities, perhaps coordinating the organization's strategy with privileged access to resources provided by the state. Alternatively, the adaptive strategy is to try to compete on the basis of productive capabilities inherited from the past.[24] Strategic managers of enterprises that have already accumulated considerable capital may see it in their interests to pursue an adaptive strategy if they sense that their own organizational capabilities cannot be developed to match those of rising international competitors.

In the face of competitors who are actively developing *and* utilizing their productive resources, the economic viability of the adaptive strategy may be prolonged by degrading product quality and by demanding longer and harder work as well as pay concessions from employees. Depending on the extent of its prior competitive advantage, the productive capabilities of its competitors, the bargaining power and mobility of its employees, the quality requirements and brand loyalty of its customers, and the serviceability of its plant and equipment, the old leader may be able to make adequate profits for a period of time. In the long run, however, the once-dominant organization will eventually reach the limits of the adaptive strategy as it loses productive employees and customers, as well as its productive capital base.

The adaptive strategy entails living off accumulated capital. It is not, therefore, open to enterprises that have not yet developed productive resources. As a general rule, the more dominant the position the incumbent organization has attained – that is, the greater its prior competitive advantage – the greater the profitability, and hence attractiveness, of the adaptive strategy in the face of new competition.

With the emphasis on making the best of existing profitable opportunities as opposed to creating new ones by the development of productive capabilities, managers who are adept at financial manipulation may replace managers adept at planned coordination of the specialized division of labor. With the loss of competitive advantage, however, the replacement of "financiers" by "producers" at top management levels may not be sufficient to enable the firm to turn from an adaptive strategy to an innovative strategy. To regain competitive advantage, the business organization requires more far-reaching privileged access to productive resources, which will be forthcoming *only* if those who participate in the enterprise expect that competitive advantage can conceivably be reattained over an acceptable time horizon.

Myriad interests might be required, and if so must be willing, to renew their grants of privileged access to resources – financial, physical, and human – if further enterprise development is to occur. Strategic managers must stand ready to confront uncertainty by pursuing an innovative investment strategy rather than attempt to avoid uncertainty by pursuing

---

[24] See Chapters 3 and 6.

an adaptive strategy that lives off the organization's past success. For the sake of the innovative strategy, shareholders might be required to reduce pressures on management for the immediate distribution of profits. Creditors might be called on to restructure the organization's liabilities and accept lower returns in the short run in order to subsidize an attempt at corporate renewal. Employees might have to work longer and harder for less pay for the sake of possible regeneration of the enterprise. The involvement of the state in the future of the enterprise might be needed in order to keep people employed and organizational capability intact during developmental periods.

Even then, in renewing their grants of privileged access to resources to the organization, shareholders, creditors, employees, and the state may only enable the firm's management to prolong the viability of an adaptive strategy. The implementation of an innovative strategy requires that those who control the allocation of productive resources within the enterprise view the development of the enterprise's productive resources for the sake of uncertain returns in the future as the rational course to pursue. For the profit-seeking enterprise as for the private individual, the adaptive strategy – that is, living off accumulated productive resources – might make very good economic sense. Certainly, an individual cannot be expected to go on developing productive resources indefinitely. If an individual does, some of those resources that are inseparable from his or her mind and body will ultimately go unutilized. It may be quite rational for individuals to accumulate human, physical, and financial capital during the earlier stages of their lives and to live off it for the rest.

The basic rationale for the corporate form of enterprise, however, is that the time horizon of the business organization is not limited by the time horizons of any particular individuals. Ostensibly, the industrial corporation stands ready to instigate and undertake the development and utilization of productive resources in perpetuity. But in practice, even the activities of the corporate organization are dependent on the interests of the people who give it access (privileged or not) to their resources. What is rational for the strategic managers of an enterprise, or for any other participants in the enterprise who exercise control over the allocation of the organization's resources, may not promote the development and utilization of the productive resources of the economy as a whole. A capitalist society relies heavily on private-sector organizations to develop productive capabilities. If all these organizations were to choose simultaneously just to live off their accumulated capital, then investment in productive resources would grind to a halt. With it too would cease the opportunities for individuals who are in the accumulating stage of their lives to develop their productive capabilities and to partake of the future benefits that economic development could bring.

In contrast, it may be for the "highest common good" that enterprises in *certain* industries be encouraged to pursue adaptive strategies – particularly labor-intensive industries that employ a large number of workers who could not be easily retrained and reabsorbed into other productive employment. It may be in the common interest, broadly construed, to utilize these resources rather than throw them back on the market with little chance of reemployment. State policies, such as the destruction of tariff walls, that subject declining industries to market forces without any plan for the generation of new jobs and careers may entail a greater drain on the economy's resources than alternative policies that seek to prolong the economic viability of the utilization strategy.

But if the benefits of further economic development are wanted, a national economy *as a whole* cannot rely on adaptive strategies, however much capital it has accumulated in the past. The promotion of innovative strategies is especially important in industries that compete on international markets, that provide capital goods and materials to other industries in the national economy, that rely on resources that have to be imported, and that present opportunities for technological change.

The key structural issues for a national development strategy concern (1) which enterprises and industries should be encouraged to pursue adaptive strategies and which should be encouraged to pursue innovative strategies; (2) whether encouragement should take the form of the provision of external economies, available to all enterprises in an industry, or the promotion of internal economies in a smaller number of dominant organizations; and (3) whether the fixed costs and organizational capability required to create value in certain industrial areas might not extend beyond the bounds of existing managerial enterprises, thus making it necessary to create new units of strategic decision making that can eventually develop the organizational capability required to attain and sustain competitive advantage in the global economy.

The once-dominant economies of Britain and the United States face, however, a prior problem in planning a national development strategy and building appropriate organizational structures to carry it out – that is, the intellectual dominance in both academic and political discourse of the myth of the market economy. As will be argued in Chapters 4 and 5, the problem is *not* a lack of intellectual traditions relevant to Britain and the United States with which to confront the myth of the market economy and develop a conceptual framework for exploring the historical dynamics of advanced capitalist development. The problem is rather the persistent intellectual dominance of an outmoded market mentality that systematically fails to make use of our knowledge of the history and theory of capitalist development.

3

Business organization and competitive advantage

The value-creating enterprise

A capitalist economy relies on private-sector enterprises to make investments in the technological capabilities that are essential to economic growth. Through its investment activities, an enterprise commits financial resources to specific processes to make particular products with the expectation of reaping financial returns. Once committed, the productive assets of the enterprise represent *fixed costs* that must then be recouped by the production and sale of its output.

The basic challenge that faces the capitalist enterprise is to transform the fixed costs inherent in its investments into revenue-generating products. To do so, the enterprise must *create value:* It must produce goods that buyers desire at prices they can afford. Value-creating enterprises are those that can produce *high-quality* (desirable) *products at low unit* (affordable) *costs*.

In a dynamic world economy, competitive standards for high-quality products and low unit costs are constantly changing. For consumer products, the definition of "high quality" depends on the needs and wants of buyers, which in turn depend on a wide array of cultural factors as well as the general evolution of living standards. Both the moral and material bases of consumer preference are to some extent shaped by the activities of the business enterprises that, taken as a whole, service these preferences. For capital goods – products that serve as inputs into the value-creating process – the preferences of buyers are shaped by the organizational and technological requirements of their enterprises. For both capital inputs and consumer products, the definition of "high quality" depends on the level of affluence that the relevant buyers have achieved.

In this book I am concerned with the role of business enterprise in creating the new standards of value – *higher*-quality products at *lower* unit costs – that are the essence of economic growth. Reference has and will be made to the role of the nation-state in creating an environment and building institutions (such as the educational and financial systems) that support the productive activities of business enterprise. But my perspective on capitalist development takes as central to the achievement of higher standards of material welfare the capabilities of business enterprises to generate higher-quality products at lower unit costs. Without a relevant conception of how business enterprises create value, one cannot understand the wealth of any particular nation, let alone why some nations are wealthier than others.

Business investment does not in and of itself create value. Business enterprises invest in productive resources with the expectation of creating value, but many fail to do so. Enterprises that incur the fixed costs of investments in organization-specific productive resources and do not then transform these resources into high-quality products at low unit costs according to prevailing competitive standards waste existing value rather than create new value. For a national economy to experience sustained economic growth, its business enterprises must be more adept at creating than wasting value.

The conventional theory of the business enterprise

How might a business enterprise generate higher-quality products at lower unit costs? Conventional microeconomics textbooks do not ask this question, primarily because (as I shall argue in later chapters) Anglo-American mainstream economists have defined the nature of the business enterprise in a way that in effect eliminates its role as an engine of economic development. The textbook "theory of the firm" simply takes as given the technological and organizational capabilities of the business enterprise. Yet it is *changes* in these capabilities that are the essence of the development process.

Many mainstream economists recognize the limitations of the standard theory of the firm for analyzing the relation between business organization and economic outcomes. They recognize that the basic assumptions of the standard theory – easily substitutable factor combinations, independence of factor price and factor productivity, perfect information – are generally contradicted by reality. Yet the standard theory is still the stock-in-trade of the economics textbooks and is the only theory of the business enterprise that millions of economics students ever learn.

The conventional theory also continues to pervade the thinking of most professional economists – even many of those who recognize that it fails to capture key aspects of real-world institutions and outcomes. There is a general unwillingness to accept the proposition that the ability of the business enterprise to shape the economic environment in which it operates might result in *beneficial* economic outcomes. Rather, conventional theory assumes that the ability of the business organization to shape its economic environment is a market imperfection that reduces economic welfare. To recognize that the business organization's power to influence market processes and outcomes might be a basic condition (as I argue is increasingly the case) for superior economic performance would be to confront the prevailing ideology that, in a well-functioning economy, business organizations are subordinate to market forces rather than vice versa. Only by ignoring the increasingly important role of business organization in generating economic growth can it be maintained that a modern capitalist economy is essentially a market economy.

To grasp the intellectual limitations of the standard theory of the firm, let us consider what happens when we drop its fundamental assumptions and place its basic concepts in developmental perspective. In the standard theory, a "U-shaped" cost curve is invariably postulated. Inherent in the technology that the enterprise takes as given are certain fixed costs of technology ("plant and equipment") and organization ("management") required to produce a particular product. As the enterprise sells more of its products, it spreads out total fixed costs over more units of output, causing average unit costs to fall. But as the enterprise transforms more inputs into more outputs, it experiences difficulties in maintaining the productivity of the ever-growing number of variable factor inputs (typically associated with material inputs and labor) that it must employ. As a result, average variable costs, and with them marginal costs, rise. When the increase in average variable costs of producing more output outweighs the decrease in average fixed costs, average total costs (fixed plus variable) begin to rise, and the cost curve assumes its U shape. In the terminology first developed by the British economist Alfred Marshall, internal economies of scale are outweighed by internal diseconomies of scale.[1]

The productivity difficulties that the enterprise faces in increasing its scale of output are attributed to the limitations inherent in applying more and more variable inputs to fixed inputs. These limitations (on which I shall later elaborate in my theory of the innovative enterprise) are posited as either technological or organizational. In the *technological* version, internal diseconomies of scale result from the need to resort to the use of lower-quality variable factors of production as the enterprise expands its output. In the *organizational* version, internal diseconomies of scale result from management's increasing difficulty in coordinating the productive activities of ever-larger quantities of variable factors (particularly, but not necessarily, labor). Some combination of technological and organizational constraints causes average productivity to fall and average costs to increase.

As any economics undergraduate knows (or soon finds out), the manager of the enterprise will continue producing more output to the point

[1] Alfred Marshall, *Principles of Economics*, 9th (variorum) ed. (London: Macmillan Press, 1961), vol. 1 (text), bk. 4, chs. 9–13.

where marginal cost, as determined by the shape of the enterprise's average cost curve, equals marginal revenue, as determined by the demand (or average revenue) curve that the enterprise faces. As every introductory economics student learns, and relearns, it is at the point where marginal cost equals marginal revenue that the enterprise's level of output, average cost, and profitability will be determined.

The internal logic of the marginalist argument is impeccable. Unfortunately, for the purpose of understanding the role of the business enterprise in the process of economic development, the argument is trivial precisely because it assumes that the enterprise takes as given technology, organization, and factor prices – that the enterprise's own productive activities play no role in shaping its own cost curves. For anyone trying to understand the process of economic development, the standard textbook theory asks the wrong questions about the nature of the business enterprise.

What are the right questions, and what are the implications of the answers for the "theory of the firm" as well as economic performance? To indicate how my perspective with its focus on the process of economic development differs from the conventional approach with its focus on optimization subject to given organizational, technological, and market constraints, let us consider the forces that determine the position and shape of the enterprise's cost structure.

The high-fixed-cost strategy

What determines an enterprise's fixed costs? Its business strategy. On the basis of its business strategy, an enterprise chooses the industry – the supply of a particular type of good or service – in which to produce and compete. Some industries are by the nature of their product and process technologies more capital intensive than others. But even within a particular industry, business strategy may involve investments that entail either low fixed costs (LFC) or high fixed costs (HFC), as depicted in Figure 2. Assume that the LFC and HFC enterprises are competing in the same *industry* because, even though their products may be qualitatively different, both types of business strategy can fulfill the same needs or wants for buyers. Output q in Figure 2 is measured in units of use-value so that the costs of both HFC and LFC enterprises are expressed in terms of the same unit. Thus avoided are the analytical complications that would arise if the outcomes of the two strategies were compared in terms of both quality and cost.

Why would a business enterprise choose an HFC strategy when an LFC strategy is an option? It is these HFC investments in technology and organization, and their interaction within the enterprise, that permit the

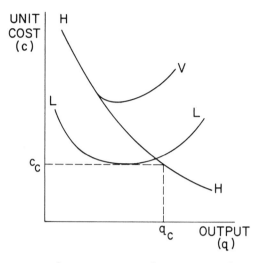

Figure 2. Fixed-cost strategies and competitive advantage.

business organization to *develop* productive resources that can yield higher-quality products and more efficient processes. Cost curve *HH* in Figure 2 represents the *outcome* that evolved out of an HFC strategy while cost curve *LL* was already in place. During the evolutionary process, the HFC strategy places the enterprise at a cost disadvantage at low levels of output but carries the *potential* of yielding a competitive advantage at high levels of output if the firm can indeed transform high fixed costs into low unit costs.[2]

If both *LL* and *HH* in Figure 2 were *known* average cost structures, it would be rational to choose the HFC strategy that generates *HH* as long as the enterprise could supply a market demand equal to q_c. Except for the case when industry demand is simply not large enough to enable an HFC enterprise to supply this output, *HH* will displace *LL* as the best-practice cost structure.

Assume, however, that at the outset, when the investments that entail fixed costs are made, only *LL* is a known cost curve. Unlike the inputs received by the HFC strategy, the inputs that enter into the LFC strategy can be purchased "ready made" on factor markets. (Perhaps in a previous time period, *LL* was the result of what was then an HFC strategy that rendered obsolete a cost structure based on even lower fixed costs). *HH* is unknown because the higher-quality products at lower unit costs

---

[2] To capture the evolutionary process in the formation of a cost structure, unit cost could be portrayed as a function of *cumulative* output. In effect, Figures 2–5 translate such cumulative cost functions into short-run cost functions. The reader must keep in mind that these short-run cost functions have long-run histories.

have yet to be developed. The rationale for an HFC investment strategy is the possibility that, through the development and utilization of productive resources, *HH* will come into existence. The enterprises that make the HFC investments and bring *HH* into existence will gain competitive advantage.

But because the productive potential of the HFC strategy is only a possibility while that of the LFC strategy is already a reality, the HFC strategy will put the enterprise that adopts it at a competitive disadvantage if it does not develop and utilize its productive resources sufficiently to lower unit costs below c_c in Figure 2. By definition, the process of bringing *HH* into existence involves *innovation* (however major or minor) because it creates quality–cost outcomes that previously did not exist. I shall, therefore, call business enterprises that make these developmental investments *innovative* and those that eschew developmental investments *adaptive*.

To make the HFC strategy work, therefore, the enterprise must augment the industry's best-practice quality and/or cost standards. A theory of economic development is a theory of the creation of higher-quality products at lower unit costs. To comprehend the process of economic development, we require a theory of the innovative business organization.

An innovative investment strategy does not in and of itself transform the industry's best-practice cost structure. An innovative HFC strategy places the enterprise at a competitive disadvantage unless it can achieve lower costs per unit of output than its LFC competitors. To do so the HFC enterprise has to develop and utilize its productive resources in ways that drive down unit costs, as depicted by curve *HH* in Figure 2. At output greater than q_c, the HFC enterprise has a cost advantage. But how does the HFC enterprise cut its unit costs sufficiently (i.e., to the point c_c in Figure 2) to transform competitive disadvantage into competitive advantage?

In the conventional theory of the firm, the question is not asked, because it is assumed that all cost structures relevant to competition are known at any point in time and that any firm will produce up to a profit-maximizing level of output. Hence, the *comparison* of the LFC and HFC strategies becomes irrelevant. If *HH* exists and enterprises that adopt *HH* can sell at q_c, no enterprise will choose the LFC strategy with its cost curve *LL*. But in the world of competitive strategy and innovation, *how* a new cost structure comes into being and *whether* old cost structures no longer secure competitive advantage are the critical issues for economic analysis.

Of course, if, relative to existing cost structures, an innovative strategy were to be an LFC strategy, fixed costs would not pose a problem for the enterprise that is engaging in innovation. Even at low output, the innovative enterprise would have a competitive advantage. But given factor prices, innovation invariably involves an HFC strategy precisely because the innovative enterprise must *develop* the productive resources that can generate higher-quality products and cost-reducing processes. Innovation generally entails higher fixed costs than existing methods of production because of not only the size but also the duration of the developmental investments that the innovative strategy requires. The size of the developmental investment is larger than with *LL* because the HFC enterprise must plan and coordinate the development of a more complex specialized division of labor – interrelated activities not only in research and development, but also in marketing and vertically related production processes. The duration of the developmental investment makes fixed costs larger than with *LL* because it takes more *time* for the innovative enterprise to transform its investments into products of sufficiently high quality and processes that can yield sufficiently lower unit costs. The innovative enterprise must develop its productive resources before they can be utilized, whereas the adaptive enterprise relies on productive resources that have already been developed, either internally or externally to the business organization itself.

For an investment of any given size, the longer the duration between the commitment of resources and the emergence of productive capabilities that can generate returns, the higher the fixed costs that must ultimately be recouped. In terms of Figure 2 a shortening of the time from the commitment of resources to the generation of returns reduces fixed costs and, all other things equal, shifts the *HH* cost curve downward and to the left, thus making competitive advantage attainable with a smaller market share.

The development process also generally requires that the enterprise enter into production and use of its product *as a basis* for generating high-quality products at low unit costs. Learning by doing and using often enhance the quality of new processes and products. Additional fixed costs of the developmental strategy are incurred when the innovative enterprise decides to sell its new products at a loss in order to expand its market share. But insofar as this competitive strategy actually speeds up learning, these calculated losses are offset by shortening the duration of the developmental process, and hence reducing fixed costs.

Both the standard theory of the firm and conventional accounting practice view fixed costs as investments in physical facilities. For an innovative business enterprise, however, investments (with their attendant fixed costs) in particular people with the requisite technical capabilities are even more fundamental. Whatever the prior education of the personnel that it recruits, the innovative enterprise must train these people to comprehend the characteristics of, and potential for, the organization's specific products and must also pay them salaries to perform their developmental work. The enterprise must also employ managerial personnel to plan and coordinate the efforts of these technical specialists. Modern accounting generally treats these investments in human capabilities as current operating costs. But because the returns, if any, on these developmental expenditures can be realized only in the future, these expenditures in human capabilities represent fixed costs to the enterprise that makes the developmental investments.

The main reason accountants treat the costs of investments in human capabilities as current expenses is that, unlike plant and equipment, the company does not own the human beings it employs. Hence, much more than in the case of physical assets, the business organization has no assurance that it will be able to *utilize* the human capabilities that it has developed. But this very fact – the ability of any employee to exit from the organization, taking with him or her the enhanced productive capabilities in which the innovative enterprise has of necessity invested – only increases the need for the enterprise to plan and coordinate not only the *development* but also the *utilization* of the investments in human capabilities. It is only by utilizing the productive resources, both human and physical, that it has developed that the innovative enterprise can transform high fixed costs into low unit costs – to achieve what economists call "economies of scale."

Fundamental to the achievement of economies of scale, as depicted by *HH* in Figure 2, is the innovative enterprise's capability as an organization to manage its human and physical assets. If the innovative enterprise does not manage its investments in human resources, its ultimate cost curve is more likely to be *HV* in Figure 2, not *HH*. With the cost curve *HV*, the enterprise cannot gain competitive advantage. Whatever the developmental intent of its HFC strategy, it is a high-cost enterprise, not an innovative enterprise.

As with the development of productive resources, the utilization of productive resources to achieve economies of scale has a critical time dimension. By definition, the enterprise incurs its fixed costs in a given time period regardless of how many of the productive services inherent in the underlying human and physical assets are used during that time period. To achieve economies of scale, therefore, the enterprise must produce and sell a high volume of output per unit of time – it must achieve a high level of *throughput*. Because time is of the essence, we can follow the business historian Alfred D. Chandler, Jr., in attributing economies of scale to the "economies of speed" that result from the administrative coordination of the flow of work from purchased inputs into sold outputs.[3]

---

[3] Alfred D. Chandler, Jr., *The Visible Hand: The Managerial Revolution in American Business* (Cambridge, Mass.: Harvard University Press, 1977). See also Alexander J. Field,

The ability of a business organization to utilize its productive resources (be they human or physical) at any point in time is dependent on the degree to which it has previously developed those productive resources. The ability of the organization to achieve high throughput during any period of time is dependent on developmental investments in a *combination* of organization and technology – specifically a combination of managerial organization that can plan and coordinate the rapid flow of work from purchased inputs to sold outputs and technological changes that can overcome existing physical constraints on the speed of productive transformation.[4]

High throughput is particularly potent in driving down unit costs if it can be achieved without degrading the quality of the product. (With output measured as units of use-value as in Figure 2, quality degradation would entail a rise in costs per unit of use-value.) The need for the enterprise to develop productive resources so that high levels of utilization can be achieved without quality degradation is an important source of high fixed costs. "Scaling up" often requires the quantitatively most significant developmental expenditures to put in place high-quality plant and equipment that can *mass-produce* a high-quality product. The high-volume production and distribution of a high-quality product requires further investments in – and makes the business organization all the more reliant on – internal management to coordinate a specialized division of labor that may include not only scientists, engineers, and salespeople, but also first-line supervisors and production workers on the shop floor. The investments in mass-production technology and organization required for the high-volume transformation of inputs into high-quality outputs increase the enterprise's fixed costs, and hence the degree of utilization of productive resources required for the enterprise to achieve low unit costs.

Note that the transformation of high fixed costs into low unit costs as depicted by *HH* in Figure 2 says nothing about the prices that the innovative enterprise charges its buyers. Figure 2 depicts a theory of costs, not a theory of returns. What will be the pricing strategy of the innovative enterprise? As both the advocates and critics of big business have recognized, the more dominant the enterprise in its market, the more power it has to charge higher prices. But to use that power and actually charge high prices can undermine the success of an HFC strategy. By passing on some of the benefits of lower unit costs to consumers, the innovative enterprise can increase its market share and lower unit costs still further. As in standard theory, the innovative enterprise has a short-run interest in

"Modern Business Enterprise as a Capital-Saving Innovation," *Journal of Economic History*, 47 (June 1987), 473–85; William Lazonick, *Competitive Advantage on the Shop Floor* (Cambridge, Mass.: Harvard University Press, 1990).
[4] See Lazonick, *Competitive Advantage*.

lowering its product price as long as marginal revenue is greater than marginal cost.

But an innovative enterprise's pricing strategy might also reflect long-run considerations. To charge high product prices might invite the entry of innovative rivals who might develop the organizational and technological capabilities to take away market share from the innovative enterprise. Low product prices, however, can rid the industry of existing competitors whose low fixed costs can block the innovative enterprise from gaining the extent of the market required to develop and utilize its productive resources so that HH comes into existence – as will be the case when learning by doing enables the innovative enterprise to develop the productive resources that permit it to achieve lower unit costs than had previously been attainable.[5] The innovative enterprise might be willing to price below average cost when it has developed only that portion of the cost curve to the left of q_c in Figure 2 in order to develop the productive capabilities that permit it to *create* some or all of the portion of the cost curve to the right of q_c. In the theory of the innovative enterprise, product price is itself a strategic variable that can contribute to the transformation of high fixed costs into low unit costs. In the standard theory of the firm, by contrast, product price is independent of product costs.

Transforming diseconomies into economies

But what happens if, as depicted by the cost curve HV in Figure 2, the enterprise that pursues the HFC investment strategy fails to transform its high fixed costs into low unit costs? The HFC enterprise has failed to develop and utilize its productive assets sufficiently to transform the competitive *disadvantage* inherent in the HFC strategy into a competitive advantage. HV arises because, at a relatively low level of output, internal diseconomies of scale outweigh internal economies of scale. The enterprise's cost curve takes on the U shape that the economics profession has made so familiar to its students.

For the would-be innovative enterprise, its cost curve HV appears to be worse than useless in industrial competition. Even if the company has been willing to sustain "short-run" losses in order to expand its market share, it has only succeeded in transforming high fixed costs into *high* unit costs. One might conclude, therefore, that the HFC strategy was misconceived; that the enterprise would have been better off adopting the tried-and-true methods for transforming inputs into outputs inherent in LL.

---

[5] See A. Michael Spence, "The Learning Curve and Competition," *Bell Journal of Economics*, 12 (Spring 1981), 49–70.

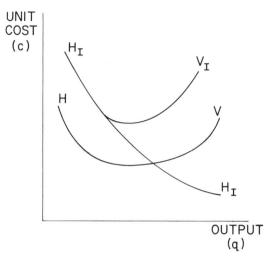

Figure 3. Transforming internal diseconomies into internal economies.

Such a critique of the attempt at innovation would be justified if *HV* represented the *final* cost outcome of the enterprise's HFC strategy. In practice, however, the very experience of internal diseconomies of scale focuses the attention of HFC managers on problems in implementing the innovative strategy. Precisely because innovation is involved, these problems could not be foreseen at the outset. That is, the experience of increasing costs inherent in *HV* may well be an essential stage in the process of discovering problems and solutions – the learning process – that characterizes the successful implementation of an innovative investment strategy. As depicted in Figure 3, the HFC enterprise that has experienced *HV* can, by incurring even more fixed costs, take strategic action to "unbend" the U-shaped cost curve and transform internal diseconomies of scale into internal economies of scale. If the enterprise is successful, H_IH_I results; if not, H_IV_I results. But even H_IV_I might be a prelude to further developmental expenditures. The business organization's innovative strategy is not fixed at the outset, but rather evolves.

What does the business organization have to do to unbend the cost curve and drive down unit costs as output expands? The answer to this question requires knowledge of why internal diseconomies of scale have arisen. As in the conventional theory of the firm, internal diseconomies of scale occur because the enterprise cannot sustain the material productivity of its resources as it employs more *variable* inputs – that is, inputs that the enterprise purchases "ready-made" on the market to complement its fixed investments in inputs, both technological and organizational.

In the "technological" version of internal diseconomies, the enterprise finds itself constrained by the deteriorating quality of materials and labor that the factor markets stand ready to supply as the demand for these materials and labor increases. Difficulties in securing the larger quantities of high-quality material and labor inputs cause production delays, down-time, and rejects that thwart the quest for economies of speed. True, the enterprise need not ordinarily pay as much for the lower-quality inputs as it has paid for the higher-quality inputs. But particularly in high-throughput production processes in which the productivity of fixed inputs is highly dependent on the productivity of variable inputs, the factor price savings from using inferior inputs are more than offset by the consequent productivity losses. Hence, unit costs rise.

How can the enterprise rectify the problem of scarcity of high-quality inputs? The most straightforward way is by stockpiling inputs of the requisite quality as they become available on the market, so that in effect variable costs are transformed into fixed inventory costs. A more innovative way is for the enterprise to undertake to generate a sufficient supply of high-quality inputs itself – an investment strategy that is generally called vertical integration. It makes economic sense, moreover, for the enterprise to incur the fixed costs of vertical integration when it has achieved high throughput. The vertically integrated enterprise still uses the same technology as it did when it embarked on the HFC strategy inherent in *HV*. But the enterprise no longer relies on *the market* to supply it with the "variable" inputs that were previously the source of increasing unit costs.

To overcome internal diseconomies of scale, therefore, the enterprise must incur more fixed costs to develop "in house" the productive capabilities of the "variable" inputs for use in its own production processes. *Technologically*, these factors of production are still variable because they are divisible; more or less of the inputs can be employed in the production process, depending on desired output. *Economically*, however, these inputs that the enterprise has undertaken to develop and utilize no longer give rise to variable costs; rather, they represent fixed costs.

Alternatively, and most innovatively, the enterprise can invest in the development of a new technology that reduces its demand for the scarce variable inputs that resulted in internal diseconomies of scale as in *HV*. The new technology can permit the use of variable inputs that are in more plentiful supply. As with the less innovative responses to internal diseconomies that involved either the stockpiling or the in-house production of high-quality variable inputs, the enterprise incurs additional fixed costs in order to develop and utilize its productive resources and drive down unit costs. Cost curve H_1H_1 in Figure 3 represents the result of a successful augmented (or evolving) HFC strategy that makes the enterprise more dependent on internal organization to develop and utilize its productive resources and less dependent on market supply. By superseding market forces, the enterprise has in effect taken control over – we might say "managed" – its technological and economic environment.

Whether or not the augmented HFC strategy results in a cost curve such as $H_I H_I$, however, depends on whether the enterprise's investment strategy in fact creates the superior organizational and technological resources that can resolve the problem of increasing costs and obtain internal economies of scale. As depicted by cost curve $H_I V_I$, it may well be that, despite the augmented HFC strategy, the enterprise does not develop or utilize its productive resources sufficiently to drive down unit costs. Indeed, the enterprise's attempt to replace the factor market with internal organization has left it at even a greater competitive disadvantage than had been the case before. It may well be that further investments that augment its HFC strategy can unbend the cost curve. But precisely because these are innovative strategies, abstract theory cannot provide either a priori expectations or conclusions concerning ultimate success or failure. One has to know more about the socioeconomic context and the actors involved.

In the "organizational" version of internal diseconomies, the enterprise finds that its existing managerial capabilities result in a *loss of control* over the utilization of labor and material inputs as output per unit of time – that is, throughput – expands. Internal diseconomies occur, not because the market cannot supply sufficient quantities of high-quality inputs (as in the technological version), but rather because of the limitations of existing management – limitations that some organizational theorists have called "bounded rationality."[6] To solve the problem, the enterprise must make further investments in internal organization. These investments may be in better managerial organization, a strategy that increases fixed costs for the sake of directly controlling variable costs. But for the purpose of inducing workers to identify with organizational goals, these investments may also take the form of long-term employment commitments to workers whose labor services had previously been treated as variable costs.[7] In this case, the result is an augmented HFC strategy that transforms variable costs into additional fixed costs with a view to unbending the U-shaped cost curve. In the process, it becomes all the more imperative to transform high fixed costs into low unit costs to gain competitive advantage.

Internal economies and diseconomies of scale are not, however, the

[6] See Oliver Williamson, *The Economic Institutions of Capitalism* (New York: Free Press, 1985); see also Chapter 6, this volume.
[7] Lazonick, *Competitive Advantage*, ch. 7.

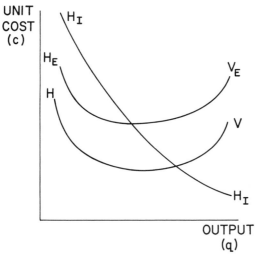

Figure 4. Transforming external diseconomies into internal economies.

only way that an enterprise can experience changes in its unit costs. As I shall elaborate in Chapter 5, Alfred Marshall drew the distinction between internal and external economies of scale.[8] Internal economies and diseconomies have to do with changes in factor *productivity* (as measured by output per unit of factor input) that result from the internal organization of the enterprise and that determine the *shape* of the cost curve. External economies and diseconomies have to do with changes in market-determined factor *prices* that *shift* the whole cost curve either down or up.

External diseconomies of scale result from the appearance of a general shortage of one or more variable inputs because of a growth of market demand for these inputs that outruns the growth of supply. The appearance of external diseconomies does not alter the productivity performance of the enterprise in the transformation of material inputs into material outputs (as measured by total factor productivity). Unlike the case of internal diseconomies, the enterprise that experiences external diseconomies can still acquire all the inputs of a requisite quality that it demands, but to do so it has to pay a higher price than previously. As a result, the cost curve shifts up, as depicted by $H_E V_E$ in Figure 4.

Figure 4 also depicts how an enterprise might respond to the appearance of external diseconomies. It can make investments that integrate the provision of the input into its internal organization with a view to expanding its own privileged supply of the input at a lower unit cost than that

[8] Marshall, *Principles of Economics*, bk. 4, ch. 9.

inherent in H_EV_E. Alternatively, and again more innovatively, the appearance of external diseconomies might induce the enterprise to invest in new technologies that reduce its reliance on the factor that, by becoming more expensive, has resulted in the shift of the cost curve to H_EV_E. The higher fixed costs of the investments in (as the case may be) either vertical integration of the existing technology or the development of a new technology are inherent in the cost curve H_IH_I in Figure 4. In either case, in order to overcome external diseconomies, the enterprise must make investments in the internal development of productive resources that are superior to productive resources available from vertically related enterprises that supply the market.

The innovative enterprise must then utilize the superior processes sufficiently to transform its high fixed costs of innovation into lower unit costs. The larger the cost of the variable input as a proportion of the enterprise's total costs, the longer the expected duration of the input's high price, and the smaller the costs of superseding the market in the supply of the input, the greater the incentive of the enterprise to incur fixed costs in order to overcome external diseconomies.

Although the sources of internal and external diseconomies are clearly distinguishable – the one arising from a decline in material productivity and the other from a rise in market price – the two sources of increasing costs can go hand in hand, particularly when the factor of production that is the source of the diseconomies is labor. Labor that is able to command a higher price than previously because of the appearance of tighter labor markets is, by definition, labor that is more highly mobile via the market. And labor that is highly mobile via the market is labor whose supply of effort is difficult for managers to control in the production process.[9] Hence, the advent of tight labor markets generally results in more rapidly rising average costs (internal diseconomies) as well as upward shifts in the average cost curve (external diseconomies).

The combined impact of internal and external diseconomies may induce the enterprise to embark on an augmented HFC strategy. Alternatively, however, as the recent experiences of many Western capitalist economies show, the inflationary impacts of tight labor markets may result in state intervention to generate unemployment for the purpose of tempering wage increases and restoring labor discipline on the shop floor.[10] Insofar as these interventions are successful in restoring previous cost conditions, the business enterprise can continue to rely on the market to supply it with labor inputs and avoid the alternative of investing in tech-

---

[9] Lazonick, *Competitive Advantage.*
[10] The classic statement is M. Kalecki, "Political Aspects of Full Employment," *Selected Essays on the Dynamics of the Capitalist Economy* (Cambridge University Press, 1971), 138–45.

nological change. Indeed, if in Figure 4 H_EV_E is the cost curve before
government policy creates unemployment and HV is the result of the
slackened labor markets, in effect state intervention generates external
economies. Most mainstream economists would contend that such market-
oriented public policies help to restore the international competitiveness
of domestic enterprises. Yet from a developmental perspective on the
nature of the enterprise and its potential role as an engine of economic
growth, by making it possible for enterprises to cut costs on the basis of
existing technologies, such state intervention to restore "market flexibility" undermines the inducement for business organizations to invest in
technological change.[11]

External economies and organizational rigidity

As the potential impact of state intervention on enterprise costs and investment activity indicates, not all cost reduction results from the impact
of the internal organization of the enterprise on the utilization of its productive resources. As Alfred Marshall argued almost a century ago, business enterprises can also reap "external economies" because the growth
of an *industry* spreads out the fixed costs already invested in the economy
as a whole over a larger volume of output.[12] By definition, external economies derive from the availability of cheaper inputs that can be purchased
on the market, not from the superior utilization of resources within the
producing enterprise.

As in the movement from LL to L_EL_E in Figure 5, external economies
result in a downward shift of the cost curve. An enterprise experiences
external economies when the price of an input that it purchases on the
market falls. The price decline occurs when the growth of the market for
an input spreads out the fixed costs of existing investments in producing
that input, and a portion of the economies of scale – the reductions in
unit fixed costs of production – are passed along to buyers in the form of
lower price. In effect, the extent of the decline in input price that accom-
panies the decline in input costs determines the extent to which the economies of scale in the production of the input are appropriated by the
producer as internal economies or by the user as external economies.
However these cost reductions are shared, what is important is that the
spreading out of fixed costs over a larger output creates a positive-sum
situation that permits both producers as sellers and users as buyers to
gain. In the presence of economies of scale, higher profits to producers
and lower prices to users are mutually consistent outcomes.

[11] See Lazonick, *Competitive Advantage*, ch. 10, for an elaboration.
[12] Marshall, *Principles of Economics*, bk. 4, ch. 9.

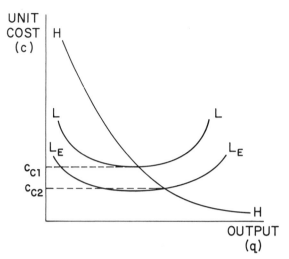

Figure 5. Adaptive strategy and competitive disadvantage.

The fixed costs that are distributed over a larger output need not be the fixed costs of private enterprise. In capitalist economies, important sources of external economies to business firms are public-sector investments in education, communication, and judicial systems. In this case, the prices that business enterprises pay for public-sector inputs into their production processes are the results of public-sector rather than private-sector pricing strategies, but the conceptual origins of external economies remain the same. The source of external economies at one vertical level is the investment in productive resources on the part of organizations, both business and government, that are suppliers of inputs.

Some of the cost reductions appear as external economies rather than internal economies because the relations between the producers and users of the inputs are mediated by the market rather than by internal organization. There are no economies, external or internal, however, unless there are investments in productive resources that are developed and utilized. Markets can facilitate the utilization of investments, thus permitting the realization of both internal economies for the producer and external economies for the user. But it is organizations (again both private sector and public sector), not markets, that develop and utilize productive resources.

External economies can enable an LFC enterprise to cut costs and remain competitive against an HFC enterprise that is *in the process* of transforming its high fixed costs into low unit costs. Assume, as in Figure 5, that the initial cost curve of the LFC enterprise is *LL*, and that *HH* is the cost curve that the HFC enterprise will *ultimately* develop. The LFC enterprise remains competitive as long as the HFC enterprise has not driven unit costs below c_{c1}. External economies that shift the LFC cost curve from LL to $L_E L_E$ enable the LFC firm to remain competitive in the cost range between c_{c1} and c_{c2} as well. Indeed, if the HFC enterprise starts to experience increasing costs within this range, as indicated by HV in Figure 2, external economies may result in sustained competitive advantage for the LFC enterprise.

If in the reality of industrial competition these results were to be general – if HFC strategies and internal organization exhibited limited power to drive down unit costs – then a market-coordinated economy made up of LFC enterprises could well remain relevant as the institutional characterization of a successful capitalist economy. The history of successful capitalist development and shifts in international competitive advantage that I have summarized in Chapter 1 argue otherwise. HFC enterprises have driven out the LFC enterprises because cost cutting on the basis of internal economies has been much more powerful than cost cutting on the basis of external economies. Organizations (and not necessarily just individual enterprises, but perhaps organized collectivities of enterprises) have increasingly replaced markets in the relations between producers and users, and internal economies have increasingly replaced external economies in the cutting of costs.[13] The basic reason for the supersession of markets in capitalist development is the growing organizational and technological complexity of the specialized divisions of labor required for the development and utilization of new products and processes.

Thus far, the analysis has centered on the strategies and structures of business organizations on the grounds that these institutions are central to the development and utilization of productive resources under capitalism. Yet, as I have argued in Chapter 2, these strategies and structures take on a national character because the relevant business organizations do not develop and utilize resources in a political and cultural vacuum. Shifts in international industrial leadership have occurred on the basis of more or less coherent national development strategies that have, through public infrastructural investments, tariff protection, financial subsidies to key industries and enterprises, and assorted other industrial policies, permitted HFC enterprises to transform themselves from high-cost to low-cost producers.

The theoretical framework that I have presented in this chapter provides a basis for understanding the shifts in international industrial leadership that I have outlined historically in Chapter 1. Assume that in Figure 5 HH represented the cost structures of U.S. enterprises and $L_E L_E$

---

[13] See Michael Best, *The New Competition: Institutions of Industrial Restructuring* (Cambridge, Mass.: Harvard University Press, 1990).

represented the cost structures of British enterprises in a particular industry (say, machinery manufacture) at a particular time (say, 1900). With *HH* in place, the U.S. enterprises had gained competitive advantage. At an earlier date (say, 1880), however, only some portion of *HH* above c_{c1} existed, and U.S. enterprises had been at a competitive disadvantage compared with their British rivals, whose cost curves *LL* were based on the use of what had by then become traditional technologies.

In line with the classic infant industry argument, tariff protection provided U.S. enterprises with the privileged access to product markets that enabled them to exclude British competition, while by developing and utilizing their productive resources during the intervening time period, they put the lower portion of the *HH* cost curves in place. Even as they did so, British enterprises benefited from learning effects in supplier industries – benefits that accrued to them in the form of lower input prices, causing the shift from *LL* to $L_E L_E$ over the two decades. Nevertheless, by the turn of the century, U.S. enterprises had gained competitive advantage over the British; U.S. enterprises had put the lower portion of *HH* in place.

How did British enterprises respond to the shift of competitive advantage to their American rivals? They might have pursued their own HFC strategies. Such strategies would have required the British to protect their markets while they transformed the high fixed costs of these innovative strategies into low unit costs. As the historical analysis in Chapter 1 revealed, however, the British economy lacked the educational, financial, and managerial institutions required to support such strategies. In addition, the very ability of the LFC British enterprises to remain competitive for a time by cutting costs (from *LL* to $L_E L_E$) on the basis of their traditional modes of organization and technology reduced their incentives to challenge U.S. dominance by transforming their own organizational and technological structures into more powerful engines of economic growth.

Rather, under pressure from innovative U.S. competition, they pursued the *adaptive strategy* of seeking to recapture competitive advantage by cutting costs even further on the basis of traditional organization and technology. Even after the British enterprises had exhausted the developmental cost reductions on the basis of the traditional technologies, they could often reduce costs further by failing to replace worn-out plant and equipment, wringing wage concessions from immobile workers fearful of losing their jobs, and taking a lower rate of return on their invested capital – all of which would appear as reductions in factor prices, and hence as shifts in the cost curve downward from $L_E L_E$.

At some point (say, 1930) the ability to cut costs on the basis of existing productive capabilities ran out. Tariff protection and government subsidies were sought but would not help. For a half-century, while U.S. enterprises built organizational structures to implement their HFC strategies, British enterprises had been able to avail themselves of external economies and continue to adapt on the basis of traditional organization and technology. As a result, as they moved into the middle decades of the twentieth century (and the precise timing varied from industry to industry), British enterprises and British society were ill-prepared to build the organizations and develop the technologies required to make the transition from proprietary to managerial capitalism.

The shift of international industrial leadership from the United States to Japan over the past few decades represents a transition from the highly organized managerial capitalism to an even more highly organized collective capitalism. Yet I believe that the same basic analysis that I have laid out from the British–U.S. comparison applies in this case as well. As Japanese business organizations have gained competitive advantage on the basis of innovative HFC strategies and the generation of internal economies, U.S. industrial corporations have tended to rely on adaptive LFC strategies to remain competitive – strategies that seek to cut costs on the basis of existing organizational and technological structures. In the process, U.S. business organizations have increasingly ignored innovative HFC strategies that, on the basis of planned coordination, might put in place wholly new trajectories of decreasing costs.

PART II

Intellectual foundations and intellectual constraints

4

The theory and history of capitalist development

Economics and history

Writing in the mid-twentieth century, toward the end of a long academic career, Joseph Schumpeter advised that "if, starting my work in economics afresh, I were told that I could study only one of [the fundamental fields of economic analysis: economic history, statistics, or theory] but could have my choice, it would be economic history that I should choose."

And this, on three grounds:

First, the subject matter of economics is essentially a unique process in historic time. Nobody can hope to understand the economic phenomena of any, including the present, epoch who has not an adequate command of historical *facts* and an adequate amount of historical *sense* or of what may be described as *historical experience*.

Second, the historical report cannot be purely economic but must inevitably reflect also "institutional" facts that are not purely economic: therefore it affords the best method for understanding how economic and non-economic facts *are* related to one another and how the various social sciences *should* be related to one another.

Third, it is, I believe, the fact that most of the fundamental errors currently committed in economic analysis are due to the lack of historical experience more often than to any other shortcoming of the economist's equipment.[1]

Schumpeter had started his career some four decades earlier by writing *The Theory of Economic Development,* an abstract theoretical investigation that sought to deduce a theory to comprehend the vast expansion of productive capabilities that had occurred in national economies such as those of Britain, Germany, and the United States. By the end of his career, Schumpeter had learned the lesson that a relevant theory of how economies develop must comprehend the history of institutional change.

Over the four decades that have passed since Schumpeter emphasized the critical role of economic history in the study of economics, U.S. economists have done anything but adopt "historical experience" as a tool – let alone a fundamental tool – of economic analysis. In the post-World

---

[1] Joseph A. Schumpeter, *History of Economic Analysis* (New York: Oxford University Press, 1954), 12–13, emphasis in original.

War II decades, the mainstream of the U.S. economics profession stressed, and indeed became obsessed with, constrained optimization as the fundamental analytical tool. At the same time, with their theoretical vision constrained by the marginal significance of their analytical equipment, these economists idealized the market-coordinated economy as the optimal (if not always attainable) form of economic organization.

In the 1950s and 1960s a field of inquiry called *economic development* was deemed relevant for studying the poorer nations of the world. But in sanctioning this endeavor (which by the 1970s had in any case been banished to the periphery of economics), the implicit assumption of the economics profession was that the economic successes of the already developed "market economies" were well understood. For purposes of "modern" economic analysis at least, there was no need to construct a theory of economic development. With the search for the nature and causes of the wealth of nations swept under the deductive, mathematical, and statistical rug, mainstream economists lost the ability to think historically. Indeed, the current generation of mainstream economists, schooled as they are in the "techniques" of economic analysis, may even have acquired a trained incapacity to understand the process of change.

In their neglect of history, mainstream economists not only lost touch with evolving economic reality, but also ignored (and then forgot) the theoretical insights into the development process of some of their most illustrious predecessors, including Schumpeter himself. And if they could not savor the insights of the conservative Schumpeter, it is not surprising that they could not stomach the works of Karl Marx. Schumpeter recognized Marx as the pioneer in the integration of theory and history in economic analysis. But during the postwar decades, mainstream economists cautioned against taking Marx seriously. "A billion people, one-third of the world's population," Paul Samuelson warned millions of college students reading their very first page of economics text, "blindly regard *Das Kapital* as economic gospel."[2]

Some students of economics managed to ignore Samuelson's message, and the radical economics movement that emerged in the late 1960s and early 1970s created an opportunity for academic economists to study and debate the dynamics of advanced capitalist development, as Marx and Schumpeter had done. At the same time, from outside the economics profession, or at best on its periphery, historians of industrial evolution were uncovering and making accessible the reality of the development process in the advanced capitalist economies; they were providing the foundations of "historical experience" that Schumpeter had deemed so important.

Indeed, back in the 1950s, even as the mainstream of the economics

[2] Paul A. Samuelson, *Economics*, 7th ed. (New York: McGraw-Hill, 1967), 1.

profession was ignoring Schumpeter's call for historically based economic analysis, his ideas were exerting a profound influence on a generation of historians who viewed the entrepreneurial decision as central to the development process. Two who stand out are David S. Landes and Alfred D. Chandler, Jr. Landes's *The Unbound Prometheus*, published in 1969, and Chandler's *The Visible Hand* (1977) and *Scale and Scope* (1990) are landmarks of historical synthesis on the development process in advanced capitalist economies.

Both Landes and Chandler are alumni of the Research Center in Entrepreneurial History, located at Harvard University for a decade beginning in 1948. Schumpeter was a senior member of the center from 1948 until his death in early 1950, but it was not his creation; that honor belonged to Arthur H. Cole. Although inspired by Schumpeter's emphasis on the economic role of the entrepreneur, much of the center's work focused on the sociology and psychology of the entrepreneur – his or her social background, personality, and social status – rather than on the impact of entrepreneurial activity on economic outcomes.[3] Nevertheless, the center left an intellectual legacy that should have helped today's economists avoid (to use Schumpeter's words) "most of the fundamental errors currently committed in economic analysis." The research center closed down in 1958, but over the longer run the academic institution at which Schumpeter had spent the last sixteen years of his career was to be, as it turned out, the main beneficiary of what might be called the Schumpeterian historical legacy. By the beginning of the 1970s, both of its most important bearers of "historical experience" – Landes and Chandler – had returned to Harvard.

As distinguished Harvard professors, Landes and Chandler, with their historical perspectives on the dynamics of advanced capitalist development, might have, to paraphrase Schumpeter, overcome the most serious shortcoming of the modern economist's analytical equipment. Among economists, there was at Harvard and elsewhere in the early 1970s a receptive audience: a significant group of radical economists bent on recapturing and renovating the historical tradition of Marx, in part by taking note of the work of Schumpeter, in order to comprehend the dynamics of capitalist development. If ever there was an academic setting in the United States at which the confluence of theoretical traditions and historical analysis could have at least made the "theory of economic development" a *matter of debate* among economists of different points of view, it was at Harvard in the 1970s.[4]

[3] Hugh G. J. Aitken, ed., *Explorations in Enterprise* (Cambridge, Mass.: Harvard University Press, 1965); Steven A. Sass, *Entrepreneurial Historians and History: Leadership and Rationality in American Economic Historiography, 1940–1960* (New York: Garland, 1986).

[4] For this story of intellectual failure, see William Lazonick, "What Happened to the Theory of Economic Development?" in Patrice Higgonet and Henry Rosovsky, eds., *Tech-*

For reasons that will become apparent in the rest of this book, not at Harvard or at any other leading American university was the mainstream of the economics profession during the 1970s and 1980s willing to enter into debate over the theory of economic development. Indeed, for lack of "historical experience" – training and practice in historical analysis – mainstream economists became increasingly unable to deal with such issues. Intellectual progress in understanding the historical dynamics of advanced capitalist development did not, however, stand still, mainly because historians carried out research of relevance to the analysis of economic development while some economists opted out of (or, as in my own case, never entered) the mainstream. Indeed, the comparative historical analysis in Chapter 1 could not have been written without the growing body of knowledge, both theoretical and historical, that has been generated over the past twenty years or so by those who take as their intellectual focus institutional and economic change. In the concluding chapter, I shall consider the contribution of these positive intellectual currents and the impacts they might potentially have on economists' understanding of the economic problem and economic process. In this chapter, however, my purpose is to evaluate critically some key intellectual foundations – the theoretical work of Marx and Schumpeter and the historical work of Chandler and Landes – on which a historically relevant theory of advanced capitalist development can be built.

The utilization of effort-saving technology

More than one hundred years ago, Karl Marx argued that to understand capitalist development requires an analysis of the evolution of the production process. Starting from a general theory of social change that emphasizes the dynamic interaction of the relations and forces of production, Marx's theory of capitalist development analyzes the impact of technological change on labor productivity within the capitalist enterprise.

By analyzing the interaction of social organization and productive capabilities in the historical context of the British Industrial Revolution, Marx sought to extend and deepen the theories of economic growth that had been propounded by the classical economists, particularly Adam Smith and David Ricardo. Even as Marx wrote, the classical perspective on economics contrasted sharply with the growing tendency among economists, ultimately to be called neoclassical, to ignore the role of production in economic growth. Rather, they depicted the capitalist economy as simply a general equilibrium of exchange relations.

nological Constraints and Entrepreneurial Responses: Essays in Modern and Contemporary Economic History (Cambridge, Mass.: Harvard University Press, forthcoming).

To accentuate the contrast in analytical focus, Marx's examination of the capitalist economy *begins* by depicting an economic system consisting of market exchanges in general equilibrium. All commodities, including labor power (human productive capability), exchange at their values.[5] The measure of value is a unit of labor time of given levels of skill and effort, and the value of commodities is the amount of socially necessary labor time embodied in them.

But, Marx asked, if all commodities exchange at their values, what is the source of the surplus value out of which are paid interest, rent, and profits to financiers, landlords, and industrial capitalists? He located the answer in the special position of labor power as a commodity when it enters the capitalist production process. The capitalist gets access to the productive capabilities (labor power) of workers for a wage that will command the amount of labor time socially necessary to reproduce the worker. But labor power is not the same as labor effort. One represents the productive capability of the worker, while the other connotes the actual utilization of that capability in the production process.

Given the wage, the greater the utilization of labor power, the lower the unit labor costs. In addition, given the capitalist's investments in plant, equipment, and material that are dependent on complementary labor inputs to transform them into products, the greater the utilization of labor power, the lower the unit capital costs. Given prevailing factor prices, surplus value depends, therefore, on the ability of the capitalist to extract labor effort from the worker. In essence, these internal economies (to use Alfred Marshall's term) that give rise to surplus value are what Alfred Chandler has called "economies of speed" – scale economies that result from speeding up the flow of work.[6] The faster the transformation of purchased inputs into sold outputs per unit of time – what Chandler has called "throughput" – the greater the utilization of capacity and the lower the firm's unit fixed costs.

The capitalist can try to influence two quantitative dimensions of labor effort: the duration and intensity of work. The first involves lengthening the hours of work, while the second involves increasing the speed of work. Marx assumed that if workers were not dependent on capitalists to earn a living, they would not willingly submit to longer and harder work for the same pay. He therefore viewed labor immobility as the source of the exploitation that results in economies of speed. Marx argued quite correctly that, although British capitalists met considerable resistance from skilled, adult male workers in the early stages of the Industrial Revolu-

---

[5] Karl Marx, *Capital* (New York: Vintage, 1977), vol. 1, pts. 1 and 2.
[6] Alfred D. Chandler, Jr., *The Visible Hand: The Managerial Revolution in American Business* (Cambridge, Mass.: Harvard University Press, 1977), ch. 8.

tion, they were nevertheless able to exploit the labor of women and children by lengthening the hours of labor. Workdays in excess of twelve hours and workweeks in excess of seventy, however, provoked reactions from various quarters to regulate the working hours of children and women in the factories. Ultimately, state legislation limited this form of exploitation. But if capitalists could no longer increase the duration of labor, the introduction of machinery provided them with an even more potent means of extracting labor effort and appropriating surplus value.

Because of its effort-saving and skill-displacing nature, mechanization increased the potential productivity of given amounts of labor effort and skill. According to Marx, however, it also gave capitalists the social power over workers to extract and appropriate those productivity gains for themselves. The *effort-saving* nature of the new technologies meant that mechanization could have lightened the load of labor even while raising labor productivity. But the *skill-displacing* nature of the same technologies meant that the once-intransigent skilled workers became dispensable. Mechanization not only permitted the use of more docile and cheaper unskilled labor, but also, by augmenting the reserve army of unemployed workers competing for the unskilled jobs, made those who did have jobs all the more dependent on their employers.[7] Marx concluded that, in the modern factories of the British Industrial Revolution, mechanization had given capitalists the power to intensify a unit of labor power to the physical limits of its productive capability.

Marx left a valuable conceptual framework for analyzing the conflicts between capitalists and workers over the generation and appropriation of productivity within the enterprise. But the historical record reveals that he overemphasized the impact of machinery in enabling capitalists to control their workers. Even in the presence of effort-saving and skill-displacing technological change, key groups of workers maintained considerable control over the organization of work on the shop floor. On the basis of this control, these workers built unions that gave them substantial power over the determination of the relation between effort and pay in operating a given technology, and hence over the determination of unit labor and capital costs.[8]

Marx's error was to attribute too much influence to technology and too little to organization in determining economic outcomes. On the one hand, the technology of the time was not as skill displacing as he thought. On the other hand, the organizational capability of capitalists to extract effort from even unskilled workers was not as potent as he assumed. In histori-

---

[7] Marx, *Capital*, pts. 3 and 4.
[8] William Lazonick, *Competitive Advantage on the Shop Floor* (Cambridge, Mass.: Harvard University Press, 1990), chs. 1–6.

cal retrospect, even within the factories that were central to the British Industrial Revolution, the relative underdevelopment of both technology and managerial organization left key groups of skilled workers – who collectively became known as the labor aristocracy[9] – with control over the recruitment, training, and supervision of unskilled workers, the repair and speed of machinery, and the division of labor on the shop floor.

Historical research has also revealed that Marx overemphasized the independent role of technology in determining the competitive structure of industry.[10] In the Marxian analysis, the first firms to introduce a labor-saving technology can effect greater internal economies and gain competitive advantage. But the technology diffuses relatively quickly throughout an industry, the diffusion resulting in a new competitive equilibrium based on the new cost structure that has become common to all firms. Implicit in Marx's view is the notion that all firms have the same organizational capability to exploit labor power because that capability is embodied in the labor-saving qualities of the machine. Hence, he assumed the diffusion of not only the new technology but also the social organization of production that makes use of it.

Marx argued, nevertheless, that the development of industrial capitalism results in the concentration and centralization of production into a relatively small number of enterprises.[11] The prediction is right for some industries in some national economies, but the explanation is inadequate. Like modern economists of industrial organization who attribute high concentration ratios to "economies of scale" inherent in supposedly indivisible technology, Marx simply argued that "the productivity of labour . . . depends in turn upon the scale of production," and "therefore the larger capitals beat the smaller."[12]

Thus, despite his own emphasis on social relations of production, Marx ended up portraying the ongoing process of capitalist development as a technological imperative. Believing that the introduction of machinery during the Industrial Revolution had completed the domination of employers over employed, Marx ceased to analyze the evolution of the social relations of production within the capitalist enterprise. Just as he missed out on how the need for the internal coordination of production determined the utilization of technology on the shop floor within the British factory, so Marx understood neither the role that enterprise-specific organizational capability would play in the emergence of oligopolistic indus-

[9] E. J. Hobsbawm, *Workers: Worlds of Labor* (New York: Pantheon, 1984), chs. 11–14.

[10] William Lazonick, "Industrial Organization and Technological Change: The Decline of the British Cotton Industry," *Business History Review*, 57 (Summer 1983), 195–236; Bernard Elbaum and William Lazonick, eds., *The Decline of the British Economy* (Oxford: Clarendon Press, 1986).

[11] Marx, *Capital*, chs. 25 and 32.   [12] Ibid., 777.

try in the United States and Germany nor how, in the absence of such capability, highly fragmented industrial structures would persist within the British economy itself.

As we shall see in our discussion of Chandler's contribution to the theory of economic development, it was organizational capability that enabled firms to develop and utilize the new technologies of what many have called the Second Industrial Revolution. The resulting internal economies enabled the "organizational" enterprise to capture a large market share, and hence grow. The economies of scale, which most economists (Marx included) view as the result of indivisible technology, were in fact the result of the organizational capability of the enterprise in planning and coordinating technologically separable production processes.

Institutional transformation and capitalist innovation

In his first work, *The Theory of Economic Development*, Joseph Schumpeter argued that "changes of technique and productive organization require special analysis." He went on to say that "non-recognition of this is the most important single reason for what appears unsatisfactory to us in [neoclassical] economic theory." Deeply influenced by Marx's historical approach, if not by his theory of surplus value, Schumpeter added that his own view of the problem of economic development "is more nearly parallel to that of Marx" than to that of contemporary neoclassical economists (he cited in particular the American, J. B. Clark). "For according to [Marx] there is an internal development and no mere adaptation of economic life to changing data." Schumpeter concluded by stating somewhat cryptically that his own "structure covers only a small part of Marx's ground."[13]

Schumpeter published *The Theory of Economic Development* in German in 1911 and reiterated his approach to economic analysis in the opening chapters of his two-volume work *Business Cycles*, published twenty-eight years later. In both works, Schumpeter's method reflects the influence of Marx; for just as Marx constructed his labor theory of value in order to depict an exchange economy in which development is absent, so too did Schumpeter set up a general equilibrium model of the economy at rest as a prelude to propounding a dynamic theory of economic change.

In *The Theory of Economic Development*, Schumpeter entitled the static model "Circular Flow of Economic Life as Conditioned by Given Circumstances." Schumpeter's notion of the nature of the firm in the "circular flow" is, however, very different from that underpinning Marx's labor

---

[13] Joseph A. Schumpeter, *The Theory of Economic Development* (New York: Oxford University Press, 1961), 60n.

theory of value. The difference is central to understanding their contrasting analyses of the role of the capitalist enterprise in generating productivity growth. In Marx's labor theory of value, the special nature of the labor market, and the resultant ability of the capitalist to extract surplus value from the worker, are already assumed and taken as given. But in his circular flow, Schumpeter adopted the perspective characteristic of the various brands of neoclassical economics being formulated in the late nineteenth century and that remains dominant today, in which no special role is accorded to labor as the human input into the production process. To be sure, labor provides a qualitatively different productive input than any given physical input, but then any two physical inputs can be distinguished from one another in precisely the same way.

In effect, Schumpeter's circular flow – or "Equilibrium and the Theoretical Norm of Economic Quantities" to use the description of the static model in *Business Cycles* – is the Walrasian theory of the market economy that forms the microeconomic foundations of modern neoclassical economics. Whereas in Marx's general equilibrium system, businesspeople are already vested with a degree of social power over workers that enables them to extract a certain amount of surplus value, in the neoclassical system that constitutes Schumpeter's circular flow the exercise of social power in the internal operation of the enterprise is absent. Rather, in the circular flow, the role of the businessperson is to adapt the quantities of inputs purchased and outputs produced in response to changes in market prices over which the firm is too small to have any influence. The level of productivity in such a stationary system is determined by the state of technology in conjunction with whatever amount of labor effort the preferences of the owners of labor services lead them to supply.[14] In the neoclassical world of competitive equilibrium, all markets, including that for labor, clear so that there is no involuntary unemployment, and hence none of the dependence of workers on capitalists that could result in Marxian exploitation.

For modern neoclassical economists, the elaboration of the theory of the circular flow has become an end in itself. Indeed, they tend to view what goes on within this framework as the extent of relevant economic activity. In Schumpeter's work, however, the main purpose of the circular flow is to show what *cannot* be explained by the Walrasian system; for his critical contribution is to identify what he called the "Fundamental Phenomenon of Economic Development" – a phenomenon that is fundamental precisely because it disrupts the "Circular Flow of Economic Life" to bring about economic change.

The "Fundamental Phenomenon" is entrepreneurial activity that re-

[14] Lazonick, *Competitive Advantage*, app.

sults in innovation, a concept that includes the introduction of a new process or product, entry into a new market, access to new supplies of inputs, and creation of a new organization, by which Schumpeter essentially meant building up or breaking down a barrier to entry.[15] In *Business Cycles*, Schumpeter specifically included under the heading of innovation such things as "Taylorization of work, improved handling of materials, [and] the setting up of new business organizations such as department stores."[16]

Schumpeter's entrepreneur is a businessperson who is not caught up in the circular flow of economic life, but rather is able to create new profitable opportunities for the firm by the "setting up of a new production function [which] covers the case of a new commodity, as well as those of a new form of organization such as a merger, of the opening up of new markets, and so on."[17] Innovation, according to Schumpeter, "dominates the picture of capitalistic life" by causing the "intrusion into the system of new production functions which incessantly shift existing cost curves."[18]

The resultant internal economies form the basis for entrepreneurial profits, a return that Schumpeter viewed as resulting from entrepreneurial leadership in "carrying out New Combinations" of means of production.[19] The determination of entrepreneurial profits, therefore, occurs outside the complex of interacting market forces that constitute the circular flow.[20] With entrepreneurial innovation seen as the essence of capitalist development, economic analysis takes leave of the neoclassical theory of the market economy.

Schumpeter's theory of economic development, however, contains at best an incipient conception of the innovation process. Entrepreneurs "conceive and work out with varying promptness plans for innovations associated with varying (and ideally correct) anticipations of profits, and set about struggling with the obstacles incident to doing a new and unfamiliar thing."[21] The success of the entrepreneurial strategy appears to depend solely on the energy and ability of the entrepreneur. Certainly in his early work, *The Theory of Economic Development*, Schumpeter adopted the perspective of another great economist, Alfred Marshall, who in his *Principles of Economics* had already recited the aphorism "from shirtsleeves to shirtsleeves in three generations."[22] Those who inherit a successful business are not likely to have the energy and creative genius of the original entrepreneur, and therefore, as Marshall argued, "a business

[15] Schumpeter, *The Theory of Economic Development*, 66.
[16] Joseph Schumpeter, *Business Cycles* (New York: McGraw-Hill, 1939), 84.
[17] Ibid., 87.   [18] Ibid., 91.
[19] Schumpeter, *The Theory of Economic Development*, 143; idem, *Business Cycles*, 88.
[20] Schumpeter, *The Theory of Economic Development*, 153–4.
[21] Schumpeter, *Business Cycles*, 130.
[22] Alfred Marshall, *Principles of Economics*, 9th (variorum) ed. (London: Macmillan Press, 1961), vol. 1 (text), 621.

firm grows and attains great strength, and afterward perhaps stagnates and decays."[23] Quite literally clothing Marshall's notion of the rise and decline of firms in different garb, Schumpeter said, "An American adage expresses it: three generations from overalls to overalls."[24]

It was on the basis of this view of the rise and decline of firms that Marshall introduced into economic analysis the concept of the "Representative Firm" – a concept that then permitted him and his followers to focus on the cost-minimizing adaptations of the firm in response to changing market forces rather than on the innovative activities of the firm that could indeed shape market forces. In *Business Cycles*, Schumpeter referred to Marshall's "concept of the Representative Firm [as] one more of those devices used to hide the fundamental problem of economic change."[25] Writing in 1928 in the *Economic Journal* as part of a debate over increasing and decreasing returns in the Marshallian firm, Schumpeter recognized that a transition from nineteenth-century competitive capitalism to twentieth-century *"trustified," "organised," "regulated,"* or *"managed"* capitalism had taken place.[26]

In "trustified" capitalism, he argued that "innovation is . . . not any more embodied *typically* in new firms, but goes on, within the big units now existing, largely independently of individual persons."[27] In the 1930s, however, Schumpeter was still grappling with the issue of the growth of the firm, much as Marshall did during the first two decades of this century in writing his book on comparative industrial organization, *Industry and Trade.*[28] In contrast to his predepression view of "trustified" capitalism as an engine of innovation, Schumpeter made what he deemed to be the realistic assumption that all innovations are "embodied in New Firms founded for the purpose," arguing that "everybody who looks around knows the type of [old] firm we are thinking of – living on the name, connections, quasi-rent, and reserves acquired in their youth, decorously dropping into the background, lingering in the fatally deepening dusk of respectable decay."[29] He went on to speak of "that process of incessant rise and decay of firms and industries which is the central – though much neglected – fact about the capitalist machine."[30]

In *Capitalism, Socialism, and Democracy*, first published in 1942, however, Schumpeter restored to the large corporation the leading role in what he now called the process of creative destruction – citing, somewhat

[23] Ibid., 323.   [24] Schumpeter, *The Theory of Economic Development*, 156.

[25] Schumpeter, *Business Cycles*, 92n.

[26] Joseph A. Schumpeter, "The Instability of Capitalism," *Economic Journal* 48 (September 1928), 361–86, cited at 362.

[27] Ibid., 384.   [28] Alfred Marshall, *Industry and Trade* (London: Macmillan Press, 1919).

[29] Schumpeter, *Business Cycles*, 94, 95.

[30] Ibid., 96; see Carolyn Shaw Solo, "Innovation in the Capitalist Process: A Critique of the Schumpeterian Theory," *Quarterly Journal of Economics*, 65 (August 1951), 417–28.

ironically, U.S. Steel as a prime example.[31] He now admitted that "technological 'progress' tends, through systemization and rationalization of research and of management, to become more effective and sure-footed" and becomes "the business of teams of trained specialists who turn out what is required and make it work in predictable ways."[32] In a 1949 paper entitled "Economic Theory and Entrepreneurial History" that was presented to the participants of the Research Center in Entrepreneurial History, Schumpeter explicitly recognized the evolution of entrepreneurship into a cooperative activity that even the state might successfully carry out:

[As] has been often pointed out, the entrepreneurial function need not be embodied in a physical person and in particular a single physical person. Every social environment has its own ways of filling the entrepreneurial function. For instance, the practice of farmers in [the United States] has been revolutionized again and again by the introduction of methods worked out in the Department of Agriculture and by the Department of Agriculture's success in teaching these methods. It is another most important point in our research program to find out how important this kind of activity has been in the past or is in the present. Again the entrepreneurial function may be and often is filled co-operatively. With the development of the largest-scale corporations this has evidently become of major importance: aptitudes that no single individual combines can thus be built into a corporate personality; on the other hand, the constituent physical personalities must inevitably to some extent, and very often to a serious extent, interfere with each other. In many cases, therefore, it is difficult or even impossible to name an individual who acts as an "entrepreneur" in a concern.[33]

In his life's work, therefore, Schumpeter not only recognized the need for a *theory* of economic development, but also came to understand that such a theory would have to deal with the impacts of transitions from individual to collective entrepreneurship on the process of technological change. Beginning his work as what might be called a pure theorist, Schumpeter ended up seeing the importance of historical analysis in order to elaborate his theoretical arguments and establish their relevance. To repeat Schumpeter's argument in *Capitalism, Socialism, and Democracy:* "The essential point to grasp is that in dealing with capitalism we are dealing with an evolutionary process. It may seem strange that anyone can fail to see so obvious a fact which moreover was long ago emphasized by Karl Marx."[34]

Yet despite his overriding theoretical concern with the forces that disrupt tendencies to competitive equilibrium and his ultimate recognition

[31] Joseph Schumpeter, *Capitalism, Socialism, and Democracy,* 3d ed. (New York: Harper, 1950), 82.
[32] Ibid., 118, 132.
[33] Joseph Schumpeter, "Economic Theory and Entrepreneurial History," in Aitken, ed., *Explorations in Enterprise,* 45–64, cited at 52–3.
[34] Schumpeter, *Capitalism, Socialism, and Democracy,* 82; see also Chapter 2, note 10.

of the long-lived enterprise as a potential generator of innovation, Schumpeter had barely any conception of the nature of the relation between entrepreneurial strategy and managerial structure in the innovation process. As a result, he left no theory of how and under what circumstances the corporate organization would fulfill the entrepreneurial role of generating process and product innovations. Furthermore, he did not even begin to think about how and under what conditions the organization could generate internal economies through the utilization of those already developed productive resources at its disposal. In *Business Cycles*, he incorrectly argued that "internal economies" are due only to innovation and asserted that "no firm which is merely run on established lines, however conscientious the management of its routine business may be, remains in capitalist society a source of profit."[35]

For understanding the *development* of productive resources – that is, the innovation process – what Schumpeter lacked was the access to historical perspectives of the likes of Chandler and Landes as well as more detailed business histories that are only now becoming available.[36] For understanding the *utilization* of productive resources, Schumpeter would also have been helped immensely by such historical works as *The Unbound Prometheus* and *The Visible Hand*. But even in his own time, Schumpeter might have recognized the importance of workers' efforts on the shop floor in generating economies of speed had he not followed his neoclassical teacher, Eugen von Böhm-Bawerk, in rejecting out of hand Marx's theory of surplus value.[37]

Among neoclassical economists, Böhm-Bawerk made the most concerted attack on the labor theory of value as a theory of static price determination – an attack that completely missed the point that Marx's static exercise was a prelude to a dynamic analysis of the creation of value by means of the diffusion of technology throughout the economy and the utilization of labor power within the firm.[38] In any case, Böhm-Bawerk had his own theory that attributed the origins of the return to capital to "roundabout" methods of production – methods he viewed as the characteristic features of capitalism. Böhm-Bawerk's point of departure was the observation that economic progress under capitalism was linked to

[35] Schumpeter, *Business Cycles*, 92, 95.
[36] See David A. Hounshell, *From the American System to Mass Production, 1800–1932* (Baltimore, Md.: Johns Hopkins University Press, 1984); Leonard Reich, *The Making of Modern Industrial Research* (Cambridge University Press, 1985); David A. Hounshell and John Kenly Smith, Jr., *Science and Corporate Strategy: Du Pont R&D, 1902–1980* (Cambridge University Press, 1988).
[37] Joseph A. Schumpeter, *Ten Great Economists: From Marx to Keynes* (New York: Oxford University Press, 1965), ch. 6.
[38] Paul Sweezy, ed., *Karl Marx and the Close of His System*, by Eugen von Böhm-Bawerk, and *Böhm-Bawerk's Criticism of Marx*, by Rudolf Hilferding (New York: Kelley, 1949).

high fixed costs in capitalist production. To explain this link Böhm-Bawerk coined the notion of "roundaboutness": the longer the time period required in a production process from the purchase of inputs until the generation of revenues, the more productive the process. Hence, he explained the *origins* of a return to capital in the form of interest for those people who are willing to forgo present consumption and wait for roundabout methods to yield them returns.

In rejecting Marx, Schumpeter did not necessarily abide by Böhm-Bawerk. Rather, Schumpeter argued that, contrary to Böhm-Bawerk, what matters "is not the *running* of production of a degree of roundaboutness . . . but the act of *introducing* greater 'roundaboutness' " in the form of innovations.[39] But Schumpeter himself missed the more fundamental critique of the theory of "roundabout" production and, in doing so, failed to confront the more general problem of fixed costs in capitalist development. In and of themselves, fixed costs do not create value. Rather, value creation depends on how investments that entail fixed costs are developed and utilized once in place. Internal organization of vertically related processes – what Böhm-Bawerk mistook for roundaboutness – may create a greater technological *potential* for the generation of productivity. But as indicated in Chapter 3, the large capital commitments may place the investing enterprise at a competitive *disadvantage* if it does not have the organizational capability to reap the technological potential by speeding the flow of work in progress through the so-called roundabout processes of production and distribution. To gain competitive advantage, the firm must *shorten*, not lengthen, the time period that elapses between the purchase of inputs and the sale of outputs. What creates the lag between investments and returns is not roundaboutness but rather the time the business organization requires to develop and utilize its productive capabilities. Capital investments, among which are included the fixed costs of bureaucratic management itself, may be a necessary, but never a sufficient, condition for returns to "waiting" to occur.

As we have seen, the phenomenon of what, following Chandler, can be called economies of speed is inherent in the distinction between labor power and labor effort that is fundamental to the Marxian theory of surplus value. In following his Austrian teacher's rejection of the Marxian theory, Schumpeter failed to recognize the need for an alternative theory of the utilization of productive resources. Rather than make the attempt to reconcile the Marxian theory of economic development with his own, Schumpeter adopted the neoclassical theory of the market economy as an adequate depiction of the economy at rest. But in the neoclassical economy, the social organization of the enterprise has no impact on the utilization of its productive resources. By adopting the neoclassical concep-

---

[39] Schumpeter, "The Instability of Capitalism," 367n.

tion of equilibrium as the relevant "theoretical norm," Schumpeter had little choice but to posit the development, as distinct from the utilization, of productive resources as the only source of enterprise-specific productivity and profits. As a result, he left himself with inadequate static foundations on which to build a dynamic theory that could analyze the interaction between the development and utilization of productive resources.

Ultimately, Schumpeter's main contributions to our understanding of capitalist development are not so much theoretical as conceptual and methodological. Like his own conception of the impact of innovation, moreover, his legacy is both creative and destructive. On the creative side, Schumpeter clearly demonstrated the need to understand the nature of the innovation process in order to analyze the performance, stability, and institutional evolution of the economy. Schumpeter himself ultimately came to recognize – particularly in *Capitalism, Socialism, and Democracy* – the importance of corporate organization in the innovation process, even if he still lacked any notion of the transformation of investments in innovation into low unit costs.

On the destructive side, Schumpeter laid bare the inability of neoclassical theory to analyze the process of economic development. What was in *The Theory of Economic Development* merely a distinction between statics and dynamics became in *Capitalism, Socialism, and Democracy*, written some thirty years later, a critique of the methodology of orthodox economics. As we have seen, Schumpeter chastised mainstream economists for failing to grasp the essential point that capitalism is an evolutionary process, even though (or is it because?) "so obvious a fact . . . was long ago emphasized by Karl Marx."[40] In a critique that remains relevant today, he found fault with

economists who, *ex visu* of a point in time, look for example at the behavior of an oligopolist industry – an industry which consists of a few big firms – and observe the well-known moves and countermoves within it that seem to aim at nothing but high prices and restrictions of output are making precisely [the] hypothesis [that there is a perennial lull in innovation]. They accept the data of the momentary situation as if there were no past or future to it and think that they have understood what there is to understand if they interpret the behavior of those firms by means of the principle of maximizing profits with reference to those data. . . . In other words, the problem that is usually being visualized is how capitalism administers existing structures, whereas the relevant problem is how it creates and destroys them. As long as this is not recognized, the investigator does a meaningless job.[41]

The job is meaningless because economists tend to view the perfectly competitive economy as the epitome of economic efficiency, and hence

---

[40] Schumpeter, *Capitalism, Socialism, and Democracy*, 82.
[41] Ibid., 84.

deduce that imperfect competition – generally considered under the heading of "monopoly" – results in restrictive practices that are injurious to the consuming public. But such a perspective ignores the role of market power in creating conditions conducive to innovation. Indeed, Schumpeter argued, the very restrictive practices that economists decry may "provide the baits that lure capital on to untried trails" that result in innovation.[42] Put differently, so-called restrictive practices may promote the development of resources by assuring the innovating enterprise that it will indeed get to utilize those resources in which it has invested, and hence be in a position to appropriate the returns.

Or to quote Schumpeter directly:

What we have got to accept is that [the large-scale enterprise] has come to be the most powerful engine of [economic] progress and in particular of the long-run expansion of total output not only in spite of, but to a considerable extent through, this strategy that looks so restrictive when viewed in the individual case and from the individual point of time. In this respect, perfect competition is not only impossible but inferior, and has no title to being set up as a model of ideal efficiency.[43]

From the theory to the history of capitalist development

The role of economic theory is to provide a simplified framework with which to analyze complex economic phenomena. Even though a particular analysis, such as that of Marx or Schumpeter, may arrive at untenable conclusions, the underlying conceptual framework may yet serve as a solid foundation on which to build a more adequate theoretical structure. As in the cases of Marx and Schumpeter, when an economic theorist asks relevant questions and creates a coherent conceptual framework designed to answer those questions, it is possible to learn as much from the shortcomings of his or her work as from its strengths.

Looking at the British Industrial Revolution, Marx saw the conflict between capitalists and workers over the amount of effort expended in the production process as the key determinant of economic development. Capitalist investment in mechanization generated economic development, in Marx's view, not just because the new technologies were effort saving and skill displacing, but also because they permitted a shift in social control over the production process from workers to capitalists. Although Marx asked the relevant questions and focused on key causal relationships, he overestimated the extent to which the introduction of mechanized technology enabled British capitalists to render the shop-floor worker the "mere appendage of a machine."

[42] Ibid., 90.   [43] Ibid., 106.

With his focus on machinery as the solution to the problem of labor effort, Marx failed to analyze how the persistence of worker control in the organization of the nineteenth-century British enterprise secured the co-operation of labor in the development and utilization of human and physical resources. These errors in the application of the theoretical framework, however, do not vitiate the insights that can be drawn from it. By focusing on the development and utilization of resources within the production process, Marx's conceptual framework captured a critical dimension of economic development in a way that no other economic theorist has since done.

Schumpeter, as we have seen, had little conception of the utilization of resources as a source of productivity growth, and indeed rejected precisely that part of Marx's work that provided a framework for analyzing the operation of the production process. Undoubtedly influenced by the momentous technological and organizational changes that were occurring in the late nineteenth and early twentieth centuries, not so much in Britain as in Germany and the United States, Schumpeter focused on the development, as distinct from the utilization, of productive resources as the prime determinant of the process of economic development.

In line with prevailing individualist ideology, however, he initially saw innovation as an entrepreneurial accomplishment, and hence made no attempt to analyze the relation between the internal organization of the enterprise and technological change. Indeed, he weakened his own conception of innovation by treating changes in both technology and organization as aspects of the same general phenomenon. Over the years, however, as Schumpeter sought to elaborate his theory of economic development through empirical investigation, he increasingly recognized the collective, and indeed often cooperative, nature of the innovation process.

In the process, he came to recognize the evolutionary and dynamic character of economic development, and hence the vital need for historical research to test existing hypotheses and, more importantly, to generate new ones. As he stated in his 1949 address at the Research Center in Entrepreneurial History (after discussing the various existing definitions of "the entrepreneur"):

Whether we define the entrepreneur as an "innovator" or in any other way, there remains the task to see how the chosen definition works out in practice as applied to historical materials. In fact it might be argued that the historical investigation holds logical priority and that our definitions of entrepreneur, entrepreneurial function, enterprise, and so on can only grow out of it *a posteriori*. Personally, I believe that there is an incessant give and take between historical and theoretical analysis and that, though for the investigation of individual questions it may be necessary to sail for a time on one tack only, yet on principle the two should never lose sight of each other. In consequence we might formulate our task as an attempt to write a comprehensive history of entrepreneurship.[44]

If by the "history of entrepreneurship" Schumpeter meant the role of business enterprise in modern economic development, then the most comprehensive histories to date have been written by two alumni of the research center. Even if the direct impact of Schumpeter on Chandler or Landes was slight, *The Visible Hand* and *The Unbound Prometheus* take us a long way in imbuing economic analysis with the "historical experience" of which Schumpeter spoke.

Innovative organization and economies of speed

Of the two historians, Chandler makes a more clear-cut contribution to the theory of economic development because of his focus on the evolution of one type of economic institution, the large-scale industrial enterprise.[45] Already by the early 1960s, Chandler had drawn on his detailed research into business history to enunciate the "strategy and structure" framework that forms the core contribution of his work. The Chandlerian framework, as introduced in *Strategy and Structure* and subsequently developed in *The Visible Hand* and *Scale and Scope*, provides an analysis of the relation between entrepreneurial strategy and organizational structure in the development of productive resources.[46] By emphasizing economies of speed in the success of the industrial enterprise, moreover, Chandler offered considerable insight into the institutional arrangements that permit greater utilization of productive resources.

Chandler's theory of economic development focuses exclusively on the role of business firms that undertake investment strategies in response to new market and technological opportunities and that then put in place organizational structures to ensure economic success. Chandler did not, moreover, analyze the strategies and structures of all business enterprises, but only those in manufacturing industries in which the high fixed costs required to respond to market and technological opportunities create the potential for substantial economies of scale. The justification for the focus on the growth of "big business" in manufacturing is that the success of capital-intensive industrial enterprises in transforming high fixed

---

[44] Schumpeter, "Economic Theory and Entrepreneurial History," 55–6.
[45] See Thomas K. McCraw, "The Intellectual Odyssey of Alfred D. Chandler, Jr.," Introduction to Thomas K. McCraw, ed., *The Essential Alfred Chandler* (Boston: Harvard Business School Press, 1988), 1–21.
[46] Alfred D. Chandler, Jr., *Strategy and Structure: Chapters in the History of the American Industrial Enterprise* (Cambridge, Mass.: MIT Press, 1962); idem, *The Visible Hand;* idem, *Scale and Scope: The Dynamics of Industrial Capitalism* (Cambridge, Mass.: Harvard University Press, 1990).

costs into low unit costs has been critical to rapid economic growth in the twentieth century.[47]

What determines the ability of these capital-intensive enterprises to transform high fixed costs into low unit costs? The simplistic response of the conventional economist is "indivisible technology." With its multi-plant operations and the vertical integration of technologically separable processes, however, the modern enterprise far exceeds the size of invest-ments dictated by indivisibility. Indeed, even the size of a single plant is, within limits, a strategic variable that depends on the entrepreneur's ex-pectations of capturing market share or, in the case of "second movers," a lower-bound parameter set by the successful strategies of the "first mov-ers." These are industries, moreover, in which not only is the necessary investment in plant and equipment – "minimum efficient scale" – large, but the processes and products are technologically "complex." High-quality goods produced at low cost cannot immediately be put on the market but *must be developed after the initial investments in plant and equipment have been made.* Technological complexity therefore creates the oppor-tunity for the business organization to engage in Schumpeterian innova-tion by combining and developing resources in new ways to achieve su-perior processes and products. To take advantage of this opportunity, the enterprise must invest in a number of vertically related processes, the planned development of which is necessary for technological break-throughs. In addition, it must employ technical and managerial personnel who are able and willing to combine and coordinate their specialized tal-ents to bring the innovations to fruition.

Even if an innovation is ultimately successful, all this investment in plant, equipment, and personnel may take years to generate reasonable returns. It is the lag between investment in innovation and the realization of revenues, and not technology per se, that subjects these enterprises to the problem of fixed costs. Unless the business organization is willing to incur these fixed costs, however, it cannot hope to generate the process and product innovations that will set it apart from its existing and poten-tial competitors.

Investment in innovation therefore creates both an economic problem and an economic possibility for the enterprise. The economic problem is that, given the high fixed costs incurred, the innovating enterprise will be at a competitive disadvantage relative to its less venturesome compet-itors if it does not succeed in capturing a large market share. But the economic possibility is that success in developing superior processes and

[47] For the evidence on the importance of "Chandlerian" firms to the growth of the U.S. economy, see Richard Tedlow, "The Process of Economic Concentration in the American Economy," in Hans Pohl, ed., *The Concentration Process in the Entrepreneurial Econ-omy since the Late 19th Century* (Stuttgart: Steiner, 1988); Chandler, *Scale and Scope.*

products will provide it with a basis for increasing *its* extent of the market – for achieving high levels of utilization of its productive resources – in ways that its competitors cannot.

Superior products enable the enterprise to charge a price premium – until competitors imitate the innovation – or forgo some or all of the price premium to extend its market share. Superior processes enable the enterprise to speed up the flow of work through its production facilities without sacrificing quality, thus cutting unit production costs by spreading out its fixed costs. It is this cost-cutting phenomenon that Chandler called economies of speed. In a dynamic interaction of supply and demand, as the enterprise captures a larger market share it spreads out its fixed costs, thus lowering unit costs and making it possible to gain an even greater extent of the market.

Such a dynamic is not automatic, however, even for the innovative enterprise. To maintain product quality and coordinate the flow of work at high throughput requires further investments in, and development of, managerial organization. The function of such organization is to spread out fixed costs by achieving high throughput while controlling variable costs, so that, as in the standard textbook depiction of the Marshallian firm, increasing costs do not occur as throughput expands.

Provided that the enterprise has developed the organizational capability that can coordinate still higher throughput, the most potent way to control variable costs is to transform them into fixed costs. Rather than rely on the market for the purchase of inputs and the sale of outputs, these activities are vertically integrated into the operations of the enterprise. As throughput expands, pressures build for the enterprise to integrate backward into material supplies in order to ensure a steady and planned flow of inputs of requisite quality. Similarly, pressures build for forward integration into distribution in order to ensure the aggressive marketing of the enterprise's output required to transform mass production into mass sales.

But controlling variable costs increases the problem of fixed costs, so that the success of such vertical-integration strategies depends on the organizational capability that the enterprise has developed. By achieving economies of speed, the dynamic interaction of organizational capability and ever-increasing investments in technology transforms what would otherwise be the problem of high fixed costs into long-term competitive advantage.

In *The Visible Hand,* Chandler focused primarily on the planned coordination of the flow of work through the processes of production and distribution of the modern industrial enterprise, without, as he put it in his introductory chapter, "[trying] to describe the work done by the labor force in these units or the organization and aspirations of the workers."[48] Yet to achieve *economies* of speed, the firm must elicit labor effort of employees at various levels of the corporate hierarchy while retaining some of the productivity gains to be passed on to buyers in the form of lower prices in order to increase market share.

Chandler's framework can be elaborated to analyze the social relations that permit the business enterprise to secure the cooperation of labor in the high-throughput investment strategy.[49] To cope with technological complexity, the enterprise has to invest in the skills of key employees. But having incurred these fixed developmental costs, it must then ensure that it retains these workers if it hopes to utilize the human resources in which it has invested. Even if successful in retaining these human resources, however, the enterprise must also motivate its employees to put forth the labor effort necessary to develop high-quality processes and products and to achieve high throughput. If the business enterprise, as distinct from its employees, is to reap economies of speed from its investment strategy, it must gain control over a portion of the resultant productivity gains. The surplus value that accrues to the enterprise will depend not only on the amount of labor effort of requisite quality that employees contribute, but also on the share of productivity gains that employees require to secure their cooperation.

To train, retain, and motivate employees whose combined skills enable the enterprise to conquer technological complexity, the extraction of surplus value cannot be "Marxian exploitation" in which capitalists win and workers lose. Rather, surplus value must result from an institutionalized process of sharing the benefits of enhanced productivity. The most potent benefits the enterprise can offer its employees are not simply high wages and salaries, but long-term job security and social mobility within the organization. In effect, as in the case of key physical resources, the creation of value through the development and utilization of human resources requires that the enterprise integrate key personnel into its organization through long-term planning.

The historical experience of successful capitalist development over time and across national economies reveals, moreover, that the definition of the "key" employee has moved further and further down the corporate hierarchy to include not only administrative personnel but also production workers.[50] Increasingly, the need for the business enterprise to make long-term commitments to its employees has transformed variable costs into fixed costs, which in turn requires that the enterprise secure the

[48] Chandler, *The Visible Hand*, 6.   [49] See Lazonick, *Competitive Advantage*.
[50] See Chapter 1.

long-term commitment of its employees to organizational goals if economies of speed are to be generated.

The integration of employees into the long-term planning of the enterprise creates pressures for the further growth of the already successful enterprise if it is to make good its promises of job security and social mobility in return for labor effort. The saturation of existing product markets or competitive product innovation may limit the growth of the enterprise on the basis of existing product lines. For sustained growth, the enterprise must build on those organizational and technological capabilities acquired in capturing existing product markets to move into new product lines. To do so, it must make further investments in physical and human resources, including facilities for systematic research and development. Such investments increase the problem of fixed costs. But such investments can also generate the product innovations that create opportunities for the enterprise to achieve *economies of scope* by spreading some of its fixed costs over a number of related product lines. Within each product line, however, economies of scale remain critical for success as high fixed costs must be transformed into low unit costs by extending market share.

Chandler's historical analysis therefore fills a large gap in the theory of innovation and, in so doing, creates a link with the theory of production. Entrepreneurship, whether individual or collective, is not enough to generate economic development. Innovative entrepreneurial strategies must be followed by the building of organizational structures to plan and coordinate innovation and throughput. The success of organizational capability in generating economies of scale and scope depends on the development and utilization not only of physical resources but, even more fundamentally, of human resources. The individual efforts of those involved in the enterprise's specialized division of labor must be planned and coordinated – in effect, collectivized – to create a powerful productive organization.

Changing industrial leadership

If, as Chandler's account implies, the dynamic interaction of organization and technology determines the course of industrial development, why have some national economies been more successful than others in setting the process in motion? And what accounts for the passing of industrial leadership from one nation to another? By placing the historical analysis of technological change in cross-national comparative perspective, David Landes has made pioneering attempts to answer these questions.

Like Schumpeter, Landes began the analysis of economic development with entrepreneurial activity. In the industrialization of Western Europe, he argued, technological change was the outcome of private enterprise engaged in the "rational manipulation of the human and material environment" – a process that could be achieved by either "mastery over man and nature" or the "adaptation of means to ends" (a distinction that bears a resemblance to Schumpeter's important distinction between creative and adaptive response).[51] In comparative historical perspective, it is clear that where and when entrepreneurial activity emerged cannot be understood in abstraction from the social context that created opportunities for private investment and accumulation; for even within Western Europe, the timing, rate, and direction of technological change varied across national economies. The comparative economic history of Western Europe, therefore, challenges the analyst to identify those aspects of the social environment that support or impede entrepreneurial activity. As Landes said, "If history is the laboratory of the social sciences, the economic evolution of Europe should provide the data for some rewarding experiments."[52]

Let us therefore look at Landes's arguments concerning the interaction of entrepreneurship and social context in determining the nature and timing of technological change. For present purposes, the analysis begins with the rise of the factory system in Britain in the late eighteenth century and ends with the long-run relative decline of the British economy from the late nineteenth century. What social forces account for the technological changes that characterized the British Industrial Revolution, and why did the advent of the factory system propel the British economy into a position of industrial leadership? What problems did Germany – ultimately the most successful of the Continental economies – face in trying to emulate Britain, and how did it confront these problems? How and when, in historical retrospect, did Germany ultimately achieve success? And finally, why was Britain, the industrial leader as late as the 1870s, so unsuccessful in responding to the German challenge?

The technological basis of the British Industrial Revolution was a series of innovations that substituted machines – "rapid, regular, precise, tireless" – for human skill and effort.[53] The inventions themselves were the result of craft-based, as distinct from science-based, activities in which practical "tinkerers" found, by trial and error, workable solutions to mechanical problems. Because the new technologies were craft based, they

---

[51] David S. Landes, *The Unbound Prometheus: Technological Change and Industrial Development in Western Europe from 1750 to the Present* (Cambridge University Press, 1969), 15, 21; Joseph A. Schumpeter, "The Creative Response in Economic History," *Journal of Economic History* 7 (November 1947), 149–59.
[52] Landes, *The Unbound Prometheus*, 39.   [53] Ibid., 41.

were easily imitated and diffused, at least once the original patents ran out.[54]

But, as Landes argued, even when the relevant inventions are ready at hand, "technological change is never automatic."[55] The main reason is that, in replacing human skill and effort with machines, technological change creates only the *potential* for saving on resources and lowering unit costs. Insofar as investments in a new technology transform what were variable costs into fixed costs, the entrepreneur must then utilize the new technology in ways that permit it to outcompete the old. If not, he will become, as Landes put it, "a prisoner of his investment."[56]

The task of outcompeting labor-intensive methods is all the more difficult because of the tendency for those with vested interests in the old technologies to accede in "compressing the costs of the human factors of production."[57] A successful adaptive response requires some combination of lower profits to those capitalists who, because of financial or managerial limitations, continue to produce on the basis of the old technologies and lower wages to those workers who stand to have their skills devalued by the success of the new technology.

A prime example of adaptive response is the putting-out system of textile manufacture that both preceded the rise of the machine-driven factory system in Britain and expanded alongside it.[58] Rather than transform the organization of the labor process, capitalists simply made use of existing rural labor supplies and relied on the head of the household to plan and coordinate the division of manufacturing labor.

In contrast, the early factory system was an innovative response because, in an era in which labor that was ready and willing to work in the factory setting was as yet in short supply, factory organization overcame the constraints that domestic industry under the putting-out system placed on the generation of throughput. An impetus to the early investments in the factory system came from the problem of throughput in the putting-out system. Particularly during periods of boom, when profitable opportunities were greatest but labor was in short supply, putters-out found that they lacked control over the flow of work. With the production process carried out in their homes, workers had the power to tie up the capital, primarily raw materials, supplied by the putters-out, as well as to appropriate some of that capital as their own. Putters-out sought to use the force of law to speed up the flow of work and reduce embezzlement of materials. But especially in good times, the control of work remained with the workers.

The factory system overcame these internal contradictions of the old mode of production. Despite the higher fixed costs of the factory, it

[54] Ibid., 62–6.   [55] Ibid., 42.   [56] Ibid., 43.   [57] Ibid., 42.   [58] Ibid., 42–4.

triumphed because the capitalist gained control over the disposition of materials and the pace of work. In Landes's words:

> The machine imposed a new discipline. No longer could the spinner turn her wheel and the weaver throw his shuttle at home, free of supervision, both in their own good time. Now the work had to be done in a factory, at a pace set by tireless, inanimate equipment, as part of a large team that had to begin, pause, and stop in unison – all under the close eye of overseers, enforcing assiduity by moral, pecuniary, occasionally even physical means of compulsion. The factory was a new kind of prison; the clock a new kind of jailer.[59]

These words could be right out of Marx, all the more so because Landes recognized the resistance of British workers to the loss of independence of action inherent in factory work. Indeed, the expansion of the putting-out system in weaving alongside the factory system in spinning during the first four decades of the nineteenth century manifested the willingness of many workers to accept lower wages to work at home rather than submit to factory discipline.

The factory system ultimately won out. By achieving higher throughput and generating economies of speed, it was able to offset both its higher fixed costs and the adaptive response of the putting-out system. To some extent these economies of speed could be achieved by utilizing relatively docile and low-wage segments of the labor force, primarily children and women, even without any radical changes in technology. Over the longer run of the Industrial Revolution, however, the introduction of effort-saving and skill-displacing technology enabled firms to achieve economies of speed even while paying relatively high wages to some of their workers, mainly men, who, judging from their union organization and strike activity, were anything but docile.[60]

Like Marx, however, Landes did not take the analysis of the triumph of the factory system far enough. In particular, he paid little attention to the contribution of the "aristocracy of labor" to its success. Instead, he placed all the emphasis on the entrepreneurial motivation to invest – "what distinguished the British economy," Landes argued, "was an exceptional sensitivity and responsiveness to pecuniary opportunity"[61] – combined with the disciplinary impact of the machine. But as Landes himself recognized as he carried the story of industrialization forward in time, the mechanized technology of the Industrial Revolution had a long

---

[59] Ibid., 43; see also David S. Landes, *Revolution in Time: Clocks and the Making of the Modern World* (Cambridge, Mass.: Harvard University Press, 1983), 229, where the depersonified clock becomes a lock.

[60] Hobsbawm, *Workers*, chs. 11–14; William Lazonick, "Industrial Relations and Technical Change: The Case of the Self-Acting Mule," *Cambridge Journal of Economics*, 3 (September 1979), 231–62.

[61] Landes, *The Unbound Prometheus*, 66.

way to go before skilled labor became dispensable – hence the notion that, in contrast to the marriage of science and technology later in the nineteenth century, the technology of the Industrial Revolution was craft based. Landes picked up the story of the "aristocracy of the labour force" only in the late nineteenth century, when these craftsmen had become, in his words, "an obstacle to innovation." Nevertheless, he eloquently described the productive roles they played in an era of less complex technology:

Masters of their techniques, able to maintain their tools as well as use them, they looked upon their equipment as their own even when it belonged to the firm. On the job they were effectively autonomous. Most of them paid their own assistants, and many played the role of subcontractors within the plant, negotiating the price of each job with management, engaging the men required, and organizing their work to their own taste and convenience. The best of them "made" the firms they worked for.[62]

In comparative historical perspective, alongside entrepreneurship and mechanized technology, then, a critical factor in the success of the British Industrial Revolution was the emergence of an abundant supply of skilled operatives who performed many of the day-to-day organizational functions that in later times and other places were taken to be the prerogatives of management. These labor aristocrats were important not only for the utilization of machine technologies on the shop floor during the Industrial Revolution, but also, through on-the-job apprenticeship systems, for reproducing and expanding the human resource capabilities on the basis of which Britain became, in the third quarter of the nineteenth century, the "workshop of the world."

Continental emulators had no trouble gaining access to the machine technologies of the Industrial Revolution. What they lacked was the skilled labor and shop-floor organization of the British factory system. Unable simply to imitate, the creative response of Germany from the first half of the nineteenth century was to make the industrial investments and build the supportive institutions that would ultimately permit its economy to challenge and then surpass the world's first industrial nation.

The investments with the most long run significance for the shift in national leadership were those that developed human resources. As Landes argued, "The lack of requisite technical skills posed an obstacle to innovation that only time could overcome."[63] In the short run, British immigrants came to the Continent as capitalists or highly paid employees and "trained a generation of skilled workers, many of whom became entrepreneurs in their own right." Landes continued: "The growing technological independence of the Continent resulted largely from man-to-man trans-

---

[62] Ibid., 306.   [63] Ibid., 139.

mission of skills on the job. Of less immediate importance [in the mid-nineteenth century] was the formal training of mechanics and engineers in technical schools."[64]

As posited by Alexander Gerschenkron's model of economic backwardness, the state, motivated by "a passionate desire to organize and hasten the process of catching up," played the major role in planning and financing these investments in human resources, the return to which was too long term and uncertain for private firms or individuals to undertake.[65] From the 1850s on, these investments in formal education laid the foundations for a new science-based technology: "What had once been compensation for a handicap turned into a significant differential asset."[66]

But for the reasons outlined in my discussion of Chandler's contribution, the advent of science-based technology greatly increased the problem of fixed costs. Landes referred to a "gradual institutionalization of technological advance" in which "the more progressive industrial enterprises were no longer content to accept innovations and exploit them, but sought them by deliberate, planned experiment."[67] Because the technological opportunity became more complex, innovation required greater integration of production activities, firm-specific investments in training of technical specialists, the building of a managerial organization, as well as longer lags between the commitment of resources and the reaping of uncertain returns. As the problem of fixed costs increased, so too did the problem of financing the necessary investments.

Even in the British factory system, which itself posed the problem of fixed costs when compared with putting-out, private individuals and close partnerships had been able to mobilize the resources to invest in the craft-based technologies. In Germany, however, early on, powerful investment banks played a leading role in industrial development. Citing the authority of Schumpeter and Gerschenkron, Landes argued that, in contrast to the insignificant role of investment banks in the finance of British industry, "Germany is the best illustration of the generous yield of systematic investment in a backward economy of high potential."[68] The German banks not only supplied the initial finance to German industry, but also assumed strategic decision-making roles, while encouraging and permitting the firms that they controlled to organize cartels within their industries to ensure that individual enterprises would have access to sufficient market shares to transform high fixed costs into low unit costs.[69]

---

[64] Ibid., 150.
[65] Alexander Gerschenkron, *Economic Backwardness in Historical Perspective* (Cambridge, Mass.: Harvard University Press, 1962); Landes, *The Unbound Prometheus*, 151, 151n.
[66] Landes, *The Unbound Prometheus*, 151.   [67] Ibid., 325.   [68] Ibid., 208.
[69] Ibid., 350.

Within the German enterprises themselves, the flow of work – what Chandler called throughput and Landes called the "logistics of production" – became all-important in the achievement of economies of scale.[70] "The basic principle of industrial organization," asserted Landes, "is smooth and direct work flow from start to finish of the manufacturing process; detours, returns, and halts are to be avoided as much as possible."[71] Elsewhere in *The Unbound Prometheus*, he succinctly enunciated the dynamics of the relation between fixed costs and throughput. "Efficiency promotes efficiency: indeed, it makes it necessary."[72] The very size of plants in the German steel industry required the rational organization of work, which in turn required further mechanization to handle the flow of work, which in turn required the standardization of materials and products.[73] In the metal-using industries, investment in special-purpose machinery to make interchangeable parts was critical for accelerating the flow of work, a theme on which Landes expanded in *Revolution in Time* in discussing the rise of the U.S. watch industry.[74]

The success of "high-throughput" technologies, however, depended on the restructuring of production relations within the firm. As Landes, referring to the triumph of German industry, went on to argue, "Reorganization of work entailed reorganization of labour: the relationships of the men to one another and to their employers were implicit in the [rationalized] mode of production; technology and social pattern reinforced each other."[75]

Summing up, Landes argued, "the reasons for German success in the competition with Britain were not material, but rather social and institutional."[76] What then accounts for the failure of Britain, already an industrial power, to make the necessary social and institutional responses? There was the intransigence of the skilled workers, the very same men who, as I earlier argued, contributed to Britain's rise to industrial supremacy. But in the context of the new international competition based on planned coordination of high-throughput processes, the "skill and virtuosity" of these craftsmen became, to quote Landes, "incompatible with the fundamental principle of industrial technology – the substitution of inanimate accuracy and tirelessness for human touch and effort."[77] The "fundamental *principle* of industrial technology" had, of course, been the same during the British Industrial Revolution. The social organization of German (as well as U.S.) industry, however, had brought the principle closer to practical perfection.

But if, in the late nineteenth century, craft control posed an obstacle

---

[70] Ibid., 301.   [71] Ibid., 303.   [72] Ibid., 267.   [73] Ibid., 264–8.
[74] Landes, *Revolution in Time*, ch. 19.
[75] Landes, *The Unbound Prometheus*, 317; see also 321.   [76] Ibid., 334.   [77] Ibid., 307.

to innovation in Britain, why were British industrialists unable to over-come the prevailing institutional constraints? Social power played a role: The craft workers were well organized; their employers were not. At the national level, when Parliament and the judiciary sought to weaken the union movement – most notably by the Taff Vale decision that signaled financial ruin for any union engaged in a prolonged strike – the creative response of the workers was to build a political party that would represent their interests. At the industry level, even when the collective power of employers was sufficient to defeat the unions, as in the Engineering Lock-out of 1897–8, employers nevertheless remained dependent on craft con-trol to run their individual workplaces because they had no organizational alternative to put in its place. During the tight labor-market conditions of the 1910s, the power of the engineering unions reemerged stronger than ever.[78] As employers who had long relied on their independently orga-nized workers for the supply of technical skills and managerial coordina-tion, British industrial capitalists simply lacked the organizational capa-bility required to coordinate the use of the new high-throughput technologies, even when, as was the case in British engineering, firms were pressed by international competition to invest in them.

But why then didn't British industrialists develop this organizational capability? Here the typical British capitalist found himself in much the same position as the craft worker who jealously protected his particular job. The capitalist himself had developed specialized managerial skills appropriate to running his particular type of business and would have had no role to play in a modern corporate structure. He did not have the ability to make a success of the corporate investment strategy – and he knew it. As a result, he was unable to introduce new technological pro-cesses that went beyond the vertically specialized purview of his existing enterprise. If, as Landes argued, the British industrialist often faced the problem of "technical inter-relatedness," it was because, unlike his more technologically and organizationally advanced competitors abroad, he would not undertake the vertically integrated investment strategy that was a prerequisite for overcoming the problem.[79] He succumbed to the prob-lem of interrelatedness rather than confront the problem of fixed costs.

If the restricted managerial ability of the British industrialist led him to avoid the problem of fixed costs, his prior investments in plant and equip-ment presented him with the alternative of an adaptive response. Rather than invest in managerial organization and new technologies, he could

[78] Jonathan Zeitlin, "The Labour Strategies of British Engineering Employers, 1890–1922," in Howard Gospel and Craig Littler, eds., *Managerial Strategies and Industrial Relations* (London: Heinemann, 1983), 25–54.

[79] Landes, *The Unbound Prometheus*, 335. For a case study, see Lazonick, "Industrial Or-ganization and Technological Change."

seek to survive in international competition by cutting costs on the basis of the existing capabilities, organizational and technological, at his disposal. He could use inferior materials, seek wage concessions from his workers, accept lower profits, and deplete his existing capital stock.[80] In the long run, of course, he would and did lose out. But depending on the immobility of his workers and the durability of his plant and equipment, the long run could be a matter of decades – by which time he might well be dead. For him, the strategy of living off his industrial capital was rational. But for British society as a whole, it meant that the opportunity to invest in superior productive resources, both human and physical, had passed it by.

Yet had the adaptive response been confined to old British industries – textiles, iron and steel, shipbuilding, mechanical engineering – it might have represented a rational social policy that permitted the expansion of new dynamic industries while avoiding catastrophic unemployment in the old industrial centers. But the backwardness of the old industries retarded the development of the social institutions that would support technological change in the new.[81] Because late-nineteenth-century industrialists did not demand science-based technical specialists, the educational system was slow to orient its activities to supply them. In the new mechanical industries, such as automobile manufacture, shop-floor control on the craft model became dominant in the first half of the twentieth century even in the absence of unions, because industrialists relied on shop-floor workers to coordinate the flow of work, while they failed to integrate professional engineers into the managerial structure.

Moreover, because late-nineteenth-century industrialists did not look to financial interests to reorganize their industries, the British banking system, as powerful and concentrated as it was, did not orient its activities toward the mobilization of long-term investment capital. What the British banking system, based in London and handling the world's portfolio investments, did produce was a new wealthy elite that merged with the landed aristocracy and had no interest in technology. Rather than restructure the system of education to effect the marriage of science and technology, the new elite sought to use the system to ratify and reproduce its class privilege. In striving to join the new aristocracy, even those British industrialists who had attained wealth on the basis of technological inno-

---

[80] See, e.g., William Lazonick and William Mass, "The Performance of the British Cotton Industry, 1870–1913," *Research in Economic History*, 9 (Spring 1984), 1–44.

[81] Elbaum and Lazonick, eds., *Decline of British Economy*; William Lazonick, "Strategy, Structure and Management Development in the United States and Britain," in Kesaji Kobayashi and Hidemasa Morikawa, eds., *Development of Managerial Enterprise* (Tokyo: University of Tokyo Press, 1986), 101–46; see also Chapter 1, this volume.

vation sought to partake of this elite culture rather than attempt to rid it of its antitechnology bias. One result of such attitudes was to imbed the British class structure even in the largest British firms in ways that made it difficult for top management to gain the commitment and coordinate the activities of technical specialists, thereby preventing the organizational cohesion that was becoming increasingly necessary for technological change and international competitive advantage.[82]

I believe that the preceding summary of the impact of institutional structure on British decline is consistent with the arguments that Landes made in *The Unbound Prometheus* under the heading "Some Reasons Why."[83] In the end, however, it is not social institutions that Landes emphasized. Rather, he argued that "the decisive consideration was one of attitudes and values."[84] "Even when the British entrepreneur was rational," said Landes, "his calculations were distorted by the shortness of his time horizon, and his estimates were on the conservative side."[85]

But if the profit calculations and time horizons of the British industrialist were adequate to the task in the early nineteenth century, why had they become inadequate by the late nineteenth century? The key to the answer is, in my view, the dramatic transformation of the social determinants of technological change. In the earlier period, the industrial capitalist did not have to engage in an innovative investment strategy or build a cohesive managerial structure. With abundant supplies of skilled labor ready at hand and craft-based technology readily accessible, the fixed costs of setting up shop were small. He could rely on the market to supply him with inputs and take his outputs. The industrial capitalist could remain an individualist, and yet participate in an industry that was in the forefront of technological change.

In the later period, however, the British industrialist found himself confronted in international competition by the growing power of collective organization in the development and utilization of productive resources. To set in motion the dynamic interaction between organization and technology now required qualities of human resources and commitments of financial resources readily available to his foreign competitors but not to him. Inherent in his own social environment, moreover, were vested interests, including those that derived from his own limited capabilities combined with his desire to control his own enterprise, that stood in the way of the necessary collective response. Compared with his international competitors, his time horizon was short because he was but an adaptive *individual*, not a creative *organization*. His estimates of returns

---

[82] Lazonick, "Strategy, Structure and Management Development"; see also Chapter 1, this volume.
[83] Landes, *The Unbound Prometheus*, 326–58; see also 468–77.
[84] Ibid., 543.   [85] Ibid., 354.

were conservative because his organized competitors had the power to shape their economic environment in ways that he, as an individual proprietor, could not. It should be added that, in his comparative analysis of the watch industry in *Revolution in Time*, Landes seemed to concur in this analysis; for in contrast to the individualism rampant in British watchmaking, Landes called for (with his own emphasis) "a model of *collective* effort and performance" to explain the passing of leadership to the Swiss.[86]

Given the organized power of the new competition, the combination of short planning horizons and conservative profit projections was not a recipe for the quick economic death of British industry but rather one for prolonging its economic life. Because British industrialists and workers had already accumulated plant, equipment, and industrial skills, they could for a time live off their physical and human capital. Meanwhile, however, by investing in new technologies and by creating organizations to transform high fixed costs into low unit costs, German, U.S., and then Japanese enterprises would leave their British competitors further and further behind.

[86] Landes, *Revolution in Time*, 303.

5

The making of the market mentality

The neglect of history

The twentieth-century experiences of successful capitalist development and relative economic decline reveal that organizational coordination has increasingly replaced market coordination in the value-creation process. Within the capitalist enterprise, planned coordination of the specialized division of labor has become increasingly important for the development and utilization of resources. Within national industries, enterprises with greater organizational capability have been able to gain and sustain competitive advantage not only through the development and utilization of resources within the enterprise, but also through privileged access to external resources both within and beyond the boundaries of the national economies in which they are based. Within successful national economies, the state has promoted the competitiveness of particular industries by investing in resources such as education, communications, and financial institutions on which the nation's business enterprises can draw in building their organization-specific productive capabilities.

In the early decades of this century, the managerial revolution in U.S. industry overcame the competitive advantage of the British economy based on market-coordinated industry. In the post-World War II decades, even more profound organizational coordination has enabled Japanese industry to surpass U.S. industry in an ever-broadening array of pursuits. As argued in Chapter 1, Japanese planned coordination is not entirely new; it can be viewed as a more integrated elaboration of the managerial enterprise that brought U.S. industry to economic dominance in the first half of this century.

The history of capitalist development in the twentieth century challenges the outlook of those economists who continue to propound, and indeed elaborate, the vision of the market-coordinated economy. Since the late nineteenth century, a necessary, and increasingly important, condition for successful capitalist development has been that industrial enterprises exercise control over market forces – not only product markets but also factor markets. Without substantial control over market forces, manufacturing enterprises in all the major industries would not have the incentives to make the large-scale investments in plant, equipment, and personnel necessary to participate in global competition. Nor would these enterprises have the organizational capabilities to develop and utilize these investments to create value and attain competitive advantage.

To be sure, existing or potential market competition may be critical for inducing an enterprise to develop further its organizational capabilities and undertake innovative investments. But in an international economy dominated by powerful organizations, behind every competitive challenge is an enterprise with superior organizational capabilities. Success in responding to "market forces" depends on whether the challenged organization can surpass its competitors by improving its own value-creating capability.

As argued in Chapter 1, we can characterize as market-coordinated the British economy that dominated world markets in the late nineteenth century because of the extensive reliance of the process of economic development on external economies. But in the twentieth century the role of the visible hand in successful capitalist development has expanded to the point where the label "market economy" might well be used to refer to a capitalist economy that is at a serious competitive disadvantage rather than one that is thriving. With their belief in the efficacy of market coordination, however, economists may be unwilling, and perhaps even unable, to comprehend the theoretical implications of the rise of the Japanese economy. On the contrary, if the elaboration of the theory of the market economy by U.S. economic theorists concomitant to the rise of managerial capitalism earlier in this century is any indication, the response of mainstream economists to the intellectual challenge posed by the Japanese "miracle" may well be to elaborate the theory of the market economy even more vigorously and abstractly as an alternative to coming to grips with evolving institutional reality.

Indeed, the static and ahistorical theory of the market economy that economists have elaborated in the twentieth century cannot even comprehend the developmental character of a market-coordinated economy such as Britain's that existed in the nineteenth century. The fact is that since the turn of the century the leading economists in Britain and the United States have failed to develop a theory of economic development that can explain the nature and causes of the wealth of nations, irrespective of whether the institutions that drive economic development are coordinated by markets or organizations. As a result, they have failed to understand the roles of organizational coordination in U.S. and Japanese success and those of market coordination in British and U.S. decline.

As this chapter will illustrate, the vision of economic activity that has dominated the thinking of academic economists during this century has retained a steadfast commitment to the notion that market coordination is the best guarantor of superior economic performance. The main thrust of a theoretical training in economics is to look for ways to achieve the optimal allocation of scarce resources by creating conditions that, given the supposed imperatives of large-scale technology and the inherent greediness of economic man, will move economic activity closer to the ideal of the market economy. In the absence of a systematic theory of value creation to accompany their systematic theory of scarce-resource allocation, neoclassical economists lack a sound basis for even asking, let alone answering, whether their "ideal" of market coordination is or is not compatible with the institutional requirements for rapid and sustained economic development.

As suggested by our discussion of the intellectual legacies of Marx and Schumpeter, the conceptual shortcomings of modern economic theory are not inherent in the history of economics. Following the leads of Marx and Schumpeter, economics could have become a discipline that combined theory and history to comprehend the institutional dynamics of advanced capitalist development. Ironically, one economist who made a serious attempt to do just that was Alfred Marshall, *the* leading economist during the decades around the turn of the century when international economic leadership passed from British proprietary capitalism to U.S. managerial capitalism. Yet in the end, Marshall's legacy was used to provide critical foundations for *neoclassical* economic theorizing in the twentieth century.

The impact of Marshall could have been very different. His influence on neoclassical economics notwithstanding, Marshall's own work demonstrates that he saw historical and institutional analyses as basic to the generation of economic theory, and that he viewed a theory of economic development as basic to understanding the world in which he lived. Yet methodologically, Marshall differed from Marx and Schumpeter in one critical respect. As we have seen, for Marx and Schumpeter the purpose of a static equilibrium conception of the capitalist economy was to lay the foundation for a dynamic analysis of how the economy escaped from equilibrium to generate economic development. In sharp contrast, Marshall began with a dynamic theory of the capitalist economy, but then undermined his own efforts by making assumptions that enabled him, and then his followers, to place the central economic institution – the capitalist enterprise – in equilibrium.

In so doing, Marshall may well have been motivated by his undoubted ideological commitment to the survival of fragmented, and hence individualistic, structures of industrial organization. But in placing the business enterprise in equilibrium, Marshall was also capturing an important dimension of the reality of British industrial structure in the late nineteenth and early twentieth centuries. Unfortunately, however much Britain's fragmented and individualistic structures of industrial organization may have contributed to British economic success in the nineteenth century, the same structures posed formidable obstacles to value creation in the twentieth century in an international economy dominated by concentrated and collectivized structures of industrial organization such as had arisen in Germany and the United States. Whatever Marshall's own motivations, in the process of moving from dynamics to statics, Marshall's economics and the neo-Marshallian version elaborated by the master's followers contributed to the making of an outmoded market mentality that pervades mainstream economics today.

From internal economies to the representative firm

As the preeminent economist of his time, Marshall presided over the transition from classical economics, which focused on the causes and consequences of economic growth, to neoclassical economics, which would focus on how market forces could optimally allocate scarce resources among competing ends. Although the Marshallian influence on twentieth-century economics was to be primarily in the neoclassical direction, in his definition and approach to economics, Marshall himself was much more classical. He defined economics as the study of "that part of individual and social action which is most closely connected with the attainment and with the use of the material requisites of well-being,"[1] and he studied the institutional evolution of the relations between firms and markets in order to provide realistic foundations for his theory of economic activity.

Writing in England during the half-century from the early 1870s to the early 1920s, Marshall saw the British economy consolidate its position as "workshop of the world," only to be confronted from the 1880s on by the rise of the German and U.S. economies based on powerful managerial enterprise. Marshall is best remembered for his neoclassical synthesis of marginal cost and marginal utility theories to derive the market equilibrium of commodity supply and demand. But underlying his theory of markets is a central concern with the causes and limits to the growth of the firm in order to understand the future of Britain's market-coordinated economy in a changing international environment.

Marshall considered *Principles of Economics*, published in eight editions between 1890 and 1920, to be the static foundations of economic theory on which he could build a dynamic, "superstructural" analysis. Toward that end, Marshall ultimately produced two volumes, *Industry and Trade* and *Money, Credit, and Commerce*, both published near the

---

[1] Alfred Marshall, *Principles of Economics*, 9th (variorum) ed. (London: Macmillan Press, 1961), vol. 1 (text), 1.

end of his life.[2] In *Principles,* the central concepts for analyzing the relations between firms and markets are external and internal economies. External economies are "dependent on the general development of the industry," while internal economies are "dependent on the resources of the individual houses of business engaged in it, on their organization, and the efficiency of management."[3]

For Marshall, "the concentration of specialized industries in particular localities" creates external economies that are favorable to small firms by giving them easy access to supplies of skilled labor, subsidiary trades, and communications networks.[4] Localization may promote the economic utilization of expensive machinery by a small firm because of the regional concentration of aggregate demand for a specialized product.[5] Over time, localization also promotes the development of productive resources within the industrial community as skilled workers perfect and pass on their crafts and develop machinery to "relieve the strain on human muscles" and take over "monotonous work in manufacture."[6] The Lancashire cotton textile industry, which was central to Britain's rise to international industrial dominance in the nineteenth century, provided the foremost example of an industry that relied on external economies or, as Marshall described it in *Industry and Trade,* "perhaps the best present instance of concentrated organization mainly automatic."[7]

As for internal economies, Marshall argued that the initial growth of the firm is dependent on the resourcefulness of its entrepreneur, and he suggested that firms that generate internal economies can cumulate their advantage by making better use of the market than their rivals.[8] Within firms that have grown large, Marshall noted that "the central problem . . . relates to the advantages and disadvantages of the subdivision of the work of business management," and he drew the general distinction between the roles of strategic and operational managers.[9]

In addition, he revealed some insight into a potential source of sustained competitive advantage in asserting that "the large manufacturer has a much better chance than a small one of getting hold of men with exceptional natural abilities, to do most of the difficult part of his work."[10] But as his reference to "natural abilities" indicates, he displayed no conception of the firm as an institution for developing resources, human or otherwise. In any case, he spoke of markets for what he called "business ability in command of capital," thereby suggesting that even the large

[2] See ibid., xiv; Alfred Marshall, *Industry and Trade* (London: Macmillan Press, 1919); idem, *Money, Credit and Commerce* (London: Macmillan Press, 1924).
[3] Marshall, *Principles of Economics,* 266.   [4] Ibid., bk. 4, ch. 4.   [5] Ibid., 271.
[6] Ibid., 261–2, 271.   [7] Marshall, *Industry and Trade,* 600–1.
[8] Marshall, *Principles of Economics,* 311, 318; also idem, *Industry and Trade,* 167–8.
[9] Marshall, *Principles of Economics,* 283–4.   [10] Ibid., 283.

manufacturer who had access to men with superior natural abilities would not be able to *appropriate* internal economies from employing them and that, indeed, his own profits reflected a market rate of return rather than firm-specific gains to enterprise.[11]

In *Industry and Trade*, Marshall added considerable institutional insights beyond what can be found in *Principles* into the advantages of the large-scale enterprise: standardization, marketing of technically sophisticated products, the development of human resources and technology within the firm (including an argument that higher prices today may make it possible for the firm to undertake investments in plant and equipment that will make consumers better off tomorrow), and the need for administrative fusion to make an amalgamation of firms result in economies.[12]

Marshall did not put forth an explicit notion of what I have termed "privileged access to resources" – the ability of a business enterprise to retain access to resources irrespective of the prevailing market rates of return that these resources could reap. Rather, as in the case of "business ability in command of capital," he succumbed to the neoclassical tendency to reduce all monetary appropriations to market-determined prices rather than firm-specific returns. Yet Marshall's summary of the role of internal economies in the growth of the firm reflects admirably the cumulative process of sustained competitive advantage that derives from privileged access to resources:

An able man, assisted by some strokes of good fortune, gets a firm footing in the trade, he works hard and lives sparely, his own capital grows fast, and the credit that enables him to borrow more capital grows still faster; he collects around him subordinates of more than ordinary zeal and ability; as his business increases they rise with him, they trust him and he trusts them, each of them devotes himself with energy to just that work for which he is specially fitted, so that no high ability is wasted on easy work, and no difficult work is entrusted to unskillful hands. Corresponding to this steadily increasing economy of skill, the growth of his firm brings with it similar economies of specialized machines and plant of all kinds; every improved process is quickly adopted and made the basis of further improvements; success brings credit and credit brings success; credit and success help to retain old customers and to bring new ones; the increase of his trade gives him great advantages in buying; his goods advertise one another and thus diminish his difficulty in finding a vent for them. The increase of the scale of his business increases rapidly the advantages which he has over his competitors, and lowers the price at which he can afford to sell.[13]

---

[11] Ibid., 313.
[12] Marshall, *Industry and Trade*, 140–62, 167, 170, 216, 274, 304–5, 327, 597, 603.
[13] Marshall, *Principles of Economics*, 315.

Marshall, moreover, did not stop with this depiction of the growth of the firm. He also recognized that the generation of internal economies could well result in oligopoly – albeit over a rather prolonged time frame – and that, if these giant firms persisted in the pursuit of innovative investment strategies, their market power might redound to the common good. As Marshall continued:

This process may go on *as long as his energy and enterprise, his inventive and organizing power retain their full strength and freshness,* and so long as the risks that are inseparable from business do not cause him exceptional losses; and if it could *endure for a hundred years,* he and one or two others like him would divide between them that branch of industry in which he is engaged. The large scale of their production would put great economies within their reach; and provided they competed to their utmost with one another, the public would derive the chief benefit of these economies, and the price of the commodity would fall very low.[14]

Marshall's 1919 publication of *Industry and Trade* with its extensive discussions of contemporary industrial developments in Germany and the United States should have at least revealed to him that the rise of oligopoly need not take a century. In *Industry and Trade,* however, he made no attempt to revise his contributions to economic theory contained in *Principles* in the light of evolving reality. When Marshall undertook the last major revision of *Principles* in 1907, his only response to the U.S. merger movement that had taken place since the prior major revision in 1891 was simply to delete the phrase "the growing democracy of trade" from the assessment that "America . . . supplies many of the most instructive instances of the latest economic tendencies of the age, such as the growing democracy of trade, and the development of speculation and trade combination in every form, and she will probably before long take the chief part in pioneering the way for the rest of the world."[15]

In *Principles,* Marshall argued that "external economies are always growing in importance to internal economies in matters of trade knowledge" and that "the tendency of large firms to drive out small ones has already gone so far as to exhaust most of the strength of these forces by which it was originally promoted."[16] Neither he nor his followers integrated back into the core of economic theory anything approaching the notions of innovation or sustained competitive advantage. In constructing his static theory of supply and demand, which *is* the part of his work that his followers were to take up, Marshall invoked and ultimately retained

---

[14] Ibid., my emphasis.
[15] Ibid., 752; see also Alfred Marshall, *Principles of Economics,* 9th (variorum) ed. (London: Macmillan Press, 1961), vol. 2 (notes), 734.
[16] Marshall, *Principles of Economics,* vol. 1, 284, 286–7.

the assumption that the growth of the firm through internal economies is limited by the "energy and enterprise, inventive and organizing power" of its founder. As summed up in the dictum "shirtsleeves to shirtsleeves in three generations,"[17] those who inherit a successful business are not likely to have the energy and creative genius of the original entrepreneur. Therefore, Marshall argued, "a business firm grows and attains great strength, and afterwards perhaps stagnates and decays."[18] Even a joint-stock company, in which managerial succession is not based on familial inheritance, is not likely to sustain its vigor:

It may retain the advantages of division of labour, of specialized skill and machinery: it may even increase them by a further increase of its capital; and under favourable conditions it may secure a permanent and prominent place in the work of production. But it is likely to have lost so much of its elasticity and progressive force, that the advantages are no longer exclusively on its side in its competition with younger and smaller rivals.[19]

It is the notion of the rise and fall of individual firms that permitted Marshall to introduce the concept of the "representative firm" into economic theory. The concept recognizes that, within any industry at any point in time, firms vary in productive capability. But because of the entrepreneurial limits on the growth of the firm, one can assume that the "representative firm"

is one which has had a fairly long life, and fair success, which is managed with *normal* ability, and which has *normal* access to the economies, external and internal, which belong to that aggregate volume of production; account being taken of the class of goods produced, the conditions of marketing them and the economic environment generally.[20]

The concept of the representative firm enabled Marshall to integrate the business organization into a static theory of the equilibrium of supply and demand in a competitive market economy. The definition of the representative firm as one "which is managed with normal ability, and which has normal access to [internal and external] economies" eliminates from the analysis the *theoretical* possibility of sustained competitive advantage of an enterprise within a national industry. For the sake of theory, all firms in an industry are assumed to be alike – hence the theoretical vision of the firm and industry structure that persists in today's microeconomics textbooks. The firm is depicted as a passive actor that takes technology as

[17] Ibid., 621.   [18] Ibid., 323.   [19] Ibid., 316.
[20] Ibid., 317, my emphasis. For a historical investigation and critique of the validity of Marshall's notion of the rise and decline of firms, see R. Lloyd-Jones and A. A. Le Roux, "Marshall and the Birth and Death of Firms: The Growth and Size Distribution of Firms in the Early Nineteenth-Century Cotton Industry," *Business History*, 24 (July 1982), 141–55.

given and reacts to changes in supply and demand by substituting at the margin.[21] The firm is incapable of attaining and sustaining competitive advantage.

Marshall was aware of the dangers of the static, competitive equilibrium model. He argued that "the theory of stable equilibrium, of normal demand and supply helps indeed to give definiteness to our ideas, and in its elementary stages it does not diverge from the actual facts of life." But he recognized that "it is especially needful to remember that economic problems are imperfectly presented when they are treated as problems of statical equilibrium, and not of organic growth."[22] He might also have added that an essential problem of the British economy in the twentieth century was that "statical equilibrium" rather than "organic growth" was *too* representative of economic reality; for in *Industry and Trade*, Marshall indicated that he was cognizant of Britain's relative decline and set out a research agenda for British economists:

[Britain] has in some respects lost leadership. Her best methods are now the common property of the Western World; and recent advances in them have been very largely due to the enterprise and inventive faculties of other countries. The maintenance of her material well-being above that of other countries of Europe, in spite of some *relative* slackening of the industrial initiative by which she achieved her success, cannot be expected to last for ever. That it should have been maintained till now is marvellous, and calls for study. We need to know on what Britain's industrial leadership was based; and how it may be conserved, and perhaps even enlarged again.[23]

Given Marshall's institutional approach to justifying his theoretical assumptions, his distinction between internal and external economies, and his interest in comparative economic development, his work could have led to a very different analysis of the capitalist economy than that embodied in the theory of the market economy to which his work in the end provided powerful support. Marshall had considerable insight into the relations between firms and markets and the dynamic process of the growth of the firm. Nevertheless, he used the device of the representative firm to abstract from dynamics in order to focus on the statics of competitive equilibrium, and he justified this theoretical focus on the grounds that external economies were likely to outweigh internal economies in the development of capitalism. He had a point for Britain in the nineteenth century, but not for Britain's competitors in the twentieth.

In moving from dynamics to statics, moreover, Marshall differed not only from Marx but also from Schumpeter; for as outlined in Chapter 4, both Marx and Schumpeter took economic analysis in just the opposite

---

[21] Marshall, *Principles of Economics*, vol. 1, bk. 5, ch. 3, and bk. 6, ch. 7.   [22] Ibid., 461.
[23] Marshall, *Industry and Trade*, 3.

direction by showing how a theory of competitive equilibrium – a theory
of how the economy *ceases* to change – could not provide an analysis of
capitalist development as a historical process of change. In a theory of
economic development, the transformations of organization and technology not only *undermine* tendencies to settle into equilibrium, but also
make prior equilibrium "solutions" irrelevant to the new economic environment.

The firm in equilibrium

Despite the way in which Marshall transformed his own analysis from one
of "organic growth" to one of "statical equilibrium," his attempts to address the issues of economic development indicate that he had a measure
of what Schumpeter called "historical experience."[24] He derived his initial conception of capitalist development from his study of the British
economy in the nineteenth century. When the rise of big business abroad
became apparent, he sought to understand its implications for economic
development. Nevertheless, insofar as there is an empirical basis for Marshall's theory of economic activity, it is to be found in the British experience. In choosing to use the device of the representative firm to abstract
from the implications of internal economies and settle down into the statics of competitive equilibrium, Marshall may well have been overly influenced by the reality of a market-coordinated British economy that, from
the late nineteenth century, was falling behind its rivals both organizationally and technologically. In effect, the institutional rigidities in the
British system of business organization – a system that was, as I have
argued, a major factor in British long-term relative decline – became con-
cretized in Marshallian economic theory.

During the interwar years, a prime focus of the work of Marshall's followers was to refine the master's theory of the firm in equilibrium. They
showed little concern with continuing his work on comparative institutional evolution or the dynamics of economic development. Rather, they
became concerned – indeed, almost obsessed – with the extent to which
the Marshallian theory of decreasing costs was compatible with "competitive conditions," by which they meant conditions of perfect competition.[25] Insofar as empirical reality informed their choices of questions and
economic models, that reality was the British economy, which for neo-
Marshallians became the "representative economy." For example, again

[24] Joseph A. Schumpeter, *History of Economic Analysis* (New York: Oxford University Press, 1954), 12–23.
[25] See Piero Sraffa, "The Laws of Returns Under Competitive Conditions," in George Stig-
ler and Kenneth Boulding, eds., *Readings in Price Theory* (Homewood, Ill.: Irwin, 1952), 180–97; originally published in *Economic Journal*, 36 (December 1926), 535–50.

and again they referred to the highly fragmented Lancashire cotton textile industry to make a point about the "optimum" size of the firm.[26] With the help of the Smithian vision of the invisible hand taken to its neoclassical extreme, they then accepted as axiomatic the conclusion that a market-coordinated economy leads to the highest common good. As is already evident in the work of A. C. Pigou, Marshall's successor as professor of political economy at Cambridge, the notion of perfect competition as the ideal state of economic affairs, and of monopoly as a deduction from the "national dividend," became unquestioned axioms of economic analysis.[27]

The belief in the efficacy of the market economy led the neo-Marshallians of the interwar period and beyond to construct a theory of economic activity in which the nature of the firm was consistent with the *stability* of equilibrium in the product market in which the firm sold its goods. A theory of the firm in equilibrium required an analysis of the response of supply to given demand in *one* hypothetical market that, as defined by a particular product that was homogeneous across firms, represented one hypothetical industry. Much, although by no means all, of the analysis focused on product-market equilibrium, with equilibrium in labor and capital markets being viewed as derivative. Because of its focus on the equilibration of supply and demand in a particular market, this brand of theoretical economics became known as partial equilibrium, in contrast to general equilibrium, in which the economy is characterized by the simultaneous interaction of, and equilibrium in, all its markets for inputs and outputs.

In partial equilibrium, market demand for a product is taken as given, so that the main task of theory is to show how much of the commodity the "representative firm" will be willing to supply at any given price. Two types of product-market equilibria are identified: the short run, during which time each firm seeks to maximize profits with its fixed capacity taken as given, and the long run, during which new investments in plant and equipment can be put in place.

Today, the diagrams depicting the short-run and long-run U-shaped cost curves are such standard stuff in economics textbooks that the assumptions that underlie the neo-Marshallian short-run and long-run equilibria are rarely questioned. In the process the analytical potential of Marshall's distinction between internal and external economies for understanding the changing relation between economic institutions and economic outcomes was lost to mainstream economic theory. The ways in which Marshall's followers, beginning with Pigou, reconceptualized the

---

[26] See, e.g., E. A. G. Robinson, *The Structure of Competitive Industry* (Cambridge University Press, 1953), 15, 23.

[27] A. C. Pigou, *Wealth and Welfare* (London: Macmillan Press, 1912).

theory of the firm to reconcile Marshallian concepts with the analysis of the firm in equilibrium tell us much about the making of the twentieth-century market mentality.

Chapter 3 has already explored the distinction between internal and external economies of scale. Together, these two types of economies – the one being experienced by the organization that produces and sells the good or service and the other by the organization that buys and uses it – give rise to decreasing costs in vertically related industrial sectors. Conversely, internal and external diseconomies of scale give rise to increasing costs. Note that the literature on decreasing costs and increasing costs often uses the terms "increasing returns" and "decreasing returns." This terminology assumes, however, that there is a strict relation between a firm's costs and revenues, as indeed there is if it is assumed that the firm always produces and sells at the level of output at which marginal cost equals marginal revenue. As discussed in Chapter 3, however, in a dynamic theory of the firm in which gaining market share is both a cause and an effect of competitive advantage – and in which *to be able* to equate marginal costs and marginal revenue means that the firm has *already solved* this basic competitive challenge – the firm may adopt a pricing strategy that results in no simple relation between changes in revenues and changes in costs as the firm's saleable output expands. Hence, throughout this discussion I shall (except when quoting) use the terms "decreasing costs" and "increasing costs" even though the participants in the post-Marshallian debate over the theory of the firm tended to talk in terms of returns.

Terminology aside, a proponent of the theory of the market economy might argue that the internal–external distinction is unimportant – that all we need to ask is whether an industry, taken as the sum of its vertically related parts, is experiencing decreasing or increasing costs. From this perspective, it is inconsequential which firms in the vertical chain benefit from the cost decreases or are burdened by the cost increases, which is tantamount to saying that the vertical structure of an industry has no bearing on economic outcomes. In effect, such a position ignores the potentially critical distinction between organizational coordination and market coordination in the generation of decreasing costs, and hence in the ability of particular industries, characterized by particular structures of business organization, to generate decreasing rather than increasing costs.[28]

Post-Marshallian debate on the implications of Marshall's framework was launched in the 1920s in the pages of the *Economic Journal* when the economic historian John Clapham challenged Pigou, as Marshall's successor, to fill in the "empty economic boxes" by telling him which industries

---

[28] See Chapter 3.

(in Britain and elsewhere) were subject to decreasing costs and which were subject to increasing costs.[29] Clapham argued that Marshall's *Industry and Trade* had only barely scratched the surface of identifying the cost characteristics of different industries, and that Pigou was using deductive analysis to cover up the empirical scratches that Marshall had made rather than to dig deeper into the substance of industrial life. Referring to Pigou's *The Economics of Welfare* (a work first published in 1919, the same year as *Industry and Trade,* and a revision of Pigou's earlier work, *Wealth and Welfare*), Clapham contended that "in nearly a thousand pages, there is not even one illustration of what industries are in which boxes, though many an argument begins – 'when conditions of diminishing returns prevail,' or 'when conditions of increasing returns prevail.' "[30]

Clapham's challenge evoked a spirited reply from Pigou, who argued that "the point at issue is whether the concepts of increasing and diminishing returns are instruments of service in the construction of a realistic economic science" and interpreted Clapham's objection to be "that they can serve no purpose of this kind."[31] Clapham quickly issued an even more spirited rejoinder that he had been misunderstood – his problem was not so much with the categorization of returns, but more fundamentally with the methodology of economics because it provided little guidance as to what types of facts and statistics were needed to fill the boxes.[32]

In 1924, D. H. Robertson joined (as he put it) the "battle of the giants."[33] He rightly insisted that the combatants should speak in terms of "costs" and not "returns." More importantly, Robertson took Pigou to task for recognizing only "external economies" as a source of decreasing costs, internal economies "having vanished into thin air."[34] With external economies as the source of decreasing costs, of course, it could still be maintained that a market-coordinated economy and economic progress went hand in hand. Robertson raised the problems that internal economies created for the theory of competitive equilibrium, saying that he "would

[29] J. H. Clapham, "Of Empty Economics Boxes," in Stigler and Boulding, eds., *Readings in Price Theory*, 119–30; originally published in *Economic Journal*, 32 (September 1922), 305–14.

[30] Ibid., 120.

[31] A. C. Pigou, "Empty Economic Boxes: A Reply," in Stigler and Boulding, eds., *Readings in Price Theory*, 131–9; originally published in *Economic Journal*, 32 (December 1922), 458–65.

[32] J. H. Clapham, "The Economic Boxes: A Rejoinder," in Stigler and Boulding, eds., *Readings in Price Theory*, 139–42; originally published in *Economic Journal*, 32 (December 1922), 560–3.

[33] D. H. Robertson, "Those Empty Boxes," in Stigler and Boulding, eds., *Readings in Price Theory*, 143–59, cited at 143; originally published in *Economic Journal*, 34 (March 1924), 16–30.

[34] Ibid., 151.

prefer to offend the mathematical theory of competition than to follow [Pigou] through this logical hole in his own logical net."[35] Robertson confessed that his criticisms of Pigou's (and Clapham's) failure to recognize the importance and implications of internal economies were "negative conclusions."[36] A quarter-century later (in a note to the 1952 reprint of his 1924 piece), Robertson identified his earlier perspective as what had by that time become known as "workable" competition,[37] a conception of economic activity that, even if not integrated into a theory of economic development, at least allowed for the possibility that the activities of the business enterprise might influence its market environment.

In the 1952 reprint of his article, Robertson also noted that his 1924 article "belongs to the pre-Sraffa, pre-Chamberlin age";[38] for in 1926, Piero Sraffa wrote his famous article "The Laws of Returns under Competitive Conditions" in which he argued that the existence of decreasing costs required that economists "abandon the path of free competition and turn in the opposite direction, namely, towards monopoly."[39] In challenging the precepts of "free competition," however, Sraffa was not concerned with how decreasing costs are generated – that is, he displayed no interest in elaborating Marshallian developmental dynamics. Rather, his concern was whether the existence of decreasing costs vitiated Marshall's static analysis of the equilibrium of the firm. What Sraffa wanted was a theory of imperfect competition, and he challenged the neo-Marshallians to devise such a theory.

In moving toward a theory of imperfect competition, Sraffa stressed the constraining influence of demand for the firm's products on the growth of the firm. "Everyday experience," Sraffa argued,

shows that a very large number of undertakings – and the majority of those which produce manufactured consumers' goods – work under conditions of individual diminishing costs. Almost any producer of such goods, if he could rely upon the market in which he sells his products being prepared to take any quantity of them from him at the current price, without any trouble on his part except that of producing them, would extend his business enormously. . . . The chief obstacle against which they have to contend when they want gradually to increase their production does not lie in the cost of production – which, indeed, generally favors them in that direction – but in the difficulty of selling the larger quantity of goods without reducing the price, or without having to face increased marketing expenses.[40]

---

[35] Ibid., 151n.   [36] Ibid., 158.
[37] J. M. Clark, "Toward a Concept of Workable Competition," *American Economic Review*, 30 (June 1940), 241–56; Robertson, "Those Empty Boxes," 158.
[38] Robertson, "Those Empty Boxes," 143n.
[39] Sraffa, "The Laws of Returns," 187.   [40] Ibid., 189.

Over the next few years, a spate of articles on the implications of decreasing costs appeared in the *Economic Journal* – contributions by Pigou, G. F. Shove, Lionel Robbins, Schumpeter, and Allyn Young,[41] as well as a symposium entitled "Increasing Returns and the Representative Firm" that offered (as the editor of the *Economic Journal* put it) "a partial rehabilitation of Marshallian orthodoxy on conservative lines by D. H. Robertson, [as well as] some negative and destructive criticisms by Piero Sraffa, and [concluded] with constructive suggestions by G. F. Shove."[42]

In the presymposium articles, Pigou, Shove, and Robbins, each in his own way, conducted the search for competitive equilibrium, while Schumpeter and Young, also each in his own way, sought to draw a distinction between, on the one hand, a theory of competitive equilibrium that assumes that the relevant cost structures are known and, on the other hand, a theory of economic development that focuses on how new cost structures come into existence. I have already dealt with Schumpeter's view that, as he put it in the 1928 article, "the discontinuous character of the [innovation] process . . . does not lend itself to description in terms of a theory of equilibrium."[43] It was in this piece that Schumpeter recognized that a transition was occurring from "competitive" capitalism to "trustified" capitalism.[44] Young saw things very differently, agreeing with Pigou that external economies were the prime source of decreasing costs, and hence envisioning (as I shall critically elaborate in Chapter 8) "economic progress" occurring on the basis of a highly fragmented market-coordinated economy.

Pigou, in contrast, continued in his attempt to reformulate Marshallian concepts into (as Joan Robinson put it some four decades later) "a neat, logical system."[45] Robbins and Shove sought to make the logical system even neater by arguing that the free mobility of resources would ensure that all industries would compete for the same resources, and hence rents would be imposed on decreasing cost industries that would bring the whole

---

[41] A. C. Pigou, "The Laws of Diminishing and Increasing Cost," *Economic Journal*, 37 (June 1927), 188–97, idem, "An Analysis of Supply," *Economic Journal*, 38 (June 1928), 238–57; G. F. Shove, "Varying Costs and Marginal Net Products," *Economic Journal*, 38 (June 1928), 258–66; Lionel Robbins, "The Representative Firm," *Economic Journal*, 38 (September 1928), 387–404; Joseph A. Schumpeter, "The Instability of Capitalism," *Economic Journal*, 38 (September 1928), 361–80; Allyn Young, "Increasing Returns and Economic Progress," *Economic Journal*, 38 (December 1928), 527–42.

[42] D. H. Robertson, Piero Sraffa, and G. F. Shove, "Increasing Returns and the Representative Firm," *Economic Journal*, 40 (March 1930), 79–115, cited at 79; see also John C. Wood, ed., *Alfred Marshall: Critical Assessments* (London: Croom Helm, 1982), vol. 3.

[43] Schumpeter, "The Instability of Capitalism," 64; see Chapter 4, this volume.

[44] Schumpeter, "The Instability of Capitalism," 70.

[45] Joan Robinson, *The Economics of Imperfect Competition*, 2d ed. (London: St. Martin's, 1969), v.

economic system into general equilibrium. Robbins and, following him, Shove argued, therefore, that Marshall's notion of the "representative firm" was irrelevant.[46] Through competitive market processes, superior economic *resources* would be able to appropriate rents in their roles as factors of production, thereby leaving the firms that employed these superior resources with the same cost structures as their competitors. As Shove put it, "The costs of a representative firm are useless as a means of discovering the costs of the industry, if we can only find out what they are when we already know the costs of the industry."[47] In effect, the likes of Robbins and Shove deemed a theory of the firm irrelevant to the analysis of a "market economy."

Shove, a champion of marginal analysis, took the "costs of the industry" as given, and his entire general equilibrium framework could have been challenged on the grounds that the problem for economic analysis is precisely to discover how new cost structures are put in place – that (as Schumpeter and Young had argued) economic analysis should be concerned with the determinants of economic progress rather than (as was Shove's concern) with the optimal allocation of scarce resources. Robertson, however, was not the man to make this argument. He was bent on defending Marshall's concept of the representative firm as "essential to an understanding of increasing returns."[48] As we have seen, the representative firm was the conceptual device that Marshall used to make the transition from dynamic to static analysis. Indeed, as Robertson argued:

Some writers, including Professor Schumpeter, deny altogether the validity of the so-called long-period descending supply-curve. Such a curve, they hold, can only represent a record of historical events, and not – as a true supply-curve should – a series of conditional sentences. This seems to be a counsel of despair, which Marshall considered and rejected.[49]

In a footnote to this statement, Robertson stated, "I regret that in my article in the *Economic Journal*, 1924, I capitulated to [Schumpeter's] view as regards certain kinds of increasing returns."

Although Robertson disavowed any notion that he was interested in how new cost structures were created, he was still willing to consider the competitive *process* that occurred "if we take an increasing return industry which is out of equilibrium, with demand price in excess of supply price, and watch its progress towards equilibrium." To use my terms, he was interested in the process of adaptation but not in the process of innovation. "The main factor in this process," Robertson went on to argue,

[46] Robbins, "The Representative Firm"; Robertson, Sraffa, and Shove, "Increasing Returns," 94–9.
[47] Robertson, Sraffa, and Shove, "Increasing Returns," 100.   [48] Ibid., 84.
[49] Ibid. Robertson referred to Schumpeter, "The Instability of Capitalism," 367.

is the scramble by individual firms, regardless of the actions of their neighbours, to reap the direct advantages of large-scale organisation and plant – advantages which have always been obvious and are in no sense being brought into existence, either through the medium of increased specialisation or in any other way, by the growth in the output of the industry as a whole. The question is whether this process, which admittedly does not always end in the abandonment of competition, can or cannot be played upon by the mind with any success without abandoning the *theory* of competition.[50]

In his reply to Robertson, Sraffa made it abundantly clear that he was not interested in this "competitive process," in "progress toward equilibrium," as Robertson had put it. Sraffa, unlike Pigou but like Robertson, was willing to contemplate the idea that internal economies played an important role in economic reality. But unlike Robertson, Sraffa was not interested in a process of adaptation, much less a process of innovation. What he wanted to know were the conditions, if any, for equilibrium, given the presence of internal economies. He was interested in the analysis of "states," not "processes." Sraffa posed the questions: "If the new firms can turn out a larger output at a lower cost than the old firms, why didn't they come into existence before? Why in the new, and not in the old position of equilibrium?"[51]

Schumpeter could have answered these questions by replying that competition is a historical process in which existing firms or new firms *create* new cost structures. Sraffa's interest in economics, however, does not appear to have been in building a new theory (although after the publication of his book *The Production of Commodities by Means of Commodities*, about thirty years later, some argued that he had done just that).[52] Rather, Sraffa's purpose was simply to confront the Marshallian theory of static equilibrium with the reality of internal economies. "I am trying to find out what are the assumptions implicit in Marshall's theory," Sraffa declared.

If Mr. Robertson regards them as extremely unreal, I sympathise with him. We seem to be agreed that the theory cannot be interpreted in a way which makes it logically self-consistent and, at the same time, reconciles it with the facts it sets out to explain. Mr. Robertson's remedy is to discard mathematics, and he suggests that my remedy is to discard the facts; perhaps I ought to have explained that, in the circumstances, I think it is Marshall's theory that should be discarded.[53]

[50] Robertson, Sraffa, and Shove, "Increasing Returns," 87.   [51] Ibid., 92.
[52] Piero Sraffa, *The Production of Commodities by Means of Commodities* (Cambridge University Press, 1960); see Maurice Dobb, *Theories of Value and Distribution since Adam Smith* (Cambridge University Press, 1973), ch. 9; Ian Steedman, *Marx after Sraffa* (London: Verso, 1977); for a critique, see R. E. Rowthorn, "Neo-Classicism, Neo-Ricardianism, and Neo-Marxism," *New Left Review*, 86 (July–August 1974), 63–87.
[53] Robertson, Sraffa, and Shove, "Increasing Returns," 93.

When Joan Robinson published her *Economics of Imperfect Competition*, she referred to Sraffa's 1926 article "as the fount from which my work flows, for the chief aim of this book is to attempt to carry out his pregnant suggestion that the whole theory of value should be treated in terms of monopoly analysis."[54] She did not, however, discard Marshallian static equilibrium but made the "economics of imperfect competition" consistent with it. In doing so, she acknowledged the influence of Shove, from whom she borrowed her marginal analysis, as well as E. A. G. (Austin) Robinson, whose book *The Structure of Competitive Industry*, first published in 1931, provided her with an analysis of the "optimum size of firms" that she took as the foundation of her treatment of competitive equilibrium.

In *The Structure of Competitive Industry*, Austin Robinson hypothesized that, with increases in the firm's output, internal economies of scale would give way to internal diseconomies of scale because of the "managerial limit."[55] Although he acknowledged that the managerial limit could be altered by building a managerial structure, he still couched his arguments in terms of *optimum* sizes – that is, he assumed that the managerial limit would be reached before the extent of the market constrained the size of the firm.[56] In Chapter 3 I argued that, in a dynamic analysis of enterprise growth, the experience of internal diseconomies can be part of a process for focusing new innovative investments in organization and technology designed to unbend the cost curve, and that the success of the innovative investments could extend the managerial limit and create new "optimum" sizes of the enterprise. Many, if not most, of the particulars of Austin Robinson's analysis in *The Structure of Competitive Industry* are consistent with the dynamic scenarios that I described. But he neither advocated nor conducted a dynamic analysis. The analytical message that he left to economists like Joan Robinson whose concern was the determination of static equilibrium was that the expansion of the firm would be constrained by the managerial limit and resultant increasing costs, and hence could be depicted by the U-shaped cost curve.

The theoretical result was that even the cost structure of the monopolistic firm could result in the equilibrium of the firm. Despite the firm's monopolistic position, it was assumed that it was subject to increasing costs. In the process, however, the neoclassical theorists implicitly assumed something that went far beyond this assumption alone. They assumed that the monopolist maximizes profits subject to the *same cost*

---

[54] Robinson, *The Economics of Imperfect Competition*, xiii.
[55] Robinson, *The Structure of Competitive Industry*, ch. 3.
[56] E. A. G. Robinson, "The Problem of Management and the Size of Firms," *Economic Journal*, 44 (June 1934), 242–57; Nicholas Kaldor, "The Equilibrium of the Firm," *Economic Journal*, 44 (March 1934), 60–76.

structures as would perfect competitors in the same industry.[57] Adopting an analytical perspective that is exclusively static, *The Economics of Imperfect Competition* does not ask how "imperfect competitors" came to be imperfect competitors in the first place. The theory of the firm, based on the assumption that perfect competitors are subject to the same cost structures as imperfect competitors has come to be known as the "monopoly model." According to the monopoly model, compared with the economic outcomes that would occur under competitive conditions, the monopolist restricts output and raises prices. Yet in the dynamic model of the emergence and growth of the dominant firm that I have presented in Chapter 3 – a model in which the path to dominance is to drive down unit costs – the "imperfect competitor" increases output and can potentially decrease price relative to the outcomes that would occur when competitive conditions are less "imperfect." It is the superior ability of firms to lower costs and increase output that results in "imperfect competition."

More dead ends

During the 1930s, two theoretical revisions to the neo-Marshallian analysis – one by Edward Chamberlin in 1933 and the other by Ronald Coase in 1937 – promised to place the theory of the firm on more realistic foundations. In *The Theory of Monopolistic Competition*, Chamberlin challenged the assumption that the firm "can sell as much as [it] pleases at the going price," by arguing that, even in a competitive environment, each firm possesses monopoly elements (or what I have called privileged access to resources) that become embodied in the nature of its product.[58] The "peculiarities of any individual establishment which cannot be duplicated," and hence constitute elements of monopoly, may take the form of patents, trademarks, the personality of the proprietor, or location.[59] Monopoly *elements*, however, do not constitute product-market *monopoly* because of the existence of close product substitutes – hence the notion of monopolistic competition.

In monopolistic competition, the firm is constantly trying to build on its differentiated product to increase its extent of the market. The prime way of doing so is to incur advertising costs, which increase not only short-run fixed costs but also the amount of the firm's product demanded at any given price. Chamberlin viewed his theory of monopolistic competition

[57] A. C. Pigou, *The Economics of Welfare*, 4th ed. (London: Macmillan Press, 1932); Robinson, *The Economics of Imperfect Competition;* for this criticism, see Joseph A. Schumpeter, *Capitalism, Socialism, and Democracy*, 3d ed. (New York: Harper, 1950), 100–1; Edward Chamberlin, *The Theory of Monopolistic Competition*, 7th ed. (Cambridge, Mass.: Harvard University Press, 1956), ch. 9.

[58] Chamberlin, *The Theory of Monopolistic Competition*, 71.   [59] Ibid., 111–13.

as a significant departure from conventional wisdom.[60] In subsequent editions of *The Theory of Monopolistic Competition*, he published bibliographies of books and articles related to his theory – in the 1956 edition there are 1,497 citations – to let the reader know the far-reaching impact of his contribution to economic theory.

In positing (for reasons that are barely mentioned, let alone explored) that firms that compete in the same general product markets will differ from one another to some extent, Chamberlin's theory just added a new wrinkle to the standard neoclassical story. As in Robinson's *Economics of Imperfect Competition*, Chamberlin argued that the existence of monopoly elements means that "the price is inevitably higher and the sale of production inevitably smaller under monopolistic competition than pure competition."[61] For Chamberlin, the perfectly competitive neoclassical economy remained the economic ideal.

Monopoly elements are not therefore seen as foundations on which an enterprise might drive down costs and prices, increase output, and gain sustained competitive advantage. Indeed, even when he introduced advertising into the picture, Chamberlin's main concern was to derive the conditions under which the firm would be in equilibrium. He had no interest in advertising as an investment activity that might enable the monopolistic competitor to attain and sustain competitive advantage. For Chamberlin, when the firm engages in advertising, costs and prices are higher than they would be under perfect competition, while the comparative level of output depends on the extent of the relative shifts of the firm's cost curve and the demand curve for its product. Advertising is simply an additional fixed cost that, by influencing the extent of the market, permits the firm to charge higher prices but not necessarily expand its output.

By the book's end, the realistic assumptions of product differentiation and sales effort have been integrated into the standard neoclassical analysis. "Imperfect competition" is viewed as a restrictive practice that prohibits the economy from achieving the ideal level of efficiency that uninhibited market coordination could supposedly bring. However innovative Chamberlin himself may have considered his theory of monopolistic competition to be, his methodological approach is nothing but conventional. He accepted the perfectly competitive model as the epitome of efficient resource allocation and sought to show how the equilibrium of the firm under conditions of monopolistic competition departs from that ideal.

In a book of essays published in the 1950s, Chamberlin recognized that Schumpeter sought to make the notion of monopolistic competition part

---

[60] Ibid., ch. 1.   [61] Ibid., 68.

of his theory of (as Chamberlin called it) "dynamic, disturbing forces."[62] He also acknowledged the pervasiveness of oligopoly in the economy and argued that insofar as it "interjects indeterminateness into the system it is certainly the job of the scientist to say so." Indeed, citing the contrary view of the noted British economist John Hicks, Chamberlin warned of the need "carefully to avoid the temptation of formulating problems with the *objective* of assuring a determinate answer." After a brief discussion of the Schumpeterian hypothesis, Chamberlin went on to speak of the "world of economists jaded by equilibria."[63]

Yet anyone who took Chamberlin's own approach to economic theory seriously (and, with his 1,497-item bibliography on work related to his theory, he certainly took himself seriously) could not help but be jaded by equilibria. One opportunity for his own escape from equilibrium occurred in *The Theory of Monopolistic Competition* when he considered the implications of the vertical integration of production and distribution – a phenomenon that is, as Alfred Chandler has shown, central to the process of sustained competitive advantage.[64] Chamberlin recognized that "it would be disastrous for [the manufacturer] to create a consumer's demand and trust this to be communicated to him automatically through the intervening middlemen." "The manufacturer must be as attentive to winning [the] favor of [dealers] as to winning that of consumers through direct advertising. Especially must the price of the product be high enough to reward adequately, even generously, all those who control the distributive outlets."[65] He went on to mention the possibility of retailing through exclusive agencies or through the manufacturer's own outlets.[66]

Chamberlin had no conception, however, that these nonmarket relations might be central to a dynamic process that results in innovation and competitive advantage – as indeed they were central in U.S. industrial history. Rather, he took the static view based on the theory of the market economy that such attempts at securing competitive advantage simply add to the costs of running the economic system. As Chamberlin argued:

All of these types of integration erect barriers in the way of competitors securing distribution except by integrating themselves. The result is much duplication of distributive machinery, and higher margins of profit which attract more people into the field and bring still more waste, always subtly concealed by the fact that the average profit per business man or per business unit is held down by the

[62] Edward Chamberlin, *Towards a More General Theory of Value* (New York: Oxford University Press, 1957), 10; see also 219–25.
[63] Chamberlin, *The Theory of Monopolistic Competition*, 61–4.
[64] Alfred D. Chandler, Jr., *The Visible Hand: The Managerial Revolution in American Business* (Cambridge, Mass.: Harvard University Press, 1977).
[65] Chamberlin, *The Theory of Monopolistic Competition*, 120, 122.   [66] Ibid., 122.

increase in numbers. In the last analysis, these costs borne by the consumer must be counted as selling costs – costs of *altering* his demands, rather than as production costs – costs of satisfying them.[67]

Since World War II, Chamberlin's approach has provided theoretical foundations for the applied field of industrial organization. Viewing the market allocation of resources as the ideal, industrial organization economists have sought to analyze the implications for pricing and economic performance of monopolistic elements – or barriers to entry – in the real-world economy.[68] If an explanation of the size of the firm is posited, it is that technological indivisibilities "create" economies of scale. Lacking a theory of business organization as an engine of economic development, the "structure–conduct–performance" approach that came to dominate the field of industrial organization in the postwar decades posited perfect markets and the passive firm as the institutional foundations of ideal economic outcomes.

This adherence to the *ideal* of the market-coordinated economy holds as well for the proponents of the transaction cost approach that, over the past two decades, has arisen to challenge the "monopoly model" inherent in neo-Marshallian theories of imperfect competition. According to the transaction cost approach, the supersession of market coordination is a manifestation not of restrictive practices but of the integration of functions into the firm on a more efficient basis than if the market continued to coordinate the specialized firms that performed these functions.

The seminal article in the development of the transaction cost approach is "The Nature of the Firm," published in 1937 by Ronald Coase. Influenced by the neo-Marshallian debates on the theory of firm, Coase's aim was to construct a theory of the firm that would be not only tractable using prevailing tools of economic analysis – specifically Marshall's notion of substitution at the margin – but also realistic.[69] For Coase, the real world was one in which coordination of economic activities took place by the price mechanism as well as by internal organization. The firm differs from the price mechanism because central planning or "conscious power" –

---

[67] Ibid., 123.

[68] Edward Mason, *Economic Concentration and the Monopoly Problem* (Cambridge, Mass.: Harvard University Press, 1957); Joe Bain, *Industrial Organization*, 2d ed. (New York: Wiley, 1968); George Stigler, "The Division of Labor Is Limited by the Extent of the Market," in *The Organization of Industry* (Homewood, Ill.: Irwin, 1968), 129–41, originally published in *Journal of Political Economy*, 59 (June 1951), 185–93; Richard Caves, *American Industry: Structure, Conduct, Performance*, 5th ed. (Englewood Cliffs, N.J.: Prentice-Hall, 1982).

[69] Ronald Coase, "The Nature of the Firm," in Stigler and Boulding, eds., *Readings in Price Theory*, 331–51, cited at 331–2; originally published in *Economica* n.s., 4 (November 1937), 386–405.

what Oliver Williamson has called the "authority relation"[70] – is used to allocate resources. As Coase argued, "If a workman moves from department Y to department X, he does not go because of a change in relative prices, but because he is ordered to do so."[71]

"But," Coase asked, "in view of the fact that it is usually argued that coordination will be done by the price mechanism, why is such organization necessary?"[72] "Our task is to attempt to discover why a firm emerges at all in a specialized exchange economy."[73] Coase answered by pointing out that there are costs of using the market. Participants have to discover what relative prices are, they have to incur costs of negotiating and concluding contracts for each separate market transaction, they face uncertainty in relying on market relations when planning is required, and they may be able to avoid taxes on market transactions by organizing these transactions internally.[74] The firm arises and then augments its coordinating functions when the cost of organizing these functions internally is less than the cost of using the market.

Coase's main contribution to the theory of the firm was to raise the question of the causes of vertical integration, including the integration of wage labor into the enterprise that distinguishes the firm from a "household" in a capitalist economy. But as a depiction of the "nature of the firm," there are a number of problems with Coase's approach, all of which stem from his basic adherence to the theory of the market economy. He adopted the view that "in the beginning there were markets"[75] and then sought to find a rationale for the firm within a market economy. The history of twentieth-century capitalist development shows, however, that as a dynamic process firms create markets, not vice versa. By definition, Coase's approach casts the firm as a passive player that arises out of "market failure" rather than "organizational success."

Coase had a crude perspective on the internal organization of the firm, characterizing it as simply an authority relation. He had no theory of why or how those whose activities are "integrated" into the firm respond in ways that are consistent with the goals of the firm. He had no conception of the development of organizational capability or of its implications for the development and utilization of productive resources.[76] At the end of

---

[70] Oliver Williamson, *Markets and Hierarchies: Analysis and Antitrust Implications* (New York: Free Press, 1975), ch. 9.
[71] Coase, "The Nature of the Firm," 333; see also 349–50.
[72] Ibid., 333.   [73] Ibid., 335.   [74] Ibid., 336–8.
[75] The quote is from Oliver Williamson, *The Economic Institutions of Capitalism* (New York, Free Press, 1985), 87; see also Chapter 6, this volume.
[76] For a critique of Coase, see William Lazonick, "The Cotton Industry," in Bernard Elbaum and William Lazonick, eds., *The Decline of the British Economy* (Oxford: Clarendon Press, 1986), 18–50, cited at 40–5.

his article, Coase stated that his analysis had "clarified the relationship between initiative or enterprise and management."

Initiative means forecasting and operates through the price mechanism by making new contracts. Management proper merely reacts to price changes, rearranging the factors of production under its control. That the business man normally combines both functions is an obvious result of the marketing costs which were discussed above.[77]

Like the managers of neoclassical theory, Coase's businesspeople merely respond to market forces.

Indeed, Coase announced that, given his definition of the nature of the firm, "the whole of the 'structure of competitive industry' [i.e., horizontal combination and vertical integration] becomes tractable by the ordinary technique of economic analysis."[78] By this, he meant Marshall's principle of substitution at the margin. Like the neo-Marshallian view and its Chamberlinian variant, Coase's approach maintains the firm in equilibrium, as managers are constantly balancing the cost of using the market with the cost of internal organization:

The question always is, will it pay to bring an extra exchange transaction under the organising authority? At the margin, the costs of organising within the firm will be equal to the costs of organising in another firm or to the costs involved in leaving the transaction to be "organised" by the price mechanism. Business men will be constantly experimenting, controlling more or less, and in this way, equilibrium will be maintained. This gives the position of equilibrium for static analysis.[79]

Coase then recognized that "dynamic factors are also of considerable importance, and an investigation of the effect changes have on the cost of organising within the firm and on marketing costs generally will enable one to explain why firms get larger and smaller."[80] But wedded as he was to the "ordinary technique of economic analysis," he introduced no conceptual framework that would enable one to carry out such an investigation. Indeed, he appeared to have only comparative statics in mind, for he claimed that, once "dynamic factors" are taken into account, "we thus have a theory of moving equilibrium."[81] Fixing on the notion of substitution at the margin as the essence of economic analysis, Coase totally ignored Marshall's distinction between internal and external economies. That the analysis of "why firms get larger and smaller" might require historical research into why some firms are able to escape from equilibrium while others remain its prisoners never appears to have entered Coase's mind.

[77] Coase, "The Nature of the Firm," 351.   [78] Ibid., 344.   [79] Ibid., 350.   [80] Ibid.
[81] Ibid.

In typical neoclassical fashion, neither Chamberlin in his analysis of "monopolistic competition" nor Coase in his analysis of the "nature of the firm" offered any analysis of the role of technological change. Theirs are short-run theories that assume that plant and equipment are in place, not long-run theories in which plant and equipment can change. Perhaps on these issues, the neoclassicals would have nothing to say, leaving the field open to dynamic historical analyses.

Not so. In 1931, in a classic article entitled "Cost Curves and Supply Curves," Jacob Viner managed to integrate technological change into the theory of the equilibrium of the firm. Viner defined "internal economies of large-scale production [as] primarily a long-run phenomenon, dependent upon appropriate adjustment of scale of plant to each successive output." As he went on to argue:

Internal economies may be either technological or pecuniary, that is, they may consist either in reductions of the technological coefficients of production or in reductions in the prices paid for the factors as the result of increases in the amounts thereof purchased. Illustrations of technological internal economies would be savings in labor, materials, or equipment requirements per unit of output resulting from improved organization or methods of production made possible by a *larger scale of operations*. Pecuniary internal economies, on the other hand, would consist of advantages in buying such as "quantity discounts" or the ability to hire labor at lower rates, *resulting from an increase in the scale of purchases*.[82]

As a static *description* of internal economies at a point in time, Viner's statement has much to commend it. But as a description of a "long-run phenomenon dependent upon appropriate adjustment of scale of plant to each successive output," the "explanation" of the growth of the firm manifests the market mentality; for in Viner's analysis, it is merely assumed that the firm can achieve a "larger scale of operations" necessary to reap "technological and pecuniary internal economies" because, as in any given short run, the firm can sell all it wants at a given price. For economists, the neoclassical theory of the firm has the "virtue" of containing the firm in equilibrium, and hence yielding a determinate solution to the size and (in Viner's version) growth of the firm. By the same token, the assumptions of market determination of the scale of the firm in the presence of exogenous technology that underlie the neoclassical theory of the firm stand in the way of an analysis of the historical dynamics of the capitalist enterprise.

Neo-Marshallian theory has no conception of the *process* of sustained competitive advantage. Rather, the long run is viewed as a series of dis-

[82] Jacob Viner, "Cost Curves and Supply Curves," in Stigler and Boulding, eds., *Readings in Price Theory*, 198–232, cited at 213, my emphasis; originally published in *Zeitschrift für Nationalökonomie*, 3 (1931–2), 23–46.

crete short runs, each new short run being characterized by the evolution of best-practice technology that permits the introduction of fixed capacity of a *larger scale* that lowers unit costs. There are, however, managerial limits to economies of scale. Analogous to increasing costs in the short run, at some point in the long run the limits of organizational capability make it impossible to achieve lower unit costs on the basis of the larger plant sizes that are becoming technologically possible. With increases in plant size, internal diseconomies of scale eventually outweigh internal economies of scale, thus causing the minimum attainable average costs to rise. In effect, a long-run U-shaped cost curve is generated that represents the locus of the profit-maximizing coordinates of price and output for a series of short runs characterized by successively larger plant sizes.

Even if, at the outset, the industry was perfectly competitive, it is possible (although by no means necessary) that, with the installation of plant sizes of greater and greater "minimum efficient scale," an evolution to imperfect competition might take place. If so, in long-run equilibrium, monopolistic firms would raise prices and restrict output relative to the price and output levels that would have prevailed in the presence of perfect competition.

In the light of the history of capitalist development as well as the historical methodology that I have set forth in this book, it is not too difficult to see what is wrong with the neo-Marshallian theory of the firm in both short-run and long-run equilibria. Let us accept that, in any short run, the industrial capitalists *would like to* squeeze every last bit of potential profit out of their businesses by employing additional variable factors of production up to the point where marginal cost just equals marginal revenue. Marx himself would have had no problem with this proposition.[83] The critical issue is, however, *what the capitalist must do* to achieve this goal. Put another way, what is the nature of managerial activity? In the neoclassical theory of the firm, marketing presents no problems – firms can sell all the output they wish at the going price. Managers just have to observe the relation between the market price of the variable factor and its value added in production and continue to expand output as long as the former is less than the latter. By doing so, they reap internal economies of scale as they spread their fixed costs over more units of output.

In this neoclassical story, the critical assumption about the relation between the firm and its product market is that, in any given short run, it can sell any amount of output that it deems worthwhile to produce. But business history suggests that the key managerial role within the enterprise is to ensure the utilization of its resources once they are in place,

[83] Stephen Marglin, *Growth, Distribution, and Prices* (Cambridge, Mass.: Harvard University Press, 1985), 317–18.

and that this relation between organization and technology is central to the struggle to gain market share. The basic short-run objective of the enterprise is to extend the market for its output. In any given short run, if the enterprise finds that it has been so successful in extending its market that marginal costs have risen above marginal revenues, it can easily restrict its output to eliminate its losses. But the real concern of the business enterprise – and the prime role for management – is to pursue strategies that will secure a large extent of the market.

Once the business enterprise has solved this basic problem – once its extent of the market has enabled it to drive down its unit costs – *then* it can engage in the relatively easy exercise of substituting at the margin. Even then, however, if such an adaptive enterprise is in an innovative industry, it will soon find that its "profit-maximizing" equilibrium between marginal cost and marginal revenue has been rendered irrelevant by innovative competitors.

The enterprise that has superior organizational capability in the short run, moreover, will also tend to be at a competitive advantage in the long run because, when making decisions to invest in new plant and equipment, it will be able to choose a larger "minimum efficient scale" than competitors who cannot expect to achieve the same throughput on the basis of new fixed investments. Hence, contrary to the neo-Marshallian assumption that the monopolist faces the same cost conditions as would the perfect competitor – the critical assumption for the standard neoclassical conclusion that "imperfect competition" results in efficiency losses – a "monopolistic" position may be the outcome of organizational capability that, by developing and utilizing productive resources more effectively than its competitors, has secured to the enterprise the large extent of the market.

Once oligopoly emerges in an industry, one should not assume that sustained competitive advantage will be maintained forever. But the history of twentieth-century capitalist development shows that, contrary to Marshall, oligopoly need not take a century to emerge. Moreover, once achieved in any given product market, oligopoly creates barriers to entry that can be overcome only by the development of even more powerful forms of business organization that can plan and coordinate even more complex specialized divisions of labor.

By assuming that the enterprise can sell as much output as it wants at any given price, therefore, neoclassical economists avoid analyzing the dynamic interaction of organization and technology in the determination of short-run costs as well as the impact of the business organization's ability to reap economies of scale on its decision to invest in new processes and products. Lacking a dynamic theory of enterprise growth, economists fall back on the device of comparative statics – a device that has become their analytical stock-in-trade – to "analyze" the relation between the enterprise and its product market over the long run. Not unlike Böhm-Bawerk's notion of "roundaboutness," which contained no analysis of the potential unit-cost advantages and disadvantages of high fixed costs, the neo-Marshallians simply posited that technological progress entailed increased fixed costs and that the very availability of capital-intensive technology was the *cause* of the growth of the enterprise. Far from viewing organizational capability as the driving force in the growth of the enterprise, they posited it only as a limit on the introduction of capital-intensive technology.

The market mentality

The obsession of economists of the interwar period with constructing theories that would maintain the firm in equilibrium was part and parcel of the quest for a science of economics that would make it unnecessary to justify one's assumptions on the basis of empirical detail. By asserting that the capitalist economy is essentially a market economy, the "nature of the firm" could be analyzed in terms of impersonal market forces, with technology and organizational capability introduced as unexplained phenomena that the economist could (or, lacking an appropriate methodology, had to) take as given. As the quest for determinate solutions based on deductive theory came to define the methodology of economics, theoretical economists tended to lose both interest in and the ability to undertake historical analyses of the dynamics of change.

For example, in his influential book *Value and Capital*, first published in 1939, John Hicks generalized the Marshallian analysis of supply and demand on product markets into a theory of the market economy. "What begins as an analysis of consumer's choice among consumption goods," Hicks argued, "ends as a theory of economic choice in general. We are in sight of a unifying principle for the whole of economics."[84] Later Hicks made it clear that he was going to analyze production in terms of the laws of exchange:

In deciding to treat the general theory of exchange before dealing with production, we are following the example of Walras rather than Marshall . . . A certain parallelism . . . exists between the case of the firm and that of the private person. It is this parallelism which will enable us to put the laws of market conduct of the firm into a similar form to that familiar to us in the [case of the consumer]; and ultimately to extend the theory of exchange set out in the last chapter to take account of production as well.[85]

[84] John Hicks, *Value and Capital* (Oxford: Clarendon Press, 1939), 24.   [85] Ibid., 57, 78.

In order to construct the theory of the market economy, Hicks advocated a separation of theoretical and historical work, although he allowed that the economic historian might learn something from the economic theorist:

> I consider the pure logical analysis of capitalism to be a task in itself, while the survey of economic institutions is best carried on by other methods, such as those of the economic historian (even when the institutions are contemporary institutions). . . . The purely theoretical economist becomes unable to say that any opportunities or dangers he diagnoses are or are not present in the actual world, at any particular date. He is bound to leave that to a separate investigation. But he will at least have helped that other investigator in showing him some things to look out for.[86]

The divorce between theory and reality went even further in the United States than in Britain. Indeed, the elaboration of the theory of the market economy in the United States occurred alongside the rise of big business from about the 1880s. Borrowing the general equilibrium approach of Walras, in which an omniscient auctioneer ensured that all markets would clear and in which business organizations as such had no place, the first U.S. systematizer of the theory of the market economy was J. B. Clark. In 1899, in the midst of the merger movement that was transforming the structure of U.S. business, Clark announced that all markets, whether for labor, land, capital, or final products, operated according to the same principles of supply and demand, and that the combined action of these market forces determined the organization of production.[87] Subsequently, Walrasians such as Frank Knight and Paul Samuelson argued that, for the sake of scientific generality, we should not speak of "factors of production," an expression that might endow inputs with social content. Rather, we should speak more generally of inputs, which differed in terms of their physical contributions to the production process but not in terms of the social relationships that ownership of such inputs entailed.[88]

By distinguishing incalculable uncertainty that forms the basis for entrepreneurial profits from calculable risk, Knight apparently put the business enterprise at the center of his analysis. But as I have already indicated in Chapter 2, Knight had no theory of the management of uncertainty by the firm. He viewed "business organizations [as] but groups of ignorant and frail beings, like the individuals with whom they deal." For Knight, the extent of productive capacities under the control of any individual (or

[86] Ibid., 7.
[87] J. B. Clark, *The Distribution of Wealth* (London: Macmillan Press, 1899), 19–20.
[88] Paul Samuelson, *Foundations of Economic Analysis*, enlarged ed. (Cambridge, Mass.: Harvard University Press, 1983), 84.

organization) were derivative of an "uncertain mixture of conscientious effort, inheritance, pure luck, force and fraud."[89]

Knight's followers, and in particular George Stigler, stressed the role of luck in the evolution of the enterprise. Because luck is not something that is amenable to analysis, the implication was that the issue of the internal growth of the business organization warranted little empirical or theoretical attention.[90] In *Production and Distribution Theories*, published in 1941, Stigler was critical of Alfred Marshall for putting forth a "theory of production that is well-nigh exclusively historical" and then queried whether it was "expedient to attempt to achieve (as Marshall did) a high degree of realism, without first establishing the very much simpler theory of stationary economics." Stigler answered his own question by arguing that Marshall's historical work served only "to diminish his contribution to theoretical economics."[91] As I have also argued in Chapter 2, Stigler's claim that "the portion of the productive process carried on in a particular unit is an accidental consideration" amounted to a rejection of the analytical value of the Marshallian distinction between external and internal economies, while his complaint that Marshall's emphasis on internal economies makes it difficult to explain the "very existence of competition" revealed his aversion to dynamic economic analysis characterized by firms that create value by breaking out of equilibrium.[92] For Stigler, it was imperative to keep the firm in equilibrium.

If Marshall is to take any blame for the sins of his successors, however, it is – contrary to Stigler – for putting *too little emphasis on,* and spending *too little effort exploring,* the nature and extent of internal economies in the comparative development of capitalist economies. The more the theory of the market economy was elaborated as economic science, the further removed were economists from contemplating the process of economic development, and the more difficult it became for them to question the myth of the market economy – namely, that the market coordination of economic activity leads to the highest common good. When, in the 1950s, economists began to try to measure the extent of productivity growth in the U.S. economy in the twentieth century, they were left with a huge unexplained residual that could not be attributed to the growth of inputs and that Moses Abramowitz aptly termed a "measure of our ignorance."[93]

[89] Frank Knight, "Some Fallacies in the Interpretation of Social Cost," in Stigler and Boulding, eds., *Readings in Price Theory*, 160–79, cited at 179; originally published in *Quarterly Journal of Economics*, 38 (August 1924), 582–606.

[90] George Stigler, Introduction to reprint of Frank Knight, *Risk, Uncertainty, and Profit* (Chicago: University of Chicago Press, 1971).

[91] George Stigler, *Production and Distribution Theories* (London: Macmillan Press, 1941), 62.

[92] Ibid., 74, 76.

[93] Moses Abramowitz, "Resource and Output Trends in the United States since 1870,"

Much of the work by economists on productivity growth over the past three decades has involved highly aggregated measurement, with little attention being paid to the development of a theoretical perspective on the sources of productivity growth.[94] As I indicate in Chapter 8, attempts that have been made to understand the microeconomics of productivity growth suggest the need to reject the theory of the market economy. Yet the rejection of the neoclassical view of the world has been something that mainstream economists have been unwilling or, given the pervasiveness of the market mentality, unable to do. I shall demonstrate this point by discussing two prime examples of contributions by well-known economists in recent decades that could have been used to challenge the market mentality. Despite their valid insights into the *organizational* determinants of the development and utilization of human resources, both Gary Becker in his analysis of investment in organization-specific human capital and Harvey Leibenstein in his elaboration of the notion of X-efficiency have continued to profess the market-coordinated ideal.

Behind Becker's notion of specific human capital is the concept of "human capital" introduced into economics by Theodore Schultz in 1961. Schultz argued that "the *quality* of human effort can be improved and its productivity enhanced" by expenditures on education, health, movements to better jobs, and on-the-job training. Schultz went on to assert that "laborers have become capitalists not from a diffusion of the ownership of corporation stocks, as folklore would have it, but from the acquisition of knowledge and skill that have economic value."[95] By viewing investments in human capital as just one type of asset that yields an economic return, thereby transforming individuals as income earners into the equivalent of capitalist firms, Schultz apparently made the concept of human capital consistent with the theory of the market economy.

What Schultz ignored entirely was the growing importance of internal job structures in capitalist economies for both acquiring human capital and reaping the returns on investments in human capital. This omission appeared to be overcome in Gary Becker's well-known treatise on human capital.[96] Becker distinguished two types of on-the-job training: general

American Economic Review, 46 (May 1956), 5–23, cited at 12; see also Robert Solow, "Technical Change and the Aggregate Production Function," *Review of Economics and Statistics,* 39 (August 1957), 312–20.

[94] For a recent example, see Dale W. Jorgenson, "Productivity and Postwar U.S. Economic Growth," *Journal of Economic Perspectives,* 2 (Fall 1988), 23–41; for a balanced assessment, see Richard Nelson, "Research on Productivity Growth and Productivity Differences: Dead Ends and New Departures," *Journal of Economic Literature,* 19 (September 1981), 1029–64.

[95] Theodore Schultz, "Investment in Human Capital," in M. Blaug, ed., *Economics of Education* (Harmondsworth: Penguin Books, 1968), 13–33, cited at 13, 15–16; originally published in *American Economic Review,* 51 (March 1961), 1–17.

[96] Gary Becker, "Investment in On-the-Job Training," in Blaug, ed., *Economics of Educa-*

and specific. General training can be used in many firms, while specific training can be used only in the firm within which it is acquired. Over the past two decades, the distinction between general and specific training has become standard in conventional labor economics.

Becker had little to say about why specific training occurs. He did not, for example, mention the firm-specific nature of productive capabilities created by the ways in which the enterprise collectivizes the specialized division of labor. Nevertheless, if economists accept that specific training is an important phenomenon in the economy – and Becker's emphasis on this type of training gives the impression that he thought it was significant – one might expect that they would be led to explore the impact of organizational coordination as opposed to market coordination on the development and utilization of human resource capabilities, along the lines put forth in this book.

With his Chicago school credentials, nobody would accuse Becker of being anything but an ardent believer in the market economy. But his discussion of the implications of employer–employee relations for investment in specific training flies in the face of the view that a capitalist economy is essentially a market-coordinated economy. Becker emphasized that firms have an interest in investing in training that is specific but leave the acquisition of general training to the workers. He then went on to consider the problems that firms face in making investments in specific training because of the possibility that firms have to pay workers in whom they have invested a premium in order to reduce the probability of labor turnover. The ways in which the costs and benefits of specific training are allocated between employer and employee determine how much investment in specific training takes place. If Becker's emphasis on specific training is to be taken seriously – as I think it should – then the relevance of the theory of the market economy for understanding how investment in firm-specific productive capabilities takes place must be called into question. Becker, however, has not appeared to have comprehended the intellectual challenges that his own insights raised.

A similar failure to confront the myth of the market economy is found in Leibenstein's elaboration of the notion of X-efficiency in the two decades since he introduced the term in an article entitled "Allocative Efficiency vs. 'X-Efficiency'."[97] Leibenstein recognized that orthodox neoclassical theory did not deal with the problem of the extent to which resources are utilized in the production process. Leibenstein called the more complete utilization of resources in production "X-efficiency" and

tion, 183–207; excerpted from Gary Becker, *Human Capital* (New York: Columbia University Press, 1964), 7–29.
[97] Harvey Leibenstein, "Allocative Efficiency vs. 'X-Efficiency'," *American Economic Review*, 56 (June 1966), 392–415.

compared evidence on the apparently large productivity gains achieved by means of X-efficiency with estimates of the apparently small gains achieved by allocative efficiency.

In effect, Leibenstein argued that neoclassical theory lacks a dynamic theory of how individual choices regarding the amount of effort expended change over time. He linked X-efficiency gains to the "degree of competitive pressure, as well as . . . other motivational factors." As he stated in his 1966 contribution:

For a variety of reasons people and organizations normally work neither as hard nor as effectively as they could. In situations where competitive pressure is light, many people will trade the disutility of greater effort, of search, and the control of other peoples' activities for the utility of feeling less pressure and of better interpersonal relations. But in situations where competitive pressures are high, and hence the costs of such trades are also high, they will exchange less of the disutility of effort for the utility of the freedom from pressure, etc.[98]

Leibenstein's 1966 article is rich in ideas concerning the importance of labor effort in the process of economic development. But his numerous subsequent articles and books on the subject of X-efficiency, written over a period of two decades, contain no empirical work to establish the mechanisms underlying productivity increases. He has not documented the assertion that increased competitive pressures will induce greater labor effort, nor has he made any attempt to explore the specific structures of industrial organization and industrial relations that are conducive to X-efficiency gains.

As a result, he has been unable not only to take the X out of X-efficiency, but also to demonstrate the *relation* between X-efficiency and allocative efficiency. In the conclusion of his 1966 article, Leibenstein stated:

Two general types of movements are possible. One is along a production surface towards greater allocative efficiency and the other is from a lower surface to a higher one that involves greater degrees of X-efficiency. The data suggest that in a great many instances the amount to be gained by increasing allocative efficiency is trivial while the amount to be gained by increasing X-efficiency is frequently significant.[99]

This formulation leaves open the question of where the "neoclassical" production surface lies relative to the "X-efficiency" surface at any point in time. Do X-efficiency gains bring us closer to the neoclassical production possibility surface or further beyond it? Put another way, do X-efficiency gains occur as we move closer to the neoclassical ideal of a market-coordinated economy, or do they rely on organizational coordina-

---

[98] Ibid., 413. [99] Ibid.

tion that requires control over market forces, and hence subvert the neoclassical "ideal"?

Leibenstein's subsequent writings strongly suggest that he took the theory of the market economy as the productive ideal. He spoke of *X-inefficiency*, thus giving the impression that a world of *X*-efficiency is well understood. In a book entitled *General X-Efficiency Theory and Economic Development*, he argued:

> When an input is not used effectively, the difference between the actual output and the maximum output attributable to that input is a measure of the degree of *X*-efficiency. In this context *X*-efficiency is to be contrasted with allocative efficiency, the latter being the form of efficiency commonly considered in neoclassical economics.[100]

He then went on to illustrate his argument about *X*-efficiency gains by means of production isoquants. But more than a decade after his original contribution, he failed to clarify the location of the production isoquant associated with the theory of the market economy relative to those associated with *X*-efficiency. In the opening paragraph of a more recent paper, however, he finally admitted his adherence to the neoclassical ideal:

> Standard neoclassical microeconomics, with its emphasis on equilibrium and its employment of a maximization postulate, may be viewed as the study of optimal conditions. It is the study of those circumstances where everything goes right. But it is equally important to understand deviations from optimality. . . . We will present a framework for viewing nonoptimal decision making, [and] suggest briefly how suboptimal decisions contribute to *X*-inefficiency.[101]

I would argue, however, that a market-coordinated economy will tend to give the *lowest* level of labor effort consistent with nonzero profits precisely because, in their choices of employers or even modes of production, workers neither are dependent on a particular employer nor have any expectation that hard work today will yield them greater benefits tomorrow. The behavior modification indicated by Leibenstein as the source of *X*-efficiency – that is, more or better labor effort – occurs when workers as individuals see a particular organization as the guarantor of their future interests, and hence cooperate in the development and utilization of their productive resources within the enterprise.[102] Had Leibenstein

---

[100] Harvey Leibenstein, *General X-Efficiency Theory and Economic Development* (New York: Oxford University Press, 1978), 17.

[101] Harvey Leibenstein, "On Relaxing the Maximization Postulate," *Journal of Behavioral Economics*, 14 (1985), 5–20, cited at 5; reprinted in *The Collected Essays of Harvey Leibenstein*, Kenneth Button, ed. (New York: New York University Press, 1989), vol. 2, 142–57, cited at 142.

[102] Lazonick, *Competitive Advantage on the Shop Floor* (Cambridge, Mass.: Harvard University Press, 1990).

seen fit to come to grips with the *neoclassical* theory of labor effort, he might have been better positioned to see the direction that an alternative theory of labor effort would have to take. In my view, such a theory stresses the role of organizational coordination in attaining greater productivity, and as such confronts rather than accepts the myth of the market economy.

Given their acceptance of the myth of the market economy, it is perhaps not surprising that neither Becker with his focus on specific training nor Leibenstein with his focus on labor effort sought to use their insights to replace the neoclassical theory of the firm with a more cogent alternative. Even when alternative theories of the business organization have been propounded in the post-World War II decades, the myth of the market economy has typically been uncritically accepted, as was the case with Chamberlin and Coase in the 1930s. For example, much of the literature on managerial discretion adopts the view generally held by economists that "market imperfections" result in a misallocation of economic resources. There may be debate over what managers who enjoy a degree of protection from the dictates of the market do with their freedom: maximize sales, growth, salaries, and so on. But there is tacit acceptance that whatever managers do, economic outcomes would be superior if their organizations did not exercise control over market forces.[103] The history of twentieth-century capitalist development shows, on the contrary, that a degree of market power has provided a necessary condition for the managerial coordination of a specialized division of labor and that this managerial coordination is critical to the value-creation process.

Perhaps the most explicit as well as oft-cited attempt to make a new theory of the firm consistent with the theory of the market economy is that of Armen Alchian and Harold Demsetz. Along with Coase's 1937 piece on the nature of the firm, their 1972 article, "Production, Information Costs, and Economic Organization," has become the standard citation for showing why business organizations exist in a capitalist economy. Alchian and Demsetz's misuse of both theory and history demonstrates the methodological dangers of an ideological commitment to the myth of the market economy.

Adopting the neoclassical ideology that all markets operate according to the same principles, Alchian and Demsetz argued at the outset:

It is common to see the firm characterized by the power to settle issues by fiat, by authority, or by disciplinary action superior to that available in the conventional market. This is delusion. The firm does not own all its inputs. It has no power of fiat, no authority, no disciplinary action any different *in the slightest*

---

[103] See, e.g., Kalman Cohen and Richard Cyert, *Theory of the Firm: Resource Allocation in a Market Economy*, 2d ed. (Englewood Cliffs, N.J.: Prentice-Hall, 1975).

degree from ordinary market contracting between any two people. . . . The single consumer can assign his grocer to the task of obtaining whatever the customer can induce the grocer to provide at a price acceptable to both parties. . . . To speak of managing, directing, or assigning workers to various tasks is *a deceptive way* of noting that the employer continually is involved in renegotiation of contracts on terms that must be acceptable to both parties.[104]

Further on they repeated:

The employee can terminate the contract as readily as can the employer, and long-term contracts, therefore, are not an essential attribute of the firm. Nor are "authoritarian," "dictatorial," or "fiat" attributes relevant to the conception of the firm or its efficiency.[105]

Alchian and Demsetz did not identify who it was that had put forth the position they opposed, thus depriving the reader of the possibility of evaluating the alternative arguments. Rather, they relied on a trite and formalistic ideology of the freedom inherent in market relations, an ideology that Marx (for one) attacked ingeniously and, in my view, profoundly over a century ago. The prime conclusion of the Alchian and Demsetz analysis is that "the firm serves as a highly specialized surrogate market."[106] They argued that the impetus for the creation of the firm is the emergence of team methods of production that are implicitly assumed to be more productive than nonteam methods. Team production makes it difficult to "meter" the efforts of individual workers to ensure that the rewards that each receives are commensurate with the value that each adds to output.

Without metering, a "free rider" problem arises, as each individual worker has an incentive to shirk. As posed by Alchian and Demsetz, the problem is not shirking per se but the relation between effort and pay. As in the neoclassical theory of the firm, the role for management is to monitor the relation between marginal revenues and marginal costs. The Alchian and Demsetz wrinkle to the story is that information on the value of the marginal product of labor may be difficult to obtain. Indeed, they posited this difficulty as the reason that hierarchical firms exist in the first place.

The story has it that some workers (apparently the nonshirkers) see it in their interest to hire an agent to monitor team production in order to ensure that each worker is paid only according to his or her productivity. Alchian and Demsetz did not tell us why all team members are not shirkers, nor did they consider power struggles between shirkers and nonshirkers over the issue of hiring a manager to monitor their work. Never-

---

[104] Armen Alchian and Harold Demsetz, "Production, Information Costs, and Economic Organization," *American Economic Review*, 62 (December 1972), 777–95, cited at 777, my emphasis.
[105] Ibid., 783.   [106] Ibid., 793.

theless, by the elimination of payments to shirkers for work they do not perform, a "residual" is created that constitutes the reward of the monitor. If the costs of metering are not too great, everyone – except possibly the shirkers – can be made better off. In any case, if the unit costs of metering outweigh the unit costs of shirking, the "firm" as a whole will be a more efficient competitive unit.

It is plausible that a group of input owners who have chosen to combine their inputs in production hire an independent agent to monitor the relation between their own individual efforts and rewards. What remains implausible, however, is the claim that, in the presence of alienated labor (as manifested by its propensity to shirk), the monitor could do his or her job in a nonauthoritarian manner. Indeed, Alchian and Demsetz themselves argued that "to discipline team members and reduce shirking, the residual claimant must have power to revise the contract terms and incentives of *individual* members without having to terminate or alter every other input's contract."[107] In other words, the monitor can hire and fire individual inputs! What is more, Alchian and Demsetz recognized that in order to have this right the monitor himself cannot be fired. He can, however, decide to sell his *right* to be the monitor that the input owners have bestowed on him.

To give someone the right to hire and fire an input vests that individual with considerable power over that input unless it is costless for the input to move; that is, unless the input is perfectly mobile – hence the insistence of Alchian and Demsetz that long-term contracts (read commitments) are not essential characteristics of the firm. But perfect mobility of *labor* causes problems for the *capitalist* enterprise insofar as production involves a *fixed commitment of the capitalist's resources;* for under conditions of perfect labor mobility, workers are not at all dependent on a particular capitalist, and as a result the level of labor effort is determined solely by the individualistic decisions of workers rather than by managerial coordination. The Alchian and Demsetz model assumes that managers do not use the promise of long-term employment security to ensure that their workers supply the high levels of effort necessary to achieve high throughput and low unit (labor and capital) costs. Nor can the monitor use the threat of firing to increase effort, and hence throughput, because perfect mobility makes the worker immune to the threat.

But even such problems in the utilization of capital resources can be resolved by assuming away fixed costs. In the *neoclassical* firm embedded in a neoclassical economy – clearly the model that Alchian and Demsetz have in mind – fixed capital poses no problem, because a basic assumption of the theory is perfect mobility of *all inputs*. Hence, precommit-

[107] Ibid., 782.

ments of resources by some resource owners (read capitalists) can be assumed away – although by the same token the *capitalist* enterprise is
assumed away as well!

The crux of the problem with the Alchian and Demsetz theory of the
firm as applied to a *capitalist world* is that they implicitly denied that
there is any difference between the position of capital inputs and labor
inputs in the production process. On the one hand, they liked to talk
about input owners (presumably both owners of capital inputs and labor
inputs), while on the other hand, they lapsed into talking about team
members as employees. It may be that, in a *neoclassical* firm, it makes
no difference if capital hires labor or labor hires capital, as Paul Samuelson has argued.[108] But that is just to admit that a neoclassical firm is not a
capitalist enterprise. The owners of capital are not employees of the firm.
If, as shareholders, they can easily sell their ownership rights, they clearly
have the right to quit the firm. But no centralized contractual agent can
claim the right to fire them. Nor is there any monitoring problem involved with shareholders because, beyond having provided the business
enterprise with finance capital, they have no responsibility as individuals
to perform any services for the organization. Finance capital does not shirk!

Nor does industrial capital. The essence of capitalist production (and
any type of production for that matter) is the long-term *commitment* of
resources to produce particular products. Once committed, the owners
of these resources have an interest in attaining high throughput. To achieve
high throughput, they are dependent on the efforts of employees. Workers and managers shirk; capital (whether financial or physical) does not.
To attain not only low unit labor costs but also low unit capital costs, the
owners of capital have an interest in ensuring that the workers they employ do not shirk.

As those who have a long-term interest in the performance of the enterprise, the owners of capital might agree to pass on control over the
utilization of assets and the disposition of profits to managers whose job it
is to prevent shirking. The carrots of promotion and profit sharing or the
stick of losing their managerial positions may give managers the incentive
to extract as much effort as possible from each worker for a given wage.
On a given technology (and, again, assuming alienated labor that is prone
to shirk), there is a conflict of interest between managers and workers
over the relation between effort and pay. The hierarchical – "authoritarian," "dictatorial," "fiat" – relations of the capitalist enterprise are designed to resolve this conflict in favor of the representatives of capital, the
claimants of the residual. Managers of a capitalist enterprise are not content simply to respond to the dictates of the market by equating the wage

---

[108] Paul Samuelson, "Wages and Interest: A Modern Dissection of Marxian Economic Models,"
    American Economic Review, 47 (December 1957), 884–912, cited at 894.

to the value of the marginal product of labor. Once the worker has entered the production process, the forces of the market have, for a time at least, been superseded. The effort–pay relation will depend not only on market relations of exchange but also, and where fixed costs are important, I would argue, more profoundly, on the hierarchical relations of production – on the relative power of managers and workers within the enterprise.[109]

The only way to gain insight into the operation of the capitalist enterprise, and the structure of social relations within it, is to study its historical evolution. Relying instead on their presupposition that the market for labor and the market for food are not "any different in the slightest degree" – and hearing nary a murmur of disagreement from their neoclassical colleagues – Alchian and Demsetz saw little need for historical investigation. Some anecdotal evidence would do. They offered the reader two examples of technological changes that ostensibly resulted in "team production," thereby creating the shirking problem and necessitating the monitoring solution. The two examples were the introduction of power-loom weaving into the factory system and the emergence of the modern assembly line:

When the "putting out" system was used for weaving, inputs were organized largely through market negotiations. With the development of efficient central sources of power, it became economical to perform weaving in proximity to the power source and to engage in team production. The bringing in of weavers surely must have resulted in a reduction in the cost of negotiating (forming) contracts. Yet, what we observe is the beginning of the factory system in which inputs are organized within a firm. Why? The weavers did not simply move to a common source of power that they could tap like an electric line, purchasing power while they used their own equipment. Now team production in the joint use of equipment became more important. The measurement of marginal productivity, which now involved interactions between workers, especially through their joint use of machines, became more difficult though contract negotiating cost was reduced, while managing the *behavior* of inputs became easier because of the increased centralization of activity. The firm as an organization expanded even though the cost of transactions was reduced by the advent of centralized power. The same could be said for assembly lines. Hence the emergence of central power sources expanded the scope of productive activity in which the firm enjoyed a comparative advantage as an organizational form.[110]

The key empirical point in the Alchian and Demsetz story is that with the rise of centralized power sources, "the measurement of marginal productivity . . . became more difficult." It will be of no help to us to examine the empirical sources that Alchian and Demsetz used to support this contention – they did not cite any. (Students take note: A belief in the

---

[109] For a theoretical and empirical elaboration, see Lazonick, *Competitive Advantage*.
[110] Alchian and Demsetz, "Production," 784.

market economy, not empirical verification, is the key to publication in major economics journals.) Nor is it likely that they would have found any support if they had bothered to look. The assertion concerning the monitoring problems created by centralized power sources is simply wrong – as are most of Alchian and Demsetz's other statements in the preceding passage.

In weaving, each worker tended his or her own looms. It was easy to measure individual output, and indeed weavers were paid on a piece-rate system. Even given unit labor costs, however, the investment in a centralized power source as well as other plant and equipment gave capitalists an interest in getting as much effort from workers as possible per unit of time in order to lower unit capital costs. Hence, if anything, the advent of the factory system increased the need for the maintenance of hierarchical control from the point of view of capitalists.[111]

It should also be noted that, contrary to popular belief, the use of centralized power sources did not dictate the emergence of large-scale firms. Quite common in British weaving into the twentieth century was the "room and power" system. Owners of *plant* (factories and steam engines) would rent their facilities to the owners of equipment (looms) so that, say, four different firms would operate off a shared power source (like tapping an electric line to adopt Alchian and Demsetz's ill-used analogy).[112] Ribbon weavers in Coventry even used a steam engine in common to power the looms in their own individual "topshops" above their individual row houses.[113]

Nor did investment in a centralized power source per se necessarily reduce transaction costs relative to the putting-out system. In Britain, the owner of the power source (and factory site) still had to recruit weavers, who, by all accounts, were ill-disposed to enter the factories precisely because of the authoritarian work environment that prevailed within.[114] The widespread availability of labor willing to accept extremely low wages in handloom weaving accounts for the expansion of domestic industry and the putting-out system in the first four decades of the nineteenth century, despite the availability of the steam engine and the powerloom. The wage

---

[111] William Lazonick, "Industrial Relations and Technical Change: The Case of the Self-Acting Mule," *Cambridge Journal of Economics*, 3 (September 1979), 231–62; William Mass, "Technological Change and Industrial Relations: The Diffusion of Automatic Weaving in Britain and the United States" (Ph.D. dissertation, Boston College, 1984).

[112] D. A. Farnie, *The English Cotton Industry and the World Market* (Oxford: Clarendon Press, 1979), ch. 8.

[113] John Prest, *The Industrial Revolution in Coventry* (London: Oxford University Press, 1960); Lazonick, *Competitive Advantage*, ch. 1.

[114] E. P. Thompson, "Time, Work-Discipline, and Industrial Capitalism," *Past and Present*, 38 (December 1967), 56–97; Duncan Bythell, *The Handloom Weavers* (Cambridge University Press, 1969); Maxine Berg, *The Age of Manufacturers, 1700–1820* (London: Fontana, 1985).

premium for work in the factory over work in the home can be counted as a transaction cost necessary to induce weavers to forgo the relatively independent work environment of domestic industry. In the United States, Lowell capitalists had to bear the costs of boardinghouses and a clean work environment in order to attract Yankee farmgirls into the mills. With the coming of the Irish in the late 1840s, such transaction costs were no longer necessary because the Irish were much more dependent on factory work for their sustenance than were the Yankee farmgirls.[115]

If anything, it was the closer supervision of the workers afforded by the factory setting that, *despite* its higher capital costs, ultimately made it more profitable than domestic industry. As Stephen Marglin has argued, a distinct advantage of the factory over the putting-out system in Britain was that within the more centralized setting the rate of throughput and hence the turnover of capital as well as the embezzlement of materials could be more readily controlled by capitalists.[116] *Once* a dependent labor force could be recruited, time discipline could be imposed within the factory setting with positive impacts on unit costs. A recent study of a Lowell, Massachusetts, weaveroom has shown that, relative to Yankees, for whom factory work yielded supplemental income rather than basic family income and who retained their option to exit to the family farm if work conditions and pay were not to their liking, the Irish (and to a lesser extent proletarianized Yankees) experienced an intensification of labor effort while real wages declined.[117] At least in weaving, it is the dependency relation between employer and employed rather than (apparently nonexistent) monitoring problems inherent in team production that, given technology, is the key to understanding productivity growth as well the relation between output and rewards.

Nor does the Alchian and Demsetz tale fare any better when applied to the assembly line, their second "empirical" example. If anything, team production and the problem of assessing individual output was *greater* before the introduction of the assembly line than after. The effect of the assembly line, as introduced, for example, in the automobile industry, and indeed one of its great advantages from the point of view of management, was that it confined individual workers not only to a single repetitive task but also to a single position on the shop floor.[118] If any given worker did not conform to the speed of the line, the supervisor could

[115] Thomas Dublin, *Women at Work: The Transformation of Work and Community at Lowell, Massachusetts, 1826–1860* (New York: Columbia University Press, 1979); William Lazonick and Thomas Brush, "The 'Horndal Effect' in Early U.S. Manufacturing," *Explorations in Economic History*, 22 (January 1985), 53–96.
[116] Stephen A. Marglin, "What Do Bosses Do? The Origins and Functions of Hierarchy in Capitalist Production," *Review of Radical Political Economics*, 6 (Summer 1974), 33–60.
[117] Lazonick and Brush, "The 'Horndal Effect.' "
[118] Lazonick, *Competitive Advantage*, ch. 7.

readily pinpoint the source of the slowdown. Moreover, whereas before the introduction of the assembly line the *team worker* might appropriate "on-the-job leisure" by taking his or her time in moving between tasks or in fetching materials, the *assembly line worker*, confined as he or she was to a particular task and post, had no such opportunity. As Horace Arnold, perhaps the closest outside observer of Henry Ford's introduction of the assembly line in 1914, commented:

[Before the introduction of flow techniques] the straw boss could never nail, with certainty, the man who was shirking, because of the many workpiles and general confusion due to shop floor transportation. As soon as the roll-ways were placed the truckers were called off, the floor was cleared, and all the straw boss had to do to locate the shirk or operation tools in fault, was to glance along the line and see where the roll-way was filled up. As more than once before said in these stories, mechanical transit of work in progress evens up the job, and forces everybody to adopt the pace of the fastest worker in the gang.[119]

Contrary to Alchian and Demsetz, by moving tasks and materials to workers rather than vice versa, the assembly line greatly simplified the problem of supervision and the measurement of individual performance. The successful introduction of the assembly line exemplifies, moreover, the interaction between organization and technology that generated internal economies and gave mass producers such as Ford and General Motors competitive advantage in the first decades of this century.

But in historical perspective, automated production processes represent just the beginning, and by no means the culmination, of the rise of organizational coordination – witness the failure of "Fordism" and the success of "Sloanism" in the 1920s, as the need for product innovation and diversification increased the importance of the planned coordination of a specialized division of labor if the high-fixed-cost investments in automated production processes were to remain economically viable.[120] That neoclassical economists such as Alchian and Demsetz have not understood the rise and consolidation of the American managerial enterprise can be explained by the obvious fact that they have not studied it. That their arguments have received such widespread attention among modern economists, despite the absence of any attempt at empirical verification, can be explained only by economists' deep-seated ideological adherence to the myth of the market economy.

[119] Horace Arnold, "Ford Methods and Ford Shops," *Engineering Magazine*, 48 (December 1914), 349; quoted in Wayne Lewchuk, *American Technology and the British Vehicle Industry* (Cambridge University Press, 1987), 62.
[120] Alfred D. Chandler, Jr., *Strategy and Structure: Chapters in the History of the American Industrial Enterprise* (Cambridge, Mass.: MIT Press, 1962), ch. 3; idem, *Giant Enterprise: Ford, General Motors and the Automobile Industry* (New York: Harcourt, Brace & World, 1964); David A. Hounshell, *From the American System to Mass Production, 1800–1932* (Baltimore, Md.: Johns Hopkins University Press, 1984), chs. 6 and 7; Lazonick, *Competitive Advantage*, ch. 7.

PART III

The "marvels of the market" versus the "visible hand"

6

The innovative business organization and transaction cost theory

History and theory

Far from serving as a "highly specialized surrogate market," as the market mentality leads Alchian and Demsetz to contend,[1] the capitalist enterprise represents attempts by individuals *to gain a measure of control over market forces* through the ownership of productive resources other than their own labor power. As elaborated in Chapter 2, entrepreneurial individuals invest in their own firms so that they will not be dependent on the labor market to earn a living.

The history of capitalist enterprise also shows that in order to ensure the continuity of control over the productive assets in which they have invested, entrepreneurs avoid reliance on impersonal capital markets until they have transformed their firms from new ventures into going concerns – that is, firms that are generating sufficient value to finance *internally* their current operations. It is on the basis of this privileged access to productive and financial resources that the industrial capitalist becomes willing and able to seek funds from the capital market to finance further expansion.[2]

It is also on the basis of control over a going concern that owner-entrepreneurs can monetize the value of their past investments by selling shares to the wealthholding public while handing over de facto control of their enterprises to career managers. As the historical argument in Chapter 1 shows, the successful transformation of a proprietary firm into a managerial enterprise required that managers, and not those who had acquired ownership by virtue of stock-market investments, retain privileged access to the organization's financial resources. During its era of greatest success, the modern managerial corporation has exercised considerable control over market forces rather than being controlled by them.

I have also argued that the most important scholarly work for understanding the evolution of the modern managerial enterprise, particularly

---

[1] Armen Alchian and Harold Demsetz, "Production, Information Costs, and Economic Organization," *American Economic Review*, 62 (December 1972), 177–95, cited at 193.

[2] William Lazonick, "Controlling the Market for Corporate Control: The Historical Significance of Managerial Capitalism," paper presented to the meetings of the Third International Joseph A. Schumpeter Society, Airlie, Va., June 3–5, 1990.

in the U.S. context, is that of Alfred D. Chandler, Jr.[3] Drawing on Chandler's historical analyses as well as other historical research (including my own) that builds on his strategy–structure framework, I have in Chapter 3 sketched out a theory of successful capitalist enterprise – a theory of what I call the innovative organization.

As we have seen in Chapter 4, the notion of the innovative organization is not new to the history of economic thought. Some forty years ago, Joseph Schumpeter made the critical distinction between innovation and adaptation in economic activity.[4] Through its investment activities, the innovative organization plays a role in shaping its economic (and social) environment, while the adaptive organization just tries to minimize costs while taking the environment as given. The innovative organization is central to a process of change.

Chandler's work provides the empirical foundations and historical generalizations necessary for elaborating a dynamic theory of the innovative organization. In *Strategy and Structure*, Chandler argued that when a corporation undertakes an investment strategy to expand into new regional or national markets or to diversify into new product lines, it must also put in place an organizational structure that is capable of administering the more complex set of business activities in which it has invested.[5] Chandler identified the multidivisional structure as the type of organization that, from the 1920s, has permitted multiregional and multiproduct U.S. industrial corporations to administer effectively more diverse sets of investments.

The key features of the multidivisional structure are (1) centralized control by the firm's chief executives over strategic decision making concerning investment in new markets and products and (2) the delegation of operational decision making to divisions to be monitored as profit centers. By separating out strategic decision making from operational responsibilities, the multidivisional structure permits the diversified corporation to retain, and often extend, its competitive advantages, despite the higher fixed-cost commitments and increased administrative complexity inherent in its diversification strategy.

In *The Visible Hand*, published some fifteen years after *Strategy and Structure*, Chandler provided the longer-run historical perspective in which to consider the emergence of multidivisional, multiregional, and multi-

[3] Alfred D. Chandler, Jr., *Strategy and Structure: Chapters in the History of the American Industrial Enterprise* (Cambridge, Mass.: MIT Press, 1962); idem, *The Visible Hand: The Managerial Revolution in American Business* (Cambridge, Mass.: Harvard University Press, 1977); idem, *Scale and Scope: The Dynamics of Industrial Capitalism* (Cambridge, Mass.: Harvard University Press, 1990).
[4] Joseph A. Schumpeter, "The Creative Response in Economic History," *Journal of Economic History*, 7 (November 1947), 149–59.
[5] Chandler, *Strategy and Structure*.

national enterprises.[6] When the historical origins of the business organizations that emerged as dominant in the twentieth century are analyzed, the process of vertical integration holds center stage. The focus on vertical integration is already evident in the earlier book. In the four case studies that form the core of *Strategy and Structure*, Chandler referred to the importance of backward integration as a strategy meant to ensure that an adequate supply of necessary inputs would be available at a reasonable price, as well as of forward integration into marketing as a strategy to ensure that mass production would indeed be transformed into mass sales.[7]

In *The Visible Hand*, Chandler explored more generally how, once the large-scale investments in plant, equipment, and personnel were made, the modern industrial enterprise managed to transform high fixed costs into low unit costs. His basic answer was: "economies of speed" made possible by administrative coordination of the vertically integrated production and distribution processes.[8]

Chandler recognized that his emphasis on administrative coordination was counter to the general thrust of the conventional theory of the firm:

Although administrative coordination has been a basic function in the modernization of the American economy, economists have given it little attention. Many [of them] . . . see the natural response to improved technology and markets as one of increasing specialization in the activities of the enterprise and vertical disintegration in the industries in which these enterprises operate. . . . Besides ignoring the [U.S.] historical experience [after 1850], such a view fails to consider the fact that increasing specialization must, almost by definition, call for more carefully planned coordination if volume output demanded by mass markets is to be achieved. . . . [Moreover,] far more economies result from the careful coordination of flow through the processes of production and distribution than from the increasing size of producing or distributing units in terms of capital facilities or number of workers. Any theory of the firm that defines the enterprise merely as a factory or even a number of factories, and therefore fails to take into account the role of administrative coordination, is far removed from reality.[9]

One economist who, by exploring the causes and consequences of administrative coordination, has sought to bring the theory of the firm closer to reality is Oliver E. Williamson. A product of the "behavioral school" that, beginning in the 1950s, sought to analyze how the managerial enterprise operates in a world of less than perfect market competition, Williamson sought during the 1970s and 1980s to elaborate the transaction cost approach into a relevant theory of the firm. In *Markets and Hierarchies*, published in 1975, Williamson elaborated a preliminary version of the transaction cost framework. In *The Economic Institutions of Capital-*

---

[6] Chandler, *The Visible Hand.*
[7] Chandler, *Strategy and Structure*, 82, 84, 116, 171, 228.
[8] Chandler, *The Visible Hand*, 235–9, 281–3.   [9] Ibid., 489–90.

194   *The "marvels of the market" vs. the "visible hand"*

ism, published a decade later, he collected his most pertinent articles written in the interim and synthesized his approach.[10]

In *The Economic Institutions of Capitalism*, Williamson stressed his intellectual indebtedness to Alfred D. Chandler, Jr.:

In many respects [Chandler's] historical account of the origins, diffusion, nature, and importance of the multidivisional form of organization ran ahead of contemporary economic and organization theory. Chandler clearly established that organization form had important business performance consequences, which neither economics nor organization theory had done (nor, for the most part, even attempted) before. The mistaken notion that economic efficiency was substantially independent of internal organization was no longer tenable after [*Strategy and Structure*] appeared.[11]

Throughout *The Economic Institutions of Capitalism*, Williamson cited Chandler's research in support of the transaction cost approach, drawing particularly on *The Visible Hand*. Of the four hundred or so names in the Author Index, Williamson's references to Chandler are exceeded only by those to himself. Most of Williamson's citations of Chandler are in two chapters, "Vertical Integration: Some Evidence" and "The Modern Corporation."[12] The material cited runs from Chandler's analysis of the rise of administrative coordination on U.S. railroads from the 1840s to the 1880s[13] to his analysis of the integration of production and distribution in U.S. manufacturing from the 1880s to the 1920s[14] and the emergence of the multidivisional structure in the 1920s.[15]

In *The Visible Hand*, Williamson received only passing mention.[16] At a postpublication conference on *The Visible Hand*, however, Williamson contributed a paper.[17] Since that time, Chandler has taken an interest in the implications of the transaction cost approach for his own historical arguments.[18] Chandler appears to have been suitably impressed, for on the dust jacket of *The Economic Institutions of Capitalism*, he provided a glowing (and rare) endorsement: "For a historian concerned with the evo-

---

[10] Oliver E. Williamson, *Markets and Hierarchies: Analysis and Antitrust Implications* (New York: Free Press, 1975); idem, *The Economic Institutions of Capitalism* (New York: Free Press, 1985).
[11] Williamson, *The Economic Institutions of Capitalism*, 11, 280; see also idem, "Microanalytic Business History," *Business and Economic History*, 2d ser., 11 (1982), 106–15.
[12] Williamson, *The Economic Institutions of Capitalism*, chs. 5 and 11.
[13] Chandler, *The Visible Hand*, pt. 2.
[14] Ibid., pt. 4.   [15] Chandler, *Strategy and Structure*; idem, *The Visible Hand*, pt. 5.
[16] See Chandler, *The Visible Hand*, 5, 515.
[17] Oliver Williamson, "Emergence of the Visible Hand: Implications for Industrial Organization," in Alfred D. Chandler, Jr., and Herman Daems, eds., *Managerial Hierarchies* (Cambridge, Mass.: Harvard University Press, 1980), 180–202.
[18] See Alfred D. Chandler, Jr., "Evolution of the Large Industrial Corporation: An Evaluation of the Transaction Cost Approach," *Business and Economic History*, 2d ser., 11 (1982), 116–34.

lution of modern institutions this is the most valuable book written by an economist since those of Joseph Schumpeter."

Because both Chandler and Williamson focus on the relations between organizations and markets in the United States and because each obviously has respect for the work of the other, it is tempting to conclude that the two approaches – the one historical and the other theoretical, the one stressing strategy and structure, the other transaction costs – yield the same substantive arguments concerning the causes and consequences of the modern corporation. I shall argue, however, that the theory of the business organization that can be built on Chandler's strategy–structure framework and that is consistent with his historical findings provides a very different perspective on the role of the business enterprise in the operation and performance of the economy than does Williamson's transaction cost framework. I shall argue, moreover, that the theory of the innovative organization that takes Chandler's historical research and strategy–structure framework as points of departure is superior to the theory of the business organization inherent in Williamson's transaction cost approach, in the sense that the valid insights of the transaction cost approach can be integrated into the theory of the innovative organization, but not vice versa.

The primary problem with the transaction cost approach is its ahistorical and static methodology. Manifesting the most serious shortcoming of a modern training in conventional economics, Williamson's work displays no conception of the dynamics of capitalist development. By imposing a transaction cost interpretation on Chandler's historical material, Williamson failed to comprehend the nature of the dynamic interaction between organization and technology that is central to the strategy–structure approach. The transaction cost framework that unifies Williamson's work contains no theory of the role of the business enterprise in generating technological change, productivity growth, and economic development. In *The Economic Institutions of Capitalism*, one finds no notion of the creation of value as a general phenomenon nor of the role of the business organization as a value-creating institution. If Williamson's book is about the "economic institutions of capitalism," the institutions that he has analyzed seem to be a breed apart from the business organizations whose activities Chandler has documented.

It is undoubtedly because Williamson has not followed other economists in defining the firm as a factory but rather places administrative coordination – or "hierarchy" – at the center of his analysis that Chandler has found *The Economic Institutions of Capitalism* to be such an important contribution to the economics literature. Yet in *The Economic Institutions of Capitalism*, it appears that Williamson has rejected some of Chandler's main conclusions while failing to grasp some of the historian's foremost insights. After citing *The Visible Hand* no less than twenty-two times in the chapter on vertical integration,[19] Williamson made a rather astonishing assertion:

Suffice it to observe here that strategic behavior mainly has relevance in dominant firm or tightly oligopolistic industries. Since most of the organizational change reported [here] occurred in nondominant firm industries, appeal to strategic considerations is obviously of limited assistance in explaining the reorganization of American industry over the past 150 years.[20]

So much for Chandler's emphasis on the emergence of dominant business organizations as the central institutional feature of twentieth-century U.S. capitalism. And so much for the business strategies that, in Chandler's framework, create the need to build organizational structures. As for organizational structures themselves, Williamson quoted Chandler's central argument in *The Visible Hand* that "far more economies result from the careful coordination of flow through the processes of production and distribution, than from increasing the size of producing or distributing units in terms of capital facilities or numbers of workers."[21] Yet in the very next sentence, Williamson asserted, "Aside, however, from the Research Center in Entrepreneurial History at Harvard, which was established in 1948 and closed its doors a decade later, there has not been a concerted effort to work through and establish the importance of organizational innovation."[22] If Chandler's own work on organizational innovation over the past thirty years, as well as all the other historical and contemporary research that it has inspired,[23] does not add up to a "concerted effort," the scholars among us might well be advised to abandon the libraries, put our lectures on videotape, and take early retirements!

Failing as he did to recognize the intellectual achievement embodied in the strategy–structure framework, it is not surprising that Williamson missed the essence of Chandler's analysis of the impact of organizational structure on economic outcomes. Arguing that none of a number of "alternative theories of organizational structure/innovation . . . makes more than piecemeal contribution to the understanding of the reshaping of the American economy," Williamson identified Chandler with a "technological imperatives" perspective that attempts to explain vertical integration (and specifically forward integration from production into distribution) in terms of "economies of speed."[24]

It was Williamson's contention that "economies of speed remain un-

[19] Williamson, *The Economic Institutions of Capitalism*, ch. 5.   [20] Ibid., 128.
[21] Ibid., 404.   [22] Ibid.
[23] See the references in Richard Caves, "Industrial Organization, Corporate Strategy and Structure," *Journal of Economic Literature*, 18 (March 1980), 64–92; Thomas K. McCraw, ed., *The Essential Alfred Chandler* (Boston: Harvard Business School Press, 1988).
[24] Williamson, *The Economic Institutions of Capitalism*, 125–6, 128.

specified" in Chandler's work – a statement that, to me at least, seems unfathomable given the attention that Chandler devoted to explicating the process in *The Visible Hand*. If, as Williamson argued, the appearance of Chandler's *Strategy and Structure* made it untenable to maintain that the internal organization of the enterprise had no substantial impact on economic performance,[25] Williamson's treatment of *The Visible Hand* reveals a very different view than Chandler's on the relation between economic institutions and economic outcomes.

Chandler's work provides foundations for a theory of the innovative organization – an enterprise that, by generating high-quality products at low unit costs, gains sustained competitive advantage. In keeping with the preconceptions of neoclassical economic theory in which the firm plays a passive and powerless role in the determination of economic organization and outcomes, Williamson's transaction cost approach puts forth a theory of the *adaptive* organization and ignores the role of the business enterprise in the innovation process. As we shall see, the analysis of the adaptive enterprise is explicit in Williamson's focus on "adaptive, sequential decision-making" in the face of "disturbances" as the essence of managerial activity. The passive role of the enterprise in the determination of strategy and structure is also implicit in Williamson's statement that "in the beginning there were markets." "Only as market-mediated contracts break down," he argued, "are the transactions in question removed from markets and organized internally."[26]

At one point, Williamson appeared to concede that the "transactions in question" may not encompass the process of innovation:

The introduction of innovation plainly complicates the earlier-described assignment of transactions to markets and hierarchies based entirely on an examination of their asset specificity qualities. Indeed, the study of economic organization in a regime of rapid innovation poses much more difficult issues than those addressed here.[27]

Yet Chandler's historical analysis – from which Williamson supposedly drew considerable historical evidence if not conceptual insight – covers a period of rapid technological and organizational innovation in which, by the 1920s, the most innovative organizations left behind existing competitors and created immense barriers to entry for potential competitors.

To comprehend the differences between Chandler and Williamson, then, is to go some way toward understanding the conceptual and practical difference between an innovative organization that contributes to the process of economic development and an adaptive organization that merely tries to minimize its costs or maximize its profit on the basis of existing

[25] Ibid., 11.   [26] Ibid., 87.   [27] Ibid., 143.

productive resources. A comparison of the two approaches to analyzing the same economic institutions of capitalism by two scholars who have paid attention to one another's work also provides us with unique insights into the different conclusions that result from two very different methodologies – the one dynamic and the other static. In the next section of this chapter, I outline my theory of the innovative organization. I then extract the essence of Williamson's arguments in *The Economic Institutions of Capitalism* to outline the theory of business organization inherent in the transaction cost approach. Comparing and contrasting the two theories, I make the case that Williamson's transaction cost theory limits the business organization to adaptation to the exclusion of innovation and that, indeed, this limitation is inherent in Williamson's adherence to the myth of the market economy. In Chapter 7, I shall use this comparative theoretical analysis to show not only how, but also why, Williamson's theory of the adaptive organization led him to misinterpret Chandler's historical material.

The theory of the innovative organization

In Chapter 3, I have already laid out my basic theory of the innovative organization – a theory in which the organizational capability of the business enterprise influences the extent to which the enterprise can transform the high fixed costs of its innovative investment strategy into high-quality products at low unit costs. Here, at the risk of a small amount of repetition, I shall supplement that discussion by focusing on the nature of fixed costs, the different sources of uncertainty the innovative organization faces, and the relation between organizational capability and technological change.

Through its investment activities, a business organization commits financial resources to specific processes to make particular products with the expectation of reaping financial returns. Once they are committed, the productive assets of the organization represent *fixed* costs that must then be recouped by the production and sale of output. If, through the sale of sufficient output, investments could generate expected financial returns *instantaneously,* fixed costs would not represent an economic problem to the organization. But then, we would probably not call the "assets" underlying these costs "investments." Indeed, we might not even deem it appropriate to call these costs "fixed" or the entity that incurs them a "firm." The *problem* of fixed costs occurs because the production and sale of the enterprise's output occur neither instantaneously nor with certainty. The basic economic problem that confronts the capitalist enterprise is to transform fixed costs into revenue-generating products to realize financial returns. An analysis of how and with what success the business organization manages this transformation is the key to understanding technological change, value creation, and economic growth.

In making its investment decisions, the organization can choose to be either innovative or adaptive. The two distinct types of investment strategy have different implications for the role of the business organization in the generation of technological change and the creation of value. If the organization adopts an adaptive strategy, it need only combine human and physical resources according to well-known technical specifications in order to produce a saleable product at a competitive cost. When the organization chooses an adaptive strategy, it may increase the amount of human and physical resources applied to productive activity – it may add to its capital stock. But unlike the innovative organization, the adaptive organization does not enhance the productive capabilities of these resources. In contrast, if the organization chooses to adopt an innovative investment strategy, it *must* develop its productive resources in order to produce a superior product at competitive cost (product innovation), a saleable product at lower cost (process innovation), or both.

In choosing an investment strategy, the central economic problem facing the decision maker is the *uncertainty* of realizing a financial return. When undertaking productive investment, incalculable economic uncertainty cannot be avoided precisely because technology and the structure of the economy are constantly in the process of evolution. But the presence of economic uncertainty – the possibility that a particular investment will fail – should not be viewed as simply a costly economic problem; for if innovation is wanted, it is paramount that, far from seeking to *avoid* uncertainty, business organizations seek to *confront* it. The innovative strategy represents an attempt to confront economic uncertainty, the adaptive strategy an attempt to avoid it.

In making investments, there are two qualitatively different types of economic uncertainty that an organization can face: *productive uncertainty* and *competitive uncertainty*.[28] The one type of uncertainty pertains to the internal operations of the organization, the other to the organization's relation to its external economic environment.

Productive uncertainty is inherent in the unknown qualities of the product innovations and unknown productivity-enhancing impacts of the process innovations that the investment strategy is expected to yield. Once the processes and products have been successfully developed, moreover, the organization must elicit sufficient effort from its employees in order to achieve a high rate of utilization of its productive resources. Even when the skills, or productive *capabilities*, of the human resources that it em-

---

[28] Christopher Freeman, *The Economics of Industrial Innovation*, 2d ed. (Cambridge, Mass.: MIT Press, 1982), 148–50.

ploys are known, the organization cannot be certain about the extent to which employees will in fact exert productive *effort*, and hence put these capabilities to the service of the enterprise.[29] At issue is not just the productivity of labor, but also, insofar as the productivity of physical resources depends on human effort, the productivity of capital.

Competitive uncertainty is inherent in the inability of the organization to know for certain the availability of factor supplies and the extent of product demands over the period during which it is trying to transform fixed costs into financial returns. Macroeconomic demand fluctuations may intensify interindustry as well as intraindustry competition for a more limited extent of the market. Within its own industry, moreover, even for a given level of product demand, the organization cannot know for certain what innovative strategies and competitive adaptations its existing competitors will pursue and what new competitors might come on the scene. When incurring fixed costs, therefore, the organization cannot know the extent of the market that it will attain and the unit costs that it will be able to achieve.

The more innovative the strategy that the organization chooses – that is, the more the enterprise must develop its productive resources to yield process and product innovations – the more productive uncertainty it faces. Unlike competitive uncertainty, productive uncertainty is not determined by the external environment but is a matter of *strategic choice*. And in contrast to the innovative organization, the adaptive organization chooses to avoid productive uncertainty by investing only in those process and product technologies for which the required productive capabilities are known.

The adaptive organization can also try to avoid competitive uncertainty by shunning fixed costs, relying instead on variable costs – rented plant and equipment, spot versus bulk materials purchases, wage versus salaried labor, consultants and agents versus permanent staff and facilities. The adaptive organization seeks to minimize competitive uncertainty by minimizing its fixed commitments. If the organization could produce solely on the basis of variable costs, there would be no productive or competitive uncertainty for the simple reason that the enterprise would not be making any investments from which it might expect a return.

But insofar as fixed costs are unavoidable – and in the real world even those items that we generally call "variable" costs do not generate revenues instantaneously – the adaptive organization cannot completely avoid economic uncertainty. Although (by definition) the adaptive organization does not have to *develop* the productive capabilities of its resources, it

---

[29] See William Lazonick, *Competitive Advantage on the Shop Floor* (Cambridge, Mass.: Harvard University Press, 1990).

still must *utilize* them, and hence faces the productive uncertainty of how much effort it will be able to elicit from its employees. It also faces competitive uncertainty because of the ease with which other organizations can produce the same saleable products at the same competitive costs.

In an industry made up of adaptive organizations, the unpredictable anarchy of the market – the uncoordinated nature of the demand for factors of production and the supply of products in an industry characterized by easy entry and relatively small enterprises – may lead the investing enterprise (and indeed each competing enterprise) to experience not only lower product prices than had prevailed when it made its investments but also higher unit variable costs *and* higher unit fixed costs. The lower product prices may result from the well-known phenomenon of *cutthroat competition:* uncontrolled price cutting in the face of overproduction. Higher unit variable costs may result because of "excess" demand for factors of production (i.e., in excess of what the enterprise had expected when it made its investments). Such excess demand subjects the organization not only to higher factor prices but also, in the case of wage labor, to a workforce whose supply of effort, and hence productivity, is more difficult for the organization to control. Higher unit fixed costs may result because of the organization's inability to utilize its productive resources as it expected and attain its anticipated market share.

The adaptive organization also faces the competitive uncertainty that an innovative organization might enter its industry and succeed in producing a superior product at a lower cost. But in the competition between adaptive and innovative organizations, competitive uncertainty cuts both ways. The presence of adaptive organizations in an industry also creates competitive uncertainty for the innovative organization because its investment strategy invariably entails higher fixed costs than the adaptive strategy. An innovative strategy requires that the organization invest in, and develop in a simultaneous or coordinated fashion, a number of vertically related (even if technologically separable) productive activities. The innovative organization, that is, must be more vertically integrated than the adaptive organization.

It is not only vertically related investments in plant and equipment that increase the fixed costs of the innovative organization. To generate new technologies, the innovative organization must invest in specialized research and development facilities. To determine the needs of potential buyers, the innovative organization must also invest in specialized marketing facilities. And to plan and coordinate development, production, and marketing activities, the innovative organization must make further fixed investments in a managerial bureaucracy.

At low levels of capacity utilization, the innovative organization, with its high fixed costs, incurs higher unit costs than does the adaptive organization. If it can achieve high levels of capacity utilization, the innovative organization may be able to outcompete its less capital-intensive rivals. But the relatively low fixed costs of adaptive organizations may impede the innovative organization from actually gaining sufficient market share to achieve lower unit costs. The innovative organization, moreover, faces the distinct possibility that, in response to its innovative strategy, adaptive organizations will compete by accepting lower profits, running down their capital stock, using inferior materials, and extracting wage concessions and greater effort from their workers. The possibility of such adaptive responses increases the competitive uncertainty facing the innovative organization, laden as it is with fixed costs. Hence, when an organization chooses an innovative strategy, it confronts productive uncertainty and in so doing may also expose itself to competitive uncertainty. But by its very choice of investment strategy, the innovative organization also undertakes to develop the productive potential for shaping and controlling – that is, managing – its economic environment in ways designed to ensure the economic success of its innovative strategy. To manage its economic environment, the innovative organization must complement its investment strategy with an appropriate organizational structure. Indeed, to pursue an innovative strategy without building an appropriate organizational structure is to confront economic uncertainty without creating any means to overcome it.

An appropriate organizational structure enables the organization to manage two distinct stages of the value-creation process: the *development* stage and the *utilization* stage. The passage through these stages to financial success does not happen just because investments in productive resources have been made. Rather, success comes from planning and coordinating the development and utilization of the organization's investments. Some of the productive resources in which the organization invests are plant and facilities, but others are personnel.

Investment in a managerial bureaucracy is critical because it enables the organization to develop the enterprise-specific organizational capability that is in turn required to plan and coordinate its physical resources and technical personnel. By transforming previously unknown technologies into process and product innovations that are ready to be utilized, organizational capability overcomes productive uncertainty. On the basis of the organizational capability that it has developed, the organization continues to overcome productive uncertainty by utilizing its productive capacity sufficiently to achieve low unit fixed costs while controlling the rise of its unit variable costs.

But why does the innovative organization need organizational capability to ensure the success of its investment strategy? To answer this question we must pose yet another: Why does technological change enable the organization to produce superior products at lower costs?

Technological change overcomes the productive limitations that the skill and effort of human beings had previously placed on the transformation of inputs into outputs. By displacing the human skills and saving on the human effort required by a previous technology, technological change enables the organization to produce a superior product at a lower cost. In more general terms, it enables the organization to raise physical productivity. But to achieve this productive benefit, technological change requires the expenditure of productive resources on the development of new types of skills as well as the utilization of the efforts of those who come to possess those skills.

The more technologically complex the innovation, the greater the need for innovative skills and the *more extensive the specialized division of labor required to develop and utilize these skills.* The organization must not only develop these specialized skills so that they can contribute to the innovation, but also coordinate them so that they constitute a *collective* productive power. Organizational capability permits the enterprise to plan and coordinate the development of these innovative skills, integrating them into an enterprise-specific collective force. As far as the innovation process is concerned, therefore, organizational capability permits the planned coordination of the horizontal and vertical division of labor required to generate an innovation.

But even when an innovation has been generated, the organization must attain a large market share in order to transform its high fixed costs into low unit costs. To do so, it must invest in production facilities with sufficient capacity to supply a large market share, thus further increasing its fixed costs. To overcome the potential competitive disadvantage inherent in its high fixed costs, the innovative organization must use its organizational capability to plan and coordinate the utilization of the productive resources at its disposal. In particular, the organization must speed the flow of work through its vertically related production processes, so that high fixed costs can be spread out over the largest possible volume of output in the shortest possible period of time – hence Chandler's focus on throughput and economies of speed.

It is the effort-saving nature of technological change that creates the *potential* for achieving high throughput on the basis of given production facilities: the speed of the work flow can increase without *necessarily* requiring more effort from workers. But it is the organizational capability of the enterprise in coordinating the efforts of those involved in the organization's vertically related processes that transforms the potential into actuality.

The need to increase throughput to achieve low unit costs exposes the innovative organization to new sources of competitive uncertainty. The supply of inputs and the sale of outputs cannot be left to the market. As the volume of throughput expands, pressures build for the organization to integrate backward into material supplies to ensure the high-volume flow of inputs of requisite quality necessary to maintain the high through-put, which is in turn necessary to supply a large enough extent of the market to transform high fixed costs into low unit costs. Similarly, pressures build for forward integration into mass-distribution facilities in order to ensure the aggressive marketing of the organization's output required to transform mass production into mass sales.

As a result of such backward and forward integration, dictated in this case by the need to achieve high levels of resource utilization rather than superior resource development, the organization transforms what were previously variable costs into fixed costs. As a result as well, the organization transforms competitive uncertainty, inherent in its reliance on the market (the essence of variable costs), into productive uncertainty, inherent in its reliance on the organization (the essence of fixed costs).

By virtue of its strategy of forward and backward integration, however, the innovative organization has not simply replaced one type of uncertainty by another. Rather, by converting variable costs into fixed costs, the organization transforms uncertainty into a form over which, *by relying on its own organizational capability, it can exercise more control.* All the more pressure is put on organizational capability to plan and coordinate the internal division of labor in order to transform high fixed costs into low unit costs.

Once the innovative organization has captured sufficient market share to ensure the success of its investment strategy, organizational capability provides the institutional foundations for entry into new product markets. The organization's investments in systematic research and development facilities enable it to generate product innovations that create opportunities for spreading out some of its existing fixed costs over a number of technologically related product lines. As the organization undertakes these new investment strategies, it expands the scope, as distinct from the scale, of its innovative endeavors.[30] But economies of scale remain critical. To transform these new strategies into competitive advantage, the organization must, as in the case of its previous investments, develop and utilize the resources that it commits to each of its new product lines in ways that generate superior products at low costs.

Innovative organizations that choose to make investments in those technologically complex industries characterized by high levels of produc-

---

[30] See Chandler, *Scale and Scope*.

tive uncertainty will face a greater chance of failure but also the opportunity of gaining significant market power if the innovative strategy succeeds. Once the organization has gained a large extent of the relevant market, moreover, it can use its dominant position to enlarge its market share and sustain its competitive advantage – hence the phenomenon of oligopolistic market power. Generally speaking, the greater the innovative effort undertaken, the greater the market share the organization will have to secure to achieve economic success and the greater the possibility for those organizations that move first in investing in innovation to secure an oligopolistic position.

Even when the *technical* characteristics of the once-new processes and products become well known, later movers still face a degree of productive uncertainty because of the need to develop enterprise-specific organizational capability in order to implement the technological change. Even if the market can supply the organization with individual personnel with the appropriate skills and attitudes, it takes time and the commitment of resources to integrate the activities of these individuals into the organized force that constitutes the essence of organizational capability. Meanwhile, in what Schumpeter called the process of creative destruction,[31] the incumbent oligopolist may use its already developed organizational capability to undertake new innovative investments that make its own past technological successes obsolete, thus increasing the competitive uncertainty facing later movers. Furthermore, later movers face competitive uncertainty because the incumbent organizations already possess the large market shares, and they do not. To fight off the challenges of later movers, the incumbent oligopolist may use its market power to pursue an adaptive strategy of predatory pricing on the basis of its existing technological capability.

In other words, with the emergence of oligopoly, it becomes increasingly difficult for later movers to choose a strategy that avoids fixed costs. If they want to challenge the power of the first movers, they must confront uncertainty by making innovative investments in technology rather than try to adapt by imitating those strategies that have made the first movers successful in the past. Whatever the entrepreneurial drive, productive talent, and financial resources available for employment in a particular economic environment, the existence of oligopoly may render the economic uncertainty facing later movers so great that attempts to enter the industry are simply not made.

Innovative success can therefore free the oligopolistic organization not only from productive uncertainty but also from competitive uncertainty. Precisely because it has overcome uncertainty by the development and

---

[31] Schumpeter, "The Creative Response in Economic History."

utilization of its productive resources, the oligopolistic enterprise finds itself in a position to become a truly adaptive organization. It possesses considerable assets, but because it is realizing a steady flow of revenues on the basis of these past investments, it no longer faces the economic problem of fixed costs. By living off its capital, the oligopolist may be able to remain profitable for years on end, even if it makes no new investments of any kind; all the more so if it adopts a strategy of disinvestment that enables it to reap financial returns with no allowance for replacing its depleted productive resources. Rather than confront uncertainty by undertaking new innovative strategies, the oligopolistic organization may choose a comfortable existence that avoids uncertainty. The very success of the organization in overcoming productive and competitive uncertainty may create the market conditions that encourage it to turn from innovation to adaptation.

Transaction cost theory

Oliver Williamson dedicated *The Economic Institutions of Capitalism* to four "teachers": Kenneth Arrow, Alfred Chandler, Ronald Coase, and Herbert Simon. Arrow, Coase, and Simon differ from Chandler not only because they are economists, but also because their impacts on the social sciences have been entirely in the realm of theory. It is fair to say as well that, as theoretical economists, none of the three has made any attempt to develop a theory of the innovative organization. Although Williamson claims to have been influenced by Chandler's history, his conceptual framework has been shaped far more by the ideas of Coase, Arrow, and Simon.

For Williamson, Coase's critical contribution was to pose the "issue of economic organization in comparative institutional terms." In outlining the Coasian influence and shortcomings, Williamson effectively summarized the analytical task that he himself took up in *The Economic Institutions of Capitalism*:

Whereas markets were ordinarily regarded as the principal means by which coordination is realized, Coase insisted that firms often supplanted markets in performing these very same functions. Rather than regard the boundaries of firms as technologically determined, Coase proposed that firms and markets be considered alternative means of economic organization. Whether transactions were organized within a firm (hierarchically) or between autonomous firms (across a market) was thus a decision variable. Which mode was adopted depended on the transaction costs that attended each.[32]

---

[32] Williamson, *The Economic Institutions of Capitalism*, 3–4.

In this passage Williamson located "transactions," and hence "transaction costs," not only in market exchange (as Coase implied) but also within the firm. At the outset of his book he argued that a "transaction occurs when a good or service is transferred across a technologically separable interface" and that "the economic content of intraorganizational and price-mediated transactions are often similar." He went on to contend that "a common framework that applies to both is therefore indicated."[33]

In Williamson's view, the main shortcoming of Coase's seminal work was that he failed to "operationalize transaction costs." "Unless the factors responsible for transaction cost differences could be identified," said Williamson, "the reasons for organizing some transactions one way and other transactions another would necessarily remain obscure."[34] Elaborating on a framework that he had already put forward in *Markets and Hierarchies*, Williamson used the concepts of *opportunism*, derived from the work of Arrow, and *bounded rationality*, derived from the work of Simon, to operationalize transaction costs.

As a leading proponent of Walrasian general equilibrium theory, Arrow, like Coase, adopted the perspective that, but for market failures, the price mechanism would be the most efficient way to coordinate a capitalist economy. The critical institutional question is, therefore, why firms come into existence and grow. Like Coase, Arrow linked market failure to transaction costs, arguing that "market failure is not absolute; it is better to consider a broader category, that of transaction costs, which in general impede and in particular cases block the formation of markets."[35] In particular, Arrow focused on the problem of information as a reason for market failure. In market exchange, the market price does not capture all of the information about the good or service that is relevant to the parties to the transaction. Where the integrity of the parties is suspect, therefore, transaction costs will arise and market coordination of economic activity will break down.

For Williamson, the source of such transaction costs is "opportunism," a behavioral attribute of "human nature as we know it"[36] that can also be described as a "condition of self-interest seeking with guile."[37] "Opportunism," said Williamson, "refers to the incomplete or distorted disclosure of information, especially to calculated efforts to mislead, distort, disguise, obfuscate, or otherwise confuse."[38] He recognized, however, that opportunism is not unique to market-mediated transactions. It can also be present when individuals interact within the same organization. "Alternate governance structures," as Williamson called different modes of coordinating economic activity, will possess different capabilities for

[33] Ibid., 1, 9.   [34] Ibid., 4.   [35] Ibid., 8.   [36] Ibid., 391.   [37] Ibid., 30.   [38] Ibid., 47.

attenuating opportunism, and hence for economizing on transaction costs. When the market provides options for one party to choose not to transact with another, "market governance" can attenuate opportunism; "market alternatives are mainly what protects each party against opportunism by his opposite."[39] In contrast, Williamson asserted that in the absence of opportunism there would be no reason for internal organization:

> Were it not for opportunism . . . the general clause device – whereby parties agreed to be bound by actions of a joint profit-maximizing kind – would also support ubiquitous contracting. There simply is no occasion to supplant market exchange by other modes of economic organization if promises to behave in a joint profit-maximizing way are self-enforcing and if sharing rules are agreed to at the outset.[40]

The presence of opportunism is therefore a necessary condition for the choice of internal governance of economic activity over market governance. But it is not a sufficient condition, for opportunism presents a transaction cost problem only in the presence of incomplete information, or what Williamson has called "bounded rationality." Economists typically assume that economic decisions are made on the basis of all information, present and future, that is relevant to cost-minimizing economic choices. With unbounded rationality, economic decision makers would neither be, nor become, reliant on others for their information. Indeed, with no limits on their cognitive competence, decision makers would know the opportunistic propensities of other actors and could simply avoid entering into transactions with those known to be prone to "self-interest seeking with guile."

Williamson argued, however, that the assumption of unbounded rationality is unwarranted. The notion that rationality is "bounded" comes from the work of Herbert Simon – founder of what has become known as the behavioral school of economics and Williamson's own Ph.D. adviser more than a quarter-century ago. In contrast to the market-oriented perspectives of Coase and Arrow, and more along the lines of Chandler, Simon focused on the internal operation of the bureaucratic organization, and specifically sought to analyze how, in the face of bounded rationality, these organizations could be administered most efficiently. The managers of organizations must pursue their objectives in the face of incomplete access to, as well as limited ability to make use of, information that will enable them to minimize costs. Quoting Simon, Williamson argued that economic actors are "intendedly rational but only limitedly so." He explained:

[39] Ibid., 73, 74.   [40] Ibid., 50–1.

Transaction cost economics acknowledges that rationality is bounded and maintains that both parts of the definition should be respected. An economizing orientation is elicited by the intended rationality part of the definition, while the study of institutions is encouraged by conceding that cognitive competence is limited.[41]

Enterprise managers do strive to minimize costs subject to their cognitive limitations; they are "intendedly rational." But because of bounded rationality, they incur transaction costs in their attempts to coordinate economic activities; there are cognitive limits to their abilities to achieve their objectives.

Given these cognitive limitations, alternative governance structures have different impacts on the ability of managers to economize on bounded rationality and reduce transaction costs. "Ceteris paribus," Williamson argued, "[governance structures] that make large demands against cognitive competence are relatively disfavored."[42] One might then assume that, all other things equal, bounded rationality would favor market exchange because it reduces the range of activities that managers must coordinate. In response to changes in prices, product demand, and input requirements, market exchange permits managers to make business decisions in an adaptive, sequential manner rather than all at once. "As compared with the contingent claims contracting requirement that the complete decision tree be generated, so that all possible bridges are crossed in advance," Williamson argued, "the adaptive, sequential decision-making procedure economizes greatly on bounded rationality."[43] He also discussed the problem of "control loss" as the organization grows.[44]

Unlike opportunism, therefore, bounded rationality would not appear to be even a necessary condition for the existence of internal governance. And just as those with unbounded rationality could avoid the costs of opportunism, so in the absence of opportunism, economic decision makers who lack complete knowledge would not be placed at a cost disadvantage because none of the parties with whom they enter into transactions would take advantage of their cognitive limitations. For Williamson, the analytical richness of the transaction cost approach derives from the linking of the assumptions of opportunism and bounded rationality. As he asserted: "Transaction cost economics pairs a semistrong form of cognitive competence (bounded rationality) with a strong motivational assumption (opportunism). Without *both*, the main problems of economic organization with which this book is concerned would vanish or be vastly transformed."[45]

Transaction cost economics has, we are told, two branches. The "gov-

---

[41] Ibid., 45.   [42] Ibid., 46.   [43] Ibid., 339.   [44] Ibid., 134.   [45] Ibid., 50.

ernance" branch "is concerned mainly with organizing transactions in such a way as to facilitate efficient adaptations," while the "measurement" branch "is concerned with the ways by which better to assure a closer correspondence between deeds and awards (or value and price)."[46] In other words, the critical question is how economic decision makers – and in particular, business managers – cope with a changing economic environment that requires that new decisions as well as appropriate contracts and commitments be made. In making these decisions, furthermore, how do business managers ensure that the costs of bringing goods and services to market are warranted by the prices they receive? Williamson asserted that "problems of governance and measurement both vanish if *either* bounds on rationality *or* opportunism are presumed to be absent."[47] As he explained:

> Thus assume that parties to a trade do not experience bounded rationality. Assume, moreover, that this implies the absence of private information and that this competence extends to impartial arbiters. Governance problems then vanish, since comprehensive contracting is feasible. Opportunistic inclinations are simply of no account. Measurement problems likewise vanish, since a world of unbounded rationality is one in which measurement costs are zero. An opportunistic propensity to exploit private information is vitiated in these circumstances. Assume instead that parties experience bounded rationality but are not opportunistic. Incomplete contracting does not then pose a governance issue, since the general clause device assures that appropriate adaptations will be implemented without resistance by either party to a bilateral trade. Similarly, costly measurement is not a problem if neither party to a trade attempts to exploit private information to the disadvantage of the other – which neither will do if opportunism is absent.[48]

The critical phenomenon that links bounded rationality and opportunism is uncertainty. What we might call "cognitive uncertainty" inheres in the limits that bounded rationality places on foreseeing "disturbances" in the economic environment. The possibility of changes in the economic environment creates the need for "adaptive, sequential decision-making", and "[alternative] governance structures differ in their capacities to respond effectively to disturbances."[49] But for bounded rationality, the changing environment would not create uncertainty and pose problems of adaptation, because "it would be feasible to develop a detailed strategy for crossing all possible bridges in advance."[50]

The occurrence of these unforeseen disturbances creates opportunities for one party to take advantage of the other. In the presence of parties to transactions who are looking for the opportunity to seek their own self-interest in deceitful, dishonest, or guileful ways, cognitive uncertainty is transformed into what Williamson has called "behavioral uncertainty" –

---

[46] Ibid., 80–1.   [47] Ibid., 81, emphasis in original.   [48] Ibid., 81; see also 66–7.
[49] Ibid., 56–7.   [50] Ibid., 57; see also 79.

that is, "uncertainty of a strategic kind . . . attributable to opportun-ism."[51] As Williamson went on to argue, "Behavioral uncertainty would not pose contractual problems if transactions were *known* to be free from exogenous disturbances, since then there would be no occasion to adapt and unilateral efforts to alter contracts could and presumably would be voided by the courts or other third party appeal."[52]

Williamson recognized that, even under the realistic assumption of the combined presence of opportunism and bounded rationality, the trans-action cost approach is not complete. In particular, it is still not apparent whether internal governance or market governance would best attenuate behavioral uncertainty, and hence reduce transaction costs. The extent to which bounded rationality and opportunism give rise to transaction costs, as well as to the appropriate organizational response to minimize them, depends on the nature of the transactions themselves. As he argued: "Re-peated reference to bounded rationality and opportunism does not, how-ever, without more [sic], direct attention to the particular problems of economic organization that are most severe. Some transactions test bounded rationality limits more severely. Some pose greater hazards of opportun-ism. Which are they?"[53]

Although Williamson argued that, "but for uncertainty, problems of economic organization are relatively uninteresting," he also asserted that "the most critical dimension for describing transactions is the condition of asset specificity."[54] "Any attempt to deal seriously with the study of eco-nomic organization," said Williamson, "must come to terms with the com-bined ramifications of bounded rationality and opportunism in conjunc-tion with a condition of asset specificity."[55] "The absence of asset specificity," he argued further on, "[would] vitiate much of transaction cost econom-ics."[56]

Asset specificity is inherent in "transaction-specific durable assets," both human and physical, that cannot be redeployed to alternative uses (i.e., other transactions) without incurring a financial loss.[57] Williamson's own categorization of the distinct types of asset specificity is somewhat confus-ing,[58] but for present purposes it can be noted that he distinguished be-tween *physical* asset specificity and *human* asset specificity. Physical asset specificity can exist because of what he called "site specificity" – the phys-

---

[51] Ibid., 58.   [52] Ibid., 59.   [53] Ibid., 81.   [54] Ibid., 30; see also 52.   [55] Ibid., 42.
[56] Ibid., 56. For the link between "asset specificity" and concepts that Williamson em-ployed in his earlier work, see Ernest Englander, "Technology and Oliver Williamson's Transaction Cost Economics," *Journal of Economic Behavior and Organization*, 10 (Oc-tober 1988), 339–53. See also Oliver E. Williamson, "Technology and Transaction Cost Economics: A Reply," *Journal of Economic Behavior and Organization*, 10 (October 1988), 355–64.
[57] Williamson, *The Economic Institutions of Capitalism*, 34, 55–6, 95–6, 104.
[58] Ibid., 95–6.

ical immobility of invested resources – or because of "dedicated assets" – the special-purpose nature of capital goods (even if they are mobile), especially when the investments have been made to service a limited extent of the market (in the extreme, a particular buyer). Human asset specificity can exist because of the need for continuity ("learning-by-doing") or collectivism ("team configurations") in the development of human resources.[59]

Because transaction-specific assets are nonredeployable without a loss, the party that has invested in them requires continuity in its ability to make use of the assets and to generate revenues from them.[60] At the same time, however, what imbues the assets involved in any particular transaction with "specificity" is the participation of *particular* parties, as investors, workers, suppliers, or buyers, in the transaction. "Faceless contracting," characteristic of market transactions, is, according to Williamson, "supplanted by contracting in which the pairwise identity of the parties matters."[61]

The need for continuity in both the use of assets and the participation of particular individuals or firms creates cost problems in the presence of bounded rationality and opportunism. In Williamson's words: "Transactions in which continuity is valued . . . are placed under greater stress as parametric uncertainty increases. Such transactions will have to be adapted more frequently or extensively to restore a position on the shifting contract curve."[62] Committed to making use of its transaction-specific assets, the organization faces the problem of adaptive, sequential decision making in the face of uncertainty. That uncertainty in turn arises out of the combination of bounded rationality (the organization cannot foresee future "disturbances") and opportunism (the organization must deal with parties who, because of "human nature as we know it," will act opportunistically when the disturbances occur).

Those who invest in the transaction-specific assets, therefore, expose themselves to potentially costly problems that must be resolved by adaptive, sequential decision making. Alternative governance structures provide the organization with different capabilities to avoid such costs. As Williamson articulated the prime testable hypothesis that emerges from his transaction cost framework, "Transactions, which differ in their attributes, are assigned to governance structures, which differ in their organizational costs and competencies, so as to effect a discriminating (mainly transaction cost economizing) match."[63] Specifically, he argued that "market contracting gives way to bilateral contracting, which in turn is supplanted by unified contracting (internal organization) as asset specificity progressively deepens."[64]

---

[59] Ibid.   [60] Ibid., 79, 143, 242–3.   [61] Ibid., 62; see also 69, 195.   [62] Ibid., 243.
[63] Ibid., 387–8.   [64] Ibid., 78; see also 42.

But when confronted with asset specificity, bounded rationality, and opportunism, what is it that internal organization does better than market contracting? Williamson did not provide a clear answer to this question. He did, however, give a concise summary of the problem that must be solved:

> Whenever assets are specific in nontrivial degree, increasing the degree of uncertainty makes it more imperative that the parties devise a machinery to "work things out" – since contractual gaps will be larger and the occasions for sequential adaptations will increase in number and importance as the degree of uncertainty increases.[65]

The virtues of internal organization lie in its relative ability to "work things out."[66] In the next section of this chapter, in which I contrast the transaction cost perspective with the theory of the innovative organization, I outline Williamson's views on how things get worked out by and within the organization.

As Williamson recognized, in "working things out" internal organizations must overcome yet another cost problem – that posed by the very cost of the internal governance structure (the "machinery to work things out")[67] – if it is to outperform market contracting. The specialized governance structures required to deal with uncertainty in the face of asset specificity "come at great cost, and the question," wrote Williamson, "is whether the costs can be justified" – hence, alongside uncertainty and asset specificity, the need to introduce one other distinguishing characteristic of transactions: "frequency."[68] The benefits of an internal governance structure in attenuating opportunism for any *one transaction* can be multiplied by the frequency with which the transactions recur. The greater the frequency of transactions, the more the fixed-cost governance structure will be utilized, and the lower the *unit* governance costs.[69] As the frequency of transactions handled by a particular governance structure increases, economies of "scale" and "scope" appear, not as the result of indivisible technology as economists typically assume, but as the result of economizing on investments in costly governance structures.

Innovation and adaptation in the theory of the business organization

In contrast to the theory of the *innovative* organization that I have elaborated on the basis of Chandler's strategy–structure approach, Williamson's transaction cost theory is a theory of the *adaptive* organization. The prime message of *The Visible Hand* is that, by means of innovative strat-

---

[65] Ibid., 60.   [66] Ibid.; see also 79, 151, 204.   [67] Ibid., 31, 60.   [68] Ibid., 52.
[69] Ibid., 60; see also 72–3.

egies implemented by appropriate organizational structures, the organization *changes* its economic environment. In contrast, Williamson has viewed the organization as an economic institution that can *only adapt* to a given economic environment. For Chandler, the key decisions made within the organization are strategic investments in plant, equipment, and personnel that determine the *very nature* of the organization's productive resources and enable the organization to alter its relation to its economic environment. For Williamson, the key decisions made within the organization are a series of adaptations to "disturbances," taking *as given* those factors that constitute the prime elements of the organization's economic environment: bounded rationality, opportunism, and asset specificity.

Chandler would not deny the existence and importance of adaptive (or operational, or tactical) decision making. But he would argue that, among the most successful enterprises in the United States, the creation of organizational structures in which such adaptive decision making took place was for the purpose of implementing the innovative investments to which these organizations had already committed themselves. Just as structure follows strategy, so in the Chandlerian framework adaptive operational decisions follow strategic innovative decisions.[70]

Despite the fact that Schumpeter long ago made the distinction between innovative entrepreneurs and adaptive managers central to his theory of economic development, mainstream economists have continued to ignore the role of innovative investments in the performance of a capitalist economy. In line with mainstream thinking, when Williamson argued (as I have already quoted him) that "strategic behavior" has been of no account in shaping the U.S. economy over the past 150 years, he was not even considering the possibility that such strategic behavior might be innovative.[71] For him, strategic behavior represents predatory and, as he put it at one point, "reprehensible" attempts by corporations that *already have dominant market power* to bankrupt existing rivals and create barriers to entry against potential competitors.[72] In Williamson's own words, "Strategic behavior has reference to efforts by dominant firms to take up and maintain advance or preemptive positions and/or to respond punitively to rivals."[73] Within the framework that I have proposed, such attempts to use market power *solely* for the purpose of limiting competition represent *adaptive* strategies.

Williamson rationalized the absence of "strategic behavior," as he de-

[70] See Alfred D. Chandler, Jr., and Fritz Redlich, "Recent Developments in American Business and Their Conceptualization," *Business History Review*, 35 (Spring 1961), 103–30; reprinted in McCraw, ed., *The Essential Alfred Chandler*, 117–39.
[71] Williamson, *The Economic Institutions of Capitalism*, 128.   [72] Ibid., 373, 376–80.
[73] Ibid., 128; see also 373.

fined it, in American business history by simply denying the existence, past or present, of dominant firms that can do other than simply respond to market forces. In doing so, Williamson not only distorted the historical record; in company with the proponents of the "monopoly model" whom he criticized, he also avoided asking how, in a capitalist economy, a business organization might *become* dominant in the first place. Nor would he find it easy to answer the question even if he were to recognize the centrality of oligopoly to twentieth-century U.S. economic history; for holding to a theory of the adaptive organization, Williamson lacked the conceptual framework necessary to analyze the process of innovation. Although he spoke loosely of *organizational* innovation, Williamson ignored entirely the *process of technological innovation,* and hence also the impact of the dynamic interaction of technology and organization on value creation, competitive advantage, and the growth of the enterprise. These neglected issues are central to a theory of the innovative organization.

Even before a rising organization might be considered dominant, its very ability to use innovative strategies to outcompete its rivals indicates that it exercises a degree of control over market forces.[74] The acquisition of market power is a cumulative process, with dominance as a possible end result. If and when the innovative organization does indeed become dominant, it is because its innovative strategies have generated *new sources of value creation* that later movers cannot match. Successful innovative strategies, that is, may create formidable barriers to entry.

But even then, if there are ongoing opportunities for innovation, it cannot necessarily be assumed, as Williamson implicitly has done, that dominant organizations will eschew innovative strategies and seek to further their goals by means of adaptive ("predatory," "pre-emptive," "punitive") behavior. Despite Williamson's desire to distance himself from the "monopoly approaches to contract" by adding governance costs to production costs,[75] his presumption that the strategy of a dominant organization can only result in a "deduction from the national dividend" (to use Pigou's phrase) is in keeping with mainstream thinking on the economic implications of market power as it has evolved since the 1920s.

According to orthodox economic theory, conditions of "imperfect competition" lead profit-maximizing dominant firms to restrict output and raise prices compared with the levels of output and price that would prevail under conditions of "perfect" competition in which no single firm can exercise market power. These dominant firms make their price and output decisions in a purely adaptive manner: They take as given technology as well as the preferences of consumers, workers, and financiers. By ignoring the possibility that the use of market power might enable an or-

---

[74] See Chapters 2 and 3. [75] Williamson, *The Economic Institutions of Capitalism*, 23–6.

ganization to pursue innovative strategies, Williamson has followed orthodox thinking in portraying perfect competition as *ideal* for economic efficiency – as evidenced by his repeated references to the "marvels of the market."[76] His contribution to this line of thought is to add new reasons – bounded rationality, opportunism, and asset specificity – for the unattainability of this ideal.

On the assumption that organizations engage only in adaptive activity, dominant firms, if they do indeed exist, will use their market power to block entry into their industry, thus interfering with the "optimal" allocation of scarce economic resources. That is, the theory of the adaptive organization posits that successful strategies of dominant firms can only *reduce* economic efficiency. In contrast, the theory of the innovative organization posits that, by generating new sources of value, successful investment strategies result in *improved standards* of economic efficiency, in effect overcoming prior conditions of economic scarcity. By helping to assure the organization that it will indeed be able to win the extent of the market necessary for the success of an innovative investment strategy, a degree of market power may, as Schumpeter put it, "provide the bait that lures capital on to untried trails."[77] The result will be superior technologies and different cost curves – and in particular, lower unit costs at high volumes of output – than would have prevailed if the organization had forgone making the innovative investments. Entry into an industry may as a result be blocked, not because of predatory practices by dominant organizations, but because new entrants cannot put in place the value-creating capabilities that innovative incumbents have already attained.

Ignoring, as he has, the dynamic interaction of technology and organization in the growth of the capitalist enterprise, Williamson has offered no conception of how innovative organizations might attain and sustain competitive advantage by *differentiating* the quality and cost of their products from those of their competitors. Williamson's approach differs from that of most of his neoclassical colleagues by his insistence that the combination of bounded rationality, opportunism, and asset specificity necessitates governance costs that must be added to the costs of plant, equipment, and labor in considering the firm's total cost structure. But Williamson has not rejected the static analytical methodology that Schumpeter criticized, thus leaving himself no choice but to assume that, in any given industry characterized by particular types of transactions, all enterprises will be subject to the same (production plus governance) cost conditions.

---

[76] Ibid., 87, 161, 276, 318.
[77] Joseph A. Schumpeter, *Capitalism, Socialism, and Democracy*, 3d ed. (New York: Harper, 1950), 90.

Although Williamson asserted that dominant organizations have not played a major role in the evolution of the U.S. economy, he admitted that he could offer no compelling reason for the limits to the growth of the organization.[78] By claiming that only already dominant organizations can engage in strategic behavior *and* that dominant organizations have not been, and are not, important in the U.S. economy, Williamson has been able to deny that enterprise strategy *of any kind* is an important determinant of the economic institutions of capitalism. In particular, nowhere has Williamson raised the possibility that, as a fundamental decision variable, the organization may *choose the degree of asset specificity* inherent in its investments, and hence the degree of uncertainty that it is *willing* to confront in its business activities.

Once one accepts that innovative strategies underlie the development of the capitalist economy, one must reject the notion that asset specificity is simply given to the organization. Not only does the innovative organization make strategic choices concerning the types of "transactions" – that is, products and processes that are generally referred to as "technologies"[79] – in which to invest, but by definition, an innovative strategy requires that the organization also *develop* the productive resources that it controls. Insofar as the innovative organization is successful in developing, as well as maintaining control over, its productive resources, it will come to possess "organization-specific" assets, both human and physical, with unique productive capabilities.

Until the innovative organization has been able to develop and utilize its productive resources to overcome the problem of fixed costs, its assets may be "non-redeployable" (the key element in Williamson's definition of asset specificity), but only in the sense that the *current* valuation of the assets by the market may be less than the *prospective* long-term gains to be generated by the innovative strategy. Hence, the *early* sale of some or all of the assets – that is, before they have been fully developed and utilized by the organization – would involve the organization in a "loss" relative to an entrepreneurial valuation of the prospective gains from an innovative investment strategy.

One would expect that the more the further development and utilization of productive resources depend on the *unique* capabilities of the organization that has developed and utilized them in the past, the greater the prospective organization-specific gains from innovation would be. Indeed, a critical ongoing decision that faces the organization that has embarked on an innovative strategy is whether to remain innovative in the face of uncertain returns or whether to cash in on the productive advances

---

[78] Williamson, *The Economic Institutions of Capitalism*, 132–7.
[79] Englander, "Technology and Oliver Williamson's Transaction Cost Economics."

that it has already achieved. The organization's perception of the productive potential inherent in its organizational capability relative to that of its rivals is the key determinant of whether it decides to remain innovative or merely adapt to the existing environment.

In the theory of the innovative organization, therefore, what Williamson has called asset specificity *results* from an innovative strategy implemented by an appropriate management structure that develops and utilizes the organization's productive resources. The strategy commits the organization to seeking returns on the basis of specific products and processes. The structure provides the enterprise with the organizational capability that in turn renders the productive potential of these resources organization specific. Put differently, *asset specificity is not a cause of "market failure,"* as Williamson has contended, *but an outcome of "organizational success."*

Conversely, the more adaptive the investments, the less *asset specific* are resources because they do not have to be developed by a particular organization to generate revenues and yield returns. By the same token, organizational capability, and hence investment in managerial personnel, is relatively unimportant to the adaptive organization. An organization that avoids asset specificity therefore avoids the problem of fixed costs. At the same time, however, it also avoids innovation and the prospect of gaining sustained competitive advantage.

Rather than seeking to avoid uncertainty, a business organization that chooses to undertake an innovative strategy must be prepared to confront uncertainty. I have shown that uncertainty plays important roles in both transaction cost theory and the theory of the innovative organization. The two theories differ, however, in their characterizations of the nature of uncertainty. In the theory of the innovative organization, the productive–competitive dichotomy distinguishes uncertainty inherent in the activities internal to the enterprise from uncertainty inherent in the organization's external economic environment. In transaction cost theory, the cognitive–behavioral dichotomy distinguishes uncertainty inherent in bounded rationality from uncertainty inherent in opportunism, quite apart from the relations between organizations and markets.

Figure 6, charting the relationship between types and sources of uncertainty, illustrates that the cognitive–behavioral dichotomy can be integrated into the theory of the innovative organization. Productive uncertainty can be usefully subdivided into two categories: (1) the cognitive uncertainty inherent in the need for the organization to develop productive resources, a sine qua non of the innovation process; and (2) the behavioral uncertainty inherent in the need for the organization to utilize these productive resources by both maintaining access to them and eliciting effort from its employees. To use Williamson's terms, the greater

	COGNITIVE (INNOVATIVE) UNCERTAINTY	BEHAVIORAL (ADAPTIVE) UNCERTAINTY
PRODUCTIVE UNCERTAINTY	CAN THE ORGANIZATION DEVELOP PRODUCTIVE RESOURCES ?	CAN THE ORGANIZATION UTILIZE PRODUCTIVE RESOURCES ?
COMPETITIVE UNCERTAINTY	WILL RIVALS DEVELOP SUPERIOR RESOURCES ?	WILL RIVALS UTILIZE PREDATORY STRATEGIES ?

Figure 6. Types and sources of uncertainty in the theory of the innovative organization.

the bounded rationality of the organization (i.e., the less the organization's cognitive competence), the more uncertain is the prospect of achieving a marketable product innovation or a usable process innovation. Also, the greater the opportunism of the resource owners who participate in the organization, the more uncertain is the prospect that the organization will be able to maintain exclusive access to the developed resources and get employees to perform at levels of effort that approach their productive capabilities.

Similarly, the competitive uncertainty facing a particular organization can be usefully subdivided into two categories: (1) the cognitive uncertainty inherent in the possibility that the organization's rivals will, on the basis of their own innovative strategies and organizational structures, develop superior products and processes; and (2) the behavioral uncertainty inherent in the possibility that the organization's rivals will, on the basis of "predatory" strategies (i.e., market competition, given relative productive capabilities), take actions that lower the product prices that the organization will be able to command and increase the factor prices that the organization will have to pay. The less bounded the rationality facing a particular organization's rivals, the greater the uncertainty that its own innovative strategies will in fact outperform those of its rivals; and the greater the opportunism of the organization's rivals, the greater the uncertainty concerning the future prices that the organization will receive for its purchased inputs and marketed outputs.

It is possible, therefore, to integrate the "transaction cost" notions of uncertainty into the theory of the innovative organization. As I have indicated in Figure 6, given my description of the sources of uncertainty, it would be appropriate to change the cognitive label to "innovative" and the behavioral label to "adaptive." Williamson could, if he so desired, integrate the dichotomy between productive and competitive uncertainty into his transaction cost framework, but *only* to distinguish between *opportunism* internal and external to the organization. He could *not* use the productive–competitive dichotomy to distinguish between the ability of an organization and the ability of its rivals to develop productive resources for the simple reason that he has *excluded innovative strategies* and resultant technological change from his analysis. In short, the transaction cost approach does not go beyond the analysis of the adaptive organization.

The theory of the innovative organization, in contrast, is equipped to analyze the institutional conditions that favor both innovation and adaptation. It is, to put it bluntly, a richer theory; its generalizations capture a broader range of fundamental real-world phenomena than does the transaction cost framework. Much of what Williamson had to say about the *operational* tasks of enterprise structure is consistent with the Chandlerian analysis. But because he has ignored innovative strategy, Williamson has missed Chandler's main arguments concerning the relation between operational and strategic decision making and the implications of this relation for the organizational structure of the enterprise. In viewing the nature of the firm much too narrowly, that is, Williamson has failed to understand Chandler's key contributions to the theory of the capitalist business organization.

As we have seen, Williamson has claimed that, in the presence of asset specificity, bounded rationality, and opportunism, the contribution of internal governance to efficiency lies in its ability to "work things out" by means of "adaptive, sequential decision-making."[80] As he put it, "Harmonizing the contractual interface that joins the parties, thereby to effect adaptability and promote continuity, becomes the source of real economic value."[81]

Basically, he identified two distinct instruments – one carrot-like and the other stick-like – of internal governance structures that ensure this harmony of interests among the parties to asset-specific transactions. The carrot-like instruments are *incentives*, and the stick-like instruments are *safeguards*. The characterization of the nature of these incentives and safeguards represents the substantive content of Williamson's analysis of the ways in which internal governance economizes on transactions costs to become a source of real economic value.

Incentives assure parties to a transaction that they will share in the

[80] Williamson, *The Economic Institutions of Capitalism*, 60, 79, 151, 204.   [81] Ibid., 30.

revenues generated by the organization. Williamson distinguished between "high-powered" incentives, which he associated with market governance of transactions, and "low-powered" incentives, which he associated with internal governance of transactions. He identified high-powered incentives as of the "residual claimant status whereby an agent, either by agreement or under the prevailing definition of property rights, appropriates a net revenue stream, the gross receipts and/or costs of which stream are influenced by the efforts expended by the economic agent."[82]

Put more simply, high-powered incentives assure parties to a transaction returns that vary directly in proportion to productive contributions. By contrast, low-powered incentives entail returns that are independent of productive contributions. Payments per unit of output, characteristic of market transactions, represent high-powered incentives to the producer, while time payments such as salaries that characterize relations within organizations represent low-powered incentives.[83]

Given the opportunistic character of "human nature as we know it,"[84] the use of high-powered incentives to govern transactions results in economic performance that is superior to the use of low-powered incentives. But, Williamson argued, in the presence of asset specificity, bounded rationality, and opportunism, market governance characterized by high-powered incentives will not work because of the *need for continuity* in the relationship of the *particular* parties to the transaction.

In effect, the presence of asset specificity eliminates the use of market alternatives by the investing party over the time frame that continuity is required, and hence exposes him or her to opportunistic behavior by a supplier or a buyer who presumably (although Williamson does not explicitly address the conditions under which such a situation would exist) retains market alternatives.[85] The high-powered incentives that, under "ideal" conditions, market governance would put in place cannot, under conditions of asset specificity accompanied by bounded rationality and opportunism, induce at least one of the parties to make the investments necessary for the transaction to occur. The market fails to create the incentives required to warrant investments in transaction-specific assets; some "non-standard form of contracting" is needed if the transaction-specific investment is to take place.

Bilateral contracting arises in cases where both parties make transaction-specific investments and trading is recurrent.[86] Given their dependence on one another, the parties have an interest in devising a contractual relation that both sides find fair. They may also agree to build safeguards, or "credible commitments,"[87] into the basic contract by post-

---

[82] Ibid., 132. [83] Ibid., 144–5. [84] Ibid., 80. [85] Ibid., 74. [86] Ibid., 78–80.
[87] Ibid., 167.

ing security bonds with one another – what Williamson has called trading "hostages" – thus expanding the contract into a "mutual reliance relation."[88]

Bilateral contracting reaches its limits, however, as asset specificity deepens and the transaction costs of behavioral uncertainty increase,[89] and is replaced by "unified contracting" – which Williamson also identified as "internal organization" – in which "a single ownership entity spans both sides of the transaction."[90] By this definition of "unified contracting" (which in any case would appear to be a contradiction in terms), the relation between the capitalist enterprise and its employees must be one of bilateral contracting that can be superseded only by the substitution of machines for people.

Internal organization must therefore represent a combination of "unified" and "bilateral" contracting. In any case, Williamson subsequently used the terms "bilateral" and "unified" to distinguish those transactions in which both parties determine the nature of contractual safeguards from those in which only one party does so. On a bilateral or unified basis, internal organization provides a governance structure that permits the organization to put in place incentives and safeguards that attenuate opportunism and to realign these incentives and safeguards in an "adaptive, sequential" manner when transactions are beset by disturbances.[91]

Williamson claimed that "the evidence on the incentive limits of firms is not well developed,"[92] but his overriding presumption was that "internal organization is unable to replicate the high-powered incentives of markets and is subject to bureaucratic disabilities."[93] The organization can try to "mimic the high-powered incentives of markets," but not "without experiencing added costs," because internal organization creates opportunities for parties to the transactions to misuse assets and manipulate accounting information to their own benefit.[94] Because of such "bureaucratic disabilities," according to Williamson, "high-powered incentives in firms are subject to degradation."[95]

Nevertheless, the organization can succeed in attenuating opportunism and economizing on transaction costs by attaching safeguards, or credible commitments, to its contractual relations.[96] One safeguard is the taking of pecuniary "hostages,"[97] but even these may be overcome by "contrived cancellation" (essentially "work to rule," or fulfilling the letter but not the spirit of the contract), uncertain valuation (when the value of a transaction-specific asset is not well known), or incomplete contracts (when contingencies that are unforeseen cannot be safeguarded by "hostages").[98]

---

[88] Ibid., 190.   [89] Ibid., 78–80.   [90] Ibid., 78.   [91] Ibid., chs. 6–8; see also 48.
[92] Ibid., 156; see also 403.   [93] Ibid., 403; see also 138, 140, 149, 151–2.
[94] Ibid., 138ff.   [95] Ibid., 142; see also 161, 395.   [96] Ibid., chs. 7 and 8.
[97] Ibid., 176.   [98] Ibid., 176–8.

Alternatively, the organization can install "safeguards in kind" by committing itself to certain parties through its very investments in transaction-specific assets.[99]

By his own admission, Williamson had considerably more to say about how internal organization might attenuate opportunism (which he associated with the "governance branch" of transaction cost economics) than how it deals with the problems of bounded rationality (which he associated with the "measurement branch").[100] In the transaction cost framework, "measurement problems . . . vary directly with asset specificity,"[101] creating more opportunities for "self-interest seeking with guile," which in turn increases the need for internal governance to attenuate opportunism.

Yet at times – and specifically when he discussed the transaction cost benefits of the multidivisional ("M-form") structure – Williamson spoke of internal organization *economizing on bounded rationality* by enabling a division of labor "between operating and strategic decision-making"[102] as 'well as by permitting adaptive, sequential decision-making in cases when "all bridges [cannot be] crossed in advance."[103] But given that both the separation of operational from strategic decision making and incomplete information undoubtedly increase the problems of opportunism, it would seem that the transaction cost economies of internal organization revolve around the use of governance structures to attenuate opportunism.

Whatever the potential for internal organization to economize on transaction costs, Williamson's analysis of the economic institutions of capitalism portrays internal organization, with its manifold "bureaucratic disabilities," as being far from the best of all possible worlds. But for the unavoidable presence of asset specificity, bounded rationality, and opportunism, the "marvels of the market" would deliver the ultimate in economic efficiency. In Williamson's view, "the marvels of the market to which [the economist F.A.] Hayek referred in 1945 apply equally today."[104] Williamson made quite clear his basic premise concerning the relation between organizations and markets: "Only as market-mediated contracts break down are the transactions in question removed from markets and organized internally. The presumption that 'in the beginning there were markets' informs [the transaction cost] perspective."[105] He went on to argue that "this market-favoring premise . . . helps to flag a condition of bureaucratic failure that has widespread economic importance but goes little remarked."[106] In effect, the widespread existence of internal organization in capitalist economies represents an adaptive re-

---

[99] Ibid., 178–9.   [100] Ibid., 29, 112.   [101] Ibid., 211.   [102] Ibid., 296.
[103] Ibid., 339.   [104] Ibid., 87.   [105] Ibid.   [106] Ibid.

sponse to our cognitive limitations, our unsavory self-seeking, and our inability to redeploy assets without taking a loss.

At best, Williamson's transaction cost perspective explains what some *established* business organizations do to *survive* in a capitalist economy. With his focus exclusively on the adaptive organization, his perspective does not explain the existence or actions of the most successful capitalist enterprises. The transaction cost framework represents an explanation of the "economic institutions of capitalism" that indicates potential sources of market failure but does not comprehend the sources of organizational success. Specifically, Williamson's framework cannot explain how innovative organizations attain and sustain competitive advantage. If, as he claimed throughout his book, transaction cost economics relies on "comparative institutional analysis,"[107] the approach contains no conceptualization of how the institutional structures that characterize innovative and adaptive organizations might be compared.

Yet like the concept of asset specificity, the notions of bounded rationality and opportunism can be integrated into the theory of the innovative organization. As I have already argued, in this theory the choice of enterprise strategy determines the degree of asset specificity. The organization does not take asset specificity as given. Nor, if the innovative strategy is to be successful, can the organization take bounded rationality or opportunism as given. The organizational structure that successfully implements an innovative strategy *extends the bounds of the organization's rationality* and *alters the behavior of those who participate in the enterprise*. In effect, when an enterprise puts in place an organizational structure to implement an innovative strategy, it does so in order to manage its economic environment with a view to overcoming cognitive and behavioral uncertainty.

Through the process of unbounding rationality and eliminating opportunism, the business enterprise "unbends" its cost curve, thereby fending off internal diseconomies of scale. Indeed, one can conceive of the process of achieving internal economies as the unbounding of rationality *by* the elimination of opportunism. To see why, one must ask how the innovative organization uses its organizational structure to extend the bounds of rationality.

For the innovative organization, the purpose of organizational structure is to plan and coordinate the specialized division of labor required to generate a successful innovation. Toward this end, the organization not only invests in physical resources but also recruits human resources with the requisite general skills. The organization then trains its employees in the specialized skills required by its particular product and process strategies,

---

[107] Ibid., 18, 88, 155n, 179, 238, 387.

and coordinates the productive capabilities of these specialized employees to achieve desired product and process outcomes. Over time, some of the organization-specific knowledge of human resources may become embodied in innovative physical resources to which the organization has privileged access. But the organization also retains a (typically substantial) portion of the employees it has trained in order to generate new innovations as well as to employ their skills to secure a high level of utilization of the resources it has already developed.

For an innovative strategy to be successful, the *training system* within the organization must be *planned,* because the nature of product and process innovation being attempted determines the nature of the specialized division of labor the organization must have at its disposal. The development of human resources must become an integral element in the long-term planning process required to generate and implement all innovations. If the organization is successful in this planned coordination of a specialized division of labor, it in effect not only broadens the "bounds" of individual rationality but also transforms the array of individual rationalities embodied in the specialized division of labor into a *collective rationality.*[108]

In the attempt to create a training system within the enterprise that enables the organization to unbound and collectivize rationality, however, the organization must also put in place an *incentive system* to ensure that it will be able to utilize the productive resources it has developed. The incentive system must accomplish a retention function and a motivation function. The incentive system must induce the human resources whom the organization has developed to provide their services to the organization on a continuing basis as a necessary condition for the organization to utilize their resources and generate returns. At the same time, the incentive system must motivate these employees to work up to their productive potential. The primary way in which the innovative organization ensures the retention of human resources is to promise the bearers of these resources long-term employment with the organization. But this long-term employment security must not undermine the incentive of employees to contribute effort, and it must also be consistent with the training system that the implementation of the innovative strategy requires. The organizational solution to the training and incentive requirements of the organization is a system of promotion that develops human resources in a planned and coordinated way, while retaining and motivating employees by providing them with social mobility within the organization.

Promotion systems that generate successful innovations do away with

---

[108] On the notion of collective rationality, see Chester Barnard, *The Functions of the Executive* (Cambridge, Mass.: Harvard University Press, 1938).

"guileful" employees by *creating* an institutional environment in which the employee can pursue and expect to achieve his or her so-called subgoals – higher pay, better work conditions, more employment stability – by developing skills and exerting efforts in ways that conform to the goals of the organization. To convince the employees to shed their "guile," the institutional environment that the organization creates must demonstrate that the organization itself is not acting in a guileful manner in promising to cater to these subgoals. In the innovative organization, it is not safeguards such as "hostage trading" that "attenuate opportunism," but rather the *sharing of the gains of innovation* that alter "human nature as we know it" and secure cooperation.

As Williamson argued, where asset specificity is involved, continuity in the employment of resources is critical and the identity of the parties to the "transaction" matters. But because he ignored the relation between innovation and asset specificity, he did not recognize the importance of promotion systems that, by combining mutually reinforcing training and incentive systems as essential elements in the planned coordination of the specialized division of labor, enable the organization to overcome the uncertainty inherent in an innovative strategy.

As a result, Williamson did not explore the dynamic relation between the success of the promotion system and organizational growth. What is critical to the success of the promotion system in furthering the goals of the innovative organization is *not* that the organization, through its strategic behavior, be able to prevent its employees from taking up employment elsewhere or pursuing subgoals within the organization. Rather, in an innovative organization, the success of the promotion system derives from the ability of the organization to *promise* realistically its employees remuneration, work conditions, and employment security that they could not easily find elsewhere in the economy. What is critical to economic performance is how the organization deals with *relations*, not how it deals with transactions.

In effect, in making its long-term commitments to its employees, the innovative organization promises to share with them the "super-normal" gains from innovation, which in turn create the very incentives that are critical to generating those gains. Once an innovative strategy is followed by such an organizational structure, success breeds success. Successful innovation and the growth of the organization provide the material basis – higher pay, more attractive positions, more secure employment – for the recruitment, training, retention, and motivation of the organization's personnel. Given the expectations and aspirations of the personnel the organization has recruited, trained, retained, and motivated, the organization must continue to grow by expansion into new regions and new products if it hopes to continue to deliver on the promises that have made it successful in the first place. At the same time, the organizational capability that has made the enterprise successful in the past can provide it with the foundations for the continued development and utilization of new productive resources.

In the theory of the innovative organization, then, appropriately structured promotion systems constitute what, following Williamson, might be called "high-powered" incentives. Indeed, from this perspective, inherently opportunistic market relations offer no basis for the planned coordination of the specialized division of labor necessary to generate innovations. Even if one accepts that market relations provide high-powered incentives in the absence of innovation, the same cannot be said when the very goals of the organization require the long-term development and utilization of its productive resources. By adopting an "organizational success" perspective rather than a "market failure" perspective on the economic institutions of capitalism, one can argue that, when innovation is the issue, the market cannot mimic the high-powered incentives of collective organizations.

7

Lending the economic institutions of capitalism a visible hand

Scale, scope, and organizational success

A prime impetus to Williamson's attempt to elaborate the transaction cost framework is the inadequacy of the "monopoly model," which has, since the post-Marshallian era, represented the standard economic analysis of the causes and consequences of the dominant enterprise. Lacking any alternative explanation of the growth of the enterprise, mainstream economists have attributed dominant market shares to technological indivisibilities. As for the impact of the enterprise on economic outcomes, orthodox economists have argued that, relative to an industry characterized by "perfect competitors," the "monopolist" restricts output and raises prices.

As a counter to the monopoly model's technological explanation of firm size, Williamson has argued that the modern corporate enterprise is the result of *human* cognitive and behavioral limitations – namely, bounded rationality and opportunism. When combined with asset specificity, these cognitive and behavioral limitations generate market failure. As Ernest Englander has pointed out, despite Williamson's protestations that his theory is not a technological explanation of the scale and scope of the organization, the inclusion of asset specificity as a determinant of market failure brings technology into the analysis as an unexplained, exogenous variable.[1]

Nevertheless, Williamson can claim that transaction cost theory does not rely on the unsupportable notion that technological *indivisibilities* account for the scale and scope of the organization. Rather, by introducing the notion of transaction-specific assets, the *immobility* of assets becomes the technological explanation. Nor, in analyzing the consequences of the modern corporation, does transaction cost theory rely on the monopoly model's untenable assumption that the dominant enterprise faces the same cost conditions as the (hypothetical) competitive enterprise. Rather, the transaction cost framework permitted Williamson to make the plausible argument that, *given bounded rationality, opportunism, and asset specificity*, internal organization results in more efficient outcomes than mar-

---

[1] Ernest Englander, "Technology and Oliver Williamson's Transaction Cost Economics," *Journal of Economic Behavior and Organization*, 10 (October 1988), 339–53.

ket coordination. Technological and behavioral factors interact to determine organizational form.

But despite his different, and richer, explanation of the scale and scope of the organization, Williamson has adhered to the neoclassical argument that the existence of internal coordination instead of market coordination represents a market failure, not an organizational success. The "market-favoring" implication is that, if we could rid our economic system of bounded rationality, opportunism, and asset specificity, the perfectly competitive ideal could prevail. Unhampered by human limitations and transaction-specific assets, the "marvels of the market" would yield superior economic outcomes.

Plausible arguments are not, however, necessarily relevant arguments. The history of *successful* capitalist development, and the theory of the innovative organization derived from it, confront the relevance of the transaction cost analysis. As I have argued, the innovative organization enhances its value-creating capabilities *organizationally by unbounding its cognitive competence and by transforming the behavior of its participants, and technologically by committing itself to the development and utilization of organization-specific assets.* It is precisely because the innovative organization makes strategic decisions to confront uncertainty and because it builds an organizational structure to *overcome* existing cognitive and behavioral limitations that it can create value where market coordination cannot.

In *Strategy and Structure, The Visible Hand,* and the recent *Scale and Scope,* Alfred Chandler has provided us with not only the core elements of the history of organizational success in the industrial enterprise, but also a consistent and relevant set of principles for analyzing the role of organizational structure in the determination of the success of an innovative strategy.[2] For any *given* market share, successful innovation and high throughput by a single-product enterprise manifest themselves as what economists have long called "economies of scale." But it is critical that those accustomed to static analytical exercises recognize that scale economies are *economies only because of the dynamic interaction of organization and technology* that transforms high fixed costs into low unit costs. By attributing economies of scale to technological indivisibilities, orthodox economics has avoided the analysis of the roles of strategy and structure in the growth of the enterprise.

Understanding the determinants of economies of scale is also critical

[2] Alfred D. Chandler, Jr., *Strategy and Structure: Chapters in the History of the American Industrial Enterprise* (Cambridge, Mass.: MIT Press, 1962); idem, *The Visible Hand: The Managerial Revolution in American Business* (Cambridge, Mass.: Harvard University Press, 1977); idem, *Scale and Scope: The Dynamics of Industrial Capitalism* (Cambridge, Mass.: Harvard University Press, 1990).

for understanding the determinants of economies of scope in an organization that, producing for a number of technologically related markets, has adopted a multidivisional structure. Insofar as the high fixed costs that a particular product division transforms into low unit costs reflect assets of the organization as a whole as distinct from assets that only the particular division uses, the product division makes a contribution to the organization's cost reduction in the form of economies of scope. *How many* scope economies any one product division contributes to the company's cost performance depends on the extent of the market for its product – which, like the economies of scale that it achieves on the basis of its own divisional assets, in turn depends on its ability to plan and coordinate its specialized division of labor.

It must be recognized that, in Chandler's work, economies of scale and scope are not *explanations* of economic success, but simply labels for economic *outcomes* that result from the dynamic interaction of technology and organization. Chandler's key contribution to economic analysis is a conceptual framework that can comprehend how organizational capability transforms an innovative investment strategy into low unit costs and competitive advantage. By using this framework to study the history of business enterprise, Chandler has explained economic outcomes as a process of *historical change.*[3] Chandler has shown that, by using an appropriate conceptual framework for the study and synthesis of history, the institutional forces that determine economic outcomes can be understood.

Like Chandler, Williamson's goal has been to understand the relation between economic institutions and economic outcomes. And unlike his transaction cost predecessors, Alchian and Demsetz, Williamson has sought to document the validity of his propositions by reference to empirical evidence. As indicated in Chapter 6, in *The Economic Institutions of Capitalism* Williamson repeatedly cited Chandler's *The Visible Hand* in support of his arguments.

By examining how Williamson used Chandler, I shall show that transaction cost theory cannot explain key institutional features of U.S. business history – specifically (1) the rise of administrative coordination of the railroads from the 1840s to the 1880s, (2) the integration of production and distribution in manufacturing from the 1880s to the 1920s, and (3) the emergence of the multidivisional structure in the 1920s. By imposing a transaction cost interpretation on Chandler's historical material, Williamson has failed to comprehend both the causes and consequences of the dynamic interaction between organization and technology that is central

---

[3] For a statement of his own methodology, see Alfred D. Chandler, Jr., "Comparative Business History," in D. C. Coleman and Peter Mathias, eds., *Enterprise and History* (Cambridge University Press, 1984), 3–26.

to Chandler's approach. As the following textual analysis reveals, underlying Williamson's "intellectual failure" is his inability to recognize the role of the innovative business organization in U.S. economic development.

The railroads

Quoting Chandler, Williamson recognized that between the 1840s and the 1880s there occurred a "transformation from market coordination to administrative coordination in American overland transportation."[4] Chandler asserted that "the operational requirements of the railroads demanded the creation of the first administrative hierarchies in American business."[5] Williamson asked what these "operational requirements" were, and why administrative coordination was more efficient than market coordination in handling them.

In the beginning, according to Williamson, the typical railroad company operated fifty miles of track and employed about fifty employees. A simple managerial structure sufficed. But, he argued, "the full promise of the railroads could be realized . . . only if traffic densities were increased and longer hauls introduced."[6] Although "the natural railroad units of fifty miles in length" could have been, in principle, unified by contract rather than ownership to form longer routes, in fact a massive concentration of ownership occurred. By the early 1890s, each of the ten largest railroads operated more than five thousand miles of track.[7]

Williamson implied that, because of the "site specificity" inherent in transactions between any two railroad companies linked end-to-end in a chain of track, bilateral contracting was fraught with opportunism, and hence subject to high transaction costs. In contrast, unified governance of railroads that joined these end-to-end units could take advantage of an "organizational innovation . . . characterized by Chandler as the 'decentralized line-and-staff concept of organization' " – an innovation that enabled some managers to set *operational standards* while leaving other managers to make *operational decisions* at various levels in the line of hierarchical authority.[8]

Once this administrative apparatus was in place, it could also be used for "strategic purposes" – namely, to make possible the merger of competing railroads when, because of the lack of "intelligence and good faith of railroad executives" in abiding by published railroad rates, cartel ar-

---

[4] Oliver Williamson, *The Economic Institutions of Capitalism* (New York: Free Press, 1985), 279; quoting from Chandler, *The Visible Hand*, 103.

[5] Williamson, *The Economic Institutions of Capitalism*, 275; quoting from Chandler, *The Visible Hand*, 87.

[6] Williamson, *The Economic Institutions of Capitalism*, 276.   [7] Ibid., 276–7.

[8] Ibid., 277.

rangements broke down.[9] Williamson argued that the federations had to contend with opportunism by member firms in the forms of "false billing regarding weight or amounts shipped or distances sent and improper classifications of freight moved" (for the purpose of attracting more traffic to their particular roads by evading the published rates).[10] The absence of unified ownership limited the ability of the federation to attenuate opportunism by auditing the activities of member firms.[11] Williamson concluded that "in the end the railroads turned to merger [because] the high-powered incentives of autonomous ownership evidently presented too strong a temptation for cheating in an industry where sunk costs were substantial."[12]

"If Chandler's account is accurate," said Williamson, "the railroad industry illustrates the importance of hierarchy."[13] Maybe so. But the "importance of hierarchy" *for what?* Does Williamson's transaction cost theory provide an accurate interpretation of Chandler's historical account?

Chandler did argue that before the 1850s railroads in the eastern United States "were all short, rarely more than fifty miles" because they were built to connect existing commercial centers or supplement existing water transportation.[14] But he did not argue, as Williamson contended, that the inability of separate "end-to-end" companies to cooperate in the efficient operation of the longer routes played a major role in the evolution of railroad systems under unified ownership and the rise of managerial hierarchies to operate them. In particular, Chandler's evidence does not support Williamson's contention that opportunism (or at least something other than the need for "physical coordination") explains the first case of administrative coordination of end-to-end lengths of track in the early 1840s.

According to Williamson (drawing on Chandler but responding to an alternative interpretation by economists Evans and Grossman):[15]

There is more to railroad organization than "physical coordination." . . . Otherwise the natural railroad units of fifty miles in length would have remained intact. And there is also more to railroad organization than unified ownership. Thus the Western and Albany road [actually the Western Railroad connecting Boston and Albany], which was just over 150 miles in length and was built in three sections, each operated as a separate division, experienced severe problems. As a consequence a new organizational form was fashioned whereby the first "formal admin-

---

[9] Ibid., 277–8; quoting from Chandler, *The Visible Hand*, 141. Chandler was paraphrasing cartel manager Albert Fink.

[10] Williamson, *The Economic Institutions of Capitalism*, 277–8; quoting from Chandler, *The Visible Hand*, 141.

[11] Williamson, *The Economic Institutions of Capitalism*, 159–60.

[12] Ibid., 278.   [13] Ibid., 279.   [14] Chandler, *The Visible Hand*, 82; see also 96.

[15] Ibid., 96–8; David S. Evans and Sanford J. Grossman, "Integration," in David Evans, ed., *Breaking Up Bell* (Amsterdam: North Holland, 1983), 95–126.

istrative structure manned by full-time salaried managers" in the United States appeared.[16]

Chandler did argue that in the early 1840s the management of the Western – the "first intersectional railroad in the country" – was transformed from three separate operating divisions, each with its own set of functional managers, into the "first modern, carefully defined, internal organizational structure used by an American business enterprise."[17] But Chandler was also quite clear that the origin of the organizational problems that the separate divisions faced had nothing to do with opportunism. The problem was rather that, running three trains a day *in each direction over a single track*, "the Western suffered a series of serious accidents, culminating in a head-on collision of passenger trains."[18]

The administrative reorganization of the railroad was a response to an "intensive investigation of the operations of the Western" by the Massachusetts legislature and was designed to "assure safety of passengers and employees" on the single-track road.[19] The Western's management chose to invest in administrative coordination rather than a second track. By remaining a single-track road, it economized on production costs. By investing in administrative structure, the Western increased its operating costs but reduced the incidence of train wrecks and loss of human life. In effect, the investment in organizational innovation resulted in a product innovation – safer railroad travel – while avoiding substantial investments in new production facilities. Judging from Chandler's account (which I for one am willing to accept as accurate), a concern with transaction costs, as defined by Williamson, did not enter into the Western's choice of organizational form.

Nor does Chandler's evidence support Williamson's argument that, in general, end-to-end railroad units gave rise to opportunism that could be resolved only by organizational integration. Williamson himself cited evidence that in 1861 "traffic between New York City and Boston moved easily over track owned by four different companies."[20] Chandler argued, moreover, that end-to-end companies were able to engage in effective interfirm cooperation *in addition to* effective internal organization:

By the 1870s the large railroads of over 500 miles in length had perfected complex and intricate systems to coordinate and control the work of thousands of employ-

---

[16] Williamson, *The Economic Institutions of Capitalism*, 276–7; quoting from Chandler, *The Visible Hand*, 96–7.
[17] Chandler, *The Visible Hand*, 96–7.   [18] Ibid.   [19] Ibid.
[20] Williamson, *The Economic Institutions*, 277; citing George Taylor and Irene Neu, *The American Railroad Network* (Cambridge, Mass.: Harvard University Press, 1956), 19.

ees, the operations of millions of dollars' worth of roadbed and equipment, and the movement of hundreds of millions of dollars' worth of goods. By that time, too, the railroad had *worked out complicated intercompany arrangements* so that a carload of goods or produce could be moved from almost any sizable town in the country to another distant commercial center without a single transshipment. In other words, goods placed in a car did not have to be reloaded until they reached their destination.[21]

Indeed, Chandler found organizational innovation – specifically, the adoption of decentralized divisional managerial structures – *not* on those roads where end-to-end systems previously operated by separate firms had been consolidated, but on those *constructed* as long routes under unified ownership. As an example of the former type, he cited the case of the "New York Central, which had not been constructed like the [other great east–west trunk lines completed between 1849 and 1854: the Baltimore & Ohio, the Erie, and the Pennsylvania] as a single work, but [was] formed by a consolidation of many small lines, [and] continued to be operated by merchants and financiers rather than by engineers." The New York Central, Chandler continued, "contributed almost nothing to the development of modern management."[22] Even under the Vanderbilts in the 1880s, the New York Central still had "no full-time executive or set of executives [with] the responsibility for planning and coordinating the system as a whole."[23]

Because they had made substantial *new* fixed investments in double-track interregional roads, the other trunk lines were compelled to develop modern managerial structures in order to ensure that the volume and velocity of traffic over their routes transformed high fixed costs into low unit costs.[24] Indeed, it was the growth of competition for traffic from these more highly organized and technologically advanced trunk lines that provided the impetus for transforming the New York Central into a unified firm. The ten New York Central companies, of which nine had originally been constructed *between 1831 and 1842*,[25] realized that an adequate adaptive response would require substantial investments in freight facilities, the replacement of poor track, and the construction of a second track west of Syracuse.

In 1853 the stockholders of the New York Central companies agreed to unified ownership in order to expedite the raising of the necessary capital as well as to avoid the difficult contractual problems of determining the "proper" returns to a number of independently financed but interrelated

---

[21] Chandler, *The Visible Hand*, 88, my emphasis.   [22] Ibid., 99; see also 107.
[23] Ibid., 182.   [24] Ibid., 100–21.
[25] Frank W. Stevens, *The Beginnings of the New York Central Railroad* (New York: Putnam, 1926), x.

investments.[26] It may well be that transaction cost considerations can explain the decision by the New York Central stockholders to consolidate ownership. If so, however, it would also appear that the same considerations, reflecting as they did adaptive behavior by the constituent firms, explain the *failure* of the consolidated New York Central to engage in organizational innovation over the next three decades.[27]

Williamson also argued that opportunism brought down the railroad cartels in the 1870s and early 1880s, thereby resulting in the growth of railroad companies through internal organization. But was it simply, as he implied, "human nature as we know it" that overcame the "intelligence and good faith" of the railroad managers who were trying to avoid ruinous competition by controlling rates and sharing the traffic through cartels?

Chandler argued that "if a central theme can be found in the operation of the American railroads during the 1860s and 1870s, it is cooperation."[28] Intense competition for traffic in the late 1870s and 1880s led Albert Fink, along with other railroad managers and directors in the Eastern Trunk Line Association, to set up formal cartels. Chandler recognized that Fink and his associates "found to their sorrow that they could not rely on the intelligence and good faith of railroad executives" – words that Williamson reproduced in support of the transaction cost argument.[29] In quoting Chandler to this effect, however, Williamson neglected to note that Chandler went on *in the very same sentence* to identify these uncooperative railroad executives as "entrepreneurs and speculators who like [Jay] Gould had little interest in the long-term profits or operational performance of the roads whose securities they controlled."[30]

It was not the railroad's career managers, therefore, who brought down the cartels. Rather, it was those who, having secured financial control over railroad assets, sought to use the companies to serve their speculative ends. "The speculators," Chandler argued, "shattered the old strategies":

They were the first to disrupt the existing alliances. They undermined the viability of the regional railroad cartels since they often had more to gain from violating

[26] Ibid., ch. 17; Alfred D. Chandler, Jr., *The Railroads: The Nation's First Big Business* (New York: Harcourt, Brace & World, 1965), 38–9.

[27] For similar cases of institutional rigidities that blocked organizational innovation subsequent to adaptive amalgamation in twentieth-century Britain, see Alfred D. Chandler, Jr., "The Growth of the Transnational Firm in the United States and the United Kingdom: A Comparative Analysis," *Economic History Review*, 2d ser., 33 (August 1980), 396–410.

[28] Chandler, *The Visible Hand*, 143.

[29] Williamson, *The Economic Institutions of Capitalism*, 277–8.

[30] Chandler, *The Visible Hand*, 141.

than from maintaining rate agreements. Sudden price wars and unexpected peace treaties effectively depressed and raised security prices. The speculators had none of the "good faith" Fink insisted was essential to make the cartels work.[31]

The attempt to control competition through cartels was an adaptive strategy that sought to ensure returns on the participating railroads' considerable sunk costs without incurring new fixed costs. But the activities of the speculators, Chandler went on to argue, "precipitated system-building in American transportation."[32] In turning to "system-building" – a phenomenon that Williamson misleadingly described as "merger" – the initial *motives* of railroad managers were also adaptive, or, as Chandler put it, "defensive." They wanted to ensure a "continuous flow of freight and passengers across the roads' facilities."[33] But given the proclivity of the speculators to buy and sell key links in transportation routes for the sake of quick financial gains, the managers of the major railroads found that they could ensure high throughput only "by fully controlling the connections with major sources of traffic." The pioneering road was the Pennsylvania, which responded to Gould's attempt to take control of its connections west of Pittsburgh by "[creating] the first great self-sustaining system in the United States."[34] The running of this system required "significant financial, legal, and administrative innovations" that were later adopted by other system-building railroads as well as by vertically integrated industrial enterprises.[35]

Whatever the forces that initially set it in motion, therefore, system building represented an innovative strategy that, as Chandler stated, entailed "the large expense of building and buying facilities which could not yet be fully used by existing traffic."[36] The amount of building was considerable: In the 1880s, 75,000 miles of track were laid down, the greatest amount of railroad mileage ever built in a single decade anywhere in the world.[37] The high fixed costs incurred in the first round of railroad building had motivated the attempts at cartellization in the 1870s. System building, to which the railroads turned to control competition when the cartels broke down, greatly increased the problem of fixed costs facing the railroads. To transform the high fixed costs into low unit costs, something more than an adaptive response had to be forthcoming from management.

To manage the new systems, the railroads built on previous managerial structures. Even when, as happened from time to time, a major road went bankrupt, *its managerial structure remained intact* as the reorganized company resumed its system-building strategy.[38] Reading Chandler, one has the distinct impression that the key to the long-run success

---

[31] Ibid., 148.   [32] Ibid.   [33] Ibid., 147.   [34] Ibid., 135–6.   [35] Ibid., 154.
[36] Ibid., 147.   [37] Ibid., 171.   [38] Ibid., 170.

of the mammoth railroad systems that had emerged by the 1890s was organization-specific development and utilization of *human* resources.

Specifically, the major railroads generated career managers who were committed to their firms by virtue of the possibilities for rising from technical specialists to managerial generalists. As Charles E. Perkins, president of the Chicago, Burlington, & Quincy, put it, "nothing is more important in the management of our railroad properties than to make and keep good men."[39] The knowledge and loyalty of these career managers enabled top management to delegate authority without fear of losing control over the utilization of the company's assets.[40] The adoption of decentralized line and staff organizational structures manifested this ability of top managers to delegate authority without losing control.

To sum up, by precipitating the collapse of the cartels, the speculators in railroad securities compelled railroad managers to look for new ways to control competition. To remain one of the players over the long run, a railroad company had to carry out an innovative investment strategy; it not only had to make massive investments in new terminals, track, and rolling stock, but also had to plan and coordinate the development of the human resources that would manage its far-flung assets. The growth of the great U.S. railroads depended on the development of managerial teams with the knowledge, commitment, and cohesion both to build interregional systems and to operate them.

Far from using managerial hierarchies to economize on transaction costs, *given* asset specificity, bounded rationality, and opportunism (as transaction cost theory posits), the most successful railroads made good on their strategies of massive investments in organization-specific and site-specific assets by building organizational structures that unbounded, and thereby collectivized, rationality. Central to the unbounding of rationality was the offer of careers to key employees. Besides the training in railroad technology and business administration that these employees received, the "high-powered" incentives of permanent careers reduced (even if they did not eliminate) any "natural" tendencies of key employees to act opportunistically. Through innovative investment strategies and organizational structures, therefore, the major railroads transformed the cognitive and behavioral constraints, and hence the cost structures, that they faced. The transformation of the "economic institutions of capitalism" inherent in the rise of managerial structures in the nineteenth-century U.S. railroads represents a case of "organizational success," not one of "market failure."

---

[39] Quoted in ibid., 180.   [40] Ibid., 167, 170, 179–81.

Vertical integration

For Chandler, the transportation revolution was a prelude to the transformation of U.S. manufacturing that took place in the last decades of the
nineteenth century and the first decades of the twentieth. The central
organizational phenomenon in Chandler's analysis is the vertical integration of various production and distribution processes. In *The Economic
Institutions of Capitalism*, at the beginning of the chapter entitled "Vertical Integration: Some Evidence," Williamson asserted that "the evidence [including numerous references to *The Visible Hand*] supports the
proposition that vertical integration . . . is more consistent with transaction cost economizing than with the leading alternatives."[41] "In particular," he went on to argue, "the condition of asset specificity is the main
factor to which a predictive theory of vertical integration must appeal."[42]

Williamson made the distinction between "mundane integration," which
involves the integration of successive stages in a "core technology," and
the more "exotic" backward and forward integration, which occurs once
the core technology is in place. He informed the reader that he would
ignore the mundane to focus on the exotic. Drawing on Chandler's *Visible
Hand* as well as the important book by Chandler's students, Glenn Porter
and Harold Livesay, *Merchants and Manufacturers* (a book on which
Chandler relied extensively),[43] Williamson offered transaction cost explanations for a number of prominent examples of forward integration in the
late nineteenth and early twentieth centuries.

Williamson remarked that Chandler as well as Porter and Livesay "refer repeatedly to the 'inadequacies of existing markets' " as an explanation.[44] "But to what," Williamson asked, "do those inadequacies refer?"
His own answer, which he admitted "is at best suggestive," is that "scale
economy, scope economy, and transaction cost factors are operative [as
well as] a hitherto unremarked factor . . . : externalities."[45]

From a table that weights the causes of forward integration into distribution as "reported by Chandler," Williamson made it clear that asset
specificity (which in his framework gives rise to transaction costs in the
presence of bounded rationality and opportunism) is the most important
factor.[46] Next come "externalities," which on this issue refer to the inability of manufacturers to exercise quality control over their products

[41] Williamson, *The Economic Institutions of Capitalism*, 103.   [42] Ibid.
[43] Glenn Porter and Harold C. Livesay, *Merchants and Manufacturers: Studies in the
Changing Structure of Nineteenth-Century Marketing* (Baltimore, Md.: Johns Hopkins
University Press, 1971).
[44] Williamson, *The Economic Institutions of Capitalism*, 111.   [45] Ibid., 111–12.
[46] Ibid., 113.

once they have passed to independent distributors.[47] The greater the asset specificity and the externalities, the more far-reaching the forward integration into wholesaling and retailing. Scope economies may give rise to integration into relatively minor wholesaling activities, while, in Williamson's words, "economies of scale are probably [even] less relevant to a decision to integrate forward into distribution than economies of scope."[48]

Citing Chandler in particular, Williamson included the cases of Duke in cigarettes, Swift in meatpacking, Eastman Kodak in cameras and film, and Singer in sewing machines.[49] He also cited Chandler on a number of cases of backward integration into materials, such as Pabst into timber and barrel making; Singer into timber, iron, and transportation; Mc-Cormick into timber, minerals, hemp, and twine; and American Tobacco, Campbell, and Heinz into the bulk buying and storage of agricultural products. Williamson allowed that backward integration into perishable agricultural products may have been economically rational, although even in these cases he cautioned that "more detail would be needed to assess the nature of the market breakdown (if such there was)."[50] But he asserted that, because asset specificity did not appear to be present in the other cases of backward integration, they must have all been "mistakes."

It is at the end of this chapter, "Vertical Integration: Some Evidence," that Williamson attributed to Chandler "the argument that technological imperatives explain organizational outcomes" because "the main factor on which he relies in explaining forward integration is what he refers to as 'economies of speed.' "[51] Williamson went on:

Although economies of speed remain unspecified, appeal to an intuitive notion of such economies leads to a number of anomalous results. Why didn't manufacturers comprehensively integrate into distribution for the sale of cigarettes, beer, and branded packaged goods? Why were small, standardized producer durables sold through independent distributors while manufacturers sold and serviced large, unique producer durables themselves? I submit that fungible human assets were employed for the retail sale and service of cigarettes, other packaged goods, and standardized producer durables, while that was not the case for large, unique producer durables. It is this (together with the economies of scope available for the former set of products and not for the latter plus the diseconomies of bureaucracy that attend forward integration) rather than "economies of speed" differentials that explain the pattern.[52]

As with the railroads, Williamson analyzed vertical integration solely in terms of market failure to the neglect of the determinants of organizational success. He portrayed forward integration as a manufacturer's re-

---

[47] Ibid., 112.   [48] Ibid.   [49] Ibid., 107–9.   [50] Ibid., 120n.   [51] Ibid., 125, 126.
[52] Ibid., 126.

action to mercantile opportunism. He also posited that most of the cases of backward integration that Chandler cited must have been mistakes because they appear to have lacked asset specificity. He failed to consider investments in distribution facilities or in material inputs as integral to the success of an innovative strategy.

As a result, Williamson did not analyze the role that vertical integration plays in the development of productive resources by the innovative enterprise. Nor did he analyze how the innovative organization ultimately transforms the high fixed costs inherent in a strategy of vertical integration into low unit costs. If he dismissed "economies of speed" as unimportant to securing the economic advantage of vertical integration, it is apparently because he did not understand how they are achieved or the role they play in the success of the innovative organization.

The limits of the transaction cost framework are evident in the four historical examples of forward integration into distribution that Williamson drew from *The Visible Hand*. All four cases demonstrate the centrality of the vertical integration of production and distribution to an innovative strategy as well as the importance of economies of speed for the success of that strategy. The arguments that I am about to make here are clearly spelled out in *The Visible Hand*, so I shall be brief.

In 1881 James Duke, a partner in a family-run tobacco products business in North Carolina, took advantage of the appearance of the Bonsack cigarette-rolling machine to *create* a mass market in cigarettes. Before Duke's transformation of the industry in the 1880s, the production of cigarettes was labor-intensive and the market for them was limited. The high-throughput, yet inexpensive, Bonsack machine drastically reduced the unit costs of cigarette production. But if Duke had confined his innovative strategy to the adoption of this continuous-process machine, he would have had a vast quantity of mass-produced output awaiting sale to a mass market that did not yet exist. Therefore, even before he had signed a contract with Bonsack for the use of his machine, Duke was busy setting up production and distribution operations in New York City for the purpose of coordinating a costly strategy to create a national market for his product – a strategy that included among other things massive advertising and salaried sales managers in charge of offices in major U.S. cities.[53]

These high-fixed-cost investments in distribution facilities account for Duke's success in mass marketing what Chandler described as a "new and exotic product."[54] With mass production *and* distribution facilities in place, along with an organizational structure to plan and coordinate them, Duke was able to ensure a high enough volume of marketed throughput to

[53] Chandler, *The Visible Hand*, 290–2.   [54] Ibid., 290.

transform the high fixed costs that he had strategically incurred into low unit costs and sustained competitive advantage.

Williamson also referred to the misconceived attempt at the turn of the century by the American Tobacco Company (the result of an 1890 merger that was dominated by Duke) to "expand its [market] position" by mass distributing cigars.[55] Porter and Livesay (as cited by Williamson) recounted how American Tobacco's "efforts to move into the wholesale and even retail end of the [cigar] industry proved very expensive, and American Tobacco endured substantial losses in its war on the cigar trade."[56] Williamson, however, neglected to refer to the specific reason that Chandler adduced for this failure – namely, that cigar smokers were not interested in a standardized product, but rather demanded "many different brands [that] had distinctive tastes and flavors."[57] In contrast to Duke's earlier ability to create a mass market in cigarettes, which in turn enabled him to make use of mass-production methods, cigars continued to be "produced by skilled workmen in small batches" using tobacco leaves grown in specific locales and cured in special ways. There was, that is, no lack of "asset specificity" in the production of cigars.

But the reason the attempt to mass-distribute cigars proved to be "very expensive" was that, unlike the case with cigarettes, the high fixed costs of marketing could not be transformed into low unit costs by achieving economies of speed. Chandler summed up how the profit potential for an innovative strategy based on the production and distribution of cigars differed from the prior success in cigarettes:

Cigars were not a product that could be mass produced and mass distributed, nor could the raw materials be purchased in bulk. Since these processes did not lend themselves to high-volume throughput, administrative coordination did not reduce costs and so raise barriers to entry. Neither massive advertising nor effective organization could bring the dominance of a single firm in the cigar business.[58]

An enterprise that did achieve market dominance in a manner similar to Duke in cigarettes was the Eastman Kodak Company. George Eastman's invention of a continuous-process method for making photographic negatives gave him the opportunity for creating a mass market in photographic equipment. Like Duke, Eastman recognized that a dramatic process innovation did not itself make a mass market. Whatever the mass-production potential of the new process technology, masses of consumers had to be willing and able to buy the products. A consuming public that

[55] Williamson, *The Economic Institutions of Capitalism*, 111.
[56] Porter and Livesay, *Merchants and Manufacturers*, 210; Williamson, *The Economic Institutions of Capitalism*, 111.
[57] Chandler, *The Visible Hand*, 389–90.   [58] Ibid., 390.

had never taken photographs had to be delivered a sufficiently high quality product at a sufficiently low price.

To be sure, if the marketing of the product had been left in the hands of "opportunistic" distributors, the easy-to-use photographic innovation now recognized by the brand name Kodak might never have seen the light of day. But as in the case of Duke, Eastman's forward integration into mass distribution cannot be analyzed simply as a response to opportunistic wholesalers and retailers to whom he had the foresight not to entrust the critical marketing activities. As Chandler put it, "To sell and distribute his new camera and film and to service their purchaser, Eastman *immediately* created a worldwide marketing network of branch offices with managers to supervise salesmen and demonstrators and to coordinate flows of cameras, films, and funds."[59] From the start, then, Eastman's integration of production and distribution represented *the essence* of an innovative strategy that was planned and coordinated by a salaried administrative structure to ensure that throughput – the volume of Kodak sales per unit of time – would be large enough to transform high fixed costs into low unit costs.

Similarly, Gustavus Swift's creation of a national market in fresh meat took advantage of a process innovation, the refrigerated railroad car, which came into use in 1881. But the ultimate success of Swift's innovative strategy depended on forward integration into distribution to generate a new product – high-quality fresh meat that had been killed some days before thousands of miles away – and deliver it at low unit cost. Beginning with winter shipments of meat from Chicago in 1878, Swift had built his distribution network in the Northeast for some three years before the emergence of a usable refrigerator car. Once refrigeration gave him the capability to ship year-round, he extended his distribution network throughout the United States.

Swift's creation of a mass meat market had to contend with opposition from those with vested interests in the old relations between production and distribution. When the Eastern Trunk Line Association refused to carry Swift's refrigerated cars, he brought meat east by using the Grand Trunk, then outside of the association. To counter local wholesale butchers' scare campaigns to turn the public against his meat, Swift invested in advertising. Even then, in Chandler's words, "it was clearly [low] prices and [high] quality made possible *by high-volume operations and the speed and careful scheduling of product flow* that won the market."[60]

In referring to Chandler's material on Swift, Williamson demonstrated his unwillingness (or inability) to comprehend the Chandlerian emphasis

---

[59] Ibid., 297, my emphasis.   [60] Ibid., 300, my emphasis.

on high throughput and economies of speed.[61] Paraphrasing Chandler on the reasons for Swift's ultimate success, Williamson argued that "despite the opposition from the railroads and butchers, Swift's 'high quality and low prices' combined with 'careful scheduling' prevailed." Compare this statement with the quote from Chandler that I have just reproduced and emphasized. For Williamson, it was not worth mentioning the other factors – "high-volume operations and the speed . . . of product flow" – that Chandler included *in the same phrase* as "careful scheduling" (the factor that Williamson did quote) as ways in which Swift attained the "high quality at low prices" that enabled him to win the market.

Finally, the case of the Singer Manufacturing Company also illustrates how a strategy of integrating distribution with production resulted in product innovation and economies of speed that gave the firm sustained competitive advantage. In 1854 I. M. Singer Company was one of twenty-four firms organized into a patent pool to manufacture sewing machines. By 1860 three-quarters of the new industry's sales belonged to three firms, including Singer. During the late 1850s, these three firms had begun to develop their own marketing networks to demonstrate and service the machines, inform their production engineers of the specific requirements of potential buyers, and provide credit to customers to make the purchase of the machines possible. Although Singer was not the largest of the big three in 1860, it soon came to dominate the industry by, in Chandler's words, "mov[ing] more aggressively than the other two in replacing [remaining independent] regional distributors with branch stores supervised by full-time, salaried regional agents."[62]

Opportunistic practices of the independent agents appear to have motivated Singer's decision to build its own sales force.[63] As Chandler described the problems:

The independent agents had difficulty in supplying the necessary marketing services, and they failed to maintain inventories properly. They waited until their stocks were low and telegraphed large orders, requesting immediate delivery. They seemed to be always either understocked or overstocked. Moreover, the agents were frustratingly slow in returning payments made on the machines to the central office.[64]

Nevertheless, it took Singer some two decades before it was able to dispense with independent agents completely. Because sales required that

[61] Williamson, *The Economic Institutions of Capitalism*, 237.
[62] Chandler, *The Visible Hand*, 303.
[63] Andrew B. Jack, "The Channels of Distribution for an Innovation: The Sewing Machine Industry in America, 1860–1865," *Explorations in Entrepreneurial History*, 9 (February 1957), 127–32.
[64] Chandler, *The Visible Hand*, 303.

Singer demonstrate to potential buyers both the capabilities of the machine (as yet a relatively crude mechanical device) and the company's ability to provide after-sales service, the salespeople of the 1850s and 1860s had to be trained machinists.[65] As Chandler said, "Finding and training [sales personnel] took time."[66] Even as it turned to its own sales force, moreover, Singer did not necessarily eliminate the problem of opportunism – for one thing, the salaried employees whom the company trained could go to work for competitors. By instituting systematic promotion and pay increases, Singer sought to use its internal organization to gain the commitment of these key employees.[67] In addition, after 1878 the company began to develop standardized sales, accounting, credit policies, and procedures that would enable the central office to exercise formal control over the far-flung distribution network. It was only in the late 1870s that, according to Chandler, "Clark and McKenzie [Singer's top executives] perfected the procedures and methods needed to supervise and evaluate this branch office network."[68]

By making long-term investments in a sales organization, the company *created* the high-quality products and reliable sales personnel that gave it sustained competitive advantage. From the 1860s into the 1880s, as Singer captured an ever-growing share of the market in the United States and abroad, it became all the more attractive as an organization in which an aspiring manager could pursue a career. Hence the company reaped the benefits over the long run of the services of the sales force in whom it had invested.

Singer's forward integration into distribution was an innovative strategy that was critical to the success of the organization. However much the move into distribution may have been motivated by the opportunism of independent agents, the success of the strategy of vertical integration cannot be understood as simply the result of transaction cost economies. By transforming the cognitive and behavioral conditions it faced in distributing its sewing machines, Singer ensured the mass sales that made its overall investment strategy a commercial success.

With the building of its sales capability, the rapid growth of the organization put pressure on Singer's manufacturing plant and equipment to produce the volume of sewing machines needed to supply its growing market. Although by the 1870s Singer's distribution facilities had ensured that it would reap the returns from its high-quality machines, yet its production methods were far from being the most advanced in the industry. By the 1880s, however, Singer's overwhelming success in selling its prod-

---

[65] Jack, "The Channels of Distribution," 122.
[66] Chandler, *The Visible Hand*, 303; see also 403–5.
[67] Jack, "The Channels of Distribution," 123–4.   [68] Chandler, *The Visible Hand*, 304.

ucts forced its production operations to abandon the "European" manufacturing methods, characterized by the employment of cheap labor for
hand finishing of parts, that the company had been using up until then.
Instead, Singer began to invest in the special-purpose machinery that
made it an important participant in a century-long process of transforming
the "American system of manufactures" into mass production.[69]

Chandler argued that, in the late nineteenth century, "both insiders
and outsiders credited Singer's business success to its marketing organization and abilities."[70] It is highly misleading, therefore, to view Singer's
movement into mass distribution as an adaptive response to opportunistic
independent agents or even more generally, to use Williamson's words,
as an "exotic" extension of its "mundane" manufacturing activities based
on a "core technology." Rather, investment in distribution facilities and
personnel was the essence of an innovative strategy that enabled Singer
to expand its knowledge about the nature of the market, develop and
utilize a committed sales force, and in time, put pressure on its managers
to invest in process innovations that could generate the throughput required to supply the extent of the market that the organization was capable of capturing.

If the transaction cost framework cannot comprehend the central role
of the integration of distribution with production in the success of an innovative strategy, neither can it understand the dynamic contexts under
which successful mass producers might, with economic justification, integrate backward from manufacturing into the supply of material inputs.
Because many cases of backward integration involved securing the supply
of mere commodities that lacked asset specificity, Williamson supposed
that they must be "mistakes."

Even if we accept that transaction-specific assets were not involved in
the backward integrations of Pabst, Singer, McCormick, and Ford, which
Williamson called "mistakes," the theory of the innovative organization
provides reasons that these investments in supplies may well have been
economically rational. All the cases involved companies that had attained
dominance in their product markets, thus increasing their demand for
material inputs to an extent that, in the short run at least, could put upward pressure on supply prices. In addition, and more important, with
the growth of the innovative organization entailing ever greater investments in manufacturing and sales facilities and personnel, the sizable and
steady flow of these supplies became all the more critical to the achievement of the economies of speed that would transform high fixed costs into

---

[69] David Hounshell, *From the American System to Mass Production, 1800–1932* (Baltimore, Md.: Johns Hopkins University Press, 1984), ch. 2.
[70] Chandler, *The Visible Hand*, 305.

low unit costs. As Chandler described the dynamic context in which McCormick's integrated backward in the 1880s:

> As was the case in nearly all of the new large machinery companies, the reorganized and enlarged sales force encouraged expansion of output in the decade of the 1880s. McCormick's annual production rose from 20,000 to 55,000 . . . between 1880 and 1884. This increase in turn led to the expansion of the purchasing office and to the buying of sawmills and timber tracts.[71]

In line with the theoretical arguments made earlier, the success of a dominant enterprise in its product markets increases the competitive uncertainty that it faces in input markets. The dynamics of enterprise growth generate new, *organization-specific* costs. Given these increased costs of using the market, the transaction cost framework *helps* to explain what motivates the innovative organization to integrate backward. It should be noted, however, that it is the very success of the enterprise in increasing the extent of the market for the products of its *core* activities, along with the large size of the fixed-cost commitments that it has made to these core activities, that underlies the organization-specific transaction costs that prompt the backward integration. The achievement of the innovative strategy *generates* vertically related transaction costs that must then be brought under control.

Moreover, transaction cost theory does not explain how backward integration, once it has been undertaken, contributes to organizational success. The theory of the innovative organization predicts that a rapidly growing enterprise will integrate backward to transform relatively unmanageable competitive uncertainty into more manageable productive uncertainty, and then use its organizational capability to achieve the economies of speed that can transform its (now even higher) fixed costs into low unit costs and sustained competitive advantage. Both the incentive and ability to engage in vertical integration are therefore *outcomes* of the successful expansion of the enterprise beyond its original core activities.

In dynamic, historical perspective, however, a high degree of vertical integration that was cost effective for an enterprise in one era may become a cost burden at a later time, because the enterprise has failed to develop the organizational and technological capabilities to remain competitive in its core activities. Hence, one cannot just assume that an investment in vertically related facilities that imposed a competitive disadvantage at a later point in time must have been "mistaken" from the outset. Williamson appears to have made such an assumption in his discussion of

[71] Ibid., 407.

Henry Ford's investment in the "fully integrated behemoth at River Rouge," because, compared with the less vertically integrated strategies of General Motors and Chrysler, it imposed a unit cost burden on his company in the late 1920s and 1930s.

Coming on line in 1921 (at first to produce tractors but later parts and fully assembled cars), the River Rouge plant extended an innovative strategy for producing the Model T begun at Highland Park in 1908. The River Rouge plant enabled Ford to increase his sales of cars from 845,000 in 1921 (about 56 percent of the entire U.S. market) to almost 1.7 million in 1923 (46 percent of the market).[72] During the fifteen-year period, Ford was able to lower the price of the Model T from $850 to $295,[73] pay his operatives more than the going wage,[74] and add to his personal fortune, which, according to Chandler "was larger than that of John D. Rockefeller, Andrew Carnegie, or James Buchanan Duke."[75]

By 1926 Ford's books showed almost $700 million in accumulated surplus.[76] What threatened Ford's fortune in the late 1920s (the company lost more than $100 million in 1927 and 1928) and early 1930s was not his high degree of vertical integration per se, but his failure to plan and coordinate the movement of his company into new models and methods that, in the face of competition from first General Motors and then Chrysler, could have sustained the economies of speed that had made him rich and famous. Ford's failure to remain a leader in product innovation and organizational capability resulted in a dramatic loss of market share (down to 31 percent in 1929 and 21 percent in 1937) that, given his high-fixed-cost strategy embodied in River Rouge, transformed his low unit costs into high unit costs.[77]

But given the vast profits that he had made in the first half of the 1920s on the basis of these same facilities, it is difficult to argue that even over the long run these integrated investments were mistaken. Ford's mistake was rather his failure to continue to make innovative investments in products, processes, and personnel that could sustain his prior competitive advantage.

---

[72] Alfred D. Chandler, Jr., *Giant Enterprise: Ford, General Motors and the Automobile Industry* (New York: Harcourt, Brace & World, 1964), 3; see also Hounshell, *From the American System*, ch. 6; Allan Nevins, *Ford: Expansion and Challenge, 1915–1933* (New York: Scribner's, 1957), 8–11.

[73] Chandler, *Giant Enterprise*, 33.

[74] Stephen Meyer III, *The Five-Dollar Day: Labor, Management and Social Control in the Ford Motor Company, 1908–1921* (Albany: State University of New York Press, 1981).

[75] Chandler, *The Visible Hand*, 280.

[76] Chandler, *Giant Enterprise*, ch. 5.

[77] Hounshell, *From the American System*, ch. 7; Arthur J. Kuhn, *GM Passes Ford, 1918–1938: Designing the General Motors Performance-Control System* (University Park: Pennsylvania State University Press, 1986).

The multidivisional structure

General Motors, the firm that surpassed Ford, was a pioneer in the 1920s in adopting the multidivisional structure to implement a strategy of product diversification. Williamson has called the multidivisional structure (the "M-form") the "most significant organizational innovation of the twentieth century."[78] Before the appearance of *Strategy and Structure*, he argued, "leading management texts extolled the virtues of 'basic departmentation' and 'line and staff authority relationships,' but the special importance of multidivisionalization went unremarked."[79] *Strategy and Structure* changed all that by analyzing the adoption of the multidivisional structure in companies such as Du Pont and General Motors in the 1920s and its diffusion to numerous other U.S. firms in the following decades.

At General Motors, the multidivisional structure replaced a holding company – what Williamson called the "H-form" – that, under William Durant as president, functioned with little central control. Rather, as Pierre du Pont found out after his company had invested heavily in General Motors stock in the aftermath of World War I, the division managers who made up the Executive Committee determined the allocation of the company's resources by trading support with one another to secure funding for their various projects.[80]

In contrast to the H-form structure at General Motors, Williamson identified Du Pont's organization before multidivisionalization as a "U-form" structure, or what Chandler called a "centralized, functionally departmentalized" structure.[81] Williamson did not, however, provide any details on the events that led to the adoption of the multidivisional structure at Du Pont.[82] Rather, he quoted a passage from *Strategy and Structure*:

> The inherent weakness in the centralized, functionally departmentalized operating company . . . became critical only when the administrative load on the senior executive officers increased to such an extent that they were unable to handle their entrepreneurial responsibilities efficiently. This situation arose when the operations of the enterprise became too complex and the problems of coordination, appraisal, and policy formulation too intricate for a small number of top officers to handle both long-run, entrepreneurial, and short-run, operational administrative activities.[83]

According to Williamson, in this passage "Chandler summarizes the defects of the large U-form enterprise."[84] In fact, this passage is part of

---

[78] Williamson, *The Economic Institutions of Capitalism*, 279.   [79] Ibid.
[80] Ibid., 280; citing Chandler, *Strategy and Structure*, 127.
[81] Williamson, *The Economic Institutions of Capitalism*, 280.   [82] Ibid.
[83] Chandler, *Strategy and Structure*, 299.
[84] Williamson, *The Economic Institutions of Capitalism*, 280.

Chandler's *general* explanation for the adoption of the multidivisional structure, not only at Du Pont and General Motors but also at Standard Oil (New Jersey) and Sears, Roebuck. Had Williamson not omitted several words from the interior of this passage, his readers would have been informed that Chandler also applied the same general explanation to the "loosely held, decentralized holding company." It is also relevant to the theoretical arguments that I have made that, in the (unquoted) sentences immediately preceding the passage that Williamson reproduced, Chandler stressed the need to have a historical perspective on the dynamic interaction between organizational adaptation and innovation in the growth of the firm. In Chandler's words:

The building of the initial [centralized, functionally departmentalized] structures was significant in itself. In the four cases described here, an examination of the adaptive response to new administrative needs also provides the essential background for the fashioning of a new [multidivisional] structure – of the truly creative response.[85]

As I have argued, Williamson's theoretical perspective cannot comprehend the dynamic evolution of a company such as Du Pont from a U-form to an M-form structure. Limited by his constrained theoretical vision, he found in Chandler a transaction cost explanation for the organizational failure of the centralized, functionally departmentalized (U-form) company. In Williamson's words:

The ability of the management to handle the volume and complexity of the demands placed upon it became strained and even collapsed. Unable meaningfully to identify with or contribute to the realization of global goals, managers in each of the functional parts attended to what they perceived to be operational subgoals instead [at this point, Williamson cited page 156 of the 1966 edition of *Strategy and Structure*, but I have been unable to locate in Chandler's book any such evidence of subgoal pursuit at Du Pont]. In the language of transaction cost economics, bounds on rationality were reached as the U-form structure labored under a communication overload while the pursuit of subgoals by the functional parts (sales, engineering, production) was partly a manifestation of opportunism.[86]

Let us examine how Chandler analyzed the dynamic evolution of Du Pont in the first decades of this century to see why the bounds on the rationality of top management were reached, whether the administrative overload resulted in opportunistic behavior by middle managers (as Williamson claimed), and why Du Pont adopted the multidivisional structure when it did. Again, I am merely summarizing arguments that can be found in *Strategy and Structure* and *The Visible Hand*.[87] This summary, how-

---

[85] Chandler, *Strategy and Structure*, 299.
[86] Williamson, *The Economic Institutions of Capitalism*, 280–81.
[87] Chandler, *Strategy and Structure*, ch. 2; idem, *The Visible Hand*, 438–53. The reader

ever, differs dramatically from Williamson's interpretation of the same material.

In 1902 three Du Pont cousins took control of a century-old family-run explosives company that had settled into an adaptive strategy of amalgamation with major competitors to control the prices of its traditional products. Immediately, the cousins, all graduates of MIT with varied experiences in industrial management, abandoned the adaptive strategy for the sake of an innovative one involving investments in both vertically integrated facilities and an organizational structure to plan and coordinate the vertically related activities. The key to Du Pont's success over the next sixteen years was the creation of a centralized, functionally departmentalized organizational structure to plan and coordinate the quest for market dominance and enterprise growth.

The use of the decentralized line and staff organization – an administrative innovation developed by the Pennsylvania Railroad[88] – to delegate full authority and responsibility for operating decisions to the heads of functional departments enabled top managers to devote all their time and energy to planning new investments in products and processes as well as to coordinating the company's various functional activities. Indeed, as Pierre du Pont repeatedly stressed, a critical organizational role of the general office was to distinguish those business decisions that affected the organization as a whole from those that affected only certain departments and to structure the delegation of authority and responsibility accordingly.

To aid its planning function, Du Pont's Executive Committee took advice from the Development Department, which oversaw the search for new ways to use the company's existing technological expertise and facilities. To aid its coordinating function, the Executive Committee relied on a financial staff that by 1910 "had developed accounting methods and controls that were to become standard procedure for twentieth-century industrial enterprises."[89]

It was one of these staff personnel – Donaldson Brown – who developed the most critical accounting innovation: the conceptualization and measurement of return on investment (ROI). The conceptual innovation was the formal recognition that the transformation of high fixed costs into low unit costs required high throughput, yielding, in Brown's words, "a rate of return that reflected the intensity with which the enterprise's resources were being used."[90] Brown called the resultant level of sales per unit of invested capital "turnover." Rather than, as had traditionally been the case, simply relying on earnings per unit of sales as the measure of

---

might also want to consult David A. Hounshell and John Kenly Smith, Jr., *Science and Corporate Strategy: Du Pont R&D, 1902–1980* (Cambridge University Press, 1988).

[88] Chandler, *Strategy and Structure*, 58.   [89] Chandler, *The Visible Hand*, 445.
[90] Ibid., 446.

profitability with which to evaluate enterprise performance, ROI was derived by multiplying these profit margins by turnover. To calculate ROI required realistic valuations of capital invested in various departments and the company as a whole.

As Chandler argued, the turnover concept developed by Brown at Du Pont *before World War I* "helped to lay the base for modern asset accounting by effectively combining and consolidating for the first time the three basic types of accounting – financial, capital, and cost."[91] In *Strategy and Structure*, Chandler explained the "significance of Brown's formula": "it provided executives at both central and departmental headquarters with an accurate standard with which to appraise each operating unit's performance, to locate the sources of deficiencies and inadequacies, and to change and adjust present plans and policies."[92]

In *The Visible Hand*, Chandler went further, portraying the new accounting methods developed at Du Pont before World War I as a culminating achievement in the rise of modern administrative methods:

By devising the concept of turnover the Du Pont managers were able to account specifically, and again for the first time, for that part of the basic contribution made by modern management to profitability and productivity – the savings achieved through administrative coordination of flows of materials through the processes of production and distribution. With these innovations, modern managers had completed the essential tools by which the visible hand of management was able to replace the invisible hand of market forces in coordinating and monitoring economic activities.[93]

In effect, the capstone on the managerial revolution in U.S. business was a formal measure of the impact on corporate and divisional profitability of "economies of speed," to use Chandler's term. Yet as we have seen, more than six decades after Brown's ROI formula had been brought into the service of the U.S. industrial enterprise, Williamson saw fit to contend that "economies of speed remain unspecified"![94]

World War I tested Du Pont's recently developed organizational capability by generating an unprecedented growth in the demand for the company's explosives. Between October 1914 and April 1917, Du Pont's output of smokeless powder (its main product) increased by 5,400 percent. During the four years of war, the size of its labor force grew by 1,600 percent, even though its administrative personnel increased by only 275 percent. Some of the new administrators ran the central personnel department created at the beginning of the war to set policies for recruitment, training, and promotion of workers and to administer the compa-

---

[91] Ibid., 447.   [92] Chandler, *Strategy and Structure*, 67.
[93] Chandler, *The Visible Hand*, 447–8.
[94] Williamson, *The Economic Institutions of Capitalism*, 126.

ny's pension program.[95] In less than three years after 1915, the size of Du Pont's invested capital increased by about 370 percent (in part because of backward integration to supply its enlarged throughput), and its profits soared.[96] As Chandler argued: "The existing organizational structure proved admirably suited to meet the needs of the resulting phenomenal growth. Few organizational adjustments had to be made."[97]

With the end of World War I, Du Pont found itself with not only excess capacity and personnel but also ample supplies of investable funds. Before the war, only 3 percent of Du Pont's business had been outside of explosives and propellants. After the war, the company began to pursue a diversification strategy to make use of the expanded facilities and personnel.[98] In formulating its diversification strategy, Chandler recounted, "the company's top command came to realize that their personnel, trained in the techniques of nitrocellulose technology and in the methods of administrating far-flung industrial activities, was an even more valuable resource than their physical plant and equipment."[99] Building on its technological expertise in nitrocellulose chemistry, Du Pont began to produce, among other things, artificial leather, artificial silk (rayon), dyes, varnish and paint, and celluloid products.

Organizationally, the company attempted to implement the diversification strategy by the further rationalization of its centralized, functionally departmentalized structure.[100] "Yet almost at once," Chandler observed, "the company began having organizational problems":

Within two years, the carefully worked-out centralized, functionally departmentalized structure had to be scrapped. The organizational form which had so effectively stood the test of phenomenal expansion and which was then further rationalized was unable to meet the needs created by the company's postwar strategy of product diversification. The structure built to manage a single line of products proved insufficient to handle the administration of several different lines of goods.[101]

Despite their common technological base, the new products had to be sold on markets and for uses so different than those for explosives that the diversification strategy had in effect transformed Du Pont into an enterprise producing and competing in a number of different industries. An organizational structure that was superb at making and selling a single product line proved inadequate "to handle several new and different products for new and different markets."[102] And although selling the new products posed the most obvious problems, Du Pont's top managers came to realize that, as in the case of explosives, the success of *each* new and different product line required its own *unified* organizational structure to

[95] Chandler, *The Visible Hand*, 449.   [96] Chandler, *Strategy and Structure*, 83–4.
[97] Ibid., 66.   [98] Ibid., 78–91.   [99] Ibid., 90.   [100] Ibid., 66–78.
[101] Ibid., 78.   [102] Ibid., 90.

plan and coordinate its vertically related processes of production and distribution.

Chandler's explanation of the need for a new organizational structure to implement Du Pont's innovative strategy is worth quoting at length:

> The essential difficulty was that diversification greatly increased the demands on the company's administrative offices. Now the different departmental headquarters had to coordinate, appraise, and plan policies and procedures for plants, or sales offices, or purchasing agents, or technical laboratories in a number of quite different industries. The development of plans and the appraisal of activities were made harder because executives with experience primarily in explosives were making decisions about paints, varnishes, dyes, chemicals, and plastic products. Coordination became more complicated because different products called for different types of standards, procedures, and policies. For although the technological and administrative needs of the new lines had many fundamental similarities, there were critical dissimilarities.
>
> The central office was even more overwhelmed than the departments by the increased administrative needs resulting from diversification. Broad goals and policies had to be determined for and resources allocated to functional activities, not in one industry but in several. Appraisal of departments performing in diverse fields became exceedingly complex. Interdepartmental coordination grew comparably more troublesome. The manufacturing personnel and the marketers tended to lose contact with each other and so failed to work out product improvements and modifications to meet changing demands and competitive developments. Coordinating the schedules of production and purchasing on the basis of market demand was more difficult for several lines than for one, particularly when the statistical offices at du Pont had no experience in estimating types of markets other than explosives and when little of this sort of analysis had been tried by anyone in the industries du Pont had entered. Also in 1919, no one in the du Pont Company had been assigned the overall responsibility for compiling and acting on these forecasts in order to maintain an even and steady use of company facilities by preventing the piling up of excessive inventories in any one department. Each of the three major departments – Purchasing, Manufacturing, and Sales – made its own estimates and set its own schedules.[103]

It was therefore not incorrect for Williamson to argue that the case of Du Pont illustrates how the "bounds on rationality were reached as the U-form structure labored under a communication overload."[104] But this use of the passive voice – "bounds on rationality were reached" – reflects the absence of a theory of the innovative organization in the transaction cost approach. What increased the demands on the company's administrative offices, creating a "communication overload," was Du Pont's decision to use its accumulated surpluses to embark on an innovative strategy of product diversification that would enable the company to find new uses for its existing resources.

---

[103] Ibid., 91.   [104] Williamson, *The Economic Institutions of Capitalism*, 280–1.

Du Pont's innovative diversification strategy therefore *created* the strains on its existing organizational structure that motivated the search for a more appropriate structure to plan and coordinate a multiproduct enterprise. But if the innovative strategy confronted top management's cognitive limitations, there is no evidence that, as Williamson claimed, "the pursuit of subgoals by the functional parts (sales, engineering, production) was partly a manifestation of opportunism."[105] Nor, given the productive uncertainty that Du Pont's diversification strategy created in the aftermath of World War I, does it make sense to *infer* that the company's departmental managers were acting in an opportunistic fashion.

The company-wide breakdown of planning and coordination meant that *even the Executive Committee* was unable to define what specific goals they expected their subordinates in the departments to pursue and who was responsible for the outcomes of particular actions. Hence, whatever the objectives and actions of Du Pont's departmental managers during the period in which the company continued to rely on the centralized, functionally departmentalized structure to plan and coordinate its innovative strategy, it is difficult to accuse them of "self-interest seeking *with guile*" (Williamson's definition of opportunism). Even if these departmental managers acted to promote their own self-interests (and given "human nature as we know it," there is no reason to doubt that they did), they may well have viewed these actions as consistent with overall organizational goals *insofar as* top management was currently capable of defining them.

Moreover, especially given the recognition by Du Pont's top management of the value of its technical and managerial personnel and its willingness to invest in innovative strategies to keep them employed, there is no reason to believe that Du Pont's middle managers had any overriding incentives to behave opportunistically – that is, in ways contrary to what they understood to be the goals of the company. Rather, just as the success of the company's innovative strategy up to 1918 had created employment opportunities for these middle managers that offered rewards not readily available from other organizations, so too they must have seen Du Pont's continued innovation and growth as furthering whatever individual objectives for creativity, authority, responsibility, status, employment security, and accumulation of wealth they may have had.

The key to the success of a managerial hierarchy is the delegation of authority without losing control, so that the decisions made and actions taken by subordinates to whom authority has been delegated are consistent with organizational goals. In a rapidly growing and highly profitable

---

[105] Ibid., 281.

enterprise, such as Du Pont was in the first two decades of this century, success breeds success. The company secures the adherence of its managers to enterprise goals by its ability to offer them promotion to positions of increased responsibility, authority, and remuneration.[106] The manifest ability of such an organization to make long-term commitments to its key employees gives those employees a powerful personal interest in identifying with the long-term goals of the enterprise. If, in the United States in the first two decades of this century, there was any company that had the foresight and economic power to gain the commitment of its key managerial employees, it was Du Pont.[107]

Although the innovative strategy of Du Pont's Executive Committee strained the limits of their existing cognitive capabilities in the aftermath of World War I, the company did not immediately recognize the need for a new organizational structure. It sought instead to adapt the old structure to its new needs. But the depression in economic activity of 1920–1, in which Du Pont incurred losses on a number of its new products, even as single-line competitors were still making profits, made it "painfully obvious" to Du Pont's top management of the need for organizational innovation.[108] In September 1921 Du Pont adopted the multidivisional structure that, as Chandler claimed, writing some four decades later, "has served the . . . Company effectively ever since. Losses were soon converted into profits and never again – not even in the middle of the depression of the 1930s – did the company face a crisis as severe as that of 1921."[109]

Why did adoption of the multidivisional structure result in organizational success? In light of the limitations of the transaction cost framework for analyzing Du Pont's prior organizational failure in particular, and the determinants of organizational success in general, Williamson was prudent to quote Chandler on the "reasons for the success of the M-form innovation":[110]

The basic reason for its success was simply that it clearly removed the executives responsible for the destiny of the entire enterprise from the more routine operational activities, and so gave them the time, information, and even psychological commitment for long-term planning and appraisal. . . . The new structure left the broad strategic decisions as to the allocation of existing resources and the acqui-

[106] William Lazonick, "Strategy, Structure and Management Development in the United States and Britain," in Kesaji Kobayashi and Hidemasa Morikawa, eds., *Development of Managerial Enterprise* (Tokyo: University of Tokyo Press, 1986), 101–46.
[107] See Alfred D. Chandler, Jr., and Stephen Salsbury, *Pierre S. du Pont and the Making of the Modern Corporation* (New York: Harper & Row, 1971).
[108] Chandler, *Strategy and Structure*, 92–5.
[109] Ibid., 112.   [110] Williamson, *The Economic Institutions of Capitalism*, 281.

sition of new ones in the hands of a top team of generalists. Relieved of operating duties and tactical decisions, a general executive was less likely to reflect the position of just one part of the whole. . . .[111]

This summary statement, as quoted by Williamson, focuses primarily on the bounded rationality issue – the cognitive dimension of the transaction cost approach – although in referring to the "psychological commitment" of top managers, Chandler did touch on the behavioral dimension. In this regard, however, Williamson might have gone on to quote the remainder of the last sentence in the passage, which reads, ". . . even though old ties and old attitudes were often hard to break." As Chandler continued:

Moreover, the top team was now less the captive of its operating organizations than it had been, since it no longer had to base its decisions on information provided by the functional departments. Not only did the financial offices [attached to the general office] provide more and better data, but the general office advisory staff immediately took on the major task of supplying information of all kinds. In this way it provided an independent check on divisional requests, proposals, and estimates.[112]

Clearly, from this statement, the success of the multidivisional structure represented an organization's success in dealing with the problem of bounded rationality. But does Chandler's account lend itself to the transaction cost interpretation? Was the multidivisional structure successful in the 1920s in such companies as Du Pont and General Motors because, as posited by the transaction cost approach, it economized on bounded rationality and/or attenuated opportunism?

The adoption of the multidivisional structure did *not* in and of itself permit top management to *economize* on bounded rationality. A well-staffed general office that could plan the long-term expansion of the multiproduct enterprise and coordinate the activities of its various divisions enabled the multidivisional structure to *extend the bounds of its cognitive competence* (or rationality) rather than simply take these bounds as given. By relieving top management of the need to process operating information, the multidivisional structure permitted the general office to increase the amount of information it could process that was relevant to appraising the success of current product strategies and to planning the innovative strategies critical to the future of the company.

But as in the case of any innovation, organizational or technological, augmenting the cognitive competence of the company *added to its fixed costs* without any certainty of a return on the organizational investment.

---

[111] Chandler, *Strategy and Structure*, 309–10; quoted in Williamson, *The Economic Institutions of Capitalism*, 281.

[112] Ibid., 310.

Indeed, Chandler reported that twice in the 1910s attempts to set up an effective general office at General Motors failed.[113] Because the extension of a company's cognitive competence increases the problem of fixed cost, the separation of strategic from operational decision making cannot, in and of itself, serve as an explanation of the impact of organizational innovation on the economies that the enterprise ultimately achieves.

What ultimately made the multiproduct enterprise with its multidivisional structure economically successful was, first, the recognition that at the *operating* level product rather than function was the relevant organizational unit and, second, the ability of its constituent operating divisions to capture sufficient shares of their product markets to transform the company's high fixed costs into low unit costs. Insofar as a division contributed to the economic success of the company, it did so in the manner exemplified in the late nineteenth and early twentieth centuries by single-industry companies such as Duke, Eastman Kodak, Swift, Singer, Ford, pre-1920s Du Pont, and for that matter pre-1920s divisions of General Motors such as Buick and Chevrolet. By planning and coordinating the production and distribution of its particular product line, a division of a multiproduct enterprise could develop high-quality products and achieve high throughput, thus aiding the company as a whole in the transformation of high fixed costs into low unit costs. The economic success of the multiproduct enterprise in the 1920s and beyond was therefore based on the same principles as the earlier triumphs of the innovative organization in the United States.[114]

What about the attenuation of opportunism? "Self-interest seeking with guile" on the part of division heads within the multidivisional structure might very well have thwarted the ability of the enterprise as a whole to achieve economic success. Can the success of the multidivisional structure be attributed to its ability to attenuate opportunism on the part of middle managers? In the case of Du Pont, as I have argued, there is no reason to believe that opportunism as Williamson defined it was a problem in the transition from the old organizational structure to the new. In the case of General Motors, however, Williamson referred to self-interest seeking of division managers before the adoption of the multidivisional structure when Durant was still the president of the holding company but when the Du Pont Company had assumed financial control. Williamson based his argument that division managers on General Motors Executive Committee were highly politicized on a statement by John Lee Pratt, a Du Pont-trained executive who in 1919 was transferred to General Motors as assistant to Durant and as chairman of the Appropriations Committee created by Du Pont: "When one of them had a project, why he

[113] Ibid., 120–2, 125–8.   [114] Chandler, *The Visible Hand*, ch. 14.

would vote for his fellow members; if they would vote for his project, he would vote for theirs. It was a sort of horse trading."[115]

Did this "horse trading" reflect "opportunism" that the implementation of the multidivisional structure then attenuated? Not if Pratt's complaint as quoted by Williamson is placed in the context in which Chandler presented it. In Chandler's words, including his complete quotation of Pratt:

> Pratt described the situation shortly after he arrived [at General Motors] to help improve procedures. "No one knew just how the money had been appropriated, and there was no control of how much money was being spent." *Durant was largely to blame*, Pratt maintained. The Executive Committee consisted of Division Managers and:
>
> > "When one of them had a project, why he would get the vote of his fellow members; if they would vote for his project, he would vote for theirs. It was sort of a horse trading. In addition to that, if they didn't get enough money, Durant, when visiting the plant, would tell them to go on and spend the money they needed without any record of it being made."
>
> Although Pratt's committee was to bring some kind of order into the appropriations procedures, he reported "that during Mr. Durant's regime we were never able to get the thing under control."[116]

Further on, Chandler refers to "Durant's almost anarchical decentralization."[117] The problem at General Motors under Durant was *not* that division managers engaged in opportunism – the pursuit of their own "subgoals" at the expense of the goals of the firm. As members of the Executive Committee, these division managers were *setting the goals* of the firm, with the concurrence of Durant, the chief executive officer. Moreover, the success of General Motors in the 1910s was the success of divisions such as Buick, Cadillac, Olds, and Chevrolet in producing and selling cars. The problem at General Motors was Durant's unplanned accumulation of car companies and his unplanned expansion of output – that is, his failure to plan for the future and coordinate the divisions, and his consequent failure to set organizational goals to which division managers could respond.

The result was recurrent financial crisis. On the eve of the depression that began in mid-1920, the Inventory Allocation Committee was set up to stem the stocking of inventories by the divisions. But according to Chandler, "The division managers made little effort to stay within the limits set by the . . . Committee." As Chandler continued:

> The executives had full control of the funds in their divisions. They could borrow money as well as place orders for materials and equipment. No one checked to

[115] Williamson, *The Economic Institutions of Capitalism*, 280; quoting from Chandler, *Strategy and Structure*, 127.

[116] Chandler, *Strategy and Structure*, 127, my emphasis.   [117] Ibid., 133.

see how they spent the money they received or what materials they purchased and used. While [through September 1920] they continued to buy supplies, the demand for their completed products fell off precipitously.[118]

The complete lack of a general planning capability at General Motors before and during the depression of 1920–1 caused the company to write off some $84 million in inventories and other commitments.

Although, during the crisis, conflicts were growing within the company over how organizational goals should be set and by whom, the decisions of the division managers, who until December 1920 continued to form the Executive Committee, remained within the bounds of their authority. Hence, it is difficult to view their actions as "opportunistic." If division managers did not adhere to the guidelines of the Inventory Allocation Committee, it was because the company still lacked not only the cognitive competence to monitor divisional purchases but also a structure of authority that, by altering access to financial resources, could *redefine* both the goals of the organization and the decision-making powers of division managers.

As in the case of Du Pont, the depression of 1920–1 precipitated the adoption of the multidivisional structure at General Motors.[119] In 1921, under Pierre du Pont, who had replaced Durant as president, and on the basis of a plan drawn up by Alfred Sloan, the manager of the company's parts division, General Motors began to create a powerful general office. Critical to the success of the general office in planning and coordinating the company's business was the removal of the division managers from the Executive Committee and the transfer of power to define organizational goals and control finances to du Pont, Sloan, and two other former Du Pont executives.[120]

As the Executive Committee manned key staff offices to give it advice and enable it to set enterprise goals, it began to view as opportunistic the very division managers who, in an unplanned and uncoordinated way, had been determining the organizational goals in the past. As a result the Executive Committee quickly replaced the "strong and independent managers" of the Olds, Oakland, Cadillac, and Chevrolet divisions with ones who would act in accordance with the new goals of the firm and acquiesce in the installation of the accounting methods required to appraise their performance.[121] With a new structure of authority in place, two of these executives could be dismissed for "drawing of money from the Corporation that was not properly authorized."[122] The investment in

---

[118] Ibid., 129.   [119] Ibid.
[120] Chandler, *The Visible Hand*, 461; idem, *Strategy and Structure*, 157–8.
[121] Chandler, *Strategy and Structure*, 141.
[122] Ibid.; quoting Alfred Sloan.

a powerful general office enabled the reconstituted Executive Committee of General Motors both to formulate a long-term enterprise strategy and to fire those who might, because of their vested interests in the old ways of doing things, opportunistically stand in the way of the achievement of these new strategic goals. Insofar as the multidivisional structure served to attenuate opportunism, therefore, it was because of a *shift in the locus of decision-making power within the organization* that transformed what had previously constituted the "goals" of the firm into merely the "subgoals" of expendable division managers.

So much for what the multidivisional structure did. How important was it in the development of modern business enterprise in the United States? As I have already pointed out, Williamson described the multidivisional structure, as it was developed in the 1920s, as the "most significant organizational innovation in the twentieth century."[123] If one had read only *Strategy and Structure*, such a conclusion might be justified – although in the last chapter of that book, Chandler was already placing the multidivisional structure in a longer-run, historical perspective.

In *The Visible Hand*, Chandler documented the longer run of business development in the United States. In doing so, he made it clear that the advent of the multidivisional structure represented the "maturing of modern business enterprise" – the subject of chapter 14, which, among other things, summarizes the case study material from *Strategy and Structure*. "By World War I," Chandler began the chapter, "modern business enterprise had come of age."[124] He continued: "The history of the modern multiunit business enterprise after World War I becomes an extension of the story already told here. It consists of refinements in existing processes and procedures, and the continuation of basic trends that appeared before 1917."[125]

He then went on to summarize, rather succinctly, the "perfecting of the structure" at companies such as Du Pont and General Motors. Far from being the "most significant organizational innovation of the twentieth century" as Williamson contended,[126] for Chandler the multidivisional structure represented the *culmination* of the managerial revolution in innovative industrial enterprises that had taken place in the United States over the previous half century.

To comprehend the multidivisional structure as the *outcome*, rather than the essence, of the innovative organization requires what Schumpeter called "historical experience" – in this case the ability to analyze the process of organizational change within major U.S. business enterprises.

---

[123] Williamson, *The Economic Institutions of Capitalism*, 279.
[124] Chandler, *The Visible Hand*, 455.   [125] Ibid., 455–6.
[126] Williamson, *The Economic Institutions of Capitalism*, 279.

Only by viewing the coming of the multidivisional structure as the outcome of a long-run "path-dependent" process can one explain, first, why this organizational innovation took root and then diffused so rapidly in the United States and, second, why it diffused so slowly and functioned so ineffectively in Britain.[127] And as I have argued in Chapter 1, for the social scientist that story – the relation between business organization and national economic performance – is ultimately what comparative institutional history should be about.

---

[127] Derek F. Channon, *The Strategy and Structure of British Enterprise* (Boston: Harvard Graduate School of Business Administration, 1973); Leslie Hannah, *The Rise of the Corporate Economy: The British Experience*, 2d ed. (London: Methuen, 1983); Lazonick, "Strategy, Structure and Management Development"; Chandler, *Scale and Scope*, pt. 3.

PART IV

Overcoming intellectual constraints

8

Business organization and economic theory

Historians and economists

Oliver Williamson's misuse of Alfred Chandler's historical research makes it worthwhile to repeat Joseph Schumpeter's position, quoted at the beginning of Chapter 4, on the importance of historical perspective for economic analysis: "Nobody can hope to understand the economic phenomena of any, including the present epoch, who has not an adequate command of historical *facts* and an adequate amount of historical *sense* or what may be described as *historical experience.*"[1] What a historian like Alfred Chandler possesses that an economist like Oliver Williamson lacks is an understanding of the process of historical change. Without an "adequate command of historical *facts* and an adequate amount of historical *sense,*" it is impossible to comprehend the dynamics of capitalist development.

But, it might be argued, progress in the social sciences requires an intellectual division of labor. Williamson is an economist, not a historian. It is fair to say, moreover, that, in conceptualizing such phenomena as bounded rationality and opportunism and recognizing the importance (if not the substance) of asset specificity, Williamson has taken his version of economics well beyond the conceptual bounds of prevailing orthodoxy. No doubt it is this attempt to create a conceptual framework for analyzing the choice of organizational form that won Chandler's praise of Williamson's book. As Chandler put it in another context, his own scholarly approach seeks to determine "how the historian can take what he needs from the concepts of the other disciplines without in any sense being captured by them."[2]

However useful the transaction cost concepts may be to Chandler, Williamson's neoclassical economics training, manifested by his ahistorical methodology and his ideological attachment to the "marvels of the market," led him to impose his theory of the adaptive organization on a his-

---

[1] Joseph A. Schumpeter, *History of Economic Analysis* (New York: Oxford University Press, 1954), 12, emphasis in original.
[2] Quoted in Thomas K. McCraw, "The Intellectual Odyssey of Alfred D. Chandler, Jr.," Introduction to Thomas K. McCraw, ed., *The Essential Alfred Chandler* (Boston: Harvard Business School Press, 1988) 1–21, quoted at 1; see also idem, *The Essential Alfred Chandler*, ch. 18.

torical reality characterized by innovation. Precisely because the "optimal" form of economic organization is an evolving reality, those who take on the task of explicating the "economic institutions of capitalism" must be able to integrate historical analysis with economic theorizing. As Schumpeter recognized, such an integration of history and theory is what a theory of economic *development* is all about.

If to be an "economist" means that one is not expected to possess a theory of economic development or understand the process of historical change, one should not look to "economists" to explain the relation between economic institutions and economic performance. And if professional acceptance in the club of economists requires that one pay homage to the myth of the market economy whatever the lessons of history, one should not look to "economists" to explicate the dynamics of capitalist development. Only by studying the history of business organization, and its ideological and political implications, can economists gain the "historical experience" necessary to develop and apply a theory of economic change. Without the ability to analyze the historical transformation of economic institutions, economists can never hope to confront, much less comprehend (if I may once again quote so ahistorical an economist as Paul Samuelson), the "majestic problems of economic development."[3]

What distinguishes Chandler's approach to business history is his explicit objective of generating relevant theory from historical research:

The historian has at least two exacting and exciting challenges. One is that of relating specific human events and actions to the ever-changing broader economic, social, political, and cultural environment. A second is the development of generalizations and concepts which, although derived from events and actions that occur at a specific time and place, are applicable to other times and places, and are, therefore, valuable as guideposts for or as tools of analysis by other historians as well as economists, sociologists, anthropologists and other scholars.[4]

Since the 1950s, Chandler continued, "business history . . . has moved from the writing of historically specific descriptive history to the writing of comparative institutional history that can generate non-historically specific generalizations and concepts."[5]

---

[3] Paul Samuelson, *Foundations of Economic Analysis*, enlarged ed. (Cambridge, Mass.: Harvard University Press, 1983), 355.

[4] Alfred D. Chandler, Jr., "Comparative Business History," in D. C. Coleman and Peter Mathias, eds., *Enterprise and History* (Cambridge University Press, 1984), 3–26, quoted at 3.

[5] Ibid. For Chandler's role in this transformation and his influence on other scholars, see McCraw, "The Intellectual Odyssey of Alfred D. Chandler, Jr."; see also Louis Galambos, "The Emerging Organizational Synthesis in Modern American History," *Business History Review*, 44 (Autumn 1970), 279–90; idem, "Technology, Political Economy, and Professionalization: Central Themes in the Organizational Synthesis," *Business History Review*, 57 (Winter 1983), 471–93.

As I have elaborated in Chapter 4, historical work that seeks to generate relevant theory can in turn be used to evaluate the contributions of
economists who have sought to use the historical record (as they understood it at the times they wrote) to construct a theory of capitalist development. The strategy–structure framework, and the theory of the innovative business organization that I have derived from it, have important
implications for the Marxian theory of production, the Schumpeterian
theory of innovation, and the Marshallian theory of the growth of the
firm. By briefly reviewing how the conclusions to be drawn from the application of each of these theoretical perspectives must be revised in the
light of our current historical knowledge, I shall highlight the most salient
contributions of other scholars to our understanding of the dynamics of
capitalist development as well as the most critical directions for future
research into the theory and history of capitalist economies. In the following, and final, chapter of this book, I shall then go on to consider the type
of historical methodology that can enable economists to engage in the
rigorous empirical analyses required to generate relevant economic theory, and thereby to overcome prevailing intellectual constraints.

Revising the Marxian perspective

The great merit of Marx's approach to economics was his explicit attempt
to generate relevant theory through the study of history. Yet Marx himself was not immune to the "economist's vice" of letting his theory, once
formulated, take on a life of its own. As discussed in Chapter 4, Marx was
misled to predict a growing conflict between capitalists and workers in
Britain over the course of the nineteenth century. A prisoner of certain
conclusions concerning the impact of technology on capitalist work organization – conclusions that, in the highly conflictual decades of the 1830s
and 1840s, appeared to him to capture the essence of evolving reality –
Marx failed to see how the persistence of craft control, even in the presence of mechanization, contributed to Britain's successful economic performance in the nineteenth century.

Nevertheless, the historical methodology that Marx espoused and (initially at least) used, remains, as Schumpeter recognized, an invaluable
intellectual legacy. Historical analysis enabled Marx to formulate the concepts that are basic to his theory of surplus value. The great merit of the
Marxian theory of surplus value is that it provides a conceptual framework
for analyzing the impact of the interaction of organization and technology
on shop-floor value creation.[6] Within that framework, the intensification

---

[6] For a formal model of the following argument, see William Lazonick, *Competitive Advantage on the Shop Floor* (Cambridge, Mass.: Harvard University Press, 1990), app.

of labor on the basis of a given technology augments the amount of value created on the shop floor. An increase in surplus value occurs when the capitalist is able to appropriate some or all of these value gains. The capitalist's ability to extract *unremunerated* effort from workers I call "Marxian exploitation" because Marx viewed this mode of increasing surplus value as the major tendency in capitalist development as well as the major source of class conflict.

But the strength of Marx's analytical framework is that, in his explicit incorporation of effort into the "production function," he also recognized that the creation of value and the appropriation of surplus value need not depend solely on unremunerated effort. Value created on the shop floor can also be augmented by the introduction of effort-saving technology, provided that the capitalist can elicit sufficient (but not necessarily more) effort from workers subsequent to the technological change to offset the cost of investing in the new technology. If the effort-saving potential of the technology is high relative to the cost of introducing it, the possibility exists for an increase in surplus value even if workers exert less effort than previously and receive higher wages in return. If institutional arrangements exist to develop effort-saving technology and provide workers with what they consider to be a "fair" division of the value gains that come from the utilization of the new technology, then Marx's major source of class conflict under capitalism disappears.

Marx was cognizant of the potential for technological change to have this "positive-sum" impact. But his reading of the history of the British Industrial Revolution told him that, by making capitalists less dependent on the skills of shop-floor workers, the introduction of effort-saving technology had increased the power of capitalists to extract unremunerated effort from workers. In response to John Stuart Mill's observation that "it is questionable if all the mechanical inventions yet made have lightened the day's toil of any human being," Marx replied that "Mill should have said 'of any human being not fed by other people's labour,' for there is no doubt that machinery has greatly increased the number of distinguished idlers."[7] Like Mill, Marx recognized that the economic potential existed for both capitalists and workers to be better off. But unlike Mill's, Marx's message was that the social relations of production inherent in the capitalist enterprise constantly worked to subvert this potential.

There is no doubt that Marxian exploitation has been a factor in capitalist development. I would venture to say that, *if* the capitalist enterprise had to rely exclusively on unremunerated intensification of labor to increase surplus value, the persistent and ever-growing class conflicts that Marx envisioned would have indeed become endemic to advanced capi-

---

[7] Karl Marx, *Capital* (New York: Vintage, 1977), vol. 1, 492 and 492n.

talist economies long ago (just as such conflicts have indeed become endemic to many technologically backward economies both within and outside the capitalist sphere of influence). Marxian exploitation has been, I would also venture to say, a root cause of class conflict when and where it has appeared in advanced capitalist economies – for example, in the labor turbulence in the United States of the 1880s, 1910s, late 1930s, and early 1970s. But until recently at least, these conflicts have ultimately been resolved by institutional transformation and rapid economic growth that enabled key groups of workers to share in the material benefits of capitalist development, thus subverting the power of those who continued to lose out. Even in Marx's time, British proprietary capitalists learned that to generate surplus value they had to share some of the value gains with key workers – in this case more highly skilled *operatives* – by providing them with higher wages, more job security, and better working conditions than would have been the case if they as employers had treated the wage relation as simply an impersonal market relation.

In the process of seeking the cooperation of key workers, British proprietary capitalists left substantial control over the organization of production and the acquisition of skills on the shop floor. From the perspective of twentieth-century managerial capitalism, such control became generally viewed as the right of management. Managerial capitalism differs from proprietary capitalism not just because of managerial strategies to take skills off the shop floor, but also because those strategies entail investments in the technical specialists who are integrated into the managerial structure. Under managerial capitalism key workers share in value gains by becoming secure members of the collectivity known as the enterprise.

In the process of assuming control over shop-floor work organization, however, managerial capitalism rendered shop-floor work devoid of skill. As outlined in Chapter 1, the confrontation between industrial capitalists and skilled workers in the United States from the late nineteenth century created a social and political segmentation of management from labor that has persisted to this day. In contrast, important competitive strengths of Japanese collective capitalism are that it has left – and indeed has developed – skills on the shop floor and shared value gains with key shop-floor workers *without*, as in the case of the British, giving up managerial control over the shop-floor division of labor.[8] As a result, Japanese business enterprises have created more powerful incentives and more substantial abilities for shop-floor workers to cooperate in the utilization, and even the development, of effort-saving technologies than is the case in either Britain or the United States.

[8] Lazonick, *Competitive Advantage*, chs. 8 and 9.

Nor have the Japanese excluded shop-floor workers from membership in the enterprise – an exclusion that in Britain and the United States has forced blue-collar workers to build their own independent union organizations to ensure their economic security. As a result, at precisely those times when British and U.S. industrial enterprises most need the cooperation of their blue-collar workers in order to adjust to adverse changes in the macroeconomic environment, international competition, and factor markets, the managers of these enterprises are most likely to find themselves enmeshed in industrial conflicts.

Given the very different technological opportunities and organizational responses in late-nineteenth-century Britain, early-twentieth-century United States, and late-twentieth-century Japan, three very different modes of business organization – proprietary, managerial, and collective – enabled first British, then U.S., and more recently Japanese industry to achieve international competitive advantage. But in none of the cases would long-run dominance have been achieved without investments in effort-saving technologies that have made both employers and employees in the major industries better off in terms of the relation between the supply of productive resources and the returns they have received.

The notion that successful capitalist development depends on labor–management cooperation in the production and distribution of the social product does not lead one to invoke the name of Marx. Yet aside from Marx, no other economist in the history of economic thought has made the key shop-floor issues for labor–management relations – namely, effort-saving technological change and the problem of the supply of labor effort – central to a microeconomic theory of production and income distribution. In analyzing the capitalist economy, moreover, Marx pioneered in the historical analysis of the dynamic interaction of organization and technology – what he called the relations and forces of production – as the engine of economic growth. Whatever conclusions Marx might have drawn concerning the *social impact* of technological change under capitalism, his conceptual framework for analyzing the dynamic interaction between shop-floor work organization and effort-saving technology remains crucial for analyzing modern capitalist development.[9]

Since World War II, some British economists and historians have sought to use Marx's conceptual framework to analyze the historical dynamics of British capitalist development. Most prominent among them have been the economist Maurice Dobb and the historian Eric Hobsbawm.[10] Dobb's

---

[9] Ibid., chs. 1–5.
[10] See Harvey J. Kaye, *The British Marxist Historians* (Cambridge: Polity, 1984), which discusses the work of Maurice Dobb, Rodney Hilton, Christopher Hill, Eric Hobsbawm, and E. P. Thompson.

main contribution was his attempt to use Marx's historical methodology to construct a synthesis of, as he put it, "Capitalism, in its origins and growth."[11] As Dobb stated in the preface to his most important historical work, *Studies in the Development of Capitalism*, originally published in 1946, his attempt at historical synthesis derived from "the obstinate belief that economic analysis only makes sense and can only bear fruit if it is joined to a study of historical development, and that the economist concerned with present-day problems has certain questions of his own to put to historical data."[12] In taking a historical approach, Dobb was quite clear about his methodological purposes as an economist:

There are those who deny that history can do more for the economist than verify whether particular assumptions (e.g. the assumption of perfect competition) are in some simple sense true of particular periods, and that all else is facile and dangerous extrapolation of past trends into the future. Such persons seem to ignore, firstly the fact that any economic forecast must rest on certain assumptions about tendencies to change (or their absence) the probability of which cannot be estimated at all without reference to the past; secondly, that the *relevance* of the questions which a particular theory tries to answer – whether a given structure of assumptions and definitions affords an abstract model which is sufficiently representative of actuality to be serviceable – can only be judged in the light of knowledge about the form of development and the sequence of events in the past. In other words, it is not a matter simply of verifying particular assumptions, but of examining the relationships within a complex set of assumptions and between this set as a whole and changing actuality. It is a matter of discovering from a study of its growth how a total situation is really constructed: which elements in that situation are more susceptible to change, and which are most influential in producing change in others. It is a matter of putting questions to economic development in order to discover what are the correct questions to ask both of the past and of the present and what are the crucial relationships on which to focus attention.[13]

For Dobb, the critical questions were the Marxian ones of the role of class relations in the transformation of society from one based on the feudal mode of production to one based on the capitalist mode of production and the implications of this transformation for the ongoing viability of capitalism as an economic system. In emphasizing the historical conditions under which new social classes emerged and class conflicts over the existing organization of the economy arose, Dobb sought to show that "the leading questions concerning economic *development* . . . cannot be answered at all unless one goes outside the bounds of that limited traditional type of economic analysis in which realism is so ruthlessly sacrificed

---

[11] Maurice Dobb, *Studies in the Development of Capitalism* (New York: International, 1963), vii.
[12] Ibid.　　[13] Ibid., vii–viii.

to generality, and unless the existing frontier between what it is fashionable to label as 'economic factors' and as 'social factors' is abolished."[14]

For conventional economists, "economic factors" are those that have to do with the quantity of factors of production and outputs exchanged on markets. Bent on deriving an economic theory that is not bound by time and place, such economists as Lionel Robbins and Paul Samuelson deemed (as I have argued in Chapter 2) "social factors" – qualitative social arrangements – to be irrelevant to "economic" analysis. In postulating that the study of economy is separable from the study of society, conventional economists, at the time Dobb wrote and today, have in effect excluded from "economics" as a discipline any substantive analysis of the process of economic development.

Dobb's argument is that the so-called social factors have a direct impact on the operation and outcomes of the economy because they influence the conditions of supply and demand. It is because conventional economists view the capitalist economy as simply a "market economy" that they feel justified in beginning their analyses with posited conditions of supply and demand. By studying the integral relation between economic factors and social factors, however, it becomes impossible to view the capitalist economy as simply a complex of market relations. By studying the history of British capitalist development, Dobb sought to extend and, within the prevailing British intellectual context, rejuvenate Marx's attack on the theory of the market economy. As Dobb put it:

To shift the focus of economic inquiry from a study of exchange societies in general to a study of the physiology and growth of a specifically capitalist economy – a study which must necessarily be associated with a comparative study of different forms of economy – is a change in emphasis which seems, in this country at least, to be long overdue.[15]

For example, Dobb resuscitated the Marxian argument that a critical precondition for the emergence of industrial capitalism was the expropriation of British peasants from the land, thus making them dependent on employment as wage laborers to gain their subsistence. In making this historical argument, Dobb attacked

the implicit assumption [among traditional economists and economic historians] that the appearance of a reserve army of labour was a simple product of growing population, which created more hands than could be given employment in existing occupations and more mouths than could be fed from the then-cultivated soil. The historic function of Capital was to endow this army of redundant hands with the benefit of employment. If this were the true story, one might have some reason to speak of a proletariat as a natural rather than an institutional creation,

---

[14] Ibid., 32.   [15] Ibid.

and to treat accumulation and the growth of a proletariat as autonomous and independent processes. But this idyllic picture fails to accord with the facts.[16]

Quoting parts of this passage, the conventional economic historian J.
D. Chambers responded to Dobb in a well-known article entitled "Enclosure and the Labour Supply in the Industrial Revolution."[17] Chambers
argued that it was indeed the growth of population that was the source of
a labor supply that could be transferred from agriculture to industry, and
hence was a precondition for the British Industrial Revolution. As I have
detailed elsewhere, however, Chambers misunderstood the Marx–Dobb
argument concerning the "institutional creation" of a proletarianized (i.e.,
landless) workforce. Indeed, Chambers's own evidence and logic tend to
support the Marxian argument, when it is properly understood.[18] Critical
to the Marxian thesis of the origins of the industrial labor force is the
transformation of the social relations of agriculture and the creation, in
the first instance, of an agricultural wage-labor force that might eventually, perhaps through market incentives, be drawn into the industrial labor force. It can even be argued that the changed social relations of agricultural production altered the constraints on early marriage and incentives
to childbearing that contributed to the growth in population. The key
point is that transformations in social relations of production can influence, and have influenced, the quantity of wage labor supplied on both
agricultural and industrial labor markets. To argue simply that population
growth created the industrial labor supply is to ignore these momentous
social transformations.

In the 1950s *Studies in the Development of Capitalism* also set off a
now-famous debate among Marxist economists and historians on the determinants of the decline of feudal social relations in Western Europe
from the fourteenth century on. The U.S. Marxist economist Paul Sweezy
emphasized the role of increasingly national and international product
markets, while Dobb emphasized the role of social class conflicts internal
to the specific regional and national economies.[19] More recently, Dobb's
historical perspective has inspired Marxist historians to attack conventional arguments that population growth per se was the determining fac-

---

[16] Ibid., 223.
[17] J. D. Chambers, "Enclosure and the Labour Supply in the Industrial Revolution," *Economic History Review*, 2d ser., 5 (August 1953), 319–43.
[18] William Lazonick, "Karl Marx and Enclosures in England," *Review of Radical Political
Economics*, 6 (Summer 1974), 1–32.
[19] Contributions by Paul M. Sweezy, Maurice Dobb, H. K. Takahashi, Rodney Hilton, and
Christopher Hill were published in *Science and Society* between 1950 and 1953, and
then published together as *The Transition from Feudalism to Capitalism* (London: Ken-
ion, n.d.; New York: Science and Society, 1954). With new additions, the debate was
republished in Rodney Hilton, ed., *The Transition from Feudalism to Capitalism* (London: New Left Books, 1976).

tor in the transition from feudalism to capitalism (and not just in the ultimate source of an industrial labor supply, as in the case of Chambers).[20]
As Robert Brenner (the initiator of the more recent debate on the transition from feudalism to capitalism) explained:

> After some three decades Maurice Dobb's *Studies in the Development of Capi-
> talism* (1946) continues to be a starting point for discussion of European economic
> development. It does so because it remains a powerful statement of the proposi-
> tion that the problem of economic development must be approached historically,
> that any theory of economic development must be constructed in historically spe-
> cific terms. . . . It is the burden of his position that economic development, the
> growth of labour productivity and of *per capita* output, must be comprehended
> in terms of the limits and possibilities opened up by historically developed sys-
> tems of social-productive relations specific to a given epoch, that the key therefore
> to the rise of new patterns of economic evolution is to be found in the emergence
> of new social relations of production.[21]

Dobb's historical synthesis of the rise of British capitalism was profound
enough, therefore, to generate serious debate among both Marxists and
non-Marxists. He had no such success in his attempts to extend the analysis of British economic development through the nineteenth and first half
of the twentieth centuries. Conceptually, he was on the right track when
he argued that

> it would be a mistake to suppose that [the] social relations [of capitalist produc-
> tion] were the passive reflection of technical processes and to ignore the extent to
> which changes in them exercised a reciprocal influence, at times a decisive influ-
> ence, upon the shape of development. They are, indeed, the shell within which
> technical growth itself proceeds.[22]

Theoretically, he was also on the right track when he emphasized the
need to understand

> the extent to which any important changes in technique and in industrial structure
> have to take place by revolutionary leaps rather than by a gradual succession of
> small adaptations, thereby increasing at the same time the danger of the ossifica-
> tion of an existing structure owing to the reluctance or inability of entrepreneurs
> to face the cost and the risks attendant upon such large-scale change. The study
> of economic processes is increasingly being influenced by the recognition that
> what may be called the "time-horizon" of business men plays a major part in
> determining the expectations and hence the actions of entrepreneurs, and is fre-

---

[20] See Robert Brenner, "Agrarian Class Structure and Economic Development in Pre-
Industrial Europe," *Past & Present*, 70 (February 1976), 30–74; T. H. Auston and C. H.
E. Philpin, eds., *The Brenner Debate: Agrarian Class Structure and Economic Development in Pre-Industrial Europe* (Cambridge University Press, 1985).
[21] Robert Brenner, "Dobb on the Transition from Feudalism to Capitalism," *Cambridge
Journal of Economics*, 2 (June 1978), 121–40, cited at 121.
[22] Dobb, *Studies in the Development of Capitalism*, 23.

quently decisive in that choice between the short-term and the long-term view upon which so much in the development of industry turns.[23]

Indeed, in his first major work, *Capitalist Enterprise and Social Progress*, published in 1925 in the midst of (but apparently independent of) the debate on "increasing returns" discussed in Chapter 5, Dobb made the critical distinction between "adaptation," which he defined as the "regrouping of existing resources," and "innovation," which he defined as "changes as will increase the yield of human effort [including] inventions in technique, geographical discoveries which affect conditions of supply and transport, and inventions in organization."[24] But he never applied this insight to the issue of the transformation of the social relations of the capitalist enterprise that underlay the shift in international capitalist leadership away from Britain starting in the late nineteenth century.

Dobb's Marxist perspective did not allow for the comparative analysis of advanced capitalist development. Like most Marxists, Dobb just saw a tendency of "Capitalism" to evolve from its competitive to monopoly stage, with ownership of the means of production becoming more concentrated in a few hands. Hence, he rejected the notion that within the capitalist legal framework there had been a "managerial revolution" in any capitalist economy[25] – let alone that the "managerial revolution" had gone much further in the United States and Germany than in Britain. What concerned Dobb was not British relative decline within the capitalist world, but the decadence of the capitalist world in general. In his view, whatever progressive force capitalism might have once possessed for economic development had long since been spent. "Compared with previous systems," Dobb argued,

there can be no doubt that modern Capitalism has been progressive in a high degree: according to the well-known tribute paid to it by Marx and Engels in the

---

[23] Ibid., pp. 366–7.

[24] Maurice Dobb, *Capitalist Enterprise and Social Progress*, rev. ed. (London: Routledge, 1926), 32–3. Decades later, Dobb referred to this book as "an unsuccessful and jejune attempt to combine the notion of surplus-value and exploitation with the theory of Marshall (but it contained some historical material about the origins of capitalism and the role of monopoly and class-advantage which was to be developed 20 years later in [Dobb's] *Studies in the Development of Capitalism*)." Idem, "Random Biographical Notes," *Cambridge Journal of Economics*, 2 (June 1978), 115–20, cited at 117. In *Capitalist Enterprise and Social Progress*, Dobb made no reference to Schumpeter's *Theory of Economic Development* (which in the 1920s had yet to be translated into English). But many years later, Schumpeter remarked on the tendency of even some Marxists of the 1920s "to build objectively scientific structures." Referring specifically (and apparently only) to Dobb's *Capitalist Enterprise and Social Progress*, Schumpeter opined: "Maurice Dobb was never impregnated with Marxism; allowance must be made for the English environment. But his sympathies, intellectual and other, are obviously with Marx rather than with Marshall or the Fabians. Nevertheless, he cannot be described as a Marxist so far as economic analysis is concerned." Schumpeter, *History of Economic Analysis*, 884, 884n; see also 894–7.

[25] See Dobb, *Studies in the Development of Capitalism*, 351.

Communist Manifesto, "the bourgeoisie has played an extremely revolutionary role upon the stage of human history . . . (it) was the first to show us what human activity is capable of achieving . . . (it) cannot exist without incessantly revolutionizing the instruments of production, and, consequently, the relations of production." But [said Dobb] this progressive influence of Capitalism was less because, by some enduring quality of nature, the system thrives on continuous innovation, than because its period of maturity was associated with an unusual buoyancy of markets as well as with an abnormal rate of increase of its labour supply. That this should have been the case in the nineteenth century, and in America for the first three decades of the twentieth, does not justify us in supposing that this favourable constellation will indefinitely continue; and we shall see that evidence is not lacking to suggest that this may be already a thing of the past.[26]

Dobb's view of modern capitalist evolution fit well with prevailing orthodox Marxist (essentially Leninist) notions of capitalism as a system that could no longer justify its existence on the basis of its ability to develop the forces of production. In the process, contrary to his own admonition of the need to use historical analysis to explore the dynamic interaction of the forces and relations of production, Dobb failed to recognize the historical significance of the rise of managerial capitalism in the United States and Germany in creating a basis for dynamic economic growth in the 1940s and beyond. Nor, despite his own theoretical insights into the dynamics of capitalist development, did Dobb recognize (to paraphrase his own words just cited) the extent to which Britain's twentieth-century responses to the important changes in technique and industrial structure that had taken place by revolutionary leaps in the United States, Germany, and indeed Japan had taken the form of a gradual succession of small adaptations, thereby resulting in the ossification of Britain's existing institutional structures owing in large part to the reluctance or inability of British industrialists to face the costs and the risks attendant on such large-scale change. And as I have already argued, without such an analysis of the historical evolution of capitalist strategy and structure, one cannot hope to comprehend the specifically "Marxian" issues of the dynamic interaction of labor–management relations and technological change.

Dobb's historical analysis of the rise of capitalism did, however, have a considerable, and perhaps profound, impact on Marxist historical scholarship in Britain in the post-World War II decades. Over almost the same time period that, in the United States, the Research Center in Entrepreneurial History provided an intellectual base for the likes of Alfred Chandler and David Landes, in Britain, the Historians' Group of the Communist Party provided an intellectual base for the likes of Eric Hobsbawm and Edward Thompson (not to mention Christopher Hill, Rodney Hilton,

---

[26] Ibid., 26.

Victor Kiernan, and John Saville, among still others). In his reminiscences of the Historians' Group, Hobsbawm referred to *Studies in the Development of Capitalism* as the "major historical work which was to influence us crucially [and] which formulated our main and central problem" – presumably the study of capitalism.[27] Hobsbawm went on to say that "Dobb's *Studies*, which gave us our framework, were novel precisely because they did not just restate or reconstruct the view of 'the Marxist classics,' but because they embodied the findings of post-Marx economic history in a Marxist analysis."[28] Nevertheless, Hobsbawm admitted, the Historians' Group was not, "on the whole, very strong on the economic side of economic history, and our work probably did not advance as far as it might have done for that reason."[29] As a totality the work of the Historians' Group contributed greatly to social theory – how social institutions evolve and function – but relatively little to economic theory – the impact of social institutions on economic outcomes, which is the central focus of this book.[30]

Ultimately, the need is for a theory of capitalist development that comprehends the dynamic interaction of social institutions and economic outcomes to enable us to understand their reciprocal and cumulative impacts. If there was one member of the Historians' Group who was "strong enough on the economic side of economic history" to make a contribution to this endeavor, it was Hobsbawm himself. For the late nineteenth century Hobsbawm did the pioneering analysis of the emergence of the "aristocracy of labour" – workers who, through their craft organizations, were able to exercise substantial control over the relation between the effort they supplied and the remuneration they received.[31] In bringing the analysis of British economic development into the twentieth century, Hobsbawm was also the first to enunciate clearly how the attempts by British industrial capitalists to maximize profits on the basis of their firms' traditional productive resources – what, following Schumpeter, I have called the adaptive response – ensured that the British economy would *not* remain in the forefront of international industrial development.[32] In keeping with

[27] Eric Hobsbawm, "The Historians' Group of the Communist Party," in Maurice Cornforth, ed., *Rebels and Their Causes* (London: Lawrence & Wishart, 1978), 21–48, cited at 23.

[28] Ibid., 38.   [29] Ibid., 44.   [30] See ibid., 21.

[31] See E. J. Hobsbawm, *Labouring Men* (London: Weidenfeld & Nicolson, 1968); idem, *Workers: Worlds of Labour* (New York: Pantheon, 1984). For more recent research that elaborates on Hobsbawm's insights into the British labor process, see Keith Burgess, *The Origins of British Industrial Relations* (London: Croom Helm, 1975); Royden Harrison and Jonathan Zeitlin, eds., *Divisions of Labour: Skilled Workers and Technological Change in Nineteenth Century Britain* (Sussex: Harvester, 1985); Lazonick, *Competitive Advantage*, ch. 6.

[32] E. J. Hobsbawm, *Industry and Empire* (London: Weidenfeld & Nicolson, 1968), ch. 9; idem, *The Age of Empire, 1875–1914* (New York: Pantheon, 1987), ch. 2.

Dobb's remarks concerning the ossification of an existing economic structure, Hobsbawm argued:

The commonest, and probably best, economic explanation of the loss of dynamism in British industry is that it was the result "ultimately of the early and long-sustained start as an industrial power." It illustrates the deficiencies of the private enterprise mechanism in a number of ways. Pioneer industrialization naturally took place in special conditions which could not be maintained, with methods and techniques which, however advanced and efficient at the time, could not remain the most advanced and efficient, and it created a pattern of both production and markets which would not necessarily remain the one best fitted to sustain economic growth and technical change. Yet to change from an old and obsolescent pattern to a new one was both expensive and difficult. It was expensive because it involved both the scrapping of old investments still capable of yielding good profits, and new investments of even greater initial cost; for as a general rule newer technology is more expensive technology. It was difficult because it would almost certainly require agreement to rationalize between a large number of individual firms and industries, none of which could be certain precisely where the benefits of rationalization would go, or even whether in undertaking it they were not giving away their money to outsiders or competitors. So long as satisfactory profits were to be made in the old way, and so long as the decision to modernize had to emerge from the sum-total of decisions by individual firms, the incentive to do so would be weak. What is more, the general interest of the economy would very likely be lost sight of.[33]

In this passage, Hobsbawm displayed an awareness both of the growing importance of collective organization for technological change and international competitive advantage in the twentieth century and of the extent to which the individualistic structures of industrial organization that had enabled British industry to dominate in international competition in the nineteenth century had become barriers to an innovative response. He did not, however, undertake the comparative study of advanced capitalist development required to elucidate the institutional character of the new, more powerful modes of capitalist organization that transformed Britain's early start from an advantage to a disadvantage in international competition.[34] Indeed, in his most recent book on the momentous social, political, and economic changes that swept the world economy between 1875 and 1914, Hobsbawm asserted that "the important issue is not who, within

[33] Hobsbawm, *Industry and Empire*, 158. At the beginning of this passage, Hobsbawm quoted from H. J. Habbakuk, *American and British Technology in the Nineteenth Century: The Search for Labour-Saving Inventions* (Cambridge University Press, 1962), 220.

[34] For an outline of the organizational and technological changes that characterized the Second Industrial Revolution, see Hobsbawm, *Industry and Empire*, 145–9; idem, *Age of Empire*, 44–50.

the growing world economy, grew more and faster, but its global growth as a whole."[35]

The fact is, however, that during the first half of the twentieth century, while the individualistic British economy was in relative decline, the more collectivized U.S. economy was, save for the decade of the Great Depression, experiencing rapid growth. Indeed, in historical perspective it would appear that the Marxian model, with its emphasis on the subjugation of the labor force to capitalist domination fits the U.S. experience of the twentieth century much better than the British. In the United States, the economic dominance of big business, the deskilling of shop-floor labor, and the absence of a political party representing the interests of U.S. labor are undisputed facts.

The seminal Marxist work on the United States is Paul Baran and Paul Sweezy's *Monopoly Capital*.[36] When Baran and Sweezy first published their analysis in the mid-1960s, U.S. industry, through its productive (and military) power, still dominated the international economy. The purpose of *Monopoly Capital* was to expose the social irrationality of the U.S. economic system. Since then, as the U.S. economy has entered into relative decline, Sweezy and Harry Magdoff have extended the analysis to expose as well the economic fragility of the U.S. system in a period in which, with its once-dominant productive power on the wane, only increased indebtedness can stave off stagnation.[37]

The Baran and Sweezy analysis began with the Marxian assumption of capitalist domination of the labor force through the introduction of technological change. They went on to argue that the very power of the capitalist enterprise to create value *and* appropriate it as surplus value generates problems for the economic system, because market coordination of aggregate consumption and production does not necessarily result in sufficient demand to ensure the utilization of the productive resources of the giant industrial corporations. And if the giant corporations do not expect that their productive resources will be utilized, they simply cease to employ workers and invest in new plant and equipment – as indeed happened in the 1930s.[38]

In the post-World War II decades, Keynesians in the United States argued that the state needed only to "fine-tune" the economy through monetary and fiscal policies to ensure economic stability, thereby leaving the predominance of market coordination intact. In contrast, Baran and

---

[35] Hobsbawm, *Age of Empire*, 47.
[36] Paul Baran and Paul Sweezy, *Monopoly Capital* (New York: Monthly Review Press, 1966).
[37] See, e.g., Harry Magdoff and Paul M. Sweezy, *Stagnation and the Financial Explosion* (New York: Monthly Review Press, 1987).
[38] See Baran and Sweezy, *Monopoly Capital*, ch. 8.

Sweezy argued that, in a system dominated by powerful industrial corporations whose abilities to produce continually outran society's ability to consume, planned coordination had to become increasingly pervasive to overcome the deep-rooted problem of effective demand. To avoid a relapse into depression, these corporations had to engage in sales efforts to sustain the demand for their own particular products. The companies' sales expenditures in and of themselves contributed to effective demand in the economic system, as did the consumer expenditures that the sales effort generated. At the macroeconomic level, with an emphasis on military spending, the economic system became ever more dependent on state spending to create the effective demand that could fend off stagnation.[39] Increasingly, however, the reliance of the economic system on the escalation of consumer and state spending resulted in an explosion of private and public indebtedness that constituted a financially fragile basis for fending off the tendency toward stagnation.[40]

The strength of the combined contributions of Baran, Sweezy, and Magdoff is that they have accounted for pervasive macroeconomic trends in spending and indebtedness in the United States in terms of the need for U.S. business corporations to utilize the productive resources they have put in place. In addition, they have related the changing nature of state involvement to the transition of U.S. industry from its era of international dominance to its current experience of relative decline. The weakness of their approach is that they have provided only a crude microeconomic analysis (essentially a technological determinism inherited from Marx) of the evolution of the internal organization of the managerial enterprise, and hence of the evolving relation between business organizations and market forces in U.S. capitalist development. The financial explosion is a manifestation of the failure of industry to generate productivity; it is not the cause of industrial decline. Because Baran, Sweezy, and Magdoff have not provided an adequate historical analysis of how the innovative business organization in the United States became dominant in the first place, they cannot explain either the timing or reasons for U.S. industrial decline.

The microeconomic weakness of the "monopoly capital" approach is reflected in Harry Braverman's much-discussed *Labor and Monopoly Capital*. Braverman followed Marx too closely in viewing technological change as simply a means by which capitalists dominate and exploit workers.[41] For Braverman, as for Marx, management solved the labor problem by taking craft skills off the shop floor and then exploiting labor to the

---

[39] Ibid., ch. 7.

[40] Magdoff and Sweezy, *Stagnation and the Financial Explosion;* see also Paul M. Sweezy and Harry Magdoff, *The Irreversible Crisis* (New York: Monthly Review Press, 1988).

[41] Harry Braverman, *Labor and Monopoly Capital* (New York: Monthly Review Press, 1974).

hilt. In contrast, I have argued that in the most successful capitalist economies, the United States included, technological change has often served as a means for creating positive-sum solutions that, by generating cooperative labor–management relations, have prolonged both the political and economic viability of capitalism as a social system.

True enough, Braverman made a compelling, and indeed historically relevant, case for the degradation of the skill content of shop-floor labor in twentieth-century U.S. capitalism. But he eschewed an analysis of how the need to transform high fixed costs into low unit costs compelled the managers of U.S. corporations to share value gains even with the de-skilled workers in order to elicit effort from them and maintain the rapid flow of work on the shop floor.[42] In other words, in focusing exclusively on the impact of technology on "capital–labor" relations, he ignored the profound organizational transformations of capitalism in the twentieth century that formed the basis for successful economic development in the United States.

To comprehend the dynamics of capitalist development, an analysis of the deskilling of shop-floor labor, when and where it has occurred, must be combined with an analysis of the evolving relations between management and labor for the purpose of transforming high fixed costs into low unit costs. Over the past two decades, radical labor historians in the United States have taken a positive step in this direction by focusing on the shop-floor determinants of U.S. workers' economic and political movements. Yet much of this historical analysis, as evidenced, for example, in the work of a leading labor historian, David Montgomery, has gone too far in the opposite direction of Marx and Braverman by virtually excluding the impact of technology on labor (be it for better or for worse) from the analysis of the transformations of the social relations of capitalist production.[43]

The research in the Marxian "labor process" tradition closest in orientation to the analysis that I have outlined here is that of David Gordon, Richard Edwards, and Michael Reich.[44] They have sought to understand how, over the past century, the U.S. labor force became segmented into distinct groups of workers with qualitatively different attachments to their

[42] William Lazonick, "Klasserna i det kapitaliska företaget" [Class relations and the capitalist enterprise], translated into Swedish by Inger Humlesjö, *Häften för Kritiska Studier,* 19 (1986), 49–78. For such an analysis, see Lazonick, *Competitive Advantage.*
[43] David Montgomery, *The Fall of the House of Labor* (Cambridge University Press, 1987). For a critique of Montgomery, see William Lazonick, "The Breaking of the American Working Class," *Reviews in American History,* 17 (June 1989), 272–83.
[44] David M. Gordon, Richard Edwards, and Michael Reich, *Segmented Work, Divided Workers: The Historical Transformation of Labor in the United States* (Cambridge University Press, 1982); see also Richard Edwards, *Contested Terrain* (New York: Basic, 1979).

places of employment and different degrees of control over the organization of their work. They characterized different stages of U.S. capitalist development as "social structures of accumulation," arguing quite correctly that "the social structure of accumulation can be conceptualized as a durable investment that, once installed, pays off over a long period of time."[45]

But Gordon, Edwards, and Reich have not explicitly recognized the importance of managerial structure as one type of "durable investment" that has been central to U.S. economic development in the twentieth century. In my view, the organizational capabilities inherent in corporate managerial structures were critical to the rise of the United States to a position of international economic leadership. Although Gordon, Edwards, and Reich did ask why certain social structures persist even when their contributions to the accumulation process display diminishing returns[46] (a phenomenon that I call "institutional rigidity"), they provided no comparative analysis of the value-creating power of competing "social structures." For example, in *Segmented Work, Divided Workers*, they made but one brief reference to the Japanese employment system.[47] Instead of focusing on shifts in international competitive advantage, which I view as key to understanding changes in labor–management relations in the United States, they resorted to the mechanistic notion of "long swings" to "explain" the rise and decline of social structures of accumulation.[48] They did recognize the existence within the U.S. occupational structure of a group of professional, managerial, and technical workers whose remuneration, employment security, and work conditions are significantly superior to those of unionized blue-collar workers.[49] They therefore characterized the more elite group as the "independent primary segment," as distinct from the "subordinate primary segment" of the labor force. But they devoted but one page to a discussion of what "professional, managerial, and technical workers" do and provided virtually no historical analysis of the conditions under which this segment of the labor force arose.

Not surprisingly given this omission (and like virtually all Marxist accounts of capitalist development), Gordon, Edwards, and Reich offered no analysis of the importance of managerial structure to the innovation process that is so critical to successful capitalist development. They recognized and documented the *existence* of the hierarchical segmentation that divides the "working class" from the "managerial class" in the United States, and they were acutely aware of the issues of effort and shop-floor control that are central to the Marxian perspective. But lacking a theory

---

[45] Gordon, Edwards, and Reich, *Segmented Work*, 34.   [46] Ibid., 34–5.   [47] Ibid., 221.
[48] Ibid., ch. 2.   [49] Ibid., 202–3.

of the innovative business organization, they did not analyze how and with what success capitalist enterprises have made use of this hierarchical division of labor between management and workers to plan and coordinate the development and utilization of productive resources, including the development and utilization of labor itself.

Revising the Schumpeterian perspective

For analyzing advanced capitalist development, the prime weakness of the Marxian perspective is the prime strength of the Schumpeterian perspective, and vice versa. Just as Marxian analysis ignores the process of innovation that creates the need for the capitalist enterprise to transform high fixed costs into low unit costs on the shop floor, the Schumpeterian analysis ignores the utilization of shop-floor labor that an innovative investment strategy renders imperative. Yet even among those who draw their primary insights from Schumpeter, there are marked differences in the understanding of the institutional character of capitalism, depending on whether or not they recognize the importance of organizational structure as a necessary condition for implementing an innovative investment strategy.

Indeed, far from viewing (as I do) innovation as the result of the strategy and structure of the business organization, one brand of Schumpeterian economics – that put forth by economists who call themselves "neo-Austrians" – reduces "innovative activity" to, quoting Israel Kirzner, the "discovery of an intertemporal opportunity" for "pure gain" created by the existence of an "intertemporal price discrepancy."[50] Identifying with the young Schumpeter of *The Theory of Economic Development*, the neo-Austrians are intellectual descendants of the late-nineteenth-century school of neoclassical economists led by Eugen von Böhm-Bawerk, Carl Menger, and Friedrich von Wieser, under whose theoretical influence Schumpeter entered the economics profession.[51] Neo-Austrians such as Kirzner view the "Schumpeterian" entrepreneur as the *discoverer* – and not the creator – of *disequilibrium* situations that arise as a matter of

---

[50] Israel Kirzner, *Discovery and the Capitalist Process* (Chicago: University of Chicago Press, 1985), 85; idem, "The 'Austrian' Perspective," in Daniel Bell and Irving Kristol, eds., *The Crisis in Economic Theory* (New York: Basic, 1981), 111–22. For a neo-Austrian approach to institutional economics, see Richard Langlois, "Rationality, Institutions, and Explanation," in Richard Langlois, ed., *Economics as a Process: Essays in the New Institutional Economics* (Cambridge University Press, 1986), 225–55. For a neo-Austrian approach to vertical integration in particular, see Morris Silver, *Enterprise and the Scope of the Firm* (Oxford: Robertson, 1984). Silver's critique of my work on industrial organization and technological change in cotton textiles fails to recognize the distinction between innovative and adaptive responses; see ibid., 60–2.

[51] Joseph A. Schumpeter, *Ten Great Economists* (New York: Oxford University Press, 1951), chs. 3 and 6, and 298–301.

course in an unregulated *market economy* because economic actors are confronted with various degrees of uncertainty concerning present and future prices in their economic decision making. These disequilibrium situations afford the entrepreneur opportunities to make an entrepreneurial profit, until the entry of imitators restores equilibrium in that particular market.

The prime institutional implication of the neo-Austrian perspective is that it is entrepreneurial activity that is constantly adapting the capitalist economy to make optimal use of its scarce resources. In the neo-Austrian version of "Schumpeterian" economics, the building of an organizational structure plays no role in the successful implementation of an entrepreneurial strategy. By my definition, moreover, what the neo-Austrians view as an entrepreneurial strategy is not even an *innovative* strategy. Rather, it is at best what I have termed an adaptive strategy – a strategy that does not *create* economic disequilibrium but helps to move the economy *into* equilibrium. It is a strategy that seeks to optimize subject to given environmental constraints, albeit in disequilibrium situations. Lacking the collective power of organization, the "Austrian" entrepreneur does not attempt to alter environmental constraints – he or she does not create disequilibrium situations.

Not surprisingly, the neo-Austrians provide no theory of how productive resources get developed in a capitalist economy; they lack a theory of economic development. The neo-Austrian brand of neoclassical economics incorporates much more realism – for example, the existence of disequilibrium and uncertainty – than the more conventional Walrasian theory of a market economy. But in an age of managerial, and indeed collective, capitalism, the neo-Austrians still view the entrepreneur as an individualist actor who discovers and then reacts to available market opportunities. By ignoring the organizational determinants of technological change, the neo-Austrians help to perpetuate the myth of the market economy. For such economists, in the beginning there were markets – and in the end there are still markets.

As argued in Chapter 1, history shows that capitalist development is a process that combines innovative strategy with organizational structure to alter existing technological and social constraints on superior economic performance. By overcoming constraints that less powerful productive organizations take as given, the innovative organization *escapes* from equilibrium, in the process altering the economic environment that confronts its less innovative rivals. Innovative activity that *creates* new economic possibilities is the essence of the process of economic *development*. The analysis of innovative activity cannot be reduced to the "optimal allocation of scarce resources," because the activity itself creates new standards of "optimality" (as evidenced by the lowering of attainable unit costs) by overcoming prior conditions of scarcity (as evidenced by the need to incur high fixed costs to develop productive resources). Innovators succeed in transforming high fixed costs into low unit costs because they build organizational structures that can develop and utilize the enterprise's productive resources.

One may conceive of a new industry equilibrium that is ultimately achieved because of either demand constraints on industry expansion or the exhaustion of internal economies of scale on the supply side. But the very need to build organizational structures to reach the new equilibrium means that the institutional landscape of the capitalist economy has been to some extent, and irreversibly, transformed. This transformation of the economic institutions of capitalism may, moreover, establish the organizational and technological bases for pursuing further innovations that involve the planned coordination of ever more complex specialized divisions of labor.

As I argued in Chapter 4, Schumpeter's relevance to us today derives not only from his understanding (already present in *The Theory of Economic Development*) that marginal adaptations in response to market forces cannot explain the process of economic development, but also from his willingness to take historical analysis seriously and his growing appreciation of the movements *away from* market coordination of economic activity in the most successful capitalist economies in the twentieth century. His earliest work posited that the analysis of economic development lay outside the purview of the emerging neoclassical paradigm of the "circular flow of economic life." Schumpeter then spent his career trying to understand first the macroeconomics and then the microeconomics of the innovation process.

Over the course of that career he came to recognize that innovation need not, and indeed under most circumstances could not, be simply the product of an entrepreneurial individual working alone, hence (as the neo-Austrians believe) making his or her mark on the economy by interacting with market processes. By the 1940s Schumpeter had come to perceive that the individual entrepreneur needed to build an organizational structure to carry the innovation through to success; he or she had to *supersede* market processes for the sake of establishing the long-term social relations with other people that form the core and substance of a cohesive and durable organization. Schumpeter recognized that not only collective organization but also collective entrepreneurship was becoming increasingly important for the innovation process.

We have also seen that, partly through the impetus provided by the Research Center in Entrepreneurial History, historians such as Chandler and Landes have moved the Schumpeterian agenda forward: Chandler through his in-depth investigations of the building of managerial structures and Landes through his much broader social analysis of economic history in which business–government relations, educational systems, and labor organization play a role in the development and utilization of technology. These historical contributions have thus far made little impact on the ahistorical methodology or individualist ideology of mainstream economics, as I shall elaborate in the last chapter.

Recently, however, in sharp contrast to the neo-Austrian interpretation of the Schumpeterian agenda, some economists in the United States and Western Europe, inspired more by the late Schumpeter of *Capitalism, Socialism, and Democracy*, have begun to analyze the role of organization, in both the private and public sectors, in determining the relative success of innovative investment strategies.[52] Because this work focuses on the role of planned coordination of both business organizations and the state in the innovation process, and indeed stresses that innovation is a *process* that by definition becomes part of economic reality over time, the links between institutional history and economic performance have become more and more central to what is presently an evolving research agenda.

The most ambitious and influential attempt to date to construct a formal Schumpeterian model of the impact of the business enterprise on innovation and economic growth is the pioneering work of Richard Nelson and Sidney Winter.[53] In keeping with the distinction between innovation and adaptation that I have made in this book, Nelson and Winter have attacked economic orthodoxy on the grounds that, in its theoretical formulation of economic growth, "the distinction between innovation and routine operation is totally repressed."[54] Neoclassical theory assumes that all relevant technologies are known, even if not presently in use, and hence leaves "no room . . . for nontrivial uncertainty, or for differences of opinion regarding what will work best, or for recognition of the fact that the set of innovation alternatives is shrouded in fundamental ambiguity."[55]

[52] Richard R. Nelson and Sidney G. Winter, *An Evolutionary Theory of Economic Change* (Cambridge, Mass.: Harvard University Press, 1982); William Lazonick, "Industrial Organization and Technological Change: The Decline of the British Cotton Industry," *Business History Review*, 57 (Summer 1983), 195–236; F. M. Scherer, *Innovation and Growth: Schumpeterian Perspectives* (Cambridge, Mass.: MIT Press, 1984); Bernard Elbaum and William Lazonick, eds., *The Decline of the British Economy* (Oxford: Clarendon Press, 1986); Christopher Freeman, *Technology Policy and Economic Performance: Lessons from Japan* (London: Pinter, 1988); Giovanni Dosi, Christopher Freeman, Richard Nelson, Gerald Silverberg, and Luc Soete, eds., *Technical Change and Economic Theory* (London: Pinter, 1988); Michael Best, *The New Competition: Institutions of Industrial Restructuring* (Cambridge, Mass.: Harvard University Press, 1990); for a review of much of the relevant literature, see Giovanni Dosi, "Sources, Procedures, and Microeconomic Effects of Innovation," *Journal of Economic Literature*, 26 (September 1988), 1120–71. See also Chapter 9, this volume.
[53] Nelson and Winter, *An Evolutionary Theory of Economic Change*.   [54] Ibid., 201.
[55] Ibid., 202.

Nelson and Winter have gone on to argue that even the more sophisticated neoclassical growth models that attempt to make technology endogenous have been

unable to come to grips with what is known about technological advance at the level of the individual firm or individual invention, where virtually all studies have shown these aspects to be central. This has caused a curious disjunction in the economic literature on technological advance, with analysis of economic growth at the level of the economy or the sector proceeding with one set of intellectual ideas, and analysis of technological advance at a more micro level proceeding with another.[56]

Missing from the neoclassical analysis is a theory of the firm that gains competitive advantage through what Nelson and Winter have called "Schumpeterian competition" – "through innovation or through early adoption of a new product or process."[57]

What is needed to understand technological and economic change is a theory that asks what determines the differences in the technological and economic capabilities of competing enterprises. Yet to assume away all technological and economic differences among enterprises is precisely what neoclassical microeconomic theory – what I have labeled the "theory of the market economy" – not only does but is *designed* to do. As Nelson and Winter summed up the argument for a new departure in economic theory:

It is not possible to reconcile what is known about the phenomena at a micro level with the intellectual structure used to model technical advance at the macro or sectoral level by arguing that the macro model deals with the average or the modal firm. The differences among firms and the disequilibrium in the system appear to be an essential feature of growth driven by technical change. Neoclassical modelling cannot avail itself of this insight.[58]

To what extent is the alternative analytical framework that Nelson and Winter have offered consistent with the arguments I have presented in this book concerning the dynamic relation between investment strategy and organizational structure in creating competitive advantage? In their brief discussion of "analysts of firm organization and strategy," they recognized the strategy–structure connection but treated as an afterthought Chandler's argument that structure follows strategy – that is, that a firm builds an organization to plan and coordinate a high-fixed-cost strategy. Although they referred to the work of Oliver Williamson and Alfred Chandler, they did not distinguish Williamson's transaction cost framework, which, as we have seen, neglects the analysis of technological change from Chandler's strategy–structure framework, which focuses on the is-

---

[56] Ibid.   [57] Ibid., 203.   [58] Ibid.

sue of how organizations generate new cost structures.[59] As Nelson and Winter summarized the literature on "firm organization and strategy":

> Strategies differ from firm to firm, in part because of different interpretations of economic opportunities and constraints and in part because different firms are good at different things. In turn, the capabilities of a firm are embedded in its organizational structure, which is better adapted to certain strategies than to others. Thus, strategies at any time are constrained by organization. But also a significant change in a firm's strategy is likely to call for a significant change in its organizational structure.[60]

Nelson and Winter themselves informed the reader why they did not make the distinction between a theory of adaptation such as Williamson's in which structure determines strategy and a theory of innovation such as Chandler's in which strategy determines structure. "Largely in the interests of establishing an understandable linkage between individual firm behavior and industry behavior, our formal models in this book suppress considerations of internal structure and organizational change."[61] In a later discussion of the relation between strategy and structure, they defined business strategy as "heuristics": "principles that are believed to shorten the average search to solution of the problems of survival and profitability." They went on to argue that Chandler's principle that "the firm should adopt an organizational structure appropriate to its strategy" reflects "high-level managerial heuristics."[62] Once these principles have become embedded in the firm's organizational structure, strategy and structure take on a symbiotic relation to one another, so that the innovation process itself becomes routinized. The essential theoretical proposition concerning the advanced capitalist enterprise in Nelson and Winter's evolutionary theory of economic change is that "organizations have well-defined routines for the support and direction of their innovative efforts."[63]

As a critique of the myth of the market economy, there is much to commend Nelson and Winter's perspective on the nature of the modern business organization. They placed firms, not markets, at the center of the analysis of economic change – notwithstanding their willingness to embrace neo-Austrian perspectives as compatible with their own, and indeed their statement in that regard that "our theory is a theory about market processes."[64] Perhaps what they meant is that theirs is a theory of market *competition,* but not of market *coordination* for those business organizations that are most successful in that competition. They posited as the essence of the process of economic change *organizational capabilities* in the face of uncertainty (cognitive if not behavioral), as distinct from entrepreneurial activities in response to the ebbs and flows of palpable

[59] Ibid., 36–7.   [60] Ibid., 37.   [61] Ibid., 38; see also 279.   [62] Ibid., 133.   [63] Ibid., 134.
[64] Ibid., 41.

market opportunities. By the same token, they pointed to the importance of organizational continuity (which, however, they seem to envision as confined to R&D activities) for cumulative technological advance.[65]

The contribution of the Nelson and Winter model is that it focuses on critical developmental issues and captures central institutional facts of modern capitalist reality. But despite their goal of elaborating an "evolutionary theory of economic change," their model cannot analyze the conditions, internal or external, under which innovative business organizations become and remain innovative or the conditions under which they turn from innovation to adaptation. Under what conditions does the enterprise use its cumulated organizational capabilities to renew its innovative strategies and extend its competitive advantage, and under what conditions does it choose to adopt adaptive strategies that seek to avoid uncertainty and live off its past success? This question, I have argued, is at the heart of the issue of the changing institutional foundations of international industrial dominance and decline. Nelson and Winter were well aware of this shortcoming of their model of evolutionary change:

An essential aspect of real Schumpeterian competition is that firms do not know *ex ante* whether it pays to try to be an innovator or an imitator, or what levels of R&D expenditures might be appropriate. . . . Only the course of events over time will determine and reveal what strategies are the better ones.[66]

They would probably agree, however, that economists who want to understand when, where, why, and to what extent certain types of strategies have turned out to be "better ones" need not remain in the dark. Rather, they can turn to the study of business history, even very recent business history. Nelson and Winter would also undoubtedly agree that an understanding of the historical dynamics of industrial innovation and decline can provide an objective foundation for considering what types of investment strategies and organizational structures, in both the private and public sectors, might be put in place to influence the "course of events" that determine economic prosperity.

Recapturing and modernizing Marshallian dynamics

Above all, the intellectual value of Nelson and Winter's elaboration of the Schumpeterian perspective lies in their insistence that economics needs a theory of how business organizations *develop* productive resources. However, such a perspective is not enough. As I have argued, a complete theory of economic development also requires a theory of how the business organization *utilizes* productive resources – a theory for which, as I

---

[65] Ibid., 255–62.   [66] Ibid., 286.

have argued in Chapter 4, the Marxian perspective with its distinction between labor power and labor effort provides a critical point of departure.[67] What unites the Marxian and Schumpeterian perspectives on capitalist development is that both view the business enterprise as an engine of economic growth – the Schumpeterian because the enterprise organizes the innovation process that permits the development of productive resources and the Marxian because the enterprise has incentives to invest in new technologies and ensure their fullest possible utilization.

For analyzing the impact of economic institutions on economic performance, however, not even the combined elaboration of the Schumpeterian and Marxian theoretical perspectives suffices. Neither perspective speaks to the critical issue of the evolving relation between organizational coordination and market coordination in capitalist development. Even if we (as history shows that we should) accept the proposition that the internal organization of the business enterprise has become *increasingly* important to the process of capitalist development, advanced capitalist economies are still characterized by the interaction of business organization and market exchange in the development and utilization of productive resources. For any given industry, the relation between organizational coordination and market coordination that yields competitive *advantage* rather than competitive *disadvantage* is a continually evolving phenomenon precisely because new combinations of organization and technology create new possibilities for the development and utilization of productive resources, and ultimately new standards for generating high-quality products at low unit costs. In terms of the analytical framework presented in Chapter 3, given the historical evolution of organization and technology in a particular industry at a particular time, too much organization and too little reliance on markets will result in high fixed costs, which will put a business enterprise at a competitive disadvantage, while too little organization and too much reliance on markets will preclude the business enterprise from developing and utilizing productive resources to the extent necessary to gain competitive advantage.

To the insights that can be gained from the elaboration and combination of the Schumpeterian and Marxian perspectives, therefore, one must add a perspective that focuses on the relation between organizations and markets in capitalist development. As I have argued in Chapter 5, such a perspective is inherent in Alfred Marshall's distinction between internal and external economies of scale as alternative determinants of economic development. In books 1 to 4 of *Principles of Economics*, first published in 1890, Marshall himself elaborated this perspective on economic development, and indeed in doing so provided a cogent explanation of Britain's

---

[67] See also Lazonick, *Competitive Advantage*.

rise to international industrial dominance on the basis of external economies during the nineteenth century.[68]

The prevalence of external economies, and hence horizontally fragmented and vertically specialized structures of industrial organization in capitalist development, led Marshall to put forth the concept of the "Representative Firm" as characteristic of a particular industry at a given point in time. By positing an enterprise cost structure that could be taken as representative of the industry norm, Marshall was able in book 5 of *Principles* to turn his analysis from the dynamics of economic development to the statics of the industry equilibrium of supply and demand. In the presence of external rather than internal economies of scale, the normal expectation was that the representative firm would remain small relative to the size of its industry, and hence would have no option but to optimize subject to given technological and market constraints.

Even as Marshall wrote, however, the emergence of the managerial business organization was transforming the institutional foundations of capitalist development, with internal economies increasingly replacing external economies as the basis for cost reductions and economic growth. As has been mentioned, in *Industry and Trade,* first published in 1919, Marshall studied this shift in the relation between economic institutions and economic performance as it was occurring in rapidly growing national economies such as those of Germany and the United States. Yet despite his comparative research, Marshall clung to the mistaken belief that external economies and the proprietary firm would continue to predominate in capitalist development. He was undoubtedly influenced not only by his ideological proclivity for bourgeois individualism based on the proprietary firm, but also by the ability of Britain's leading industries – even one so horizontally fragmented and vertically specialized as the cotton textile industry – to remain competitive on the basis of external economies throughout his life.[69]

As outlined in Chapter 5, Marshall's followers took as their point of departure the analysis of the firm in equilibrium. They devoted virtually all of their discussion of internal and external economies and diseconomies to whether the cost structures inherent in the "theory of the firm" could be reconciled with perfectly competitive market conditions. In the process, they lost sight of Marshall's developmental perspective as set out in the first four books of *Principles* – a perspective that sought to understand how cost structures evolve rather than, as was the case in book 5,

---

[68] For an analysis of the rise and decline of British competitive advantage that uses the Marshallian approach to economic development, see William Mass and William Lazonick, "The British Cotton Industry and International Competitive Advantage: The State of the Debates," *Business History*, 32 (October 1990), 9–65.

[69] See ibid.

how a firm chooses its level of output to maximize its profits with its cost structures in place.

To take cost structures as given in economic analysis is likewise to take the technologies (capital–labor combinations) and factor prices that together determine costs as given, and hence to assume that the decisions and activities of the firm have no influence on production processes or the prices of inputs. The neo-Marshallians of the 1920s and 1930s prided themselves on the realistic focus of their partial equilibrium analysis, as distinct from the much more ethereal general equilibrium analysis of the neo-Walrasians such as John Hicks, Frank Knight, and Paul Samuelson. But by confining economic analysis to optimization subject to given technological and market constraints, even the neo-Marshallians became part of the neoclassical methodological consensus that by the 1930s had come to dominate Anglo-American economic thought. No longer was economics the study of the "attainment and . . . use of the material requisites of wellbeing" as Marshall had defined it.[70] Now "economics" was the study of the optimal utilization of the material requisites of well-being that, *by some process beyond the purview of "economics,"* had already been attained. To repeat Lionel Robbins's argument, "Whatever Economics is concerned with, it is *not* causes of material welfare as such."[71] Marshall himself probably would have argued against this definition of "economics." The neo-Marshallians of the 1930s, captivated and ultimately captured by the methods of constrained optimization, not only would not have so argued; they could not have. They had acquired a trained incapacity to contemplate the issues of economic development.

Even when, as in the case of Joan Robinson's *The Economics of Imperfect Competition*, the neo-Marshallians confronted the case of "imperfect competition," they saw the essence of economic analysis as working out the equilibrium of the firm. Robinson herself, transformed by the "Keynesian Revolution," eventually came to see the light. Some three decades after the publication of her neo-Marshallian elaboration of the theory of the firm in equilibrium, Robinson argued, "A model applicable to actual history has to be capable of getting out of equilibrium; indeed it must not normally be in it."[72] At the same time, however, neo-Keynesians such as Robinson followed Keynes, as well as the Polish economist Michal Kalecki, in focusing their economic analysis on macroeconomic problems.

---

[70] Alfred Marshall, *Principles of Economics*, 9th (variorum) ed. (London: Macmillan Press, 1961), vol. 1 (text), 1.

[71] Lionel Robbins, *The Nature and Significance of Economic Science* (London: Macmillan Press, 1932), 9.

[72] Joan Robinson, *Essays in the Theory of Economic Growth* (London: St. Martin's, 1964), 25.

They made virtually no attempt to develop microeconomic theory "applicable to actual history."

As a result the neo-Keynesians have been unable to bring Marshallian dynamics into the world of twentieth-century capitalist development even when they have come to recognize that maintaining the firm in equilibrium is not what economics is all about – that is, even when they have sought to recapture Marshallian dynamics. For example, in the 1960s and 1970s Nicholas Kaldor, a leading neo-Keynesian, stressed the irrelevance of equilibrium and the importance of increasing returns in the operation of the economy.[73] In an article entitled "The Irrelevance of Equilibrium Economics," Kaldor wrote:

> The difficulty with a new start is to pinpoint the critical area where economic theory went astray. In my own view, it happened when the theory of value [by which Kaldor meant the neoclassical theory of price determination] took over the center of the stage – which meant focusing attention on the *allocative* functions of markets to the exclusion of their *creative* functions – as an instrument for transmitting impulses to economic change.[74]

If by "creative functions," Kaldor meant the process of economic development, he pinpointed how economics began asking the wrong questions. But note that he referred to the creative functions of *markets*, not firms. Kaldor's arguments about increasing returns did not call for an understanding of the relation between firms and markets in capitalist development. Rather, he simply assumed that the economy (or industry) in question is market coordinated. Unlike Marshallian dynamics that sought to understand the evolving relation between internal and external economies, Kaldor simply did not address the issue of whether increasing returns result from organizational coordination or market coordination.[75]

Instead, Kaldor pinned his dynamic theory on "Verdoorn's Law."[76] This

---

[73] Nicholas Kaldor, "Causes of the Slow Rate of Economic Growth in the United Kingdom," in *Further Essays on Economic Theory* (New York: Holmes & Meier, 1978), 100–38; idem, "The Irrelevance of Equilibrium Economics," in ibid., 176–201.

[74] Kaldor, "The Irrelevance of Equilibrium Economics," 181, emphasis in the original.

[75] The same failure to specify the institutional foundations of "increasing returns" characterizes some of the more recent literature. See, e.g., Paul M. Romer, "Increasing Returns and Long-Run Growth," *Journal of Political Economy*, 94 (October 1986), 1002–37; W. Brian Arthur, "Competing Technologies, Increasing Returns, and Lock-in by Historical Events," *Economic Journal*, 99 (March 1989), 116–31. In contrast, some "post-Keynesian" approaches assume the managerial corporation and internal economies of scale, but reduce managerial decision making to "administered pricing" with no analysis of how investment strategy and organizational structure might lead to superior economic outcomes. Along these lines, see Alfred S. Eichner, *The Megacorp and Oligopoly: Micro Foundations of Macro Dynamics* (Cambridge University Press, 1976).

[76] Kaldor, "Causes of the Slow Rate of Economic Growth in the United Kingdom." See also "Symposium: Kaldor's Growth Laws," *Journal of Post Keynesian Economics*, 5 (Spring 1983), 341–429.

"law" asserts that the rate of growth of productivity is a function of the rate of growth of the economy – an argument that leaves intact (or at least in no way challenges) the mainstream myth that it is the market-coordinated economy that provides the microeconomic foundations for economic growth.

Indeed, rather than develop his analysis in terms of the critical Marshallian distinction between internal and external economies, Kaldor drew his intellectual inspiration from Adam Smith by way of the article "Increasing Returns and Economic Progress" by Allyn Young, a U.S. economist working in England who had originally presented the paper to the British Association for the Advancement of Science in 1928.[77] At the time, it will be remembered from our discussion in Chapter 5, economists in Britain had become obsessed with the problems that Marshallian increasing returns (decreasing costs) posed for the conventional assumption of perfect competition. As a result, they lost sight of the fact that, whatever their implications for industrial organization, decreasing costs manifested economic development.

Young rightly argued that economists' analytical apparatus for dealing with the equilibrium of supply and demand might "stand in the way of a clear view of the more general or elementary aspects of the phenomena of increasing returns, such as I wish to comment upon in this paper";[78] for he contended, also correctly in my view, that "the counter forces which are continually defeating the forces which make for economic equilibrium are more pervasive and more deeply rooted in the constitution of the modern economic system than we [i.e., economists of the 1920s] commonly realise."[79]

Young understood the need for a theory of economic development, but he did not view the internal organization of the business enterprise as fundamental to the process. In analyzing the "counter forces which are continually defeating the forces which make for economic equilibrium," Young invoked Marshall's distinction between internal and external economies to "safeguard against the common error of assuming that wherever increasing returns operate there is necessarily an effective tendency towards monopoly."[80] He went on to argue that *existing* firms are what I have called adaptive firms:

When we look at the internal economies of a particular firm we envisage a condition of comparative stability. Year after year the firm, like its competitors, is manufacturing a particular product or group of products, or is confining itself to certain

---

[77] Allyn Young, "Increasing Returns and Economic Progress," *Economic Journal*, 38 (December 1928), 527–42. See also Charles P. Blitch, "Allyn Young on Increasing Returns," *Journal of Post Keynesian Economics*, 5 (Spring 1983), 359–72.
[78] Young, "Increasing Returns and Economic Progress," 527.   [79] Ibid., 533.
[80] Ibid., 527.

definite stages in the work of forwarding the products towards their final form. Its operations change in the sense that they are progressively adapted to an increasing output, but they are kept within definitely circumscribed bounds.[81]

Where, then, does "economic progress" – what I have called "innovation" – come from? Young's answer is: external economies based on new products introduced by new firms that come to form new industries.[82] Hence, according to Young, there is no point in studying the history of individual firms to understand how capitalist economies grow. His mind untouched (as we shall see) by the rise of managerial capitalism in the United States and Germany, Young's vision was of an innovative capitalist economy based on market coordination of the specialized division of labor.

To further locate this vision of economic progress in the intellectual traditions of economics, Young combined Böhm-Bawerk's notion that "the principal economies which manifest themselves in increasing returns are the economies of capitalistic or roundabout methods of production" with Adam Smith's argument that "division of labor is limited by the extent of the market."[83] "Economies of roundabout methods, even more than the economies of other forms of the division of labour," Young argued, "depend upon the extent of the market."

In and of themselves, however, these notions of the determinants of economic progress do not necessarily support Young's argument that external economies and market coordination dominate the process of economic development. The introduction of more complex divisions of labor (so-called roundabout methods) could be the result of planned coordination, and the business organizations that introduced these more complex divisions of labor would then require a greater extent of the market to ensure that they could utilize them sufficiently to transform high fixed costs into low unit costs. Rather, Young's argument is based entirely on his *assertion* that external economies and market coordination dominate. "I have naturally been interested," said the American Young, "in British opinions respecting the reasons for the relatively high productivity (per labourer or per hour of labour) of representative American industries."[84] Young then made clear his opinion on this matter:

Those who hold that American industry is managed better, that its leaders study its problems more intelligently and plan more courageously and more wisely can cite no facts in support of their opinion save the differences in the results achieved. Allowing for the circumstance that British industry, as a whole, has proved to be rather badly adjusted to the new post-war economic situation, I know of no facts

---

[81] Ibid., 528.   [82] Ibid.
[83] Ibid., 531; for my critique of Böhm-Bawerk's argument, see Chapter 4.
[84] Young, "Increasing Returns and Economic Progress," 532.

which prove or even indicate that British industry, seen against the background of its own problems and its own possibilities, is less efficiently organised or less ably directed than American industry or the industry of any other country.[85]

In 1951, in an article entitled "The Division of Labor Is Limited by the Extent of the Market," the U.S. neoclassical economist George Stigler ventured into the analysis of the institutional determinants of economic development by elaborating on Young's argument (albeit without the encumbrance of "roundabout methods").[86] Like Young, Stigler argued that the coordination of the more complex specialized divisions of labor that were the sources of economic growth would be done by the market. Whereas Young made his argument by assertion, Stigler turned to two recently published business histories on the U.S. textile machinery industry[87] to support his argument that "if one considers the full life of industries, the dominance of vertical disintegration is surely to be expected."[88] The business histories show that, in the early nineteenth century, British bans on the exportation of machinery compelled U.S. firms in the incipient (and tariff-protected) cotton textile industry to produce their own machines. But as the nineteenth century progressed, the machinery producers became independent capital-goods producers, prepared to sell machines to far more customers than simply the textile manufacturing firms that initially owned the machine-making establishments.

Stigler's purpose in using the U.S. textile machinery example was to argue that, however a capitalist economy might have been organized in the past, advanced capitalist economies tend to become increasingly market coordinated, because it is only through vertical specialization that capital-goods producers can reap the benefits of the growing extent of the market. "Broadly viewed," Stigler argued, "Smith's theorem suggests that vertical disintegration is the typical development in growing industries, vertical integration in declining industries."[89] Following a discussion of external economies in nineteenth-century Britain and a quotation from Benjamin Franklin on the difficulty of the planned coordination of a specialized division of labor, Stigler concluded his article by arguing that "the division of labor is not a quaint practice of eighteenth-century pin factories; it is a fundamental principle of economic organization."[90]

Stigler might have noted that division of labor in the eighteenth-century

[85] Ibid.
[86] George Stigler, "The Division of Labor Is Limited by the Extent of the Market," in *The Organization of Industry* (Homewood, Ill.: Irwin, 1968), 129–41; originally published in *Journal of Political Economy*, 59 (June 1951), 185–93.
[87] George Gibb, *The Saco-Lowell Shops* (Cambridge, Mass.: Harvard University Press, 1950); Thomas R. Navin, *The Whitin Machine Works since 1831* (Cambridge, Mass.: Harvard University Press, 1950).
[88] Stigler, "The Division of Labor Is Limited by the Extent of the Market," 135.
[89] Ibid.   [90] Ibid., 141.

pin factory of Adam Smith was not market coordinated.[91] In any event, the U.S. textile machinery case is Stigler's only "modern" example of vertical disintegration (the machinery makers became independent of their parent firms in the last half of the nineteenth century). I do not intend here to enter into an analysis of the relation between organizations and markets in textile production (including machinery manufacture) in the United States. Nor do I in any way wish to denigrate Stigler's admirable attempt to draw on business history, particularly his reference to books so recently published at the time he wrote his "division of labor" article. His invocation of the historical record was especially commendable given his remarks a decade earlier that Marshall's use of history had diminished the old master's contribution to economic theory.[92] But considering, as Stigler said we should, the "full life of industries," he might have considered the following points.

First, because of the importance of the utilization of productive resources to the success of any enterprise, one would expect that a producer of durable capital goods that had for some reason or other (in this case because of the initial unavailability of alternative sources of machinery supply) arisen as a supplier in a vertically integrated structure would soon find it economically advantageous to find external buyers for its products. Indeed, a larger extent of the market might be economically necessary for reaping adequate returns to a continuation of its innovative investment strategy. The greater the fixed costs of the capital-goods producer, the longer the useful life of its products, and the slower the expansion of the integrated firm's downstream operations, then the greater the capital-goods producer's need to secure market sales. As it happens, in choosing textile production to illustrate vertical disintegration, Stigler picked a sector in which in the nineteenth century the capital-goods producers experienced relatively high fixed costs of not only plant and equipment but also research and development.[93] It was also a sector within the nineteenth-century U.S. economy in which there was a slow rate of technological obsolescence, and hence machinery replacement, in the production of a consumer good, cloth.[94] Also limiting the extent of in-house demand for

---

[91] See Adam Smith, *An Inquiry into the Nature and Causes of the Wealth of Nations* (New York: Modern Library, 1937), bk. 1, ch. 1. For a critique of this piece by Stigler that complements what follows, see Ross Thomson, "Invention, Markets, and the Scope of the Firm: The Nineteenth Century U.S. Shoe Machinery Industry," *Business and Economic History*, 2d ser., 18 (1989), 140–9.

[92] George Stigler, *Production and Distribution Theories* (London: Macmillan Press, 1941), 62; quoted in Chapter 5, this volume.

[93] William Mass, "Sustaining Technological Leadership: Innovation, Standardization, and Flexibility in Weaving Technologies, 1890–1980," paper presented at the Conference on the Process of Technological Change, New York, November 10–11, 1989.

[94] See, e.g., Paul McGouldrick, *New England Textiles in the Nineteenth Century* (Cambridge, Mass.: Harvard University Press, 1968); William Lazonick and Thomas Brush,

machinery by the consumer-goods producer from the vertically integrated capital-goods producer was the fact that, of the mass-market industries in the United States in the nineteenth century, the industrial
structure of cloth production was probably the most horizontally fragmented. Chandler's documentation of the importance of vertical integration in U.S. economic growth in the late nineteenth and early twentieth
centuries would lead one to question whether Stigler chose a typical industry on which to base his claim for the tendency toward vertical disintegration in the process of economic development.[95]

Second, the very textile machinery manufacturers who, in order to gain
larger extents of the market, separated themselves from the consumer-
goods producers with which they had been initially integrated, *themselves* engaged in vertical integration (as indeed is documented in the
business histories of Gibb and Navin that Stigler cited). The Whitin Machine Works integrated not only forward into marketing to secure sales in
the South but also backward into building a company town (which it remained right up to the time Stigler wrote) in order to secure a stable
supply of labor. In contrast, the Saco Water Power Machine Shop failed
to integrate forward into marketing and, as a result, by 1897 had become
(in George Gibb's words) a "competitive nonentity."[96] Indeed, at least
one major textile machinery firm – Draper – integrated forward into cloth
manufacture in the early twentieth century in order to develop the automatic loom.[97]

Third, moving into the twentieth century, the demand for the most
advanced textile machinery came from textile firms that were themselves
highly integrated, not only between spinning and weaving but also increasingly into marketing.[98] To advocate an examination of the "full life of
industries," as Stigler indeed proposed, is to say that the economist needs
a complete historical perspective on the cases in question. Even for Stigler's own example of U.S. textiles, if one considers the full life of industries, vertical disintegration or increased vertical specialization was not
the dominant historical tendency. Stigler did well to read *some* business

"The 'Horndal Effect' in Early U.S. Manufacturing," *Explorations in Economic History*,
22 (January 1985), 53–96; William Lazonick, "Production Relations, Labor Productivity,
and Choice of Technique: British and U.S. Cotton Spinning," *Journal of Economic History*, 41 (September 1981), 491–516.

[95] See Alfred D. Chandler, Jr., *The Visible Hand: The Managerial Revolution in American
Business* (Cambridge, Mass.: Harvard University Press, 1977).

[96] Navin, *The Whitin Machine Works*, xx, 62, 219–22, 263; Gibb, *The Saco-Lowell Shops*,
402.

[97] Mass, "Sustaining Technological Leadership."

[98] See Solomon Barkin, "The Regional Significance of the Integration Movement in the
Southern Textile Industry," *Southern Economic Journal*, 15 (April 1949), 395–411; Jesse
Markham, "Integration in the Textile Industry," *Harvard Business Review* 28 (January–
February 1950), 74–88; Lazonick, "Industrial Organization."

history. But, as someone once said, a little bit of knowledge is a dangerous thing. Would that he had read on.

It is only fair to say that, had Stigler been writing "The Division of Labor Is Limited by the Extent of the Market" in the late 1980s, the amount of relevant business history he would have been able to read would have been vastly greater than that available to him in the early 1950s when he first published the article. The interested reader can start by consulting the secondary literature cited in Chandler's *Visible Hand* and *Scale and Scope*.[99] Nevertheless, the degree to which economists who have addressed issues of economic growth have been wedded to the myth of the market economy cannot wholly be explained by their ignorance of the institutional transformations in business organization that have taken place during the twentieth century. Even with a much less adequate knowledge base concerning the historical dynamics of capitalist development, some economists working within what I have identified as the Marshallian developmental tradition had by the close of the 1950s offered cogent arguments concerning the increasing importance of organizational coordination relative to market coordination as the basis for economic growth.

Two economists in particular, P. Sargent Florence and Edith Penrose, pioneered in addressing the critical issue of how the planned coordination of the specialized division of labor can enable the business enterprise to overcome the "managerial limit" on the growth of the firm by driving down costs with the expansion of output.[100] Both, that is, explored how internal organization could make the business enterprise an engine of economic growth.

In 1933, the same year that the (undeservedly) famous works of Joan Robinson and Edward Chamberlin appeared, P. Sargent Florence published *The Logic of Industrial Organization*, an initial attempt to develop an inductive (what he called a "realistic") analysis of modern industrial structure. Over the ensuing decades in which Florence explored the facts of mid-twentieth-century industrial structure, this work evolved into a comparative analysis, *The Logic of British and American Industry*, that came out in three editions between 1953 and 1972. Florence's institutional approach lacks a specific theory of the relation between the internal organization of the enterprise and comparative economic growth – a defect that could have been remedied had he linked business strategy to his

---

[99] Chandler, *The Visible Hand*; idem, *Scale and Scope: The Dynamics of Industrial Capitalism* (Cambridge, Mass.: Harvard University Press, 1990).

[100] P. Sargent Florence, *The Logic of British and American Industry* (London: Routledge & Kegan Paul, 1972), 3d ed.; first published in 1953; Edith T. Penrose, *The Theory of the Growth of the Firm*, 2d ed. (White Plains, N.Y.: Sharpe, 1980), first published in 1959.

analysis of organizational structure. Nevertheless, the scope of his empirical inquiry covers the gamut of the relevant social relations of industry: horizontal and vertical industrial structure, financial structure, producer–consumer relations, the internal organization of managerial hierarchies, business–government relations, labor–management relations, and the uses of the educational system.

Central to Florence's analysis is the building of integrated managerial structures that permit top management to delegate authority to members of the organization and thereby unbend the U-shaped cost curve – to extend the bounds on rationality. Indeed, by showing how the "managerial limit" could be extended, Florence viewed his work as a critique of neo-Marshallians such as Nicholas Kaldor and Austin Robinson who argued that the inherent limitations of managerial capability constrained the growth of the firm, thereby resulting in rising costs that maintained the firm in equilibrium.[101]

Compared with the far-ranging, empiricist approach of Florence, Edith Penrose's *The Theory of the Growth of the Firm*, first published in 1959, is more abstract and focused.[102] Penrose's major argument is that, by building its managerial organization, a firm can grow through expansion in its original industrial activities, vertical integration, diversification, and mergers and acquisition. In Penrose's terms, "administrative integration" provides the social foundations for a "receding managerial limit."[103]

Throughout her book, Penrose stressed the centrality of internal organization to the growth of the firm. Inputs are not simply factors of production; rather, they are *services* to the firm. The productive characteristics of these services are determined by the organizational context in which they are used; they are "firm specific."[104] The productivity of any particular *human* (and in Penrose's model, especially managerial) resource depends on its role in a collectivity, because planned coordination "requires the cooperation of many individuals who have confidence in each other, and this, in general, requires the knowledge of each other."[105] Hence, the services that people as the bearers of human resources can render "are enhanced by their knowledge of their fellow-workers, of the

---

[101] Nicholas Kaldor, "The Equilibrium of the Firm," *Economic Journal* 44 (March 1934), 60–76; E. A. G. Robinson, "The Problem of Management and the Size of Firms," *Economic Journal*, 44 (June 1934), 242–57; Florence, *The Logic of British and American Industry*, 193–4.

[102] For a recent review of Penrose that emphasizes her contributions to the study of the relation between internal organization and economic success, see Best, *The New Competition*, ch. 4. Another perceptive work by an economist that combines the Chandlerian and Penrosian insights is Scott J. Moss, *An Economic Theory of Business Strategy: An Essay in Dynamics Without Equilibrium* (New York: Halsted Press, 1981).

[103] Penrose, *The Theory of the Growth of the Firm*, chs. 4–8.

[104] Ibid., ch. 4.   [105] Ibid., 47

methods of the firm, and of the best way of doing things in the particular circumstances in which they are working."[106] Learning or experience within this organizational context is critical to the development of the firm's productive resources: "The process by which experience is gained is properly treated as a process creating new productive services available to the firm."[107]

Penrose was careful to point out that there are limits to internal economies – larger is not necessarily better.[108] She also acknowledged the opportunities that the rise of dominant enterprises generally creates for smaller firms in the "interstices" of a growing economy. But referring to the U.S. evidence through the 1950s, she recognized the centrality of the dominant enterprise to long-run economic growth. In a manner reminiscent of Schumpeter (to whom, however, Penrose made only a few passing references), she argued that the large business enterprise that has achieved dominance through the building of an integrated managerial structure can achieve further "economies of expansion" because of "its ability to explore, to experiment, and to innovate [combined] with the market position (carefully cultivated by advertising) that its reputation, and the reputation of its products, can command."[109] "A strong case," she concluded, "can be made for the big firm and for 'big business' competition, especially with respect to the rate of development of new technology and new and improved products."[110] "That economists have been slow to recognize some of [the big firm's] advantages," she argued, is because the traditional theory of the firm in equilibrium "does not provide suitable tools for the analysis of the growth and, in particular, of the innovating activities of firms treated as administrative organizations free to produce any kind of product they find profitable."[111]

Penrose contended that "the theory of the *process* of growth is . . . susceptible to empirical testing against the experience of individual firms." She specifically designated business history as the type of empirical material that would be needed. But, she continued, "there is not sufficient systematic information yet to enable any comprehensive testing of the generality of the theory."[112] A few years after she wrote these words, Alfred Chandler's *Strategy and Structure* appeared.

Recently, and in an approach similar to the one I have taken in this book, Michael Best has linked the Penrosian view of the growth of the firm to the historical perspective provided by Chandlerian business history.[113] Focusing on what he calls "The New Competition" of the late twentieth century, Best has shed considerable light on the competitive advantages that derive from the dynamic interaction of business organi-

---

[106] Ibid., 52.   [107] Ibid., 48.   [108] Ibid., chs. 10–11.   [109] Ibid., 262.   [110] Ibid., 260.
[111] Ibid., 260–1.   [112] Ibid., 3.   [113] Best, *The New Competition*.

zation and technological change in social environments as different as Japan and Italy. He has documented an argument that I raise in Chapter 1: that the power of collective business organization transcends what we normally think of as firms (units of financial control). The power of collective business organization can include groups of horizontally and vertically related enterprises that, in terms of strategy and structure, operate as organizational units by tapping the combination of entrepreneurial initiative in smaller-scale undertakings and the long-term planning horizons and capabilities of dominant enterprises.[114]

These arguments about the evolving character of collective capitalism have far-reaching economic, social, and political implications, a discussion of which goes far beyond the critical objectives of this book. But for those who wish to debate the future of industrial capitalism, and in particular issues of business and government policy within the declining British and U.S. economies, two realities, one industrial and the other intellectual, must be recognized. The industrial reality is that successful capitalist development is increasingly collective capitalist development. The intellectual reality is that the vast majority of economists remain captive to the myth of the market economy, and hence are ill-prepared to enter into debates about the structures of collective business organization that are best suited to gain competitive advantage in an evolving international economy.

Recognizing the intellectual constraints, both ideological and methodological, that the myth of the market economy poses for understanding the process of economic development will not in and of itself enable the British and U.S. economies to *respond* to the challenge of collective capitalism. But it might encourage a transformation of these intellectual constraints, so that politicians and academics in these once-dominant capitalist economies can *start thinking about* how to respond to the industrial realities of the late twentieth century and beyond.

[114] Ibid., chs. 6–8.

9

Rigor and relevance in economics

Historical analysis as rigorous economics

To produce a theory of capitalist development that can account for the major changes in international industrial leadership of the past century, we can *begin* with the insights of the likes of Marx, Schumpeter, and Marshall. Then, using theory as a guide to empirical research rather than as a reason for ignoring it, we can generate the data that will enable us to confirm, modify, or reject our previously held assumptions and explanations. Model building is important for working out the internal logic of a chosen set of assumptions and relationships. But rigorous empirical analysis is needed to ensure the relevance of those assumptions and relationships.

Such a methodology that integrates the building of theory and the study of reality contrasts with the highly abstract mathematical models that fill the mainstream economic journals and sell themselves as "economic science." The ability of economists to use mathematical technique has far outrun their understanding of economic reality. Indeed, the extent to which modern economists rely on mathematical technique to establish their professional credentials generally constitutes an intellectual impediment – what one might call a "trained incapacity" – to comprehending the economy as a dynamic, historical process.[1]

The intellectual problem is not mathematical virtuosity per se; I have personally worked with accomplished mathematical economists who were adept at comprehending, and even fashioning, dynamic historical arguments. The problem is with the construction of intricate and esoteric models

---

[1] For another blunt statement on this theme, see Barbara R. Bergmann, "Why Do Economists Know So Little About the Economy?" in Samuel Bowles, Richard Edwards, and William G. Shepherd, eds., *Unconventional Wisdom: Essays in Honor of John Kenneth Galbraith* (Boston: Houghton Mifflin, 1989), 29–38. Bergmann observed: "The impoverished factual content of our thought doesn't embarrass us as economists; we are used to it. But it is somewhat embarrassing to explain explicitly to noneconomists that we find things out by sitting and thinking and mulling over a few factual crumbs, and that the systematic, firsthand observation of economic functioning has no place whatever in economic science" (31). For an excellent, and highly critical, account of how the economics profession sought to establish its "scientific" credentials by imitating the physical sciences, see Philip Mirowski, *More Heat Than Light* (Cambridge University Press, 1989).

of economic activity that are relevant to the world of *economists* but irrelevant to the world of *economics*. By virtue of the methodology and ideology that mainstream economic theorists bring to their work, what appears to be "rigorous" economics is generally irrelevant, and often obstructive, to comprehending the nature and causes of the wealth of nations.

Once the irrelevance of mainstream economic theory is accepted, the definition of what constitutes *rigorous* economic analysis must be brought into question as well. To be sure, given a certain set of fundamental assumptions and functional relationships, rigor can be defined, as is typically the case among economists, in terms of logical analysis. But rigor can also be defined as the historical analysis required to determine just what these fundamental assumptions and relationships should be.

Obviously, rigorous historical analysis is essential if an economic theory is to have descriptive value. But in contrast to the positive economic methodology proposed some time ago by Milton Friedman, I would argue that rigorous historical analysis is essential if a theory is to have predictive value as well.

Friedman argued that, because all theories involve abstraction from reality, one's choice of theoretical assumptions does not matter as long as one's predictions prove to be correct.[2] There are two basic problems with this methodological position. First, if one's predictions do not prove to be correct, then one requires a methodology that entails rigorous empirical analysis in order to discover what assumptions would yield correct predictions. Second, even when one's predictions do prove to be correct at one point in time, they may not prove to be correct at another point in time because the underlying model takes as given one or more variables that are in fact integral to the changes that have occurred over the time period. Put differently, two very different theoretical models may yield the same predictions at a point in time, but only one of the models may be able to account for changes in outcomes over time.[3] If a theory is to have predictive (and hence prescriptive) value, rigorous historical analysis is a precondition for rigorous logical analysis.

Basic to overcoming the intellectual constraints that render mainstream

---

[2] Milton Friedman, *Essays in Positive Economics* (Chicago: University of Chicago Press, 1953), pt. 1.

[3] For an example, see William Lazonick, *Competitive Advantage on the Shop Floor* (Cambridge, Mass.: Harvard University Press, 1990), ch. 4. There it is shown how a neoclassical theorist could have predicted the relative factor intensities in cotton spinning in Britain and the United States while adopting the conventional assumption that firms in both countries were making their technical choices subject to the same production functions. But because rigorous historical analysis shows this assumption of identical production functions to be wrong, the neoclassical theorist would not be able to comprehend the technical choices in the two countries that would occur when factor prices change. Yet it is the reaction of factor intensities to changes in factor prices that is central to the neoclassical theory of production.

economics irrelevant, therefore, is the ability to do rigorous empirical analysis. And when one is concerned with comprehending the process of change, that empirical analysis must be historical. Such an analytical ability is, I believe, what Joseph Schumpeter had in mind when he spoke of "historical experience."[4] To do historical analysis does not, however, mean to neglect theory. Rather, it means to make theory the servant of historical analysis rather than a substitute for it. A general theoretical "vision" (to borrow another term from Schumpeter)[5] provides us with a basis for asking certain questions of history. Historical analysis provides us with the knowledge required to make relevant theoretical abstractions or to modify our adherence to abstractions previously held, while theory provides us with a framework that directs our historical research to ask the right questions and explore the right material to provide answers. In other words, we require a methodology that brings history and theory into dynamic relation with one another and that ensures that our theoretical deductions remain anchored in our understanding of historical reality.

Economic history as constrained optimization

A willingness to engage in historical analysis is not sufficient to overcome the methodological and ideological limitations of the neoclassical approach. During the "cliometrics revolution" of the 1960s and early 1970s, economics departments in U.S. universities allocated considerable resources to the study of economic history.[6] The explicit objective of the "cliometricians," or "new economic historians" as they were also called, was to apply economic theory and statistical technique to historical data.[7] In effect, they viewed economic history as an applied field of economics more generally and entertained no notion that historical analysis might be used to generate more relevant economic theory. At the outset at least,

---

[4] Joseph A. Schumpeter, *History of Economic Analysis* (New York: Oxford University Press, 1954), 12–13. See also Chapter 4, this volume.

[5] On "vision," see Joseph A. Schumpeter, "Science and Ideology," *American Economic Review*, 39 (March 1949), 345–59. Schumpeter recognized that this "vision" had to be "preconceived"; that is, it had to exist prior to one's empirical investigations. The choice of theoretical vision is, of course, critical to one's "intellectual trajectory" because the initial adoption of a vision that is irrelevant can prevent one from exploring certain issues that may be the essence of the historical process – hence the importance of a training in alternative visions in the history of economics to enable future economists to make intelligent choices that will determine their intellectual trajectories. Given its acceptance of the myth of the market economy and its overriding concern with mathematical virtuosity, a modern graduate economics training does not provide students with a serious exposure to alternative visions in the history of economics.

[6] See the discussion in Alexander J. Field, "The Future of Economic History," in Alexander J. Field, ed., *The Future of Economic History* (Boston: Kluwer-Nijhoff, 1987), 1–41.

[7] See, e.g., Peter Temin, "Introduction," in Peter Temin, ed., *The New Economic History* (Harmondsworth: Penguin Books, 1973), 8.

the new economic historians accepted the ideological and methodological limitations of neoclassical economics.

These limitations were particularly apparent in the work of one group of new economic historians who saw as their intellectual mission the application of neoclassical price theory to the analysis of statistical data. Following the macroeconomic analyses of the sources of U.S. economic growth of Moses Abramowitz and Robert Solow, much work was devoted to estimating total factor productivity at a highly aggregated level. Despite Abramowitz's warning that this unexplained residual was a "measure of our ignorance," the new economic historians tended to use total factor productivity as a proxy for superior economic performance. The measure figured prominently in a prolonged statistical debate over whether the British economy "failed" in the late nineteenth century.[8]

This work did not attempt to explain British success or failure in terms of a theory of economic development. Rather, it measured "economic success" in terms of the observed growth in total factor productivity. But total factor productivity itself cannot be explained by the neoclassical conceptual framework, because that framework assumes that economic growth derives merely from an accumulation of standard marketable commodities that serve as inputs into the production process. In taking this unexplained residual as the measure of economic success, the new economic historians were implicitly recognizing that their own theoretical grounding contained no theory of economic development. Lacking a theory of economic development with which to evaluate the quality of inputs, they

---

[8] Moses Abramowitz, "Resource and Output Trends in the United States since 1870," *American Economic Review*, 46 (May 1956), 5–23; Robert Solow, "Technical Change and the Aggregate Production Function," *Review of Economics and Statistics*, 39 (August 1957), 312–20; Donald N. McCloskey, "Did Victorian Britain Fail?" *Economic History Review*, 2d ser., 23 (December 1970), 446–59; N. F. R. Crafts, "Victorian Britain Did Fail," *Economic History Review*, 2d ser., 32 (November 1979), 533–7; Donald N. McCloskey, "No It Did Not: A Reply to Crafts," *Economic History Review*, 2d ser., 32 (November 1979), 538–41; Stephen Nicholas, "Total Factor Productivity Growth and the Revision of Post-1870 British Economic History," *Economic History Review*, 2d ser., 35 (February 1982), 83–98; Mark Thomas, "Accounting for Growth, 1870–1940: Stephen Nicholas and Total Factor Productivity Measurements," *Economic History Review*, 2d ser., 38 (November 1985), 569–75; Stephen Nicholas, "British Economic Performance and Total Factor Productivity Growth, 1870–1940," *Economic History Review*, 2d ser., 38 (November 1985), 576–82. See also the theoretical critique of this debate in Frank Geary, "Accounting for Entrepreneurship in Late Victorian Britain," *Economic History Review*, 2d ser., 43 (May 1990), 283–7. Basing his critique of total factor productivity measurement on a neo-Austrian perspective on the nature of entrepreneurship, Geary did not recognize that social relations of production, and in particular the social relations that determine the dynamic interaction between factor prices and factor productivities, also bias the measures of total factor productivity. See William Lazonick and William Mass, "The Performance of the British Cotton Industry, 1870–1913," *Research in Economic History*, 9 (1984), 1–44. For my brief critique of the neo-Austrian perspective, see Chapter 8.

tended to use ad hoc arguments to make adjustments to the data that entered into the estimates of total factor productivity.

The theory of the market economy provides the theoretical foundation for measuring the productive contributions of the inputs that leave total factor productivity as a residual. A basic weakness of the theory of the market economy is its assumption that factor prices are independent of factor productivities, and hence that the process of economic growth is independent of both the organization of production and the distribution of income to those who supply factors of production. Yet a central argument of a dynamic theory of economic development is that the organization of production and the distribution of income are integrally related, because workers' expectations of returns to their labor power affect the quality and quantity of effort they supply to the production process, while employers' expectations of returns to capital investments affect the quality and quantity of their investments in productive resources. Moreover, the actual returns that workers receive depend on the quality and quantity of investments in productive resources that their employers have made, and the actual returns that employers receive depend on the quality and quantity of effort that their workers have supplied.[9]

The static theory of production in which factor prices are independent of factor productivities is explicit in neoclassical analyses of choice of technique. In the 1960s and 1970s this perspective provided the theoretical underpinnings of a debate among the new economic historians concerning the reliance of nineteenth-century Britain on relatively labor-intensive technologies when compared with the United States.[10] Initially, this debate on the choice of technique focused simply on whether the observed differences in British and U.S. factor intensities could be explained in terms of relative factor prices and did not address the issue of the relative performance of the two economies at a point in time or over time. In the neoclassical scheme of things, economic performance does not depend on

[9] See Lazonick, *Competitive Advantage*, esp. the appendix.
[10] The debate had originally been stimulated by H. J. Habakkuk's wide-ranging essay, *American and British Technology in the Nineteenth Century: The Search for Labour-Saving Inventions* (Cambridge University Press, 1962), in which it is argued that a relative scarcity of labor in the United States led U.S. firms to adopt technologies that were relatively capital-intensive compared with those in Britain. See also Peter Temin, "Labor Scarcity and the Problem of American Industrial Efficiency in the 1850s," *Journal of Economic History*, 26 (September 1966), 277–97; Robert Fogel, "The Specification Problem in Economic History," *Journal of Economic History*, 27 (September 1967), 288–308; Ian M. Drummond, "Labor Scarcity and the Problem of American Industrial Efficiency in the 1850's: A Comment," *Journal of Economic History*, 27 (September 1967), 383–90. For a later contribution, see Alexander J. Field, "Land Abundance, Interest/Profit Rates, and Nineteenth-Century American and British Technology," *Journal of Economic History*, 43 (June 1983), 405–32.

the nature of technological choices – whether they are capital-intensive or labor-intensive. Rather, economic performance depends on whether the "entrepreneurs" who have chosen certain techniques have been "rational" in making these choices – whether they have optimized subject to the constraints they face.

Neoclassical economic theory, therefore, can analyze what I have called adaptive response – the choice of an investment strategy that takes the technological, organizational, and market environment as given.[11] But (as was the case with Oliver Williamson's framework) neoclassical economic theory cannot analyze an innovative response; for in the case of innovation, the entrepreneur does not merely adapt to given technological, organizational, and market constraints but, by investing in organization and technology, seeks to overcome constraints.

As I argued in Chapter 3, innovative investment strategies tend to be HFC strategies because of both the length of time and the complex set of productive activities required to develop new technologies. At the outset, an entrepreneur who pursues an innovative HFC strategy may appear to be irrational in his or her technological choice – at least to those adaptive industrialists who take alternative technologies and market prices as given constraints on technical and economic choices. In retrospect, however, the entrepreneur will be recognized as an innovator if, through the development and utilization of productive resources, he or she can transform the high fixed costs of the innovative investment strategy into low unit costs and competitive advantage. Moreover, insofar as the investments required for a particular innovation constitute the organizational and technological foundations for other innovations, only those business organizations that have made the prior investments will be positioned to engage in continuous innovation.

When the new economic historians did try to relate choice of technique to economic performance, their intellectual vision was constrained by their acceptance of neoclassical price theory as a relevant theoretical framework for historical analysis. In particular, they did not question the notion that optimization subject to given constraints by business executives would result in the best possible outcomes at both the microeconomic and macroeconomic levels. For example, a major research effort of the new economic historians in the late 1960s and 1970s was to attack the "entrepreneurial-failure hypothesis" as an explanation of the decline of the British economy from the late nineteenth century. The leaders of the attack, Donald McCloskey and Lars Sandberg, rejected the hypothesis on the grounds that the empirical evidence on choice of technique demonstrated that, in making their investment decisions, British managers of

[11] See Chapter 3.

the late nineteenth and early twentieth centuries were minimizing costs subject to the constraints they faced.[12]

In taking constrained optimization as the "yardstick" for evaluating "entrepreneurship," the neoclassical economic historians ignored the Schumpeterian distinction between "entrepreneurs," who confront the constraints that are maintaining the enterprise in equilibrium, and "managers," who simply adapt to their environment. The neoclassicals used the terms "entrepreneur" and "manager" interchangeably to refer to decision makers who optimize subject to available technology and market determined prices. Yet it is just such a species of businessperson that Schumpeter relegated to the world of marginal adaptation within the "circular flow." Precisely because these managers accept the constraints they face, they cannot be performing the entrepreneurial function of innovation – a function that, by definition, requires that existing constraints be confronted and, to some degree, overcome.

This is not to argue that the analysis of constrained optimization cannot serve a useful purpose. The constrained-optimization methodology permits the exploration of the character of the constraints on managerial decision making that exist at selected points in time. When we observe that an enterprise or industry is neglecting a new technology, we can then, through empirical investigation, explore the determinants of its choice and the constraints that would have to be changed to render it rational to adopt the new technology. We can also use the constrained-optimization approach as a comparative-static methodology to see whether constraints on the choice of technology have indeed been altered between two points in time.[13] Ultimately, however, to understand the transformation of constraints – to understand how and why change occurs – requires a historical methodology.

---

[12] Donald McCloskey and Lars Sandberg, "From Damnation to Redemption: Judgments on the Late Victorian Entrepreneur," *Explorations in Economic History*, 9 (Fall 1971), 89–108. In another neoclassical contribution to the debate, Peter H. Lindert and Keith Trace posited the "cardinal rule" for judging the caliber of entrepreneurship: "The comparison must reflect the conditions faced by the individuals or firms whose performance is being judged. It will not do, for example, to fault Victorian manufacturers for not having adopted techniques that were preferable under American or German, but not British, price relationships." "Yardsticks for Victorian Entrepreneurs," in Donald N. McCloskey, ed., *Essays on a Mature Economy: Britain after 1840* (London: Methuen, 1971), 239–74, cited at 241. For McCloskey's more recent contribution to the debate, see his *If You're So Smart: The Narrative of Economic Expertise* (Chicago: University of Chicago Press, 1990), chs. 3–4.

[13] For my original statement of this argument, see William Lazonick, "Factor Costs and the Diffusion of Ring Spinning in Britain Prior to World War I," *Quarterly Journal of Economics*, 96 (February 1981), 89–109. For an elaboration of the argument as well as an application of a dynamic theory of competitive advantage, see William Mass and William Lazonick, "The British Cotton Industry and International Competitive Advantage: The State of the Debates," *Business History*, 32 (October 1990), 9–65.

Economic history as evolving constraints

The analysis of how constraints on economic activity change is the analysis of the transformation of the social institutions that determine market prices and productive capabilities. That the analysis of institutional change must be central to the study of the economy was recognized in the early 1970s by Lance Davis and Douglass North in *Institutional Change and American Economic Growth*. As Davis and North argued in the first sentence of the book, "It is difficult to believe that the exploration of long-run economic change can be achieved without the development of a body of theory that can incorporate the innovation, mutation, and demise of institutions."[14] Yet in exploring "long-run economic change," Davis and North took as exogenous "technology, market size, income expectation, prices, knowledge, rules of the game."[15] Indeed, their view of organizational change was avowedly technological determinist. "Technological change," they argued, "has produced, as a by-product of scale economies, the factory system and the agglomeration of economic activity which has led to the urban, industrial society of today."[16]

They did speak of "developmental investments," but in defining these investments as "social overhead capital" they offered no perspective on the role of the strategies and structures of business organizations in generating economic development.[17] Indeed, they dismissed organizational innovation in what Alfred Chandler has called the managerial enterprise as inconsequential for U.S. economic growth:

> [History] textbooks discuss the growth of the economy in terms of the "rise of big business," and they mean "big manufacturing business." Moreover, while the country has produced many famous men, it is the Rockefellers, the Carnegies, and the Fords – businessmen associated with the manufacturing sector – who are most often chosen to typify the nation in the period 1850–1929. Despite the importance of the growth of new manufacturing industries to the development of modern America, arrangemental innovation has played a relatively small role.[18]

That Davis and North denied that changes in business organization were central to U.S. economic growth is not surprising, for at the outset they informed (warned?) the reader that their model of institutional change "is consistent with, and built upon, the basic assumptions of neo-classical theory."[19] And in keeping with the neoclassical perspective, at the end of the book Davis and North admitted that their "model is not dynamic, and

---

[14] Lance E. Davis and Douglass C. North, *Institutional Change and American Economic Growth* (Cambridge University Press, 1971), vii.
[15] See ibid., 62.   [16] Ibid., 42.   [17] Ibid., 145.   [18] Ibid., 167.   [19] Ibid., vii.

we know very little about the path from one comparative static equilibrium to another."[20]

In subsequent writings, North has sought to extend his theory of change, referring explicitly to the need for economists to analyze how constraints evolve over time. In a 1978 piece in the *Journal of Economic Literature,* North outlined the "task of economic history":

> The cliometric revolution in economic history wedded neoclassical economics and quantitative methods in order to describe and explain the performance of economies in the past. Economic history gained in rigor and scientific pretension, but at the expense of exploring a much more fundamental set of questions about the evolving structure of economies that underlies performance. Cliometricians have turned their backs on a long tradition stretching back from Joseph Schumpeter to Karl Marx to Adam Smith. These scholars regarded economic history as essential because it added a dimension to economics. Its purpose was to analyze the parameters held constant by the economist. If economics is a theory of choice subject to specified constraints, a task of economic history was to theorize about those evolving constraints.[21]

North emphasized the importance of Schumpeter's contribution to the analysis of change, particularly as presented in its most mature form in *Capitalism, Socialism, and Democracy.* As North remarked, "The accuracy of [Schumpeter's] predictions is an impressive testimonial to his analytical powers." But North went on to argue that "it is difficult to turn his insights into any theory capable of testable implications" and that "the most basic building block missing in the Schumpeterian system is any explicit analysis of the political process."[22] Explicitly, North contended that "Schumpeter's system is flawed because it essentially assumes a Marxian two-class world in which the anti-bourgeoisie gradually gain the ascendancy over the political system."[23]

As these comments indicate, North's main interest was in grafting onto mainstream economics a theory of *political* change. He displayed no interest in the Marxian and Schumpeterian insights into the role of the capitalist enterprise in driving the process of economic change. Nor did he look to Marx or Schumpeter for a *method* of historical analysis. Subsequently, North admitted that there was "much to learn" about institutional change from "the 'old economic historian,' the institutionalist of Veblen and C. E. Ayres' persuasion, or the Marxist." But in seeking to analyze the process of change, he warned against abandoning neoclassical theory:

---

[20] Ibid., 263.
[21] Douglass C. North, "Structure and Performance: The Task of Economic History," *Journal of Economic Literature,* 16 (September 1978), 963–78, quoted at 963.
[22] Ibid., 966.   [23] Ibid., 967.

Neoclassical theory has made economics the preeminent social science by providing it a disciplined, logical analytical framework. To abandon neoclassical theory is to abandon economics as a science. The challenge is to widen its horizons to come to grips with these issues. The economic historian is uniquely qualified to meet that challenge.[24]

The existing "choice-theoretic" neoclassical approach could, he argued, be applied to the analysis of political behavior, the growth and application of scientific knowledge, and demographic change. But this approach took constraints on economic and political activity as given. To analyze institutional change in economic organization, property rights, and ideology required the exploration of how constraints change. "The ultimate direction," North advised the reader, "is towards a generalized theory of social science."[25]

In two subsequent books, *Structure and Change in Economic History*, published in 1981, and *Institutions, Institutional Change, and Economic Performance*, published in 1990, the focus of North's attempt to develop a "generalized theory of social science" has been on the determinants of property rights and ideology.[26] He has placed particular emphasis on the role of the state in dealing with the "free rider problem" – the ability of individuals to reap the benefits of a collectively determined outcome without bearing a proportionate amount of the costs of achieving that outcome. For understanding how a capitalist society operates, these political and cultural phenomena are without doubt of central importance. But legal arrangements and ideological outlooks can be consequences as well as causes of the process of economic development. If a generalized theory of social science is what we are after and if historical methodology is the appropriate way to develop such a theory, then we want to explore the dynamic interaction among economic, political, and cultural phenomena.

The particular contribution that *economists* can make to understanding the process of social change is to explain how the process of economic growth influences property rights and ideology. And if institutions are to be central to the explanation of economic growth, then we require a relevant theory of how the central economic institutions – business enterprises – develop and utilize productive resources. From my perspective, what economics needs, and lacks, is a theory of how business organization and technological change interact dynamically to develop the economy.

If North deemphasized the role of business organization in determining economic performance, he did not ignore the subject. In *Structure and*

---

[24] Ibid., 974.   [25] Ibid.
[26] Douglass C. North, *Structure and Change in Economic History* (New York: Norton, 1981); idem, *Institutions, Institutional Change, and Economic Performance* (Cambridge University Press, 1990).

Change in Economic History, he argued that "the organizational crisis of
the modern world can only be understood as a part of the Second Economic Revolution" from the late nineteenth century – an economic revolution that "created an elastic supply curve of new knowledge which
built economic growth into the system."[27] North recognized that the
"Second Economic Revolution" required large fixed-capital investments,
and he quoted Alfred Chandler on the importance of high throughput for
achieving economies of scale and the importance of vertically integrated
organizational structures for achieving high throughput. But North went
on to contend that Chandler had described only one part of the "effort to
realize the productive potential of the new technology." "A major part of
that managerial revolution," North argued, "was the attempt to devise a
set of rules and compliance procedures to reduce the transaction costs
attendant on the new technology."[28]

North addressed the issue of the determinants of economic development under capitalism. As causal factors in the generation of invention,
he mentioned the development of scientific disciplines, the willingness of
private and public organizations to invest in basic and exploratory research, and the promulgation of laws to protect intellectual property rights.[29]
The result was a series of "technological breakthroughs" that characterized the Second Economic Revolution.[30]

But why did the new technologies of the Second Economic Revolution
result in unprecedented economic growth? North asked this question,
but the perspective that he offered contains no theory of the innovative
business organization. Rather, given the new technology, North attributed the productivity gains to "occupational and territorial specialization and division of labor on an unprecedented scale," against which had
to be weighed the costs of an "exponential multiplication of exchange."
"Obviously," North argued (rather tautologically, given his framework),
"the productivity gains from specialization have exceeded the increasing
transaction costs in the process; hence the quantum leap in living standards that makes the modern Western world unique in history."[31]

In making these arguments about the importance of specialization, North
made no distinction between market coordination and planned coordination. Apparently, all relations among "specialists" can be subsumed under
the notion of "exchange." To be sure, North recognized that the terms of
exchange would differ depending on prevailing property rights and ideology.[32] But I would argue, as I have throughout this book, that it is the

---

[27] North, *Structure and Change in Economic History*, 171.   [28] Ibid., 175–6.
[29] Ibid., 172–3.   [30] Ibid., 173–4.   [31] Ibid., 175.
[32] For critiques of North's neoinstitutionalism, see Alexander J. Field, "On the Explanation
of Rules Using Rational Choice Models," *Journal of Economic Issues*, 13 (March 1979),
49–72; Alexander J. Field, "The Problem with Neoclassical Institutional Economics: A

organizational contexts at the level of the business enterprise that are key to understanding the relation between economic institutions and economic performance.

In addition, these organizational contexts themselves are often transformed in major ways, independently of prevailing property rights and ideology. To document this argument adequately would require another book. Let me just mention three examples. First, the rise of the industrial corporation in the United States was characterized by the separation of asset ownership from managerial control. Yet despite the fact that, by the early decades of the twentieth century, shareholders had generally become passive portfolio investors, property rights in the assets of corporations remained in their hands. In addition, the U.S. antitrust laws, which were supposed to protect the viability of proprietary enterprise (i.e., the integration of ownership and control), actually encouraged the concentration of U.S. industry and the separation of ownership from control. Indeed, by outlawing price cartels, the antitrust laws made survival more difficult for the small, proprietary enterprise.[33]

Second, U.S. patent law was designed to ensure that the individual inventor would reap the benefits of his or her invention. Yet from the last half of the nineteenth century, it was primarily industrial corporations that incurred the high fixed costs (including legal costs) required to develop and utilize patents. By the purchase of the rights to patents from individual inventors, an increasing proportion of patents that stood a chance of being transformed into commercial successes fell under corporate control. Through in-house research, moreover, industrial corporations themselves became the generators of patentable inventions. Yet the patent system has continued to vest property rights in inventions in individuals, not in the organizations that actually develop and utilize them. Indeed, industrial corporations have often bought up patent rights simply as an adaptive strategy – that is, to avoid the "creative destruction" of their existing products and processes.[34]

Critique with Special Reference to the North–Thomas Model of Pre-1500 Europe," *Explorations in Economic History*, 18 (April 1981), 174–98.

[33] On the ironic application and impact of the antitrust laws, see Thomas K. McCraw, "Rethinking the Trust Question," in Thomas K. McCraw, ed., *Regulation in Perspective* (Cambridge, Mass.: Harvard University Press, 1975), 1–55. See also idem, *Prophets of Regulation* (Cambridge, Mass.: Harvard University Press, 1984), chs. 3–4; Martin Sklar, *The Corporate Reconstruction of American Capitalism* (Cambridge University Press, 1988). On the beneficial impact of the separation of ownership from control on the development of U.S. industry in the first half of this century and on the adverse impact of the reintegration of ownership and control more recently, see William Lazonick, "Controlling the Market for Corporate Control: The Historical Significance of Managerial Capitalism," paper presented to the meetings of the Third International Joseph A. Schumpeter Society, Airlie, Va., June 3–5, 1990. See also the discussion toward the end of this chapter.

[34] See David Noble, *America by Design: Science, Technology and the Rise of Corporate*

Third, the land-grant college system of higher education arose in the United States from the 1860s ostensibly to enhance the educational attainment and consequent social standing of the farmer and artisan. Yet from the 1880s, the United States Department of Agriculture used the land-grant college system to build a vast and effective bureaucracy to provide leadership in, and resources for, the development of agricultural technology and the diffusion of technology to the mass of farmers. From the 1890s, moreover, the land-grant college system became the major source of technical specialists for the burgeoning managerial bureaucracies of U.S. industrial corporations. Of course, the human products of the land-grant colleges retained property rights in their own labor. But increasingly, their economic futures became dependent on lifelong attachment to a successful corporation.[35]

More generally, the ideology that individual property rights provide the only foundation for economic activity in the United States finds its intellectual expression in neoclassical economic theory – a theory that propounds the myth of the market economy despite the transformations from proprietary to managerial to collective capitalism that I have documented in Chapter 1. These social transformations in business organization in the most successful capitalist economies have no place in North's account of institutional change and economic performance. Rather than analyze the social determinants of technological change and productivity growth, North, like Oliver Williamson, invoked transaction cost explanations.

In his most recent book, North described how Williamson's transaction cost approach differs from his own:

Williamson assumes enforcement to be imperfect (otherwise opportunism would never pay), but does not make it an explicit variable in his analysis. Such an approach simply does not lead the scholar to be able to deal with the problems of historical evolution, where the key problems of institutional change, or contracting, and of performance turn on the degree to which contracts can be enforced between parties at low cost.[36]

From this perspective that enforcement of the contracts governing exchange relations is what institutional change is all about, North has claimed that the transaction cost approach enables us to understand, among many other things, the role of technology in the transformation of work in the

Capitalism (New York: Knopf, 1977), ch. 6, who relied extensively on the work of Floyd L. Vaughan, *The United States Patent System: Legal and Economic Conflicts in American Patent History* (Norman: University of Oklahoma Press, 1956).

[35] See Lou Ferleger and William Lazonick, "The Industrial District and the Developmental State: The Case of U.S. Agriculture," photocopy, Harvard University, 1991; Noble, *America by Design.*

[36] North, *Institutions, Institutional Change, and Economic Performance*, 54n–55n.

production processes of U.S. corporations in the late nineteenth and early twentieth centuries. As North asserted:

A contention of Marxist writers is that deliberate deskilling of the labor force occurred during the early twentieth century. That is, employers adopted capital-intensive technologies that eliminated highly skilled workers and replaced them with semiskilled or unskilled workers. The logic of this charge is that the bargaining power of skilled workers enabled them to disrupt the production process strategically, which, given the "high speed throughput" (Chandler's term) of modern technology was enormously costly. Employers found it reduced total cost over time to introduce technologies that used less-skilled workers who did not have the bargaining power to disrupt production. In this case, a new production technology was introduced to reduce transaction costs.[37]

Certain elements of this story occurred as North has depicted them. As I have argued in *Competitive Advantage on the Shop Floor,* the exercise of craft control by groups of skilled workers did pose obstacles to the achievement of high throughput in U.S. mass-production enterprises around the turn of the century.[38] The introduction of skill-displacing technologies, moreover, did render employers less reliant on these skilled workers. But North was wrong to accept the conventional Marxist view that the introduction of skill-displacing technology was a solution to the problem of achieving high-throughput production. The high-throughput potential of the new technologies derived not just from the skill-displacing characteristics of particular technologies, but more fundamentally from the existence of vertically integrated organizational structures that could plan the development of systems for mass production and mass distribution, and then, with these systems in place, coordinate the rapid transformation of purchased inputs into sold outputs.

Given the high fixed costs of both organization and technology inherent in these innovative investment strategies, even less skilled workers could inflict considerable costs on employers by restricting output and sabotaging the operation of the new technologies. To attain the high throughput required to transform high fixed costs into low unit costs, mass-production employers remained dependent on the supply of effort by the less skilled (generally labeled "semiskilled") operatives. To elicit effort from shop-floor workers, employers found that they could not simply treat their interactions with workers as "transactions." Rather they had to extend to semiskilled workers employed on the mass-production technologies the promise – although rarely a *contractual* commitment – of long-term attachment to the enterprise.

Only by the transformation of short-term exchange relations (with their

---

[37] Ibid., 65; see also North, *Structure and Change in Economic History,* 177–79.
[38] Lazonick, *Competitive Advantage,* ch. 7.

attendant transaction costs) into long-term production relations (with their attendant organizational costs) could U.S. managers take sufficient control over the supply of effort on the shop floor to realize the high-throughput potential of the new technologies. The basis of managerial control was not so much the enforcement of contracts – even disgruntled unskilled workers quickly learned to "work to rule" – but the emergence of cooperative relations based on mutual expectations of sharing in organization-specific value gains generated over extended periods of time.[39]

To gain competitive advantage on the basis of these new technologies required prior investments in managerial structures that could speed the flow of work from purchased inputs into sold outputs and that could gain the cooperation of workers in the supply of effort on the shop floor. It was the power of collective organization, and not simply the introduction of skill-displacing technologies, that overcame the constraints posed by craft control and resulted in superior economic performance on the basis of these technologies.

This superior economic performance cannot, moreover, be attributed to a reduction in transaction costs, because the transaction costs in question – those that arose from the unwillingness of skilled workers to cooperate in the utilization of the mass-production technologies – came into being only after these new technologies had been introduced. Indeed, in the absence of investments in the skill-displacing technologies, employers were dependent on, and valued, the productive efforts of skilled workers. The value gains from the introduction of mass-production technologies derived not from a reduction of the transaction costs that arose only when and because management confronted the existing skilled workers with the skill-displacing technologies, but from the organizational capability of the enterprise in securing the cooperation of the new, semiskilled operatives in the high-speed utilization of the new technologies.[40]

North vastly underestimated the ability of the private-sector business enterprise – particularly where "technological breakthroughs" were involved – to build internal organizational structures that could gain the cooperation of its participants in the value-creation process and thereby develop and utilize new technologies. North left little doubt about his view of the efficacy of corporate organization: "If the multiplication of rules and regulations is a device to reduce shirking and opportunism, the deadweight losses associated with bureaucracy are so familiar that they require no further elaboration here."[41]

As I argued in Chapter 1, and as is amply documented in the very work of Alfred Chandler that North cited, the view of bureaucracy as a "dead-

---

[39] Ibid.   [40] Lazonick, *Competitive Advantage*, chs. 6–10.
[41] North, *Structure and Change in Economic History*, 178–9.

weight loss" ignores the organizational successes of major U.S. industrial corporations in the planned coordination of specialized divisions of labor during the first half of this century. It was collective organization within major U.S. industrial corporations that formed the institutional foundations for the rise of the U.S. economy to international industrial leadership.

That collective organization *might* promote rather than impede economic growth has been acknowledged, albeit tentatively, in a book by Mancur Olson, *The Rise and Decline of Nations*. Olson set forth a framework for analyzing the relation between collective organization and economic growth. He argued that organizations could be either distributional or encompassing. Distributional organizations (or coalitions) increase their members' share of the social product without contributing to an increase in the social product to be shared. Indeed, in pursuing their special interests, distributional coalitions tend to encumber decision-making processes and fix those prices that favor them. As a result, distributional coalitions "slow down a society's capacity to adopt new technologies and to reallocate resources in response to changing conditions, and thereby reduce the rate of economic growth."[42]

In contrast, an encompassing organization represents a sufficiently large number of people that it identifies with the interests of a relevant productive entity as a whole. As a result, an encompassing organization may have incentives to take actions that "make the society in which they operate more prosperous."[43] An example of an encompassing organization is a "labor union that represents all the workers in some firm," such as a Japanese enterprise union:

A union that is encompassing in relation to the firm or industry for which its members work has a reason to help the host firm or industry prosper and expand. Contrast this with the situation of a craft union that controls the supply of some specialized skill a firm or industry needs, but controls only a minute percentage of the relevant employees. Such a union would have only a minute influence on the profitability of any firm and accordingly would have little incentive to avoid inefficient practices or to help the employer or industry in any other ways.[44]

Olson warned, however, that an organization that becomes *too* encompassing might use its power to raise prices and restrict output – that is, to act like a classic monopolist.[45] Hence, both narrow and encompassing organizations might act as distributional coalitions that, in seeking to pur-

---

[42] Mancur Olson, *The Rise and Decline of Nations* (New Haven, Conn.: Yale University Press, 1982), 74.
[43] Ibid., see also 42, where Olson stated that "such organizations could in some circumstances serve their members' interests by helping to make the society in which they operate more productive."
[44] Ibid., 49.   [45] Ibid., 49–50.

sue their own special interests, will create rigidities in the social system that obstruct the process of economic growth. In introducing the concept of the encompassing organization, Olson recognized that a collectivity can "in principle serve its members . . . by making the pie society produces larger" rather than simply by "obtaining larger shares [of a given] social pie for its members." But he quickly added that "our intuition tells us that the first method [making the pie larger] will rarely be chosen."[46] In Olson's view, the overwhelming impact of collective organization is to impede the process of economic growth.

There is a surface resemblance between Olson's notion of social rigidities and the "institutional rigidity" argument that I, along with Bernard Elbaum, have used to explain Britain's relative decline in the twentieth century[47] and that I have summarized in Chapter 1 under the heading "The limits of proprietary capitalism." But apart from the recognition that "social rigidities" can emerge in a successful capitalist economy, our perspective on British decline has very different analytical and ideological implications than that of Olson. Inherent in our argument is a critique of conventional microeconomic theory. We have argued that a prime cause of Britain's decline was the persistence of highly fragmented structures of industrial organization that left British industry too reliant on market coordination in an era in which competitive advantage went to those business organizations capable of planned coordination.

As part of his argument concerning the ways in which special-interest groups can impede the process of economic growth, Olson emphasized the gradual accumulation of distributional coalitions as the cause of Britain's relative economic decline in the twentieth century. The implication he drew is that "British society has acquired so many strong organizations and collusions that it suffers from an institutional sclerosis that slows its adaptation to changing circumstances and technologies."[48] In his view, Britain's problem was that its growth was thwarted by a rash of obstructive collectivities, and he explained the emergence of these distributional

---

[46] Ibid., 42.

[47] Bernard Elbaum and William Lazonick, *The Decline of the British Economy* (Oxford: Clarendon Press, 1986). In a perceptive summary of the debate over British entrepreneurship from the late nineteenth century, Peter L. Payne has argued, "In focusing attention on the question of institutional adaptation, Lazonick and Elbaum have, in effect, given substance to the generalities of Mancur Olsen [*sic*]." *British Entrepreneurship in the Nineteenth Century*, 2d ed. (London: Macmillan Press, 1988), 54. See also idem, "Entrepreneurship and British Economic Decline," in Bruce Collins and Keith Robbins, eds., *British Culture and Economic Decline* (New York: St. Martin's, 1990), 25–58; and M. W. Kirby, "Institutional Rigidities and Economic Decline: Reflections on the British Experience," *Economic History Review*, forthcoming. For a more general discussion of institutional rigidities and economic growth, see Geoff Hodgson, "Institutional Rigidities and Economic Growth," *Cambridge Journal of Economics*, 13 (March 1989), 79–101.

[48] Olson, *The Rise and Decline of Nations*, 78.

coalitions as simply the result of Britain's history of political stability. In my view, Britain's economic problem was that it lacked *sufficient* collective organization to maintain international competitive advantage, and I explain Britain's social fragmentation in terms of the persistence of the institutions of an outmoded proprietary capitalism that relied heavily on market coordination of productive activities.

It is also the case that the centrality of collective business organization to U.S. and Japanese industrial success in the first half of the twentieth century is devastating to the standard neoclassical view of the world – a view that correlates market coordination with economic success. Yet Olson informed the reader that he had no problem with standard microeconomic theory. Toward the beginning of his book, he asserted:

Most of the economics we shall use is well-established; it is mainly the widely tested "microeconomic theory" of individual firms, consumers, and industries. Many laymen suppose that economists disagree about everything, but in fact this part of economics is mainly acceptable to almost all skilled economists, be they left-wing or right-wing, Keynesian or monetarist.

Olson did allow that "to this we must add the less formal but invaluable 'Schumpeterian' insight into innovation and entrepreneurship, which is also rather widely accepted."[49] I have argued, however, that an acceptance of the Schumpeterian insight and its application to the history of successful capitalist development in the twentieth century vitiates standard microeconomic theory. Increasingly, innovation requires the planned coordination of productive activities, whereas standard microeconomic theory extolls the efficacy of market coordination.

It was his uncritical acceptance of the theory of the market economy that led Olson to deemphasize the existence, persistence, and ultimate importance of encompassing organizations in the determination of economic outcomes.[50] In particular, he never considered that the innovative business organization itself is just such a collectivity,[51] even though to have done so would not have contradicted his own description of what encompassing organizations do. To paraphrase Olson, innovative business organizations make the society in which they operate more prosperous

---

[49] Ibid., 36.

[50] Olson's only attempt at systematic empirical work was some highly aggregated, very simplistic, and inevitably inconclusive statistical exercises. See ibid., 98–117.

[51] For example, Olson argued that "the gains from encompassing – as compared with narrow special-interest – organizations would ensure that there would be a tendency for such organizations to merge in every society in much the way large firms come to dominate those industries in which large-scale production is most efficient" (ibid., 91). Apparently, Olson's view is that the large-scale firm is simply a technologically determined, as distinct from an organizationally determined, outcome. As I have argued, the scale and scope of modern business enterprise is the result of the dynamic interaction of organization and technology.

and do so by redistributing their shares of that prosperity – that is, the gains of innovation – to their members, thus encouraging their members to supply their productive resources to ensure economic success.[52]

Institutions, technology, and growth

There is a need to inquire, as Olson has done, into what types of social institutions impede and what types promote economic growth. But rather than permit a preconceived ideology of the efficacy of individualism (and the dire consequences of collectivism) to predetermine the conclusions of one's analysis, there is a need for careful historical investigation of how institutions operate, how and why they change their goals and internal organization, how institutional change affects the choices that individuals are able and willing to make, and what effects institutional organization and institutional change have on the development and utilization of productive resources, and hence on economic growth.

The empirical analysis of the role of institutions in economic development must be historical and comparative. It must be historical to explain why institutional arrangements develop and utilize productive resources and how, through their own internal dynamic, the limits to this process of value creation are reached. It must be comparative to explain why, quite apart from their own internal dynamic, institutions that have possessed the capability to promote technological change and economic development are rendered less effective by the rise of new competitors.

Some three decades ago, Walt Rostow presented a historical analysis of the wealth of different nations in *The Stages of Economic Growth*.[53] As the title of the book indicates, Rostow's purpose was to provide a general framework for understanding the successive stages of economic growth through which, as of the late 1950s, the advanced industrial nations had passed. He used some national data to chart the timing of five stages in a number of advanced industrial economies as well as the "takeoff" into sustained economic growth in a number of less developed economies. But the stage schema that Rostow adopted – traditional society, preconditions for takeoff, the takeoff, the drive to maturity, the age of high mass consumption – lacked explanatory content. He did chastise economists for simply positing a relation between a high rate of investment and a high rate of economic growth without recognizing that "the rise in the rate of investment . . . requires a radical shift in the society's effective attitude toward fundamental and applied science; toward the initiation of change in productive technique; toward the taking of risk; and toward the condi-

---

[52] See Olson's summary discussion in ibid., 74.
[53] W. W. Rostow, *The Stages of Economic Growth: A Non-Communist Manifesto* (Cambridge University Press, 1963).

tions and methods of work."[54] But beyond this broad statement, Rostow's "non-communist manifesto" (the subtitle of his book) provided no insights into the institutional and technological forces underlying successful capitalist development.[55]

One U.S. economist of the post-World War II decades who did articulate the need to comprehend the roles of technological change and institutions in economic development was Simon Kuznets. Although his own empirical work focused on the construction of national economic statistics, Kuznets saw that a more fundamental intellectual challenge was to understand the technological and institutional determinants of long-run economic growth.[56] As he put it in his 1966 volume, *Modern Economic Growth:*

> While some epochal innovations may be largely technological, the exploitation of the potential of growth provided by them usually requires much social invention – changes in arrangements by which people are induced to cooperate and participate in economic activity. . . . The interplay of technological and institutional changes is thus of the essence of the economic growth that takes place within the framework constituted by some epochal innovation.[57]

Although Kuznets recognized that the "interplay of technological and institutional changes" forms the basis for economic growth, he viewed the main line of causation as running from technological innovations to organizational adaptations. Speaking of U.S. economic growth in the nineteenth century and first half of the twentieth century, Kuznets argued:

> But the effects of technological innovations were not only on capital formation and factor productivity. They were also on the organization of economic production or

---

[54] Ibid., 20.

[55] For his statistical treatment of economic growth, see W. W. Rostow, *The World Economy: History and Prospect* (Austin: University of Texas Press, 1978). For his writings on the history of economic thought on the issue, see idem, *Theorists of Economic Growth from David Hume to the Present* (New York: Oxford University Press, 1990). As useful as these two works are in charting the statistical and theoretical history of economic growth, neither provides insights into the roles of organization and technology in the process of economic growth. For a thorough, and much-used, statistical analysis of the "stages of economic growth" in the advanced capitalist nations, see Angus Maddison, *Phases of Capitalist Development* (New York: Oxford University Press, 1982). See also idem, "Growth and Slowdown in Advanced Capitalist Economies: Techniques of Quantitative Assessment," *Journal of Economic Literature*, 25 (June 1987), 649–98. As in the case of Rostow, the dynamic interaction between organization and technology plays no role in Maddison's macroeconomic perspective.

[56] For his early work on national statistics, see Simon Kuznets, *National Income and Its Composition, 1919–1938* (New York: National Bureau of Economic Research, 1941).

[57] Simon Kuznets, *Modern Economic Growth: Rate, Structure, and Spread* (New Haven, Conn.: Yale University Press, 1966), 5. "The epochal innovation that distinguishes the modern economic epoch," Kuznets asserted, "is the extended application of science to problems of economic production" (9).

management units, in the pressure for the modern type of corporation; and they had a ramifying effect on industrial organization through the use of the discriminating power of monopoly. They affected conditions of work, with changes in employment requirements, educational levels, and the active lifespan of the working population; and they affected conditions of life, through further urbanization and modifying patterns of consumption and other elements in the modes of living associated with rising economic standards. The various institutional adjustments, and shifts in conditions of work and life, required for effective channeling of the continuous stream of technological innovations, were neither easy, nor costless. The gap between the stock of knowledge and inventions as the necessary condition, and the institutional and social adjustments that would convert the former into a sufficient condition is wide – as past history of the economically developed countries and the current history of the less developed amply show. That the United States achieved a sustained and fairly high rate of growth of per capita product over this long period is evidence of the country's capacity to modify its institutions and patterns of work and life, at rates sufficient to accommodate the technological potentials and in ways that preserved, except for the Civil War, a freely accepted social consensus.[58]

In this account, Kuznets gave no consideration to the possibility that social institutions in general and business organizations in particular might take a leading role in generating technological innovation. He did allow that "the political and social framework of a country sets the major conditions for economic growth, in formulating and monitoring rules of economic and social behavior; and changing them, when adjustments are required by new obstacles and opportunities brought by accumulated costs of the past, new knowledge, and new external circumstances."[59] But with his focus on the nation as the appropriate unit of analysis,[60] Kuznets displayed little if any intuitive grasp of the ways in which a nation's "political and social framework" could become imbedded in institutions that could promote or impede economic growth.

Nevertheless, in an essay entitled "Technological Innovations and Eco-

---

[58] Simon Kuznets, *Growth, Population, and Income Distribution: Selected Essays* (New York: Norton, 1979), 12–13. See also idem, *Population, Capital, and Growth* (New York: Norton, 1973). The view that technological change determines institutional arrangements, but not vice versa, can be found in Moses Abramowitz, "Catching Up, Forging Ahead, and Falling Behind," *Journal of Economic History*, 46 (June 1986), 385–406. As Abramowitz stated: "The state of education embodied in a nation's population and its existing institutional arrangements constrains it in its choice of technology. But technological opportunity presses for change. So countries learn to modify their institutional arrangements and then to improve them as they gain experience. The constraints imposed by social capability on the successful adoption of a more advanced technology gradually weaken and permit its fuller exploitation" (388–9). The view that social institutions constrain technological development rather than generate it echoes the perspective of Mancur Olson discussed earlier. Abramowitz made frequent references to the views of Olson.

[59] Kuznets, *Growth, Population, and Income Distribution*, 13.

[60] Kuznets, *Modern Economic Growth*, 16–19.

nomic Growth," Kuznets made it clear that he viewed economic growth as a dynamic process rather than as simply a series of institutional adjustments to exogenous technological change. "The combination of a contribution of growth to further innovation with the contribution of past innovations to growth," he stated, "forms a continuous and self-reinforcing mechanism – subject to limits, but sustainable by continuous feedback between growth and technological change."[61] More specifically, he contended that

> a related general argument would stress the effect of accumulated *experience*, and institutional innovations, through which modern economic growth may stimulate further technological innovations. The experience with past innovations has presumably yielded new ways of handling not only the organizational problems involved in the movement from conception to first successful application, but also those involved in the development of basic science and its connections with applied science.[62]

That Kuznets himself neither conceptualized nor researched these issues is not important. What is significant is his recognition of the need for economists to ask the big question concerning the dynamic interaction of organization and technology in the process of economic growth. That he had few answers is inherent in the fact that he devoted his career to resolving problems of macroeconomic measurement. As the economic historian William Parker wrote in his review of *Modern Economic Growth*, Kuznets's "generalizations about causes rest upon loose impressions of economic history."

> But on the other hand, by use of the quantitative evidence, Kuznets has established some main facts to be explained by economic historians, and – most important – has established these in a world-wide perspective. The body of the book presents not an explanation but rather an *explicandum* of modern economic history. It gives the outline of a program in which model-builders and historians may direct their peculiar efforts to produce a useful, cumulative result.[63]

From the perspective that I have offered in this book, the "useful, cumulative result" that economic historians can offer is one that, as Kuznets suggested, focuses on the dynamic interaction of organization and technology in economic development. Notwithstanding the overriding tendency of economists to ignore historical analysis in general and the process of technological change in particular, in recent years a number of economic historians (or economists who have been willing and able to

---

[61] Kuznets, *Growth, Population, and Income Distribution*, 81.   [62] Ibid., 83.
[63] William N. Parker, *Europe, America, and the Wider World: Essays on the Economic History of Western Capitalism* (Cambridge University Press, 1984), vol. 1, 182.

make use of history) have made important contributions to this intellectual project.[64]

The recent research on technological change asks two key questions concerning the strategies and structures underlying the innovation process: What are the forces that motivate strategic decision makers to invest in innovative technologies, and what are the institutional arrangements that determine the ultimate success of these innovative investments? Using the terminology of the basic theoretical framework that I set out in Chapter 3, these questions can be restated as what leads strategic decision makers to opt for an HFC investment strategy, and how are these high fixed costs ultimately transformed into high-quality products at low unit costs? I believe that, in combination, the theoretical arguments presented in Chapter 3 and the historical arguments presented in Chapter 1 provide a coherent intellectual framework within which the recent work on the dynamics of technological change can be interpreted and synthesized.

I do not intend to undertake this substantial task of interpretation and synthesis here. But drawing on the conceptual framework that I have already set forth in this book as well as the critical insights from the recent work by economists on the historical dynamics of technological change and innovation, I shall sketch the basic elements of an approach that, with adequate empirical research, can contribute to the elaboration of a theory

[64] A portion of the relevant work is cited later in the text. In recent years, among the open forums in which economists interested in exploring the relation between social institutions and technological innovation have been able to exchange ideas and share their research have been the biannual meetings of the International Joseph A. Schumpeter Society and the annual meetings of the Business History Conference. Papers presented at the Schumpeter Society meetings can be found in Horst Hanusch, ed., *Evolutionary Economics: Applications of Schumpeter's Ideas* (Cambridge University Press, 1988), and in Mark Perlman and Arnold Heertje, eds., *Evolving Technology and Market Structure* (Ann Arbor: University of Michigan Press, 1990). Forthcoming is a volume from the 1990 Schumpeter Society meetings, edited by Mark Perlman and published by the University of Michigan Press. The papers presented at the annual meetings of the Business History Conference can be found in the journal of the conference, *Business and Economic History*. The relation between institutions and innovation is also central to the workshops of the Consortium on Competitiveness and Cooperation at the University of California at Berkeley, Stanford University, Columbia University, and the Harvard Business School. See, for example, David J. Teece, "Innovation and the Organization of Industry," Consortium on Competitiveness and Cooperation Working Paper No. 90-6, Berkeley, August 1989; Richard R. Nelson, "What Is Public and What Is Private about Technology," Consortium on Competitiveness and Cooperation Working Paper No. 90-9, Berkeley, September 1990; David C. Mowery and Nathan Rosenberg, "The U.S. National Innovation System," Consortium on Competitiveness and Cooperation Working Paper No. 90-3, Berkeley, September 1990. Important international conferences have also been sponsored by Associazione di Storia e Studi sull'Impresa, based in Milan, Italy. See Giovanni Dosi, Renato Giannetti, and Pier Angelo Toninelli, eds., *Technology and Enterprise in a Historical Perspective* (Oxford University Press, 1991).

of capitalist development that is both rigorous in its fundamental assumptions and relevant to a world of organizational, technological, and economic change.

As argued in Chapter 4, the relevant intellectual framework must start with Joseph Schumpeter's critical insight into the centrality of innovation to the process of capitalist development. Yet as I have also argued, Schumpeter's own work did not answer the critical questions of what motivates investments in innovation and what determines the success of innovation, in large part because it was only late in his career (probably not until after the publication of *Business Cycles* in 1939) that Schumpeter came to recognize that to answer these questions would require rigorous historical analysis. Despite his ultimate recognition that the most fundamental "tool" of economic analysis is what he called "historical experience," Schumpeter himself never immersed himself in the historical analysis of the innovation process.[65]

Among economic historians, Nathan Rosenberg has gone furthest in identifying the phenomena that motivate investments in new technologies.[66] In *Perspectives on Technology*, Rosenberg argued that the decision to invest in a new technology cannot be understood as a movement along a production isoquant in response to relative factor prices precisely because, in the case of innovation, the relevant production isoquant is by definition not known.[67] Hence, something other than the market mecha-

---

[65] For an excellent discussion of Schumpeter's intellectual legacy to current research on innovation and productivity growth, see C. Freeman, "The Nature of Innovation and the Evolution of the Productive System," paper prepared for the OECD International Seminar on Science, Technology, and Economic Growth, Paris, June 5–8, 1989.

[66] For his survey of the relevant work on "technical progress" up through the early 1970s, see Nathan Rosenberg, *Inside the Black Box: Technology and Economics* (Cambridge University Press, 1982), ch. 1. In the concluding paragraph of this chapter, Rosenberg stated that on "the social determinants of a society's capacity for generating technical progress . . . our understanding remains, at best, rudimentary" (29). In contrast to Rosenberg's historical perspectives on the process of technological change, most economic analyses of technological change have consisted of attempts to measure inputs and outputs, with no explanation of the process that transforms one into the other. For an outline of one prominent approach to the measurement of technological change, see Edwin Mansfield, "Microeconomics of Technological Innovation," in Ralph Landau and Nathan Rosenberg, eds., *The Positive Sum Strategy: Harnessing Technology for Economic Growth* (Washington, D.C.: National Academy Press, 1986), 307–25. In the same volume, Ann F. Friedlaender criticized the failure of Mansfield and his fellow economists to provide an explanation of the role of the "environment" in determining the outcome of the innovation process. Friedlaender concluded by arguing that "greater insights into the question of how productivity growth and technical change take place . . . can only be obtained by using analytic frameworks that combine and synthesize the insights of technologists, engineers, and economists." "Macroeconomics and Microeconomics of Innovation: The Role of the Technological Environment," in Landau and Rosenberg, eds., *Positive Sum Strategy*, 327–32, cited at 332. Following Schumpeter, I would argue that, without the work of historians, such an attempt at combination and synthesis would come to naught.

[67] Nathan Rosenberg, *Perspectives on Technology* (Cambridge University Press, 1976), 64–

nism is needed to explain the decision to invest in technologies that must be developed before they can be utilized.

Rosenberg pointed to two types of environmental phenomena, one apparently technical and the other social, that might motivate an industrialist to invest in innovation. The technical phenomenon, which Rosenberg called the "inducement mechanism," derives from the fact that technological change is a highly interdependent process, with advances at one vertical stage of production creating technical imbalances at other upstream or downstream stages.[68] These imbalances constrain the development of technology, and hence "[direct] the attention of technically competent personnel to the solution of problems of obvious practical importance."[69] The social phenomenon, which he called a "focusing device," derives from a socially imposed constraint, such as a strike or a piece of legislation, that adversely affects the use of an existing technology, and hence focuses the industrialist's attention on the search for a new technology to overcome the constraint.

In effect, Rosenberg's approach views the impetus to technological change as the appearance of a constraint, either social or technical, that blocks the pursuit of the enterprise's goals. The industrialist invests in the development of a new technology in order to overcome this constraint. Critical to the success of such investments is the stock of knowledge available to the industrialist that can be used to develop a new technology. By building on the available stock of knowledge in a purposeful way, the constraint on technological innovation can be overcome.

Rosenberg's approach implicitly raises, but does not address, the question of the circumstances under which those who make strategic decisions in business organizations will choose to try to overcome constraints rather than succumb to them. To use the terminology of this book, when confronted by the appearance of a constraint on the pursuit of the "goals" of the enterprise, under what circumstances will strategic decision makers be innovative and under what circumstances will they be adaptive? The perspective that I have offered in this book is that, as a necessary condition, strategic decision makers will choose the innovative strategy when

5. Rosenberg specifically criticized W. E. G. Salter, who assumed that the economist's conventional analysis of choice of technique as a constrained maximization problem could include as potential choices technologies that had not yet been fully developed. See W. E. G. Salter, *Productivity and Technical Change* (Cambridge University Press, 1960), 43–4.

[68] Rosenberg cited Albert Hirschman, *The Strategy of Economic Development* (New Haven, Conn.: Yale University Press, 1958) as providing the basic insights into the existence and importance of inducement mechanisms. Rosenberg did not explicitly identify inducement mechanisms as technical and focusing mechanisms as social, but the distinction is implied by his examples. For Rosenberg's more fully developed arguments on technological interdependence in the U.S. economy, see *Inside the Black Box*, ch. 3.

[69] Rosenberg, *Perspectives on Technology*, 117.

they control an organizational structure that they believe provides them with the capability of developing productive resources that can overcome the constraints they face.

The willingness to confront a constraint is, however, only a necessary, and not a sufficient, condition for transforming that constraint. Innovation requires both an appropriate investment strategy and an appropriate organizational structure. The transformation of constraints requires the collective power that derives from what I have called "organizational capability." Organizational capability manifests the power of planned and coordinated specialized divisions of labor to achieve organizational goals. Through planned coordination, organizations can integrate the various types of knowledge needed to develop new products and processes. Through planned coordination, organizations can speed the flow of work from purchased inputs to sold outputs, thereby permitting the high fixed costs of developing new products and processes to be transformed into low unit costs and competitive advantage.

The basic historical thesis that I have put forward is that over the past century the growing technical and social complexity of the specialized divisions of labor that must be planned and coordinated to achieve economic success have made organizational capabilities ever more critical for attaining and sustaining competitive advantage. Increasingly and across a widening range of industries, the economic benefits of planned coordination in developing and utilizing productive resources have justified the high fixed costs of not only investments in plant and equipment but also investments in those personnel who are the essence of an organization that can do the requisite planning and coordination.

The recent research on technological change as a historical process reveals why organizational capability has become of paramount importance for sustained economic growth in the advanced capitalist economies. Giovanni Dosi has outlined the essential "stylized facts on innovation" that can be drawn from studying the process of technological change.[70] These stylized facts are (1) the uncertainty inherent in innovation, (2) the increasing importance of advances in scientific knowledge for major technological breakthroughs, (3) the increasing complexity of the search activities that lead to new processes and products, (4) the importance of "learning-by-doing" and "learning-by-using" to the generation and augmentation of innovation, and (5) the cumulative character of technological

---

[70] Giovanni Dosi, "The Nature of the Innovative Process," in Giovanni Dosi, Christopher Freeman, Richard Nelson, Gerald Silverberg, and Luc Soete, eds., *Technical Change and Economic Theory* (London: Pinter, 1988), 221–38; see also Keith Pavitt, "Sectoral Patterns of Technical Change: Towards a Taxonomy and a Theory," *Research Policy*, 13 (December 1984), 343–74.

advance within "firms, organisations and often countries."[71] In the following pages, I shall show how these stylized facts on innovation relate to one another as well as how they relate to the conceptual framework I have elaborated in this book.

As argued in Chapter 6, in investing in innovation the business organization faces two sources of uncertainty: productive uncertainty inherent in its own ability to develop and utilize the new technology and competitive uncertainty inherent in the abilities of its rivals to respond. Each source of uncertainty has its cognitive and behavioral dimensions. For successful innovation to occur, not only must productive resources be developed (the cognitive problem), they must also be utilized (the behavioral problem).

The two sources of uncertainty are interdependent. The ability of a particular business organization to overcome productive uncertainty increases competitive uncertainty for its rivals. Whether or not a rival responds with its own innovative investment strategy depends not only on the competitive uncertainty created by the "first mover," but also on the productive uncertainty inherent in its own business organization.

The greater the productive and competitive uncertainty that must be overcome, the more important is planned coordination, as distinct from market coordination, of the innovation process. The arguments that I have made concerning the growing importance of planned coordination in successful capitalist development imply that there have been increases over the past century in the productive and competitive uncertainty inherent in the innovation process. In general, the productive uncertainty inherent in an innovative investment strategy has increased because of the growing complexity of technological change. This growing complexity derives from the burgeoning stock of useful knowledge, itself a result of prior innovation, that can be used to confront new technological challenges. Increasingly, the innovation process requires the combination of ever more extensive divisions of labor in which the participants have ever more specialized knowledge that must be integrated and synthesized into a new product or process. This integration and synthesis, moreover, requires highly focused communication among the participants in the specialized division of labor, with repeated feedback from one specialist to another.[72]

Planned coordination is much more effective than market coordination in ensuring that this critical feedback occurs. Cognitively, planned coor-

---

[71] Dosi, "The Nature of the Innovative Process," 222–3.
[72] See Stephen J. Kline and Nathan Rosenberg, "An Overview of Innovation," in Landau and Rosenberg, eds., *Positive Sum Strategy*, 275–305.

dination can put in place all the specialists with the requisite training as well as the lines of communication required to integrate the specialized division of labor into collective knowledge. Behaviorally, planned coordination can ensure that the participants in the specialized division of labor have an interest in communicating with one another in order to share their knowledge and contribute their expertise.

Over the course of the twentieth century, the most obvious manifestation of the power of planned coordination in overcoming productive uncertainty has been the increasing reliance of industrial enterprises on in-house research laboratories, especially in the science-based (electrical and chemical) industries.[73] But it is not only in science-based industries that research on new products and processes occurs. Even in machine-based industries, such as textiles, that formed the basis for the earlier industrial revolutions, planned coordination by machinery makers became critical to successful innovation, because the growing complexity of technological change created the need for systematic experimentation on a large scale and over a prolonged time period.[74]

Investments in R&D, moreover, are just one component of an innovative strategy. Recent research on innovation has stressed the growing organizational as well as technological complexity of the innovation process and the resultant uncertainty of success. To comprehend how this complexity, and hence uncertainty, is confronted and possibly overcome – that is, how successful innovation occurs – students of technological change have focused on the nature of the "learning" process.[75] This research suggests that the learning process required to generate product and process innovations has become increasingly *cumulative, continuous,* and *collective.*

The learning process is cumulative when the attainment of certain types of knowledge is a prerequisite to acquiring other types of knowledge.[76] Some requisite knowledge is acquired outside the business organization,

[73] See David Mowery and Nathan Rosenberg, *Technology and the Pursuit of Economic Growth* (Cambridge University Press, 1989).
[74] See William Lazonick and William Mass, "Technology Transfer, Development, and Diffusion: An International Perspective on National Industrialization," photocopy, Harvard University, 1991.
[75] For recent research, see Ross Thomson, ed., *Learning and Technological Change* (London: Macmillan Press, forthcoming).
[76] In the history of U.S. economic thought, the main proponent of the view that technological change is the cumulative result of a large number of small improvements is Abbott Payson Usher. See his *A History of Mechanical Inventions,* rev. ed. (Cambridge, Mass.: Harvard University Press, 1954). For a useful comparison of the views of Usher and Schumpeter, see V. Ruttan, "Usher and Schumpeter on Invention, Innovation, and Technological Change," *Quarterly Journal of Economics,* 73 (November 1959), 596–606; reprinted in Nathan Rosenberg, ed., *The Economics of Technological Change* (Harmondsworth: Penguin, 1971), 73–85. On Usher, see also Parker, *Europe, America, and the Wider World,* app.

via the market. But by its very nature, innovation entails the development of a unique knowledge base within the business organization itself.[77] It is those enterprises that have made the investments necessary to embark on an innovative strategy that are in the best position to discover what technical problems must be resolved to achieve ultimate success – that is, to discover what must be learned.[78] And it is enterprises that have developed this competence that are in the best positions to acquire useful knowledge via the market.

The learning process is continuous when an interruption in the accumulation of knowledge results in a dissipation of the knowledge that has already been accumulated. As an input into the innovation process, knowledge is often perishable. Even for an individual, a discontinuity in the learning process can result in a loss of prior knowledge, and hence a wasted investment of time and effort. Discontinuity can have even greater destructive consequences when the learning process is collective – when it involves the combined and interrelated knowledge of a number of participants in a specialized division of labor. Any disruption of an individual's learning process disrupts the collective learning process as well.

The more an innovative strategy requires learning that is cumulative, continuous, and collective, the greater the advantages of planned coordination over market coordination for overcoming productive uncertainty. The planned coordination of the specialized division of labor can ensure the continuity and collectivity of the learning process in ways that market coordination cannot, thus enabling learning to accumulate rather than dissipate.

The functions that planned coordination can perform in ensuring that learning accumulates can be behavioral as well as cognitive. The behavioral dimension of productive uncertainty enters the innovation process because of the possibility that learning will dissipate rather than accumulate. Without proper incentives, key participants in the specialized division of labor will cease to supply their efforts to the achievement of organizational goals (or supply their efforts only at a price the organization cannot afford). The more continuous the learning process, the more dif-

---

[77] As I have suggested in Chapter 3, the resolution of these problems invariably entails additional investments that create even higher fixed costs that must be eventually transformed into low unit costs.

[78] In terms of product innovation, learning often occurs while one is trying to sell a new product or may result from feedback from the users of the product. In terms of process innovation, learning typically occurs in the transition from prototype to pilot plant and then in scaling up to mass production. For an important historical study by an economist, see Ross Thomson, *The Path to Mechanized Shoe Production in the United States* (Chapel Hill: University of North Carolina Press, 1989). See also Ross Thomson, "The Eco-Technic Process and the Development of the Sewing Machine," in Gavin Wright and Gary Saxonhouse, eds., *Technique, Spirit, and Form in the Making of Modern Economies: Essays in Honor of William N. Parker* (Greenwich, Conn.: JAI Press, 1984), 243–69.

ficult it is to replace a defector with another participant having the requisite cognitive competence. The more collective the learning process, the more adverse the impact of the defection of a key participant on the accumulation of learning. As argued in the critique of the transaction cost framework in Chapter 6, a key advantage of planned coordination over market coordination in ensuring successful innovation is that planned coordination can offer key participants the "high-powered" incentive of long-term attachment to the innovative organization as a necessary condition for long-term access to the gains from innovation that accrue to the organization.

Yet the very learning that has made innovation possible may eventually come to pose a barrier to further innovation. As Paul David has shown, the centrality of learning to technological development renders technological change a "path-dependent" process.[79] Given the cumulative, continuous, and collective character of learning, there are high costs to abandoning an established path of technological development for another one requiring different types of skills.[80]

Indeed, as David's well-known example of the persistence of the QWERTY typewriter keyboard illustrates, the new skill development may involve masses of individuals (in this case, the users of typewriters) who have but a market relation to the business organizations that must invest in innovation. The implication is that, given the limits that market relations impose on the ability of the business organization to engage in planned coordination, strategic decision makers opt to rely on existing learning, and

---

[79] For David's early statement of the path-dependent character of technological development, see *Technical Choice, Innovation, and Economic Growth* (Cambridge University Press, 1975), 1–16. For some of his more recent arguments and examples, see "Understanding the Economics of QWERTY: the Necessity of History," in William N. Parker, ed., *Economic History and the Modern Economist* (Oxford: Blackwell, Publisher, 1986), 30–49; idem, "Narrow Windows, Blind Giants, and Angry Orphans: The Dynamics of System Rivalries and Dilemmas of Technology Policy," in F. Arcangeli, P. David, and G. Dosi, eds., *Innovation Diffusion* (Oxford: Oxford University Press, forthcoming).

[80] The potential conflict between increasing productivity by learning on the basis of a given technological system and by innovation is stressed in William Abernathy and Kenneth Wayne, "Limits of the Learning Curve," *Harvard Business Review*, 52 (September–October 1974), 109–14. See also William Abernathy, *The Productivity Dilemma: Roadblock to Innovation in the Automobile Industry* (Baltimore, Md.: Johns Hopkins University Press, 1978). For elaborations of the "productivity–technology dilemma," see Kim B. Clark, Robert H. Hayes, and Christopher Lorenz, eds. *The Uneasy Alliance: Managing the Productivity–Technology Dilemma* (Boston: Harvard Business School Press, 1985). Case studies of "learning" on the basis of a given technological system do not typically ask whether the observed gains in productivity actually result in increases in productive *capability* (augmented skills) as distinct from increases in productive *performance* (augmented effort), taking productive capability as given. For a case study that makes this distinction, see William Lazonick and Thomas Brush, "The 'Horndal Effect' in Early U.S. Manufacturing," *Explorations in Economic History*, 22 (January 1985), 33–60. More generally, see Lazonick, *Competitive Advantage*.

its relevant technological path, instead of making the investments in the new learning required to move onto a new technological path. To move onto a new technological path, existing business organizations may have to extend the scale and scope of their planning capabilities.

Yet even within an existing business organization, prior learning may obstruct continuous innovation not only because of the high fixed costs required to develop new skills, but also because of the vested interests that those who have acquired the "old" skills have in preventing the "creative destruction" of both these skills and the particular organizational arrangements through which the skills of individuals are combined into a collective force. The existence of such vested interests in what has become a traditional technology may lead strategic decision makers to engage in adaptation rather than innovation. Again, for technological innovation to remain continuous may require the prior, or at least concomitant, transformation of the business organization itself to permit the planned coordination needed to change the "trajectory" of the organization's technology.

Indeed, to alter the path of technological development may require institutional transformations that go well beyond existing business organizations. Within a capitalist society, the business enterprise is not, and has never been, the only organized entity in which learning that is relevant to industrial innovation takes place. As Richard Nelson has outlined, the historical experience of the United States shows that the learning process that results in technological change also occurs through various arrangements among firms that enable them to share existing knowledge and cooperate in the generation of new knowledge, as well as through research conducted within universities, much of it funded by the federal government.[81] And as Christopher Freeman has argued, underlying Japan's rise to international industrial leadership has been a new "national system of innovation" – a "network of institutions in the public and pri-

---

[81] As Nelson has put these questions: "Economists, from Marx to Schumpeter, have touted capitalism as an engine of technical progress. But what kind of an engine is it? What are its key components? How does it work? . . . If technical change is far more complicated and variegated than it is depicted in standard economic theory, so too are the institutional structures supporting it." "Institutions Supporting Technical Change in the United States," in Dosi et al., eds., *Technical Change and Economic Theory*, 312–29. A revised version of this paper appears as "Capitalism as an Engine of Progress," *Research Policy*, 19 (June 1990), 193–214. See also Richard R. Nelson, "U.S. Technological Leadership: Where Did It Come From and Where Did It Go?" *Research Policy*, 19 (April 1990), 117–32. See also Edward W. Constant II, "The Social Locus of Technological Practice: Community, System, or Organization?" in Wiebe E. Bijker, Thomas P. Hughes, and Trevor J. Pinch, eds., *The Social Construction of Technological Systems* (Cambridge, Mass.: MIT Press, 1987), 223–42; Thomas P. Hughes, "The Evolution of Large Technological Systems," in Bijker et al., *The Social Construction of Technological Systems*, 51–82; Don E. Kash, *Perpetual Innovation: The New World of Competition* (New York: Basic, 1989).

vate sectors whose activities and interactions initiate, import, modify and diffuse new technologies."[82] A complete understanding of how new technologies are developed and utilized requires an analysis not only of the learning process within enterprises, industries, and universities, but also of the dynamic interaction of these learning processes within a national economy.

The analysis must be historical because the learning process in each of these institutions as well as the interconnections among institutions are subject to change. Institutions are transformed in part because of their own internal dynamics and in part because of changes in public policy as well as the rise of international competition. The analysis must also be comparative because the rise of new international competitors with more powerful learning capabilities can render inadequate a national system of innovation that was previously capable of technological leadership.

Individualist ideology and historical reality

By using a rigorous historical methodology to analyze the dynamic interaction of organization and technology in economic development, economists can begin to comprehend the nature and causes of the wealth of different nations. But as I have argued from the outset of this book, the intellectual constraints that have to be overcome are not just methodological. Wittingly or not, by employing a static, ahistorical methodology, economists have been able to ignore the increasingly important role of collective organization in generating economic development. Rather than explore the changing institutional foundations of international economic leadership, mainstream economists have continued to propound an ideology of market individualism.

In Chapter 2, I have presented a conception of the capitalist economy in which, over their lifetimes, individuals use both markets and organizations to achieve personal goals. The issue is not whether markets exist in capitalist economies – goods and services, financial securities, and even the capacity to work are exchanged on impersonal markets every day. The issue is rather how the process of economic development shapes the conditions of demand and supply and, in so doing, affects the ways in which individuals can make use of markets and the types of choices that markets can make available to individuals.

---

[82] Christopher Freeman, *Technology Policy and Economic Performance: Lessons from Japan* (London: Pinter, 1987), 1. On national systems of innovation, see also B. Lundvall, "Innovation as an Interactive Process: From User–Producer Interaction to the National System of Innovation," in Dosi et al., eds., *Technical Change and Economic Theory*, 349–69; Mowery and Rosenberg, "The U.S. National Innovation System"; Richard R. Nelson, ed., *National Innovation Systems*, forthcoming.

The perspective I have offered is that, increasingly, it is organizations, not markets, that ensure the development and utilization of productive resources. The strategies and structures of business organizations, therefore, determine the quality and quantity of market choices that individuals can make. As for entrepreneurship, individuals who are able and willing to assume leadership roles in business organizations find that their power to innovate is very much dependent on the collective power of the organizations they lead. As applied to successful economic development in nations such as Britain, the United States, and Japan, the perspective that I have presented confronts the ideology of individualism with the historical reality of a growing collectivism at the core of the capitalist economy itself.

Neoclassical economic theory espouses the ideology of individualism. According to the theory of the market economy that represents the core of neoclassical theory, markets permit individuals to make choices concerning the consumption of goods and services, the supply of their own labor power (which gives them income that can be used to purchase goods and services), and the investment of their savings (which, in any period, is what remains of disposable income that is not consumed).[83] It is the aggregation of these individual choices that, in a market-coordinated economy, determines economic outcomes. Yet institutional analyses of the U.S. economy have revealed that business organizations have had a profound impact on the ways in which individuals can use markets to purchase their goods and services, sell their labor power, and invest their money. In the following pages, I shall summarize our knowledge of the evolution of economic institutions in the United States over the past few decades to provide further support for my argument of the growing importance of collective organization for successful capitalist development.

It is in the markets for consumer goods and services that individual choice comes to the fore. According to the notion of consumer sovereignty, the aggregation of the consumption decisions of millions of individuals determines the allocation of the society's productive resources. Such a view might hold in a world in which consumers are aware of all the products that can meet their needs and desires. Yet the history of product innovation in consumer markets suggests that it is stretching the notion of consumer sovereignty to argue that the supply of products is simply a response to consumer demand. The challenge for the innovative

[83] Neoclassical economists generally recognize that the relevant unit of analysis is the household rather than the individual. But they offer no theory of the family as a collectivity. Indeed, Gary Becker has gone to great lengths to conceptualize relations among family members as market relations. See his *A Treatise on the Family* (Cambridge, Mass.: Harvard University Press, 1981). Hence, for all intents and purposes, neoclassical economists make no distinction between the allocative decisions of an individual and those of a household.

enterprise in consumer markets is to create a product that people want at a price they can afford. To do so, it has to incur high fixed costs without any assurance of a return. To generate a return, the innovative enterprise must incur even more fixed costs to make its new product both available to retailers and known to consumers. It is only through these investments in marketing that the innovative enterprise can hope to transform its high fixed costs into low unit costs.[84] In twentieth-century capitalism, innovative business organizations have created mass consumer markets, not vice versa.

In the 1950s and 1960s advertising by U.S. business came under attack as a mode of manipulating the consumer to buy inferior products at fixed prices.[85] Instead of engaging in product and process innovation – that is, instead of producing higher-quality (more reliable, durable, and usable) products that could be sold at lower prices – many U.S. corporations in oligopolistic industries sought, on the basis of advertising expenditures, to maintain their established market shares by shaping the behavior of their potential customers. Such a sales effort conforms to my definition of an adaptive strategy that utilizes existing productive resources but does not develop new productive resources.

This adaptive strategy began to falter when consumer groups organized for more truthful advertising and to demand that U.S. corporations provide higher-quality products.[86] The strategy reached its limits when, on the basis of innovative investment strategies, foreign competitors, particularly the Japanese, began to provide the U.S. consumer with higher-quality consumer products at lower prices. The sales effort remains essential to attaining and sustaining market share – and may in some contexts actually educate the consumer about the qualities of the products being

---

[84] See Susan Strasser, *Satisfaction Guaranteed: The Making of the American Mass Market* (New York: Pantheon, 1989); Richard Tedlow, *New and Improved: The Story of Mass Markets in America* (New York: Basic, 1990). Both of these books reflect an understanding that, in the first half of this century, the strategies and structures of U.S. business organizations were the driving force in the creation of the greatest consumer markets the world had ever seen.

[85] The most well-known book on advertising of the 1950s was Vance Packard, *The Hidden Persuaders* (New York: Mackay, 1957). On U.S. advertising more generally, see Michael Schudson, *Advertising, The Uneasy Persuasion* (New York: Basic, 1984). For an analysis of U.S. capitalism that views the "sales effort" as a major force in ensuring the utilization of productive resources, see Paul Baran and Paul Sweezy, *Monopoly Capital* (New York: Monthly Review Press, 1966), ch. 5.

[86] It is generally recognized that the document that galvanized the consumer movement was Ralph Nader, *Unsafe at Any Speed: The Designed-In Dangers of the American Automobile* (New York: Grossman, 1965). In his study of the determinants of competitive advantage around the world, Michael Porter has stressed the importance of "sophisticated demand" on the part of local consumers as a key initiating factor in the emergence of firms in that locality that engage in product innovation. *The Competitive Advantage of Nations* (New York: Free Press, 1990), 86–99. It remains for future research to show why demand is more sophisticated in some places than in others.

sold. But it has been the productive capabilities of a more collective capitalism on the supply side that has altered the quality–price choices available to consumers and, thereby, has undermined (even if it has by no means eliminated) the ability of industrial corporations to maintain market share through advertising alone.

For most people, the foundation for consumption is employment income; those people who have less income are more constrained in their consumption choices than people who have more income. Over the long run, the high levels of employment income that make possible high standards of living depend on successful business enterprises – that is, enterprises that through innovation have gained competitive advantage and large market shares. The people who enjoy these high standards of living are those who have secure attachments to successful business enterprises; for it is these enterprises that can pay the high incomes and provide the long-term employment security that constitute the foundations for high levels of consumer spending.

In a modern capitalist economy, individuals can choose among employers. But as I have argued in Chapter 2, they must do so judiciously if they want to obtain and retain good jobs. For most people a "good job" is one that offers not only a high income but also long-term employment security, promotion opportunities, and attractive work conditions. Indeed, in a well-functioning capitalist economy, employment opportunities that offer high remuneration tend to offer secure tenure, upward mobility, and desirable work as well.[87]

The more successful the economy, moreover, the more capable are its employers, be they in the private sector or public sector, of offering these good jobs. In the private sector, the business enterprises that are most capable of offering attractive employment opportunities are those that, through innovative investment strategies, have been able to gain marked competitive advantages, and hence large market shares. In turn, as I have argued in this book and as I have shown in detail elsewhere, the ability of the business organization to offer secure and remunerative employment opportunities is integral to its ability to develop and utilize the productive resources of its employees.[88] And a national economy in which such innovative business organizations play a major role has the wherewithal to create good jobs in the public sector as well. Within a capitalist economy, the least advantaged workers are those who, because of inade-

---

[87] For institutional labor economists, such jobs are in the primary labor market. See Peter Doeringer and Michael Piore, *Internal Labor Markets and Manpower Analysis* (Lexington, Mass.: Heath, 1971); David M. Gordon, Richard Edwards, and Michael Reich, *Segmented Work, Divided Workers* (Cambridge University Press, 1982), ch. 5; Paul Osterman, ed., *Internal Labor Markets* (Cambridge, Mass.: MIT Press, 1984).

[88] Lazonick, *Competitive Advantage*.

quate education and inappropriate socialization, are unable to gain access
to these good jobs, and hence are constantly at the mercy of finding employment on the "free labor market" that neoclassical economists so glo-
rify.

Neoclassical economists also extol the virtues of capital markets that
permit individuals to invest their savings in those pursuits that, adjusting
for risk, offer the highest possible returns. The investments might be
made in physical resources, either by taking an ownership stake in an
enterprise (with returns dependent on the success of the venture) or by
making a loan to someone else who agrees to pay a stipulated rate of
interest. According to the neoclassical story, when new opportunities arise
that promise a greater return on one's capital, individuals can choose to
withdraw their financial resources from old investments and put them
into the new, more profitable ones. Anything that stands in the way of
such financial mobility manifests a capital-market "imperfection." Unfettered capital markets bestow on wealthholders the freedom to choose what
to do with their property. And "as if by the working of an invisible hand,"
so the time-honored story goes, in exercising this individual freedom,
wealthholders also ensure that the economic system grows and pros-
pers.[89]

This perspective on the role of capital markets in a capitalist economy
ignores the financial requirements of the innovation process. From the
perspective of the innovative enterprise, what is needed is not financial
mobility as stressed by the proponents of unfettered capital markets, but
financial commitment – sustained access to financial resources so that the
business organization can continue the process of innovation to its successful conclusion. Financial commitment is critical to the transformation
of high fixed costs into high-quality products at low unit costs – the transformation that ensures the economic success of an innovative investment
strategy.[90]

Innovation requires financial commitment for both cognitive and behavioral reasons. The cognitive reason is that the business organization
must develop its productive capabilities. The cumulative and continuous
character of the learning that is the technological essence of the innova-

---

[89] During the 1980s, this view was propounded vociferously by the proponents of the "market for corporate control." See Gregg A. Jarrell, James A. Brickley, and Jeffrey M. Net-
ter, "The Market for Corporate Control: The Empirical Evidence since 1980," *Journal of
Economic Perspectives*, 2 (Winter 1988), 49–68; Michael C. Jensen, "Takeovers: Their
Causes and Consequences," *Journal of Economic Perspectives*, 2 (Winter 1988), 29–48.

[90] For an elaboration of this argument and those that follow, see Lazonick, "Controlling the
Market for Corporate Control"; see also Duncan Foley and William Lazonick, "Corporate
Takeovers and the Growth of Productivity," Barnard Economics Working Paper Series
No. 91-01, September 1990.

tion process necessitates financing that is both continuous and sustained. The behavioral reason is that, to transform high fixed costs into low unit costs, the business organization must not only develop its productive resources but also utilize them. Because the learning process is collective, as well as cumulative and continuous, the innovative organization must create incentives for those with specialized productive capabilities to make their skills and efforts continuously available to the enterprise. Financial commitment permits the business organization to reward adequately those participants in the specialized division of labor on whom the success of the innovative strategy depends. The financial capability of the business organization to share, or to make credible promises to share, the returns that accrue to its successful innovative strategies are critical for securing from participants in the organization's specialized division of labor the behavior required for continuous innovation and sustained competitive advantage.

Where, then, does financial commitment come from? Since the Great Merger Movement of the turn of the century, the institutional foundation of financial commitment in the U.S. industrial corporation has been the separation of asset ownership from managerial control. With J. P. Morgan taking the lead, Wall Street financed the mergers by selling to the wealth-holding public the ownership stakes of the entrepreneurs who had built up their companies from new ventures into going concerns in the decades after the Civil War. The result over the early decades of this century was to transfer ownership of corporate assets from the original owner-managers to a dispersed population of wealthholders. The organization of the trading activities of these wealthholders by powerful Wall Street banks created a highly liquid market in industrial stocks.[91]

The shareholder became a portfolio investor; beyond the price of the stock, shareholding did not require that the new "owners" make any further commitments of time, effort, or finance to "their" companies. It should also be noted that, contrary to the folklore of modern capitalism, the new "owners" of common stocks did not generally finance *new investments* in organization and technology. Rather, they financed the retirement of the old owners from the industrial scene.

In participating in the transfer of ownership, the shareholders in the major U.S. corporations unwittingly resolved a *managerial* problem for the growth of the firm that Alfred Marshall had posed in 1890 in the first

---

[91] Thomas R. Navin and Marion V. Sears, "The Rise of a Market for Industrial Securities, 1887–1902," *Business History Review*, 29 (June 1955), 105–38; Adolf A. Berle and Gardiner C. Means, *The Modern Corporation and Private Property*, rev. ed. (New York: Harcourt, Brace & World, 1968); Lazonick, "Controlling the Market for Corporate Control"; see also Chapter 1, this volume.

edition of his *Principles of Economics*.[92] Marshall argued that, insofar as family ties formed the basis for succession to top management, the internal dynamism of a going concern was likely to flag when the original entrepreneur gave up command to the next generation in whose hands ownership and control remained united.

Indeed, as I have outlined in Chapter 1, even in the more capital-intensive industries, the persistence of owner-management of going concerns did afflict Marshall's Britain well into the twentieth century. Britain's problem was not an absence of capital markets. At the turn of the century, well-developed markets in industrial securities had been in place for several decades.[93] Many of the stock exchanges were highly local affairs, so that, even when a British firm went public, there was not the widespread distribution of ownership that occurred in the United States. With enterprises less dominant and the demand for a company's stock less extensive than in the United States, it was more difficult to separate the original owner-managers from the control of their firms in Britain. The securities that British firms did float around the turn of the century tended to be nonvoting preferred issues for the purpose of financing direct investment. It would only be decades later that British enterprises would follow the U.S. example of issuing shares that transferred ownership rights to portfolio investors and effected the separation of ownership from control.[94]

As a result, even in more capital-intensive industries, proprietary capitalism persisted in Britain well into the second half of the twentieth cen-

---

[92] Alfred Marshall, *Principles of Economics*, 9th (variorum) ed. (London: Macmillan Press, 1961), vol. 1 (text), bk. 4. See also Chapter 5, this volume.

[93] See Lance Davis, "Capital Markets and Industrial Concentration: The U.S. and U.K., a Comparative Study," *Economic History Review*, 19 (August 1966), 255–72; Michael Edelstein, *Overseas Investment in the Age of High Imperialism* (London: Methuen, 1982), 47–65; William Kennedy, *Industrial Structure, Capital Markets, and the Origins of British Economic Decline* (Cambridge University Press, 1987). Kennedy's argument is that British economic performance was hampered by the impediments that "imperfect" capital markets placed in the way of the financing of new investment. In comparative perspective, however, the so-called imperfections in British capital markets were far less evident than those in the United States and Germany, where Wall Street and the Great Banks dominated new share issues. The key to the inadequacy of British investment in domestic production facilities was not imperfect capital markets, but business organizations that failed to build the managerial structures that were able and willing to pursue innovative strategies. As outlined in Chapter 1, Britain's problem was not "imperfect" capital markets but rather "imperfect" business organizations. In effect, as Steven Tolliday has argued in the case of the British steel industry in the interwar period, proprietary organizational structures led to adaptive investment strategies. *Business, Banking, and Politics: The Case of British Steel, 1918–1939* (Cambridge, Mass.: Harvard University Press, 1987). More generally, see Alfred D. Chandler, Jr., *Scale and Scope: The Dynamics of Industrial Capitalism* (Cambridge, Mass.: Harvard University Press, 1990), chs. 7–8.

[94] See P. L. Cottrell, *Industrial Finance, 1830–1914* (London: Methuen, 1980), 164–7.

tury. The integration of ownership and control placed severe managerial constraints on the growth of British industrial enterprise because it resulted in the segmentation of top management from technical specialists, as outlined in Chapter 1. The inability to separate ownership from control could also place financial constraints on the growth of the enterprise. Because the proprietary firm generally lacked managerial organization, it could not gain a dominant position in its industry, and hence had difficulty generating sufficient earnings for self-sustained expansion. The rise of more powerful competitors abroad, moreover, encouraged the owner-managers of British firms to choose adaptive strategies, perhaps tapping the returns from previous industrial successes to make portfolio investments and to support aristocratic lifestyles.[95]

In contrast, in the United States, the separation of ownership from control left managers with the power to allocate the enterprise's earnings. In addition, by giving institutional investors confidence in the continuity of the enterprise, the separation of ownership from control provided the basis for long-term bond financing, when required. Thus was secured the financial commitment that was, and remains, a necessary condition for product and process innovation.

Since the first decades of the century, U.S. institutional economists have investigated the relation between ownership and control and have analyzed the implications of this relation for the investment strategies of business enterprises. Thorstein Veblen recognized that, with the rise of the market in industrial securities around the turn of the century, the legal owners of corporate assets no longer possessed knowledge concerning the products and processes that gave those assets value. Yet Veblen did not think that ownership had been separated from control. Writing in the aftermath of the Great Merger Movement and in an era when public opinion railed against the Morgan-dominated "money trust," Veblen considered shareholders to be in control over output and pricing decisions. Intent on maximizing profits on the basis of the existing productive resources in which they held shares, the absentee owners instructed their managerial employees to raise prices and restrict output. In Veblen's view, the absentee owners acted like classical monopolists.

This "conscientious withdrawal of efficiency" placed the interests of absentee owners squarely in conflict with the interests of the "engineers" – those participants in the business organization who possessed the essential knowledge of products and processes.[96] Imbued with what Veblen

---

[95] See Chandler, *Scale and Scope*, 390. For a critique of Chandler's use of the notion of "personal capitalism" as an explanation of Britain's relative decline, see Leslie Hannah, "Scale and Scope: Towards a European Visible Hand?" *Business History*, forthcoming.

[96] Thorstein Veblen, *The Engineers and the Price System* (New York: Huebsch, 1921).

called the "instinct of workmanship,"[97] the engineers sought to develop and utilize the forces of production to the fullest extent possible. The clear implication of Veblen's analysis was that economic progress would be thwarted unless the engineers could wrest control over strategic decision making from owners.[98]

Yet by the early 1930s, Adolf Berle and Gardiner Means were arguing that professional managers had indeed taken control of strategic decision making in the largest U.S. industrial enterprises.[99] Berle and Means were undecided about the economic consequences of the separation of ownership from control. On the one hand, control now rested with those who were in continuous contact with, and had intimate knowledge of, the activities of the corporation. On the other hand, there was concern that managers would become a self-perpetuating group of insiders, immune to, and perhaps even in conflict with, the interests of shareholders and society at large.[100]

In *The New Industrial State*, published more than three decades after Berle and Means had documented the separation of ownership from control, John Kenneth Galbraith elaborated a perspective on modern capitalism in which the "technostructure" (essentially managerial employees) exercised inordinate power over the "planning system" (that part of the economy under control of the dominant business corporations).[101] Written at a time when (as it has turned out) U.S. industrial leadership was at

---

[97] Thorstein Veblen, *The Instinct of Workmanship and the State of the Industrial Arts* (New York: Viking, 1914).

[98] See Thorstein Veblen, *Absentee Ownership and the Business Enterprise in Recent Times; The Case of America* (New York: Huebsch, 1923). On the evolution of Veblen's thinking on owners and managers, see Malcolm Rutherford, "Veblen on Owners, Managers, and the Control of Industry," *History of Political Economy* 12 (Fall 1980), 434–48.

[99] Berle and Means, *The Modern Corporation and Private Property*. See also Robert Aaron Gordon, *Business Leadership in the Large Corporation* (Washington, D.C.: Brookings Institution, 1945). See also Thomas K. McCraw, "Berle and Means," *Reviews in American History*, 18 (1990), 578–96.

[100] As Berle and Means put it in *The Modern Corporation and Private Property*: "In examining the break up of the old concept that was property and the old unity that was private enterprise, it is therefore evident that we are dealing not only with distinct but often with opposing groups, ownership on the one side, control on the other – a control which tends to move further and further away from ownership and ultimately to lie in the hands of the management itself, a management capable of perpetuating its own position. The concentration of economic power separate from ownership has, in fact, created economic empires, and has delivered these empires into the hands of a new form of absolutism, relegating "owners" to the position of those who supply the means whereby the new princes may exercise their power" (116).

[101] John Kenneth Galbraith, *The New Industrial State* (Boston: Houghton Mifflin, 1967). The book has been reissued in several editions, with revisions being made in the second (1971) and third (1978). The fourth (1985) edition contains a valuable introduction in which, among other things, Galbraith considers the relevance of the arguments of *The New Industrial State* in an era of U.S. industrial decline.

its historical apogee, *The New Industrial State* remains a compelling attack on what I have called the myth of the market economy.[102]

Galbraith argued that those who constituted the technostructure had an overriding interest in the growth of their respective companies. To do so they had to plan production, and it was the need for planning that gave the members of the technostructure their power. To be successful in the pursuit of its goals, the technostructure also had to manage effective demand. Managing effective demand meant influencing the amounts and types of expenditures made by consumers and the government. The prime means of influencing consumer expenditures was advertising, and the prime means of influencing government expenditures was through ties with the Pentagon.

From Galbraith's point of view, it was inevitable that in an advanced industrial society the technostructure would have control. It was not, however, inevitable that its social priorities would result in rampant consumerism and militarism. The political and cultural problem was to set more rational societal goals to which the technostructure, with its inordinate control over the nation's productive forces, could respond.[103]

The ability of citizens to set social goals is a matter of political power. The ability of business organizations to respond to social goals is a matter of productive power. From the perspective that I have presented in this book, the issue for the coming decades is whether the U.S. economy will possess the organizational capabilities to respond to social goals, whatever they may be.[104] During the 1970s and 1980s, belief in the ideology of

---

[102] Toward the end of *The New Industrial State*, Galbraith wrote: "The genius of the planning system lies in its organized use of capital and technology. . . . To leave these matters to the market would be regarded by those principally involved as the equivalent of leaving them to chance. Yet, as we have seen, the myth of the system is quite different. That holds, and a large, expensive though not universally successful educational effort teaches, that all credit belongs to the market, which is a force of transcendent power" (364).

[103] Cogent arguments have been made that link military spending as a social priority with U.S. economic decline. See Seymour Melman, *The Permanent War Economy: American Capitalism in Decline* (New York: Simon & Schuster, 1974); Robert W. DeGrasse, Jr., *Military Expansion, Economic Decline: The Impact of Military Spending on U.S. Economic Performance* (Armonk, N.Y., Sharpe, 1983).

[104] In a provocative contribution to the industrial policy debate (insofar as such a debate can be said to exist in the United States), Robert Reich has argued that it is not whether business organizations are indigenous that is important for U.S. economic prosperity, but only whether business organizations of whatever national origin have incentives to employ workers in the United States. Reich contended that it is the availability of a skilled labor force that is a prime incentive for global corporations to employ labor in any nation. "Who Is Us?" *Harvard Business Review*, 68 (January–February 1990), 53–64. One problem with Reich's argument is that, in the absence of a growing demand for skilled labor by powerful business interests located in the United States, there is no reason to believe that those who control wealth and power in the United States will

individualism facilitated a vast exploitation of the wealth of the United States by financiers exercising their power through financial markets. This exploitation of the wealth of the nation is now manifest in financial fragility at the levels of the enterprise, household, and the state. This financial fragility, in turn, militates against making the financial commitments that investments in innovation require.[105]

This exploitation of the wealth of the nation is also manifest in the growth of economic inequality.[106] The relationship between the growth of economic inequality and the erosion of the organizational capabilities of U.S. business organizations remains to be studied. My view is that the growth of inequality has undermined the incentives for those who participate in the business organization's specialized division of labor to make the long-term commitments of their skills and efforts that the innovation process requires. Over the past decades, top managers have made their strategic decisions in a financial environment that, by permitting them to put their own aggrandizement ahead of the long-term viability of the organization as a whole, encourages adaptive responses.[107] At the same time, even the salaried employees of dominant corporations can no longer count on long-term employment security. Why should they commit their careers to business organizations that appear unwilling and perhaps unable to make long-term commitments to them? Blue-collar workers have even less employment security. Indeed, in an era when international industrial leadership relies ever more heavily on developing the skills and gaining the commitment of shop-floor workers, U.S. employers oppose legislation that would give these workers even a modicum of advance notice that they will be losing their jobs. What is the other side of the same paycheck, U.S. employers still regard the blue-collar worker as an "hourly em-

support private and public programs to allocate resources on the massive scale required to upgrade the quality of the U.S. labor force. More generally, Reich's argument does not analyze how the intensification of international economic competition has rendered even more critical for national economic prosperity the existence of a set of interlinked institutions that constitute a "national system of innovation." Japan and Germany, among others, are still building up their national systems of innovation. It is difficult to see how the United States can hope to compete in the decades ahead if, as appears to be the case, it allows its national system of innovation to run down.

[105] See, e.g., Alfred L. Malabre, Jr., *Beyond Our Means: How Reckless Borrowing Now Threatens to Overwhelm Us* (New York: Vintage, 1987); Benjamin M. Friedman, *The Day of Reckoning: The Consequences of American Economic Policy under Reagan and After* (New York: Random House, 1988).

[106] On the growth of economic inequality in the United States in the 1970s and 1980s, see Frank Levy, *Dollars and Dreams: The Changing American Income Distribution* (New York: Norton, 1987); Bennett Harrison and Barry Bluestone, *The Great U-Turn: Corporate Restructuring and the Polarizing of America* (New York: Basic, 1988); Kevin Phillips, *The Politics of Rich and Poor: Wealth and the American Electorate in the Reagan Aftermath* (New York: Random House, 1990).

[107] See Lazonick, "Controlling the Market for Corporate Control."

ployee," even as they ask this worker to commit his or her skill and effort to the success of the organization.[108]

Overcoming intellectual constraints

The intellectual constraints that mainstream economists must overcome to comprehend the realities of collective capitalism in the late twentieth century are therefore both ideological and methodological. The ideological problem is inherent in the myth of the market economy that I have critiqued throughout this book. Trained to believe in the economic superiority of perfect competition to all other forms of economic organization, mainstream economists have an inbred bias against the proposition that any form of collectivism, even (and perhaps especially) within a capitalist economy, could promote economic well-being.

But even for those mainstream economists who manage to overcome this ideological bias, another, perhaps more insurmountable problem remains. In becoming well-trained economists, they have acquired a trained incapacity for analyzing the process of change. In viewing economic activity as adaptive responses subject to given constraints, economists have simply not acquired the ability to analyze the evolution of those constraints. Because the constraints on economic outcomes that mainstream economists generally take as given are the very technologies that enable business organizations to transform inputs into outputs, the vast majority of economists have avoided the analysis of the process of technological change. As a result, they have not acquired the intellectual capabilities to do so.

This intellectual handicap means that even those economists who ask the right questions about the role of the business enterprise in the evolution of the economy tend to ignore the readily available historical knowledge that is critical for answering the questions. For example, in an otherwise informative and wide-ranging review of alternative perspectives entitled "The Corporation, Competition, and the Invisible Hand," with more than 150 citations of the economics literature, Robin Marris and Dennis Mueller made but one reference to a work that can be con-

---

[108] For an example of the tenacity of the ideology of the "hourly worker," an excellent book devoted to showing the benefits of focusing on the long-term for innovation and competitive advantage contains the following statement: "As the world's technology becomes more sophisticated, workers have to be more sophisticated, too. Instead of tightening the same bolt every ninety seconds, they'll be running computerized equipment. Even Third World nations like Singapore are preparing for that, investing as much in factory employees as factories. In America, however, most of our training programs focus on management alone. That's valuable, but it's not enough. We have to see what nations overseas have seen for years: that the industrial future will depend on the skills of *hourly employees*." Ira Magaziner and Mark Patinkin, *The Silent War: Inside the Global Business Battles Shaping America's Future* (New York: Vintage, 1989), 303, my emphasis.

strued as containing substantive historical perspective on the evolution of the business organization.[109] Yet the critical question that Marris and Mueller raised at the end of the essay is whether, left to itself, the evolutionary process of corporate capitalism results in the emergence of the most efficient organizational and industrial structures.[110] As I have argued in my critique of the transaction cost approach, one cannot address this question without understanding the historical conditions under which innovative rather than simply adaptive business organizations will emerge. And one cannot begin to answer the question without a comparative analysis of the historical impacts of business organization on economic performance.

An awareness of the available historical literature, however, does not necessarily solve the methodological problem. In the same issue of the *Journal of Economic Literature* in which Marris and Mueller published the piece just cited, Richard Caves, a prominent industrial organization economist, surveyed recent work in business history, business policy, and organizational behavior relevant to an understanding of the relation between corporate strategy and structure. Caves concluded his survey by arguing that "the well-trained professional economist could have carried out many of the research projects cited in this paper more proficiently than did their authors, who were less effectively equipped by their own disciplines."[111] Prominent among the authors cited was Alfred Chandler. Caves went on:

If one accepts the weak postulate that the firm is a purposive organization maximizing some objective function, it follows that its strategic and structural choice represents a constrained optimization problem. My reading is that students of business organization with disciplinary bases outside of economics would accept that proposition but have lacked the tools to follow its blueprint. Constrained-maximization problems are mother's milk to the well-trained economist.[112]

For lack of a historical methodology, economists may think that the analytical tools they have acquired are as natural as "mother's milk" for studying the economy. I would prefer to argue that bottle feeding during professional childhood with a formula of individualist ideology and static methodology has deprived these "well-trained" economists of the ability to analyze the historical dynamics of business strategy and structure.

---

[109] Robin Marris and Dennis Mueller, "The Corporation, Competition, and the Invisible Hand," *Journal of Economic Literature* 18 (March 1980), 32–63. The one reference to a work containing historical perspective is to S. J. Prais, *The Evolution of Giant Firms in Britain* (Cambridge University Press, 1976).

[110] Marris and Mueller, "The Corporation, Competition, and the Invisible Hand," 59.

[111] Richard Caves, "Industrial Organization, Corporate Strategy and Structure," *Journal of Economic Literature*, 18 (March 1980), 64–92, cited at 88.

[112] Ibid.

The result is the failure of "well-trained" economists to ask, let alone answer, what Robert A. Gordon called the "big questions."[113] Indeed, some mainstream economists have extolled the virtues of the neoclassical tendency to ask the *little* questions. For example, in 1967, in a well-known review of Galbraith's *The New Industrial State*, Robert Solow argued:

The world can be divided into big-thinkers and little-thinkers. . . . Economists are determined little-thinkers. They want to know what will happen to the production of houses and automobiles in 1968 if Congress votes a 10 percent surcharge on personal and corporate tax bills, and what will happen if Congress does not. They would like to be able to predict the course of the Wholesale Price Index and its components, and the total of corporate profits by industry. They are not likely to be much helped or hindered in these activities by Professor Galbraith's view of Whither are We Trending.[114]

Solow recognized that "little-thinking can easily degenerate into mini-thinking or even into hardly thinking at all."[115] But he left the distinct impression that intelligent "little-thinking" was what a well-trained economist not only could do but also should do.

Opinions can change. At the 1984 meetings of the American Economic Association, Solow delivered a paper in a session entitled "Economic History: A Necessary Though Not Sufficient Condition for an Economist." He articulated admirably what decades of "little-thinking" by neoclassical economists had done to the relation between economic theory and economic history. Solow recognized that, with the discipline of economics as it was currently constituted, "economic theory learns nothing from economic history, and economic history is as much corrupted as enriched by economic theory."[116] He cautioned that, in looking for a closer relation between economic theory and economic history, he was "not prepared to abandon the exhaustive study of the implications of particular axiom systems," although he admitted, quite candidly, "I do not expect a lot from that sort of theory." "What I am arguing against," Solow explained, "is the foolish belief that when it comes to studying the real world there is only one useful system of axioms and we already know what it is."[117] He went on to suggest that

it would be a useful principle that economists should actually believe the empirical assertions they make. That would require more discipline than most of us now

---

[113] Robert A. Gordon, "Rigor and Relevance in a Changing Institutional Setting," *American Economic Review*, 66 (March 1976), 1–14, cited at 1. See Introduction, this volume.

[114] Robert M. Solow, "The New Industrial State or Son of Affluence," *The Public Interest*, 9 (Fall 1967), 100–8, cited at 100.

[115] Ibid., 101.

[116] Robert M. Solow, "Economics: Is Something Missing?" in Parker, ed., *Economic History and the Modern Economist*, 21–9, cited at 21.

[117] Ibid., 22.

exhibit, when many empirical papers seem more like virtuoso finger exercises than anything else. The case I am trying to make concerns the scope and ambitions of economic model building, not the intellectual and technical standards of model building.[118]

If, through a narrow conception of rigorous analysis, economic theorists have lost touch with reality, Solow argued that economic historians have done so as well because of their attempt to conform to the prevailing standards of economics. "As I inspect some current work in economic history," Solow confided, "I have the sinking feeling that a lot of it looks exactly like the kind of economic analysis I have just finished caricaturing: the same integrals, the same regressions, the same substitutions of *t*-ratios for thought."

Apart from anything else, it is no fun reading the stuff any more. Far from offering the economic theorist a widened range of perceptions, this sort of economic history gives back to the theorist the same routine gruel that the economic theorist gives to the historian. Why should I believe, when it is applied to thin eighteenth-century data, something that carries no conviction when it is done with more ample twentieth-century data?[119]

Solow pointed to both the need for an integration of rigor and relevance in economics and the possibility of fulfilling this need through a more substantive interaction between economic history and economic theory. Because the fundamental problem is to discover how the real world works, he attributed to economic history the "more interesting" role:

If the proper choice of a model depends on the institutional context – and it should – then economic history performs the nice function of widening the range of observation available to the theorist. Economic theory can only gain from being taught something about the range of possibilities in human societies. Few things should be more interesting to a civilised economic theorist than the opportunity to observe the interplay between social institutions and economic behavior over time and place.

In turn, the economic theorist, Solow argued, has something to offer the economic historian:

If economists set themselves the task of modelling particular contingent social circumstances, with some sensitivity to context, it seems to me that they would provide exactly the interpretive help an economic historian needs. That kind of model is directly applicable in organizing a historical narrative, the more so that the economist is conscious of the fact that different social contexts may call for different background assumptions and therefore for different models.[120]

The intellectual agenda that Solow articulated is admirable, coming as it did from a leading economic theorist in the neoclassical tradition who

[118] Ibid., 23.   [119] Ibid., 26.   [120] Ibid., 23–4.

had just two decades earlier defended the "little thinkers" of the world.[121]
More than that, the agenda of integrating history and theory is essential
if the collective work of economists is to illuminate more than it obscures.
Neglecting as it has for decades the serious study of the process of economic development in the advanced capitalist economies, mainstream
economics currently propounds a view of economic activity that grossly
misconceives reality.

At the 1962 meetings of the American Economic Association, Paul
Samuelson concluded his presidential address by telling his colleagues
that they were the best judges of the economics profession's scientific
achievements. As the leading neoclassical economist of his generation,
Samuelson advised his disciples, "The economic scholar works for the
only coin worth having – our own applause."[122] This book stands as testimony that, a few decades later, not everyone is clapping. Those who, in
an age of collective capitalism, wish to influence the policies of businesses
and governments for the sake of promoting innovation and economic growth
must first confront the myth of the market economy and the meager analytical tools that the proponents of the myth have labeled "science." What
is required to reverse the decline of economics as a relevant academic
discipline is an innovative intellectual response. Instead of ignoring the
history of capitalist development, economists need a methodology that
can analyze it – a methodology that permits economists to explore, and
ultimately comprehend, the relation between individual choice and collective organization in the process of economic development. To invoke
once again the legacy of Joseph Schumpeter, economists must acquire
"historical experience" before the experience that we call history passes
them by.

---

[121] Solow made his name in economics by (1) showing that U.S. economic growth could not
be explained on the basis of typical neoclassical measures of productive inputs, and (2)
defending and elaborating a neoclassical theory of growth. More recently, however,
Solow has recognized that conventional macroeconomic models fail to capture important, if not essential, aspects of microeconomic reality. See *The Labor Market as a Social
Institution* (Oxford: Blackwell Publisher, 1990). Along with Michael Dertouzas and Richard Lester (both MIT engineering professors), Solow is a coauthor of *Made in America:
Regaining the Productive Edge* (Cambridge, Mass.: MIT Press, 1989). This book provides evidence, consistent with the arguments that I have made in Chapter 1, on how a
number of U.S. industrial sectors have lost international competitive advantage, particularly to the Japanese.

[122] Paul Samuelson, "Economists and the History of Ideas," *American Economic Review*,
52 (March 1962), 1–18, cited at 18.

Index

Abramowitz, Moses, 176, 306
accounting practice, 98–9, 250–1
accumulation, social structures of, 282
adaptation, 57, 162, 163, 275, 333; and innovation, 50, 66, 67, 192, 249, 286, 289; marginal, 66, 285; in railroad administration, 235; theory of, 288; in theory of business organization, 213–27
adaptive firms, 97, 294–5
adaptive organization(s), 206, 213–14, 220, 224, 265–6; theory of, 17, 216; and uncertainty, 200–2; Williamson's theory of, 197, 198
adaptive response, 137, 202, 277, 327, 344, 345; of British industrialists, 143–4; in managerial capitalism, 49–50; in neoclassical analysis, 308; in proprietary capitalism, 48; to technological change, 138
adaptive strategy, 88–9, 90, 91, 199, 205, 214, 250, 284; in administration of railroads, 236; and competitive advantage, 110–11; and competitive disadvantage, 108f; in consumer goods and services, 336–7; in managerial capitalism, 52, 55; by profit-seeking enterprise, 90; proprietary capitalism and, 340n93, 341
administrative coordination, 193, 195; of railroads, 194, 230, 231–7
administrative integration, 301
advertising, 166, 336, 343
agriculture, in Great Britain, 3
Alchian, Armen, 17, 181–8, 191, 230
allocative efficiency, 178, 179; see also resource allocation
"Allocative Efficiency vs. 'X-Efficiency,' " (Leibenstein), 178–9
amalgamation, 48, 56, 250
American Economic Association, 347, 349
"American system of manufactures," 27
American Tobacco (co.), 239, 241
antitrust laws (U.S.), 314
aristocracy of labor, 25, 121, 277–8; and factory system, 139–40
aristocratic status: pursuit of, by British industrialists, 48–9

Arkwright, Richard, 4
Arnold, Horace, 188
Arrow, Kenneth, 206, 207, 208
assembly line, 185, 187–8
asset ownership, separated from managerial control, 314, 339–41; see also ownership
asset specificity, 211–13, 214, 216, 220, 221, 222, 223, 265; and administration of railroads, 237; choice in, 217–18; and innovation, 226; and organizational success, 228–9; and production–distribution integration, 245; in theory of innovative organization, 224; and vertical integration, 238–9, 240
Austin (co.), 47
authority, 259; hierarchical, 60, 169
authority, delegation of, 78–9, 250, 254–5, 300; in managerial capitalism, 33–4; in U.S. railroads, 237
automobile industry: assembly line in, 187–8; England, 46–7, 144; Japan, 36, 38; U.S., 52
Ayres, C. E., 311

backward integration, 134, 193, 238, 239, 240; in Du Pont, 252; of innovative organizations, 204, 245–6
Baltimore & Ohio (railroad), 234
banking system, in England, 144
Baran, Paul, 279–80
barriers to entry, 86–7, 124, 173, 214; innovative strategies as, 215, 216
Becker, Gary, 17, 177–8, 181, 335n83
behavior modification, 180
behavioral limitations, 228–9, 237, 244, 256
behavioral school of economics, 193, 208
behavioral uncertainty, 210–11, 218, 219, 220, 222, 329
Berle, Adolf, 342
Best, Michael, 301–2
big business, 156, 175, 279, 301
bilateral contracting, 212, 221–2, 231
Blackstone, Sir William, 63
Blinder, Alan, 11–12

351

"Division of Labor Is Limited by the Extent of the Market, The" (Stigler), 296, 299
Dobb, Maurice, 270–8
dominant business organizations/firms, 70, 84–6, 87, 88, 165, 193, 215–17; in collective capitalism, 37, 38–9, 41; competitive strategies, 89; and economic growth, 301; labor relations, 35–6; in managerial capitalism, 28–30, 32, 35–6, 196; monopoly model in explanation of, 228; and vertical integration, 245, 246
Dosi, Giovanni, 328–9
Duke (co.), 239, 257
Duke, James, 240–1, 247
Dunlop (co.), 47
Du Pont (co.), 28, 248, 249–57, 259, 260
du Pont, Pierre, 248, 250
Durant, William, 248, 257, 258
dynamic analysis, 149, 164, 176; of Marshall, 150–1
dynamic theory, 16, 17

East India Company, 2
Eastern Trunk Line Association, 235, 242
Eastman, George, 241–2
Eastman Kodak (co.), 239, 241–2, 257
economic analysis, 115–16, 117, 155–6, 162, 292–3, 346–9; Chandler's contribution to, 230; importance of historical perspective in, 265–7; of Schumpeter, 122, 124
economic backwardness, model of, 141
economic change, 10, 118, 287, 311; evolutionary theory of, 288–9
economic crisis, 67–8
economic development/growth, 97, 195, 282; analysis of, 17, 67–70, 271–2, 274; business enterprise engine of, 16, 93, 132, 231, 286–7, 290, 299–301; central problem of, 64–5; collective organization in, 318–21, 334; determinants of, under capitalism, 313–14; effect on property rights and ideology, 312; entrepreneurship in, 136; evolutionary, dynamic character of, 131; as field of inquiry, 116; ignored in neoclassical theory, 10; institutional determinants of, 296–9; institutions, technology, and, 321–34; investment strategy and, 199; Landes's analysis of, 136–46; organizational coordination in, 299; productivity growth and, 294; relation with economic institutions, 1–3; value creation in, 93
economic development, theory of, 10–11, 67, 70–1, 118, 149, 284, 288, 294, 301,

306–7; in Chandler, 122, 132–6; in theory of the market economy, 7–8; in Schumpeter, 124–5, 126; in Smith, 1–2, 3, 6
economic dominance, 12–19; *see also* Great Britain; Japan; United States
economic efficiency, 64–5, 194, 223; perfect competition as ideal of, 129–30, 216
economic environment, 192, 214, 284; changing, 210–11; managing, 202
economic factors, 272
economic historians, 306–9, 324–5, 348
economic history, 10; as constrained optimization, 305–9; and economic theory, 347, 348, 349; as evolving constraints, 310–21; social analysis of (Landes), 286; in study of economics, 115–18
economic institutions, 45; development and utilization of productive resources, 312; and economic development, 1–3; and economic outcomes, 157, 197, 230; and economic performance, 15, 16, 18, 24, 71, 290–303, 314; evolution of, 335–45; visible hand and, 228–61
Economic Institutions of Capitalism, The (Williamson), 193–4, 195, 198, 206–13, 230, 238
Economic Journal, 125, 158–9, 161, 162
economic organization: optimal form of, 116, 266; value creation in, 15
economic outcomes: economic institutions and, 197, 230; impact of enterprise on, 228; impact of organizational structure on, 196; as process of historical change, 230; social institutions and, 277
economic performance, 61–2; business organization and, 94, 261; impact of economic institutions on, 15, 16, 18, 24, 71, 290–303, 314; in neoclassical theory, 307–8
economic problem (the), 155, 198–9; in neoclassical economics, 64–5, 67
economic theory, 10, 277, 304–5; ahistorical, 149; big questions in, 1, 2, 6–7, 9, 10, 347; business organization and, 9–12, 265–82; economic development excluded from mainstream, 67–70; and economic history, 347, 348, 349; historical analysis and, 18, 303; history and, 226–7; of Marx, 130–1; and process of change, 18; and reality, 6–9; role of, 130; of Schumpeter, 131–2
"Economic Theory and Entrepreneurial History" (Schumpeter), 126
economic uncertainty; *see* uncertainty
economics: defined, 150, 292; as discipline,